PRAISE FOR

JACKPOT

"Economic inequality has never been more gaping in the United States, which makes it the perfect time to read *Jackpot*, Michael Mechanic's entertaining and eviscerating peek behind the velvet curtains and into the real lives of America's super-rich. Mechanic provides an eye-opening exposé of the myriad ways in which our nation's political system unfairly enriches those at the top at the expense of those at the bottom. His myth-busting conclusion is that everyone loses, even the lucky few who have hit the jackpot."

—Jane Mayer, author of *Dark Money*

"Character-driven and far more rollicking fun than it should be, this riveting guide to how the other half lives illuminates how economic inequality leaves everyone worse off."

—*Esquire*

"Observant, funny, and discomfiting."

—*Town & Country*

Mechanic "peels back the layers of what it means to be mega-rich. . . . Following a year of reckoning with material and racial inequalities, *Jackpot*'s timing is ideal. If there were ever a moment to interrogate our collective attitude toward extreme wealth, it's now. . . . While reading about all the absurd things vast amounts of money can buy sparks a certain voyeuristic hate-reading joy, it's sobering to witness the way wealth erodes attitudes toward work, purpose, and integrity."

—*Los Angeles Review of Books*

"*Jackpot* skillfully explores the impact of great wealth on people's lives and society; an economic system driven by selfish values; and the urgent need for a more fair, equal, and sustainable capitalism that works for the greater good of everyone and the planet."

—Marc Benioff,
chair and CEO of Salesforce

"Mechanic offers such a fluent survey of the vast literature on historical inequality—indicating that he's not only read that literature but understood its implications—that I was surprised by his upbeat ending, when he suggests that transformative change could happen."

—*The New York Times*

"Having spent decades reporting and writing books in this field, I admire Michael Mechanic's book. His writing is elegant, his storytelling sublime. Well worth the time of anyone who wants to understand the effects of our make-the-rich-richer policies."

—David Cay Johnston,
Pulitzer Prize–winning journalist and author

"*Jackpot* recalls for me the muckraking reporting of America's first Gilded Age when dogged prophetic journalists exposed the giants of crooked capitalism and—voilà!—inspired progressive forces that changed the country. Michael Mechanic, you've shown us how to do it. May legions follow your example."

—Bill Moyers,
broadcast journalist

"Another important entry in the literature of the second Gilded Age, and how people on the gilded side are living, thinking, protecting themselves. You think you know, but you don't know the half of it."

—James Fallows, contributing writer,
The Atlantic

"Such great fun to read—so inside the heads and lives of its subjects—that its vital insights sneak up on you: how America's most fortunate, often despite the best intentions, perpetuate class advantages; how African Americans and women of all races are systematically excluded from wealth-building; and how rethinking our cherished myths about money and mobility could help us survive as a nation."

—Peggy Orenstein,
author of *Girls & Sex*

"A fascinating tour through this increasingly stratified society of ours by a superb reporter with an acute eye for the telling detail, and for the emotional reverberations of privilege and deprivation that a less sensitive journalist would have missed."

—Adam Hochschild,
author of *Bury the Chains*

"*Jackpot* is a rich, well-reported, compellingly told story that is not only a good read but an unsettling reminder of the absurd advantages that accrue to Americans who have won the proverbial lottery."

—Gary Rivlin,
author of *Broke, USA*

"*Jackpot* is my favorite kind of book—filled with rollicking reporting and deep thinking, bringing you into the living rooms (and the extremely weird lives) of the suddenly wealthy. It's a key document to help you grasp our screwed-up moment in history."

—Clive Thompson, contributing writer,
The New York Times Magazine

"A nimble exploration of a society obsessed with crowning winners and punishing losers. *Jackpot* makes me angry but also hits the spot."

—Gary Shteyngart,
author of *Lake Success*

"[*Jackpot*] really is great. The book is first-class therapy for anyone who was ever jealous of the rich. Veblen would be proud!"

—James K. Galbraith,
economist

JACKPOT

How the Super-Rich Really Live—
and How Their Wealth Harms Us All

MICHAEL MECHANIC

Simon & Schuster Paperbacks

NEW YORK · LONDON · TORONTO
SYDNEY · NEW DELHI

Simon & Schuster Paperbacks
An Imprint of Simon & Schuster, Inc.
1230 Avenue of the Americas
New York, NY 10020

First Simon & Schuster trade paperback edition April 2022

SIMON & SCHUSTER PAPERBACKS and colophon are registered trademarks of Simon & Schuster, Inc.

For information about special discounts for bulk purchases, please contact Simon & Schuster Special Sales at 1-866-506-1949 or business@simonandschuster.com.

The Simon & Schuster Speakers Bureau can bring authors to your live event. For more information or to book an event, contact the Simon & Schuster Speakers Bureau at 1-866-248-3049 or visit our website at www.simonspeakers.com.

Manufactured in the United States of America

1 3 5 7 9 10 8 6 4 2

Library of Congress Cataloging-in-Publication Data
Names: Mechanic, Michael, author.
Title: Jackpot : how the super-rich really live—and how their wealth harms us all / by Michael Mechanic.
Identifiers: LCCN 2020046505 (print) | LCCN 2020046506 (ebook) | ISBN 9781982127213 (hardcover) | ISBN 9781982127220 (paperback) | ISBN 9781982127237 (ebook) Subjects: LCSH: Wealth—Moral and ethical aspects—United States. | Rich people—United States. | Equality—United States. | Social stratification—United States. Classification: LCC HC110.W4 M445 2021 (print) | LCC HC110.W4 (ebook) | DDC 305.5/2340973—dc23
LC record available at https://lccn.loc.gov/2020046505
LC ebook record available at https://lccn.loc.gov/2020046506

ISBN 978-1-9821-2721-3
ISBN 978-1-9821-2722-0 (pbk)
ISBN 978-1-9821-2723-7 (ebook)

For Nikko and Ruby
The journey is no less important than the destination.
Also, it's garbage night. Please take out the trash.

CONTENTS

JACKPOT

INTRODUCTION

You realize I could spend $3 million a day, every day,
for the next 100 years? And that's if I don't make another dime.

—BILL GATES

Nick Hanauer is "NOT a billionaire." It says so right there in his Twitter profile, which also describes him as an entrepreneur, venture capitalist, civic activist, philanthropist, author, and podcast host. He included the addendum because people kept mislabeling his economic status.

One might be forgiven for such a mistake. Hanauer, a youthful sixty-one years old with nut-brown eyes and neatly cropped curly brown hair, has held significant stakes in nearly three dozen companies, including aQuantive, an online advertising firm Microsoft purchased in 2007 for $6.3 billion in cash. He hops around the globe in his Dassault Falcon 900LX, a sleek private jet that accommodates up to a dozen passengers. His children attended a prestigious private high school. He owns "a beautiful house here in Seattle and a beautiful house in Mexico and a beautiful ranch in Montana and a beautiful ski house at Big Sky and a beautiful weekend home in the San Juan Islands."

He also has a share in a large yacht harbored near the Mexico house, and co-owns, with another investor, an "absolutely beautiful" 1960s-era wooden boat, a ninety-five-footer his family plans to use for an upcoming Alaska vacation. "People think I'm a billionaire because I live like a billionaire, because practically there's no difference in terms of your lifestyle," he says between bites of salad in his downtown Seattle corner office overlooking the Puget Sound.

So how much are his assets actually worth?

"Hundreds of millions."

"More than five hundred?"

"Less than a billion."

He's being coy now, but for years, Hanauer has gone around referring to himself as a "plutocrat" and talking about his "obscene" wealth. The fact is, he doesn't know the answer to my impolite question: "How do you count it up, all the dozens of— God knows how many positions and private companies and the real estate and the art and . . . ?"

He would love to be a billionaire, he says, not because he wants a bigger jet, but because it would help him achieve his current goal— one that seems counterintuitive for a guy who owns five homes, two yachts, and the rest. He hopes to persuade government officials and fellow plutocrats to support policies that will reduce the massive wealth and income disparities between 0.001 percenters like him and the rest of America. Not long ago, he was just another rich guy getting richer. Now he's an anti-inequality crusader. And his transformation began with a jackpot.

Back in the early 1990s, Hanauer was a young capitalist doing what young capitalists do: looking for ways to turn a buck into five. The web was in its infancy, but he recognized sooner than most that it would one day revolutionize commerce, so he put up seed capital for the first online bookstore. It was he who helped convince Jeff Bezos, a friend of a friend and "the smartest, most capable person I've ever met," to move to Seattle in the first place. When Bezos needed cash to launch Amazon, Hanauer put up $45,000. In return, he got 1 percent of the company.

Incorporated in the spring of 1994, Amazon became a poster

child of the first dot-com boom, but unlike most of the era's poster children, it had a solid business model. Amazon went public on May 15, 1997, opening on the NASDAQ for $18 per share. The stock lingered under $30 for a few months before taking off like a rocket. Roughly two years after the IPO, the split-adjusted share price was spiking north of $1,200. Nick and Leslie Hanauer left for their honeymoon soon after Nick's investment went, to use his word, "parabolic." He'd just watched $45,000 turn into $20 million . . . $30 million . . . $40 million . . .

He was doing pretty well before, but nothing like this. In the late 1800s, his great-grandfather had founded a successful pillow business in Stuttgart, Germany. When the Nazis came to power and began making life miserable for Jews like the Hanauers, Nick's grandfather, Sigmund, emigrated to Seattle, where he teamed up with a cousin to revive the bankrupt Pacific Coast Feather Company. Nick's father took over the business eventually, and when Nick and his two brothers weren't in school, they could often be found at the factory doing scut work and learning the trade.

In his late twenties, Hanauer married a woman he'd been dating for years, but the match was short-lived. He met Leslie a couple of years later, just as Pacific Coast Feather was really gaining traction in the marketplace. By the time they were wed, annual sales exceeded $100 million, and Hanauer, now a part owner, was drawing a good salary. Then Amazon went bonkers. It made for a pretty surreal honeymoon. Suddenly, he was "insanely, incomprehensibly wealthy. So wealthy that it just was clear that the range of choices that I had about my future were categorically broader." Even aQuantive wouldn't feel like a big deal after this—another $350 million, *whatever*. Hanauer made a decision. He wasn't going to do what a lot of guys in his position might, which is spend the rest of their days trying to make their big pile of money even bigger. "It was like, okay, that would be just stupid. I should do other things."

Now he just had to figure out what.

———————

This is the American fantasy: the jackpot. The windfall. The exit. The payday. We dream of being whisked from the toil of the rat race into a socioeconomic realm that will end our daily grind, solve our most pressing problems, and mark the start of a fabulous new adventure. We would set our financial house in order, help out friends and relatives, and support causes we cared about. There would be perks and parties, access and adventures, and, yes, *stuff*—houses and boats and cars and clothes and jewelry and $500 sneakers. We would be blissfully unshackled. This collective fantasy, or some version of it, helps explain why nearly half of American adults play the lottery. We spent a staggering $81 billion on lottery tickets in 2019, up 6 percent from the year before. That's more than the GDPs of two-thirds of the world's nations. It is also more than ten times the amount we spend each year on books.

In this era of pandemic and political turmoil, in a nation inching toward Dickensian inequality, the wealth fantasy is tinged with desperation, but it has always been with us. From prerevolutionary times through the cryptocurrency craze, few things have captured Americans' imagination like the notion of striking it rich. The first colonists, a contingent from London's Virginia Company, sailed into Chesapeake Bay in 1607 in search of gold and silver. They found famine and misery. These precious metals were to be discovered in large quantities centuries later in the West, whose rapid development was driven by our lust for instant wealth. "Men are here nearly crazed with the riches forced suddenly into their pockets," one 49er wrote in a letter to his hometown Tennessee newspaper.

The fantasy has survived through harmony and unrest, war and peace, expansions and recessions, plagues and recoveries, and economic bubbles of all stripes. In a national survey of college freshmen, more than 120,000 full-time college and university students from the class of 2021 were asked to rate twenty life goals on a scale from "not important" to "essential." Most were lofty aspirations: becoming a community leader or an authority in one's field, launching a successful business, creating artistic works, raising a family, developing a meaningful philosophy toward life, promoting racial understanding, helping the environment, things like that. The top choice, deemed "essential" or "very important" by more than four out of five students, was "being very well off financially."

Thus the fantasy persists. But seldom do we interrupt our reveries to contemplate the social, psychological, and societal complications that come with great affluence and the reality that so few possess it. Superlative wealth is a blessing in many respects, but if not handled with care it can easily turn into a Pandora's box, not only for its bearer but for everyone in their midst. If you don't believe me, talk to sixty-six-year-old Richard Watts, a tall, silver-maned attorney who makes his living as a consigliere for some of America's richest families. Watts is privy to his clients' greatest joys and deepest sorrows. In the conference room of his wood-paneled legal offices in Santa Ana, California, he regales me with stories of aimless and ungrateful heirs, of philandering husbands and gold-digging spouses, of a client reduced to tears in her oceanfront mansion at the sight of a group of beachgoers grilling hot dogs below—because she could no longer relate. "She said, 'I don't have anything in my life that feels like that. It's always charitable dinners and fancy things. Nobody is there to just share simple pleasures.'" Another client came to him in despair after yet another person in her life had revealed a hidden agenda. "She sat here and cried and she said, 'Everybody ultimately wants something from me. *Everybody*. Even my own kids,'" Watts recalls.

We have difficulty empathizing with the pain of fortunate people because we believe, contrary to popular wisdom, that their resources would bring us contentment. But until you actually experience great wealth, you can never be sure how it will affect you. Coming into money in a culture that's obsessed with it will alter your reality. And that might be very good. It might also be very, very bad.

What do we mean by "wealthy"? I'm old enough to remember when having a million bucks meant you were crazy rich. Now it won't even get you into the wealthiest 10 percent. Decades of growth in the public equities markets and tax policies that favor investors over workers have turned millionaires into zillionaires and upper-middle-class Boomers with government-subsidized retirement accounts into multimillionaires. Tech IPOs, exotic Wall Street investments, and soaring regional real estate prices have minted even more millionaires. In 2016, researchers from the Federal Reserve Bank of St. Louis calculated that if you were college educated, middle-aged, and white or Asian, your odds of being a millionaire were greater than 1 in 5—though only about 1 in 15 if you were Black or Hispanic.

To make it into the wealthiest 10 percent, based on the latest (2019) numbers from UC Berkeley economists Emmanuel Saez and Gabriel Zucman, and Thomas Piketty, their mentor, your family needs at least $1.1 million in net assets, the combined value of everything you own minus your debts. You will be among 18.3 million U.S. households better off than most. But you're small fry, because you don't have enough *net investible assets*. That would be your net assets minus whatever money you've got tied up in your home. To get wealth advisors excited, you need net investible assets of $1 million or more: that's the 5 percenters.

Why the cutoff? Well, that spare $1 million makes you an "accredited investor." In 1933, Congress passed the legislation that created the modern stock market. The Securities Act set forth rules for companies that wanted to offer shares to the public. Among other things, they would have to register their stock offerings with the newly created Securities and Exchange Commission and disclose, in a prospectus, all the information a reasonable investor would need to evaluate the offering's merits.

Say Vinod Khosla is launching a new venture capital fund and doesn't want the government looking over his shoulder. He can raise that capital privately, in which case the law dictates that only accredited investors can take part. You and your spouse either need $1 million in the bank or a joint annual income of at least $300,000 for two years running. The government, in other words, protects the little guy by cutting him out of the action. "Reward and risk are absolutely balanced," one financial professional told me. "You are not going to make a lot of money unless you risk losing a lot of money." Conversely, if you can't take the risks, the big money is off-limits. Without accredited investments, says Jerry Fiddler, a businessman we'll meet in the pages to come, there's no way he could reliably get such solid returns on his portfolio: "To take your entire asset base and grow it by 7 percent a year, very few people could do that. Whereas I probably could." A close friend of mine who made a fortune trading stock options and investing in real estate told me he considers his accredited investments a less-risky bet than publicly traded stocks and bonds.

Ernst & Young predicted, pre-pandemic, that accredited investors in North America would hold nearly $29 *trillion* in combined assets by 2021—a 24 percent jump over 2016, with the lion's share going to the wealthiest 1 percent. But let's touch on the 5 percenters, because that's where true privilege starts to kick in. With at least $1.9 million in net assets, 5 percenters are comfortable, though not flashy. One needn't stress about the bills. As a 5 percenter, you can afford nice cars and cushy vacations, though you'll probably fly coach. Perhaps the biggest perk is your ability to easily pay your kids' way through college. And though you can't actually buy them admission to Yale, you can afford the private schools and private tutors, SAT and essay coaches, and all of that. Your children will start on second base, and you'll have a nice cushion for yourself.

Now let's meet the legendary 1 percent. The 1.83 million American families who comprise this wealthiest sliver are unequivocally rich. But those at the category's lower threshold—a tad over $5.6 million in 2019—aren't *that rich*. They are basically 5 percenters with a nicer house and a bigger security blanket, and who can afford first class.

When we hear the term "rich people," we tend to think more about the top 0.1 percent, families with assets of $29.4 million and up. This is the realm of elite private schools, private travel, stunning houses, extraordinary vacations (and vacation properties), luxury cars, and concierge doctors. At this tier, unless you enjoy mind-numbing financial arcana, you will need professional help managing your wealth. But if your advisors are worth their salt, you can supplement your substantial employment earnings with dividends and investment profits. By now, you are probably considering home security beyond your golden retriever. Estate planning is getting serious, too, because you and your spouse have assets of more than $23.4 million—the maximum, as of January 2021, that a married couple can pass to their heirs without paying any federal gift or estate taxes. To further avoid those taxes, you could put your excess assets into a tax-exempt charitable foundation or establish trusts for your children that will circumvent the tax and have the added benefit of shielding your financial legacy from lawsuits and creditors. You might even transfer some of that wealth to your grandkids through a generation-skipping trust. But will the money ruin them?

That question becomes more pressing as we move into the 0.01 percent, a cluster of 18,300 families with at least $157 million apiece—a level of wealth at which one's affairs grow substantially more complicated. In most cases you will have businesses and complex investments to oversee, philanthropic strategies to think about, and properties and personal employees to manage. Hedging, diversifying, and insuring your assets are a greater concern now—as is navigating the minefield that this level of wealth can lay down in your family relationships. You are furthermore entering a realm of legal planning focused heavily on circumventing that $23.4 million estate tax exemption. Very doable, but you'll have to keep a close eye on your accountants, lawyers, and money managers to make sure they aren't bleeding you dry.

Further up the ladder, the top 0.001 percent families, all 1,830 of them, are worth $805 million and up. Now we're talking about far-flung private and public investments and real estate holdings. Helicopters, private jets, yachts, rambling estates, fine art, Rolls-Royces, private islands—that whole fantasy is yours for the taking. Your kids will attend private school if only because your security consultants deem public too risky. Now you *can* afford to donate a building to Harvard—no guarantees, but your child's chances of getting in will improve dramatically. There's also a pretty good chance you have established a company whose sole purpose is to manage your own personal and financial affairs, where your minions will push the envelope of tax avoidance (if not evasion), because tax strategies at this level fall into lots of legal gray areas. If you're worried about the IRS, don't be. You can just call your senator and ask them to defund it further. They'll call you back.

Billionaires? They're just the 0.001 percenters with the biggest yachts.

The seed for this book was planted in the late 1980s. I was a biochemistry major fresh out of college, doing marketing for a company that sold antibodies for scientific research. The commute was long, the pay paltry, and the work unfulfilling. I wasn't happy, so I started buying the occasional lottery ticket and planning my escape. I didn't win.

Years later, having changed careers, I was hired as an editor and writer for *The Industry Standard*, a San Francisco–based magazine launched in the mid-1990s to cover the burgeoning new "internet economy." During the dot-com boom, as during the gold rush, the Bay Area was mad with hubris and visions of instant wealth. I was making $62,000 and change, which was quite decent. But every other week you'd hear stories—mostly about young, college-educated white guys—abruptly coming into seven or eight figures. Perhaps that was what prompted me to start buying lottery tickets again, at a convenience store on my daily walk to the *Standard*'s offices. The odds for California's SuperLotto Plus were 1 in 41 million. I once got three out of six, for a $10 jackpot. *Yay.* People call the lottery a tax on poverty or ignorance, but I disagree. Low-income people are actually the least likely to play, and I suspect even poorly educated players have a sense of the odds. People aren't buying a chance to win but a chance to fantasize about that most American of dreams: to become fantastically, ridiculously, irreparably wealthy. No debts. No limits. No bosses. No deadlines. Freedom—right?

But as I further interrogated the fantasy, I began considering what coming into serious wealth would truly be like. Money is complicated. We dedicate our waking hours to accumulating it, and our culture is obsessed with it. (There are almost one hundred English expressions for "money.") Yet talking openly about our personal finances is considered taboo. We harbor stereotypes around wealth or lack thereof, and use money as a yardstick to measure the social value of others— "net worth"—and even of ourselves. Our interactions and self-esteem are tangled up with our finances in strange and complex ways. Money creates rifts between friends and lovers, and tensions with relatives.

Rarely, too, have our collective wealth fantasy and public attitudes toward affluence been more worthy of examination than the present—a time of staggering economic inequality, political divisions, racial reckoning, and a global plague that has rendered undeniable the truth that America's economic game is rigged. As we will discover in the pages to come, it is rigged so powerfully, and in so many ways, that if it were an *actual* game nobody would bother to play—a game in which the winner is preordained, and the more you have, the more you receive. In which capital is crucial but few can obtain it. In which white men receive favorable treatment, while other groups are forced to play by alternative rules that leave them at a disadvantage. It is a game in which nearly all of the spoils flow to the top one-fifth of players, and the four hundred biggest winners end up with more than the 150 million biggest losers. We have reached the point at which our republic, founded upon egalitarian ideals (if not behavior), is so starkly divided into haves and have-nots, winners and losers, that some 0.1 percenters feel compelled to bribe and cheat their children's way into our nation's top colleges. Such is the fear of our progeny winding up on the wrong side of the wealth equation.

We know there is something deeply wrong with all of this, and yet still we yearn to win the proverbial lottery. And so, to better under-stand the realities of wealth in America, it behooves us to follow the fantasy to its conclusion. In doing so, we'll connect with people who have hit the jackpot in one way or another and were willing to talk about their attitudes, anxieties, and experiences, the ways wealth has affected their realities and behaviors, and how those behaviors, col-lectively, shape our society. It also behooves us to ask how and why our most fortunate citizens, often despite the best intentions, have contributed to the profound problems our nation now faces—and to explore how they can be part of the solution. This is what *Jackpot* is ultimately about.

We'll start by speaking with some fortunate folks about their jack-pot moments, the thrill of the windfall, and the trepidation that may follow. Next comes a high-end shopping spree. We'll visit with "the queen of San Francisco real estate," browse for Bentleys, and consider $300 cognac shots and $500 T-shirts. We'll gaze upon watches that cost more than your car and cars that cost more than your house, check in with physicians who cater to the 1 percent, and connect with luxury concierges who can get you virtually anything your heart desires.

In Part II, we'll explore the surprising complications that great wealth entails. We'll powwow with wealth advisors and researchers who study materialism to see why money makes some people miser-able, and how extreme wealth bears an odd resemblance to poverty in terms of the psychological malaise it inflicts. We will look into the ways our wealth differences separate us, and examine the dual ob-sessions of privacy and exclusivity that compel our most affluent to wall themselves off, build $500,000 safe rooms, and get their nannies trained in countersurveillance. We will witness the sometimes-tragic effects of grooming children for success and the massive advantages rich kids enjoy in higher education. We will play games with a psy-chology researcher to learn how our socioeconomic status affects our values and behaviors, and speak with a former senator and a sitting congressman about how money distorts our democracy.

Part III looks more deeply at how wealth is made in America, how dynasties perpetuate themselves, and why we tolerate them. We'll pay special attention to the experiences of Black Americans and women, both of whose scarcity in the ranks of the ultra-affluent is no accident. We'll also take a hard look at inheritance and philanthropy, and the extent to which charitable giving can sometimes exacerbate rather than improve our societal woes.

My goal is not to convince you that the superwealthy are villains—the villainous ones can accomplish that without my help—but to give a sense of the problems great wealth inflicts, the superpowers it imparts, and how the latter might be harnessed to make life better for all of us. Because if there's going to be another American Revolution—and heaven knows we're due—it's best if we can get everyone on board.

PART I

PART I

CHAPTER 1

JACKPOT

Suddenly you're not ugly. You're unique.

—CALIFORNIA LOTTO BILLBOARD

James Everingham has never been in his swimming pool.

He has lived in this $10 million house in America's fourth-priciest zip code—Ross, Marin County, California—for almost two years and never even a dip! To be fair, he grew up in a landlocked Pennsylvania town not known for water sports.

Everingham is among the most highly compensated coders in Silicon Valley. On a pleasant, pre-pandemic January afternoon, we settle into his den to get to know one another. His partner, Karina, is off somewhere, but we are joined by Banana, the couple's friendly black Lab. It's a long way from here to Menlo Park, where Everingham serves as VP of engineering for Novi, Facebook's cryptocurrency division. But he's got some fine vehicles in the driveway to choose from: a Porsche 911, a Tesla Model S, and a BMW touring bike. An avid cyclist and mountain biker, he also keeps a second, smaller house in the Santa Cruz Mountains.

Very few of us will ever see our fantasies of sudden wealth fulfilled, but we can ask those who have what it's like. And whom better to ask than the *Mozillionaires*. That's the nickname people gave Everingham and his former Netscape colleagues, because Netscape Navigator, the first commercial web browser, was the culmination of a top-secret effort known as the Mozilla project.

Everingham is a good guy to start out with because he experienced his jackpot as any of us might. He had no real wealth to speak of—then suddenly he did. He was one of three siblings raised in a middle-class family in rural DuBois, Pennsylvania, a town that voted overwhelmingly for Donald Trump in 2016 and again in 2020. (He's the only liberal in the family.) As a teen hacker in the late 1970s, Everingham wasn't out for money, but a community, free games and software, and the thrill of doing something quasi-illegal—like Matthew Broderick in *WarGames*. His mom thought he was headed for failure, and so did he, more or less. He never dreamed he would one day get paid to program computers, let alone strike it rich. But that's exactly what happened to him and several hundred coworkers on August 9, 1995, the day Netscape went public. Even the receptionist became an overnight millionaire.

We've grown accustomed to nerds striking it rich, but Silicon Valley wasn't awash in superwealth then. Netscape was, in fact, the IPO that launched the dot-com boom, the first start-up to have its stock hit the NASDAQ and go haywire, closing at more than double the $28 asking price on the first day of trading. Everingham had been recruited only three months earlier by a friend and fellow coder named Lloyd Tabb. His starting salary was in the high seventies, low eighties. He took whatever stock options the company offered—didn't bother to negotiate. That was a mistake, but nobody knew! He and his coworkers figured these options, at best, might buy them a car. And then, all of a sudden, their sixteen-month-old company, yet to earn a dime, was worth almost $3 billion on paper. Everingham's share, in today's currency, was about $8.5 million—at the stock's peak, it would have been well over $20 million. He was twenty-nine years old.

Everingham is fifty-five now, and still dresses like the hacker-skater kid he used to be, in blue jeans, plain black T-shirt, and black Chuck Taylors. He has receding strawberry blond hair and hip Buddy Holly glasses. He is six feet tall, but his skinny build, geek vibe, and "city kid" status made him a target for grade school bullies after his family moved from Pittsburgh to DuBois. His dad worked in advertising, making $36,000 or $37,000 tops, Everingham estimates. His mom was a homemaker, raising James and his brother and sister. The family didn't have much discretionary cash, but his parents were adamant the kids should work hard and go to college.

James was a rebel, though. At thirteen, he wanted HBO and his parents wouldn't get it for him, so he figured out how to steal it by climbing a telephone pole and removing a blocking filter on the line. To discourage the neighbors from snitching, he pilfered HBO for them, too. His mom ratted him out to the company, which promised not to press charges if the family subscribed. "So I got HBO—and I got yelled at!"

He discovered computers his junior year in high school when, one day at the mall, a friend showed him how to write a simple BASIC program on a Commodore VIC-20:

```
10 PRINT "Jim"

20 GOTO 10
```

When he hit Return, the screen filled up with his name, and James was smitten. He was soon so obsessed with writing code that he stopped going to class. He downloaded games and software from electronic bulletin boards over an ancient dial-up modem, racking up a huge telephone bill—"more than my mother's mortgage." She was distraught. So he researched how phone systems worked and wrote a program that generated access codes one could use to make free long-distance calls. He would trade these codes for software. Later, after obtaining a list of the tonal frequencies the long-distance operators used to control phone company networks, he created Wardial, a mischievous program that gave its users the awesome powers of a telephone operator.

Everingham sometimes fantasized about wealth when he was a kid. The irony, he says, is that it wasn't until he stopped trying to get rich that he actually did. After flunking out of high school, and later Penn State, he began building a library of open-source tools for software developers. Hoping to cash in on his creation, he started a company called Logical Alternatives, approaching a dozen banks before finding one that would loan him money without collateral. He flailed as a first-time businessman, but was able to sell his company at a small profit to a Georgia software firm that paid him $45,000 a year to stay on and help rewrite their products. He was recruited two years later by Borland, a software company near Santa Cruz, which offered him $72,000 a year. He bought himself a Porsche, and was always getting pulled over. "I had long hair, goatee. I wore skater shorts, wallet with a chain, combat boots," he recalls. "I looked like trouble."

One day, a Borland pal said something that Everingham couldn't stop thinking about: "He's like, 'You'll find out that your ideal income is always going to be double what you make.' That seems to be true, and that actually gave me a lot of anxiety."

The Netscape jackpot only added to the anxiety. His stock options vested over four years, so the money didn't come all at once. Morgan Stanley, the IPO manager, called him one day. "Hey, your cliff is up. What do you want us to do?" Everingham told the banker to go ahead and sell the first chunk of stock, and then promptly forgot all about the conversation. A week later, he went to an ATM to get some money out. His balance, in today's dollars, was more than $2 million. "The highest balance I'd ever seen in there was probably $4,000, and this incredible stress hit me," he recalls. "I almost passed out. Like, 'I don't know what to do with that.'"

People at work started going a little nuts. One colleague ordered enough Silly Putty to fill up his bathtub—literally. "Because he could," Everingham says. "He still rented a garage in Palo Alto. This is the only thing that he had bought. He was worth probably $30 million right out of college." Colleague Lou Montulli, whose office aquarium featured one of the web's first live cams, bought a massive new 350-gallon tank and went snorkeling in it. Some Mozillionaires bought "decked-out campers" and began living in the parking lot.

Nobody knew what to do with their windfalls, and the company wasn't helping, so they turned to one another: *How are you manag-*

ing it? How are you dealing with people? Because the people thing . . . well, the whole tech world was watching Netscape's stock price, and some of Everingham's old Borland buddies felt put out. "A couple of my closest friends completely stopped talking to me," he says. New acquaintances came around, and pretty women—they'd never noticed him before that. It was just like in the old blues songs; suddenly everybody was his friend, which was kind of fun but also super disconcerting. Even things that seemed simple turned out not to be. For instance, Everingham got excited after the IPO, so he went out and bought a Nissan Maxima for his mother, who had never owned a new car. He later learned that his brother had gotten depressed about this and had gone to their mom and apologized because he hadn't ever been able to do something so nice for her. "I'm like, 'Oh, shit! I didn't think about how that's going to make him feel,'" Everingham says.

The NASDAQ roller coaster made matters worse. The stock would shoot up suddenly. "You're doing the math, and you're like, 'That can't be. That's millions of dollars!'" He would get a number in his head—the number at which he would no longer need to work. "And then it goes right below that: 'Damn. I have to work.' And then it shoots back up, and I'm like, 'Oh! Now I *don't* have to work.' Then, a week later, 'Damn.'" But not needing to work begets a sort of existential crisis. The Mozillionaires—some of whom would never have been friends had they not bonded over their "shared trauma"—talked about this a lot.

One Mozillionaire decided he would go become a photographer. "He came to me after three or four years of being lost," Everingham says, "and he's like, 'I figured out what I want to be when I grow up.' And I'm like, 'What?' He goes, 'That I don't have to figure out what I want to be when I grow up.'"

That's even truer now. Everingham and his colleague wound up cofounding another company, LiveOps, that made call-center software. Had Everingham sold his stake at the firm's peak valuation, he'd be $80 million to $100 million richer. (It's only worth about half a million now—so it goes.) But his pal took a software utility he'd developed and spun it off into another company, which Google snapped up not long ago for $2.6 billion.

Everingham's first recruit at Netscape was a coder I'll call Jake, fresh out of college. Jake was dead set on one day starting his own company, and eventually he did—a social media aggregator that Twitter eventually took off his hands for $134 million. Jake flailed around for a couple of years, trying to figure out what to do with himself. He invested in an online shopping platform, and then, when that company started struggling, came on as general manager. Here Everingham pulls out his phone and shows me a text exchange from one week earlier. . . .

Jake: hey man . . . we sold the company for $4B.

Everingham: Wow nice! . . . Hope you made out well!

Jake: yea . . . fuck ton of money . . . I was an early investor to boot. good times! pile on the continued existential crisis!

All of this reminded me of something Nick Hanauer had told me: Anyone who hits the jackpot will quickly discover that necessity is straightforward, but choices are complicated. "When all of a sudden the world is your oyster, what are you going to do?" he said. "For a lot of people that choice—well, you see what happens when people win the lottery."

———

We should talk about the lottery, actually, if only because a lottery jackpot is so raw, so disconnected from anything real. Winning requires no smarts, education, social connections, or drive, other than a drive to the convenience store. Just dumb luck. With Powerball, you have to match five numbers from 1 to 69 and a bonus number from 1 to 26. The probability of hitting them all is 1 in 292 million. Winning Mega Millions is even less likely. These are incomprehensible odds—

we'll never win, and we know it. We've heard the horror stories, too. Attorney Richard Watts, whom we met in the introduction, tells me another: One early client, three decades ago, was a working-class guy with a lottery win of about $60 million after taxes. He came to Watts in deep trouble, but he came too late: "It was all gone in five years: bankrupt, wife gone, kids gone, kids on drugs, kids in jail—really, truly a life he could not recover from."

The conventional wisdom is that winning the lottery will ruin your life, and yet we keep buying those tickets. The last time Gallup inquired, in 2016, 49 percent of American adult survey respondents said they'd purchased at least one lottery ticket in the previous twelve months. Contrary to the lottery's reputation as a poor person's vice, those with household incomes of less than $36,000 a year were less likely to have bought a ticket (40 percent) than "middle-income" folks (56 percent) or people whose families earned $90,000 or more (53 percent). People with college degrees were more likely to play than people with high school diplomas were—and even 45 percent of respondents with postgraduate degrees had participated.

Jason Kurland, forty-seven, represented them all. In fall 2011, Kurland, then an attorney at the Long Island branch of the firm Rivkin Radler specializing in commercial real estate law, received a phone call that would determine his future. The caller, seeking legal advice, had gotten Kurland's name from another client. Payment would not be an issue because he and two coworkers had just won a $254 million Powerball jackpot. After taxes on their lump-sum payout, they would have $104 million to share. We stereotype lottery winners as financially unsophisticated. Not these guys. They were a founding partner, senior portfolio manager, and chief investment officer for Belpointe Asset Management, a financial firm in Greenwich, Connecticut, where mansions sprout from spacious lots and single-family homes list for quintuple the national median price.

Kurland was no lottery expert, but he quickly made it his business to become one. He researched how different states tax lottery winnings, whether and how big jackpot winners need to be identified (at least eight states let them remain anonymous), and the legal tricks one might use, depending on location, to claim a monster windfall. Claiming in the name of a trust or a limited liability corporation, for instance, won't reduce the initial tax hit, but it may limit a winner's public exposure. Some states let you claim using a legal entity and others don't. Some require press conferences. Some allow an attorney to claim the prize as a trustee. "In that case, the attorney signs the back of the ticket—and you have to make sure you trust that attorney," Kurland said. (We will come to see the irony in that advice.)

Four days after Thanksgiving, Kurland accompanied the Greenwich trio to their mandatory press conference at Connecticut lottery headquarters, where they were presented with a giant, ceremonial check for $254.2 million, payable to the Putnam Avenue Family Trust. The counterintuitive spectacle of a clutch of 1 percenters hitting the numbers attracted a lot of media coverage, including a piece by *New York Times* finance reporter Kevin Roose. There were even rumors the trio was a front for the *actual* winner, but Kurland denied it.

The second call, a few months later, was from a lawyer for Louise White, an eighty-one-year-old Rhode Islander who'd hit a $336 million Powerball jackpot, then the third-largest ever. White had sequestered her winning ticket within the pages of her Bible and slept with it until she could get to the bank and stash it in a safe-deposit box. She hired Kurland to set up "the Rainbow Sherbert Trust," so named because it was a relative's craving for *sherbet* that had brought White to the Newport Stop & Shop, where she'd bought her winning ticket. After paying roughly $52 million to Uncle Sam and $15 million to the state of Rhode Island, White took home about $143 million. At this point, Kurland realized he could make the lottery his niche. He built a website and began promoting himself to media outlets. Soon reporters were calling "the Lottery Lawyer" for quotes, and TV news producers were booking him whenever a huge jackpot had everybody abuzz. "Long story short," he told me, "now I get calls on almost a daily basis."

When we first spoke, in early 2019, Kurland said he'd represented about three dozen winners with $2 billion in total payouts, and individual jackpots ranging from $5 million to $330 million. He was being coy, because the winner of a $1.5 billion Mega Millions jackpot, the biggest individual prize in lottery history, stepped forward a few weeks later—or rather, Kurland did. The woman had purchased her golden ticket at a gas station in rural South Carolina, one of the states that allow winners to conceal their identity.

Kurland's clients have run the gamut. "The reality is that it's everybody. When the prize was over $1 billion, the whole country was buying tickets. Rich, poor, single, married, young, old. Every ethnicity," he said. His winners broke down about evenly into two categories. One consisted of the cautionary tales, those who succumb to temptation and go on reckless spending binges, putting themselves on a road to ruin. The second group was the kind of winners we rarely hear about, the ones who live so boringly within their means that Kurland felt compelled to remind them they could afford to cut loose. (If he were to hit the jackpot, "I'd probably live large," he admitted.) But every client has had one thing in common: "They're freaked out."

"The joyful part, the jumping around and screaming. That's the first day. I never see that. All of my clients come to me worried," Kurland said. They are nervous about their names being made public, and wondering what to do next: "Yesterday, you were living a normal life and today you're somewhat different, but you still have your old life. Do you quit your job? Do you go to work? Do you not tell anybody?"

Anonymity is precious because lottery winners are besieged. Long-lost friends and relations come out of the woodwork seeking handouts. Charities troll for donations. Sketchy financial professionals will come at you, dangling the prospect of unrealistic investment returns. Money managers see "a really easy fish to catch, and so they're getting into the high-risk stuff because the fees are big," Watts says, and the unsophisticated winner often goes with the first person who comes along. But winners who claim their prizes without first seeking professional guidance, according to Kurland, "are in real danger."

The $1.5 billion South Carolina winner called him in December

2018, about six weeks after the drawing. She wouldn't say her name and she was "very nervous, very hesitant." She sounded legit, but Kurland knew not to get too excited. Big lottery jackpots are weirdo magnets. He would field calls pretty regularly from people falsely claiming they had the winning ticket. "The first time it happened, I thought it was really crazy," he said. "Maybe they're fantasizing and want to feel what it's like to go through the steps a winner has to go through. Or they have mental problems."

Given all the emotions involved, it can be hard to tell the winners from the wingnuts, which is why Kurland asked callers to send him a picture of their winning ticket. The South Carolina woman did so, and he flew down to meet with her. Only after they spoke for several hours did she agree to retain him. She was wise to be sparing with her identity. In California, where winners have to reveal their name, the lottery handbook suggests renting a PO box, changing one's contact information, filtering calls, and channeling requests through an intermediary. The handbook doesn't mention social media: "Shut it down completely," Kurland advises. (It's not just lottery winners. Gilded Age Standard Oil tycoon John D. Rockefeller used to get hundreds of letters every day asking for money. And some contemporary billionaires have begged *Forbes* to keep them off the Forbes 400 because of the unwanted attention it generates.)

Kurland would advise his clients, before stepping forward, to have in place a team of legal and financial professionals for which he might function as "quarterback," and to be ready to spread their winnings over a range of financial institutions, since regular bank accounts are insured for only $250,000 and investment accounts for $500,000. The South Carolina woman wanted everything done right. Each week of delay in claiming her lump-sum payout (almost $500 million after taxes) was costing her $250,000 in interest, Kurland calculated, but she didn't seem too concerned.

A winner's typical first instinct is to bury their debts. That's understandable. Just prior to the pandemic, Americans owed more than $14 trillion on home mortgages, auto and student loans, and credit cards, and that debt is a huge source of family stress. What else? Lots of new cars, Kurland told me. People want to trick out friends and relatives—maybe not the best financial move, since buying someone a $30,000 vehicle, for instance, might cost you thousands more in federal gift taxes. "But they're emotional and they really want to do it. So I don't dissuade, I just educate," Kurland said.

The problem, especially with massive sums, is that it's just hard to predict how the money will change your life, and even you. Take work. "A lot of times you're a distraction for your coworkers," Kurland said. "The bosses don't want you there, 'cause you don't have the same work ethic or whatever—responsibility. You don't *need* the job."

For someone who has worked their entire life in pursuit of a big payday—or simply to pay the bills—this can be a perplexing question. What happens when there is no longer a financial incentive to work? Will the job still feel meaningful? Will you persevere through challenges, or simply bail when things get tough? Massachusetts attorney Jeff Weissglass took a career hiatus during the 1990s after both of his wife's parents passed away in the space of a year. His own father then died shortly after. Their little family was devastated—and suddenly rich, because the couple had inherited stock worth about $8.5 million in today's dollars—far more than expected—and whose value proceeded to soar in that decade's booming stock market. Weissglass, then still in his thirties, had a revelation. He no longer had "to work at jobs I didn't like for money I didn't need." Instead, he has spent the last quarter century serving on the boards of progressive nonprofits—he also did a four-year stint as the unpaid chairman of More Than Money, a group of inheritors determined "to explore the impact of money in their lives."

Was the liberation from employment a blessing or a curse? Up until a few years ago, Weissglass felt "absolutely" unmoored, he told me. Hailing from a family with a deep work ethic, in which doing business and earning money were a given, he struggled with his identity: "I didn't know what I was doing every day when I woke up." The worst were the social events, cocktail parties and such. "It's the 'What do you do?' question," he says. "I was uncomfortable. It was hard to talk about what I do without saying that I don't have to work for money. There were certainly self-esteem issues wrapped up in that. What were people going to think of me? Maybe what do I think about myself?"

Almost all of Kurland's lottery clients quit their jobs within a few months of winning. Oftentimes it was a practical matter: How prudent would it be to stay in a gig that pays you $40 an hour when your portfolio is seesawing $400,000 a week one way or the other? "You want to make it grow," Kurland says. "You want to invest in things."

Mike Depatie invested in hotels. His story is a fine example of the financial advantages that accompany business knowledge and ready access to capital in certain sectors of our economy. A fit sixty-three-year-old with an easy smile and a head of thick snow-white hair, Depatie was born and raised in Kalamazoo, Michigan, where his father ran a small company that distributed hydraulic and pneumatic products: valves, cylinders, O-rings, etc. Depatie knew he wanted to be a businessman—even as a preteen he would advise his aunts and uncles on financial matters, but he had no interest in taking over his dad's operation. After attending Michigan State and later Harvard, where he earned his MBA, he gravitated to the hospitality industry and eventually made his way up to the helm of Kimpton Hotels, a chain of boutique lodgings. The compensation was fine. In 2013, he and his wife bought a new home, listed for eight figures, in one of San Francisco's most exclusive neighborhoods. The acquisition became all the more affordable the following December, when Depatie, as CEO, orchestrated Kimpton's sale for $430 million—jackpot!

With the ink barely dry on the paperwork, Depatie took off to Hawaii, where he remembers checking and rechecking his account balance. A few days later, boom, there it was! More than enough money to pursue a life of leisure. "Like whoa! It was kind of weird. It was very liberating at first," he says. "It's like, 'Ah, euphoria!'" But the novelty wore off quickly as he began to ponder, "What's the next mountain I need to climb?"

The next mountain turned out to be a private equity partnership Depatie spun off with two fellow Kimpton alums. KHP Capital Partners raises hundreds of millions of dollars in commitments, mainly from institutional investors, and then summons that cash to purchase underperforming boutique hotels, which KHP revitalizes, rebrands, and ultimately sells. The makeovers are hands-on. A worktable outside the KHP conference room is covered with samples: woods, fabrics, tiles, flooring. The refurbished hotels are stylish, with the average room renting for about $225 a night before the pandemic ground travel to a halt.

Private equity is incredibly lucrative, under normal circumstances. A successful fund at least doubles in value within five to ten years. This means KHP's "small" $360 million fund—it had two funds incubating—would be expected to grow by at least that much. The investors would get their money back, plus a premium. The remaining profit would be split eighty/twenty between the investors and the fund managers, who also collect hefty annual fees. "I don't know why it's eighty/twenty. It's outrageous compensation for what we do," Depatie acknowledged. And the icing on the cake: Thanks to the "carried interest" rule, that 20 percent—and in some cases the management fees, too—is taxed not as wages but at the far lower prevailing rate for long-term capital gains. Depatie and his wife have a second home under construction in wine country at a cost of $11 million. "A vacation home?" I ask. He isn't sure. Their designer and a local realtor each predicted it would fetch $16 million on the open market when finished. Depatie is tempted: "I'm a capitalist," he says.

When the coronavirus hit Pause on the hotel industry, Depatie initially expressed fear for his livelihood, but it struck me that the crisis might be a big opportunity for him, with hotels selling at fire-sale prices. Indeed, he sounded much more upbeat when I checked in a few months later. He had taken a huge hit on paper, he said in an email, but his latest fund still had $320 million of untapped capital.

"That will translate to roughly $900 million worth of hotels at today's prices," he said. So, assuming the industry eventually recovers, "as it will most likely do," he should do nicely.

Depatie seems comfortable in his skin. He's good at what he does, and what he does generates a ton of money. He doesn't feel America's economic system is unfair, really. In his view, if somebody is clever and motivated, they will find a path to financial success. "Over time, the top 10 percent of smart people figure out how to get all the power and all the money," he says. "That's kind of where we are today. Then there's the redistribution; somebody comes in, kicks over the anthill: 'Hey, cut that shit out!' Then they go away and the ants start coming back."

He has two sisters still in Kalamazoo. One is a schoolteacher, the other an artist who drives Uber to cover her bills. He hasn't been helping them out financially, even amid the pandemic. He would if they needed it, absolutely, he says. Yet he fears his doing so might result in feelings of resentment. Family is complicated. "I've felt, not guilt, because I'm not a guilty person," he says. But "for the first time I've really started to feel a separation from my family of birth. I didn't realize they are actually starting to have a little anger toward me."

What's more, like a small but growing subset of his ultrawealthy peers—the likes of Nick Hanauer, Salesforce CEO Marc Benioff, and hedge fund titan Ray Dalio—Depatie has begun to feel unnerved by America's economic divisions and where they seem to be headed. People are eyeing the anthill again. "I'm starting to think more about income and equality," Depatie says. "I'm thinking they could come and burn my house down. They could come for us with pitchforks."

———

When we fantasize about being rich, we often neglect to think about how we would get there, but the journey is critical. The way we experience a windfall depends a lot on our education, politics, and family culture. It depends on our race and gender. On the kind of work we do. On where we live and whom we spend our time with. On the amount of exposure we have to people less fortunate than ourselves. Perhaps most of all, it depends on how, and *whether*, our money is earned, and at what point in our lives.

Martha's jackpot came in the form of an unexpectedly massive inheritance. This experience has defined the parameters of her life. It is her freedom and her albatross. She could afford a private jet and cooks and butlers, but what she really wants is to be rid of this *burden*. Even the small perks, like hiring gardeners to tend her yard, give her pause. She fears she's becoming one of *those* people—rich people. She doesn't think very highly of them, doesn't want to be associated with them, and yet here she is. Why, one might ask, doesn't Martha give her money away? That's what everyone says, but it's easier said than done. Handing out large sums is a big responsibility. As Andrew Carnegie, one of the wealthiest men who ever lived, wrote in his widely read 1889 essay, "The Gospel of Wealth": "It is well to remember that it requires the exercise of not less ability than that which acquired the wealth to use it so as to be really beneficial to the community."

We are sitting, on a pleasant winter day in 2019, in Martha's large and somewhat cluttered study on the second floor of one of the nicer homes in a pricey Northern California neighborhood. Martha is in her mid-fifties. She writes books, though not exactly for a living. Her readers would assume her royalties paid for this house, but they would be mistaken. Her family bought it for her when she got divorced. If people had a clue how much money she has inherited, and still stands to inherit, she fears they would no longer take her or her work seriously, which is just one of the reasons she has asked me to use a pseudonym. Does her publisher know? "Oh Christ almighty! Jesus Christ, no, no, no!" she says. "My kids don't know!"

Even she didn't know the full extent of her situation until well into middle age. Her parents divorced when she was a baby and she rarely saw her biological father. Her mother and stepfather were intellectuals—he held an academic position. The family lived in a funky three-bedroom house in a suburb one now associates with Silicon Valley wealth, but in the 1960s and '70s it was doctors and professors living there, not tech zillionaires. They didn't live extravagantly, and if it seemed odd their mother didn't work—which was common then anyway—Martha and her brother never dwelled on it. They knew their granddad was affluent, but the family culture was such that they also knew not to be overly inquisitive.

Toward the end of high school, Martha was set up with an account to cover her college expenses. Her mother said she would be getting some "small cap" shares. Martha didn't know what that meant, but she came to understand that the money that appeared in her account, as if by magic, was something called dividends, from funds administered by her grandfather's financial company. She attended an elite East Coast college, paying her way from the account. After graduating, she worked in publishing and then briefly as a teacher before earning a master's degree in creative writing. The money kept flowing all the while. It accumulated in her account throughout her twenties as she honed her writerly skills, and into her thirties. By that time, the balance was substantial, though not insane—definitely less than $1 million. It was enough to buy a very nice house one day, Martha figured.

She and her brother sometimes compared notes and scratched their heads about all this money they were getting. The quarterly statements would arrive in the mail and Martha would glance at them and shove them in a drawer. "The number would seem unrelated to me," she recalls. But the number kept getting bigger. By the late 1990s, it was growing by perhaps $200,000 a year. And then, quite abruptly, something changed with the distribution of dividends. In 2001 or 2002, without warning or explanation, the figures exploded. Martha's annual income was no longer a couple hundred grand. It was millions.

This windfall brought her, not joy, but bewilderment and confusion. Her uncle had been introduced to the family business and eventually took it over. Her mother and aunt, however, had been left out of the loop almost entirely. As a result, Martha and her brother and their aunt's children lacked knowledge and adult guidance related to the scope of the family wealth and how that wealth might affect their lives. It was don't ask, don't tell. This was deliberate, Martha would later surmise, because her mother and aunt hadn't wanted their children to be distracted. Ignorance was bliss, they probably figured, and for a long time they were right. But Martha was woefully unprepared when, in her late thirties, she learned the whole truth. About a month before we met, at a meeting with her mother's estate lawyer, she was handed a document that made her relive that moment of revelation. The document included all the details about the trusts her mother had set up for Martha and her brother. It also showed the value of another trust they stood to inherit from their octogenarian mother, in addition to the tens of millions of dollars they'd already received.

The number was shockingly large. Martha is reluctant to reveal it, and when she does, she declares that it is never to leave this room. She seems upset. I ask her what it's like to say the number out loud. "*Shameful*. It's shameful," she says, her blue eyes welling with tears. "And it makes me want to cry, because this is the fantasy. I've got the fantasy in my fucking drawer. You're going to be showered with gold. How can that be anything but the best news?"

Her fortune hangs over her like a cartoon anvil. "It's practically a daily battle to put it down so that I can actually write my books," she says. "I feel like I have a train coming at me. That's how I feel about it."

Martha was engaged to be married when her dividends hit the stratosphere. The money, perhaps inevitably, created tensions in her marriage. She's divorced now, with two teenagers. She would like to meet someone new, but her wealth anxiety has made intimacy challenging. What's more, ever since becoming pregnant with her first child, she has frequently pondered what her death would mean for her offspring. She is terrified of what will happen if, for whatever reason, she meets her maker before her mother does. "If I were to die tomorrow, the train's going to come at them and I can't do anything about that," she says. "Whereas if my mother dies first, the train hits me first."

CHAPTER 2
RETAIL THERAPY

I love money. I love everything about it. I bought some
pretty good stuff. Got me a $300 pair of socks. Got a fur sink.
An electric dog polisher. A gasoline powered turtleneck sweater.
And, of course, I bought some dumb stuff, too.

—STEVE MARTIN

Martha is an outlier in that she never had much use for the wealth fantasy. She was raised comfortably upper-middle class. Healthy. Education covered. No debt. After college, unlike her peers, she could afford to buy her own flat, so there were no landlords or roommates to squabble with. She never required a nine-to-five job to make ends meet, and she had the means to pursue a creative path she knew might never cover the bills. That's a very privileged upbringing. She had enough money to feel liberated, but not so much as to leave her questioning her role in the world. So when the jackpot landed in the form of several additional zeros on her bank account balance, her instinct was to hide, not celebrate.

For someone who has never felt the same kind of security, however, a big windfall is more likely to awaken a desire to sample the so-called good life. Having vast sums of money opens hidden doors to sparkly things and exhilarating experiences and famous people and exotic places. Most of all, it enables the twin obsessions of the superwealthy: privacy and exclusivity. It gets one away from the crowds and beyond the velvet rope. And for most of us, it's only natural to want to see what's on the other side.

One thing you will find on the other side is a host of opportunities to bask in your eliteness and display it to others. Consider, why might one buy a Rolls-Royce? Granted, it's a work of art—beautifully made, limited in number, elegant, powerful, safe, quiet, and comfortable. But if we're going to be honest, the main reason one buys a $500,000 car or a thirty-thousand-square-foot house or a $1,000 meal is to signal to our peers how special we are. Social scientists would characterize this as an "extrinsic" pursuit, a category that includes our desire for attractiveness, popularity, material things, and financial success. At the other end of the psychological spectrum are "intrinsic" goals such as self-acceptance, community-mindedness, and meaningful relationships. Researchers have long studied how the balance between extrinsic and intrinsic affects a person's well-being. Short answer: Being highly extrinsic doesn't presage good outcomes. Therefore, for the sake of authorial sanity (and the integrity of my bank account), that shopping spree I promised in the introduction will have to be a *window*-shopping spree.

Food and drinks are a good place to start. Prime 112 steak house in Miami Beach offers a 16-ounce Japanese A5 Kobe rib eye for $230—and who wouldn't be tempted to Instagram such an entrée? Masa in New York City and Urasawa in Beverly Hills offer memorable sushi experiences starting at $1,200 to $2,200 per couple. "A fundamental respect of the distinctiveness, which is naturally occurring, is observed with each act of slicing, shaving, and sprinkling," Masa's website boasts, and the food is prepared rapidly and plated immediately "to preserve the idea that each dish is still in a living, being state."

Serving the right vintages at the right temperatures is more or less a social obligation at rarified levels of wealth. Things can get ugly, though. In 2013, billionaire collector Bill Koch (one of the lesser-known Koch brothers) sued former billionaire tech consultant Eric Greenberg, claiming Greenberg knowingly sold him an auction lot with twenty-four bottles, including an 1811 Chateau Lafite and a nineteenth-century Chateau Latour, that were inauthentic. Koch, who ultimately secured a $12 million settlement, viewed such wines as "links to history," his lawyer insisted. At a certain price point, one is paying not so much for the actual quality of the wine as "the scarcity, the story behind it, the critical scores," Mark Oldman, author of *How to Drink Like a Billionaire*, explained to *Forbes*. "Or, it could simply be priced higher so we value it more— the luxury good effect."

Speaking of which, if you want to impress your billionaire pals, the High Limit Lounge at the ARIA Resort & Casino in Las Vegas offers a $1,500 cocktail called the ARIA Sazerac. I did not order one, but it was just the sort of thing that might appeal to the man I was in town to see. That was Phil Hellmuth, who won the World Series of Poker's main event at the tender age of twenty-four, and is prone to reminding a visitor that he's "the greatest poker player of all time." I won't argue with that. With a record fifteen World Series bracelets, he has lifetime tournament winnings of more than $23 million, plus substantial revenue from his non-tournament play, endorsements—the ARIA sponsors him, for instance, paying for his meals and drinks and high-rise hotel suite—book and TV deals, speaking fees, and equity stakes in companies that want him on their advisory boards.

The extrinsic life features prominently in Hellmuth's public persona. His social media followers see him schmoozing with rock stars and famous athletes and former presidents, flying on private jets, relaxing with actor Rob Lowe on a billionaire friend's yacht in the Galápagos, and sitting courtside with the owners of the Golden State Warriors, whose charity poker tournaments Hellmuth hosts. (Draymond, Steph, and Klay—"a big fan," he assures me—are on his speed dial.) He's a regular at the High Limit. During winning streaks, he says, he used to splurge on Louis XIII cognac: "I'd go out and have six shots of Louis Treize at $300 a pop—$1,800 down the tubes. You wouldn't think twice, though, because your money's flying in so fast." For a while, he made a show of drinking exclusively Dom Pérignon, champagne that retails for $150 to $400 a bottle, never mind that he doesn't even like the stuff.

———

For goods and services, the gold standard in luxury marketing circles is "bespoke." The word is often misused to imply exclusivity in general, but a truly bespoke item is one designed and manufactured for a specific client. Keeping up with the Joneses is about conformity. Keeping up with the Rockefellers means setting oneself apart. Anyone with $80,000 to $100,000 to spare can obtain a Vacheron Constantin Overseas Perpetual Calendar Ultra-Thin wristwatch, but a more discerning person of wealth might turn to the Swiss watchmaker's Les Cabinotiers division, established in 2006 to extend the company's centuries-old tradition of creating one-of-a-kind timepieces. During the 1860s, Russian tsar Alexander II and his tsarina ordered a bespoke Vacheron Constantin as a gift for their son. Other customers have included the Maharajah of Patiala and carmaker James Packard. The sometimes yearslong process starts "with a narrative: the client's private story. A history fan might ask for the reproduction of a painting by one of the great masters in *grand feu* enamel on the dial; an aspiring Romeo might want his piece to chime once a year on his Juliet's birthday; or a grand complications enthusiast might dream of owning a groundbreaking mechanical masterpiece." If you cannot afford such a thing, don't bother asking what it costs. "I wish I could give you something concrete," a journalist who wrote about Les Cabinotiers for *Robb Report*, a luxury industry magazine, informed me, "but this is where brands who do this kind of thing go all Chamber of Secrets."

Smartphones have rendered wristwatches a mere fashion accessory, but the phones themselves pose an opportunity to set oneself apart. For the well-heeled who spend time in Europe and Asia, Mobiado's PRO3 VG Fleur, limited to eighteen phones and priced at $3,442, is "a celebration of life" featuring a battery cover inlaid with a sapphire daisy "gracefully encircled by five ruby butterflies." Gresso's Hamilton line, starting at $7,000, reconfigures Apple's iPhone 11 Pro into a handcrafted "masterpiece" with titanium cladding, 18 karat gold, and crocodile leather. If you must, for about $16,000, Goldstriker International offers an iPhone 12 Pro Max featuring a diamond-studded 24-karat-gold dragon ("the oldest symbol of cosmic and supernatural power") embedded on a back panel crafted from "the highest quality leather of the Nile crocodile."

When Elizabeth, a veteran Silicon Valley product executive, came into wealth, she told me, what struck her most is that she felt like a mark. Elizabeth (a pseudonym) and her husband, a former Apple guy, are techies in their fifties whose stock options and real estate flips ripened all at once to create a jackpot moment—not ultrawealth as we're defining it, but $12 million or so, enough to retire early and comfortably. When we first spoke, in fact, the couple was in existential mode, taking time off to ponder what truly mattered to them. Elizabeth, who has a grown daughter from her first marriage, knows what it's like to scrape by as a single working mom in Silicon Valley. She is unusually disciplined with money, too—a trait inherited from her frugal father, an executive who would record all the family expenditures, big and small, on little index cards. Her husband is from modest means, she says. So for them, the sudden relief of no longer needing to worry about money felt intoxicating, and *that* was unsettling. "You are a mark because you want to just not think about a $100 dinner," she says. "And you want to say, 'Oh, I can buy that coat!' The context shift makes it unbelievably easy to blow money, and about a year into it, my husband and I looked at each other and we're like, 'Fuck no!'"

That "Oh, why not!" mindset, combined with the peddling of a superficial kind of exclusivity, makes it easy for the nouveau riche to get snookered. At Nordstrom, where I went looking for an outfit to wear to the Concours d'Elegance classic auto show at Pebble Beach, a women's sneaker display caught my eye, perhaps because the shoes looked dirty. They were intentionally scuffed. The brand was Golden Goose, and its all-white "Rainbow Superstar" shoe looked very much like my daughter's Nikes, except for the multicolored laces and the price: $565. And T-shirts, God help us. A minor scandal erupted two summers ago at Brooklyn's Pratt Institute, where my son attends art school. A student had left his shirt in a dorm laundry room and another kid tried to "adopt" it. That was my introduction to the Parisian designer brand Vetements. The pilfered item was a plain white cotton tee designed to be worn inside out. A large white tag on the back read: "This is the outside of the garment. Prohibited to wear on the inside." Below, in larger print, it said, "VETEMENTS." That's all. I found this same shirt online, in black, for $492. Vetements also sells a replica of the shirt Kurt Cobain wore on the cover of *Rolling Stone*, a plain white tee on which Cobain had scrawled in Magic Marker: "Corporate Magazines Still Suck." Vetements added the words ". . . a lot" and made the "a" an upside-down anarchy logo. This brand of anarchy will cost you $550 plus tax. Another tee, priced at $570, read: "It's my birthday and all I got is this overpriced T-shirt from Vetements."

Luxury retailers have perfected the art of making wealthy people feel special. At Galeries Lafayette Paris Haussmann, a modest fee gets you access to "Le Concierge" lounge, where "our Anglo-Saxon clients" will find "a guaranteed moment of escape in the heart of the temple of fashion . . . a hassle-free shopping getaway, a peaceful interlude in which to enjoy some well-being time." Concierge Loungers are catered to "all day long" by "a team of professionals" and treated to a gourmet lunch or afternoon tea, including wine or champagne. Los Angeles fashion consultant Bree Jacoby takes privacy and exclusivity further. Prior to the pandemic, for a flat fee and your agreement to spend at least $1,000 on clothing, she sent a stylist right to your hotel or home in L.A., San Francisco, or New York City, armed with a curated wardrobe selection from partner brands (including Golden Goose). Another $1,000 bought a "closet edit" in which the stylist helped you decide which of last season's clothing to get rid of.

But designer brands are so *new money*. In preindustrial times, all fine garments were made to order. The word "bespoke" actually comes from old tailoring jargon for a quantity of fabric a customer has reserved for their exclusive use. "Bespoke is about the experience of working directly with a skilled artisan, who will make something special for you using time-honored techniques that have all but disappeared from factories," notes the Armoury, a Hong Kong haberdasher. The process takes months and requires four in-person appointments. First the clothier collects your measurements and preferences for cut and fabric. Next, you are fitted with a "basted" garment, which resembles a wearable pattern. The rough suit is taken to near-completion at the "forward fitting." And then comes the final fitting, at which the final product is presented and tweaked to perfection. In the United States, a bespoke suit typically costs $3,000 to $5,000.

If it's bragging rights you're after, a shopping excursion at the House of Bijan is by appointment only. Bijan caters to a global elite that includes billionaires, kings, celebrities, and every former president from George H. W. Bush through Barack Obama. The boutique, opened in 1976 by the late Iranian-American designer Bijan Pakzad, is located in a Mediterranean-style palazzo on Beverly Hills' Rodeo Drive, where a bright yellow Rolls-Royce and/or a black-and-yellow Bugatti (both Bijan design collaborations) are often parked out front. Suits start at around $10,000 and ties can be had for $1,000 each. Former Trump campaign manager Paul Manafort—who pleaded guilty in 2018 to conspiracy charges related to money laundering, tax fraud, obstruction of justice, and failure to disclose a foreign bank account—reportedly spent more than $520,000 on Bijan clothing, which the store calls "wearable art."

The Manafort affair revealed another clothier so exclusive that few knew of its existence: Alan Couture relied solely on word-of-mouth advertising until proprietor Alan Katzman's son, Maximillian, was called to testify at Manafort's trial. In all, Trump's sidekick had spent nearly $1.4 million on his wardrobe from 2008 to 2014. Highlights included a $9,500 vest, a $15,000 coat made of ostrich leather, and an $18,000 python jacket. "Really, it's normal," Max Katzman told *GQ*. "The heart of our business is $12,000 per suit," his father revealed in a rare interview. "And we go up to $45,000 for pure vicuña; we made eight of those for a client in Chicago." Vicuñas, lest you have forgotten, are wild camelids from high in the Andes.

Luxury travel similarly banks on the desire of the ultrawealthy to separate oneself from the rabble. In the tiny, zero-stoplight town of Barnard, Vermont, I wrangle a pre-COVID tour of Twin Farms, a five-star getaway where rooms start at around $2,000 per night. The rustic three-hundred-acre resort, where various household names and billionaires have reportedly stayed, boasts a helipad and a private pond for boating and fishing and swimming far from the madding crowd. Chef-prepared meals and exquisite snacks with wine pairings, all-inclusive, are available when and where guests desire them. Twin Farms has a fancy spa, of course, a gift shop full of handmade Vermont crafts, and rooms adorned with notable works, such as the painting and the limited-edition print I spotted in the main lodge—of young apes dressed in period clothing—by the contemporary artist Donald Roller Wilson. The property, originally purchased by the novelist Sinclair Lewis for his betrothed, boasts miles of private hiking trails, a croquet court, and a ski mountain with six runs. Fly-fishing gear and lessons are available—the pond is "fully stocked." Vermont-y excursions are expertly curated. A bee tour is hosted by Dave, the resort's resident apiarist. A morel-hunting expedition is led by the resort's chef and two "foremost" mushroom experts; an afternoon canoe outing at nearby Silver Lake features a picnic on the water—a good Riesling would pair nicely with poached lobster. Should a guest desire a scenic drive in the countryside, a $100,000 BMW is reportedly available. It's a version of Vermont, but one that few Vermonters could ever afford. Perhaps the most telling detail? My tour guide carefully steered me away from any common area where a Twin Farms guest happened to be present.

The clientele of Twin Farms is more or less David Christiansen's target audience. On a hazy May afternoon, I sit down with Christiansen in a glass-walled sales office at Walnut Creek Luxury Cars, a Northern California dealership where he is not a salesman but a "brand manager." Our conversation is interrupted every few minutes by the guttural roar of a staffer firing up a Maserati Ghibli or Quattroporte to move it out of the showroom. He hardly notices, but I startle each time. I'm unused to such sounds, having arrived here in a Toyota minivan.

The Ghibli, the first-ever Maserati priced under $100,000, was intended as a gateway drug to hook BMW and Mercedes owners on high-end Italian driving machines. Christiansen also sells Alfa Romeos and Bentleys, and inventory is being reshuffled today to make room for additional luxury brands: Aston Martin, Lamborghini, McLaren, etc. Also on order are a few Paganis and Koenigseggs, insane supercars retailing for $2 million–plus.

The number of Americans who can afford a Pagani is higher than ever. The United States, with about 4 percent of the planet's population, boasts more than 32 percent of its ultra-high-net-worth individuals—people with assets of $30 million or more. From 2016 to 2019, according to Wealth-X, their numbers increased by 29 percent, to 93,790, with combined assets totaling nearly $11.3 *trillion*. Roughly 44 percent of this treasure is in cash and liquid assets, properties, and luxury items such as yachts, private jets, fine wines, jewelry, art, and high-end cars. Plenty of super-affluent folks couldn't give a fig about a Rolls-Royce, Christiansen says. They're fine with their Prius. But if it's flash they covet, he can offer them a wide variety of proxies for wealth, class, and conventional masculinity.

Out on the lot, with a few painful contortions, I slide behind the wheel of a low-slung 2019 Lamborghini Aventador. This charcoal Batmobile, priced at $520,000, boasts a carbon fiber monocoque, scissor doors, and massive air intakes on either flank. A rear-mounted V12 engine is partially visible through smoked glass panels. Christiansen points out the independent racing suspension, with horizontal shocks like a Formula One racer, and the single-clutch transmission with paddle shifters—another F1 innovation. A console in the small cockpit contains an ignition switch and buttons marked Strada, Sport, Corsa, and Ego. Each offers a unique driving experience. Ego makes shifting more aggressive and limits the traction control so you can drift, Fast & Furious style.

The ignition switch has a red protective cover, like in a missile silo. I flip it up and push the button. A tiger awakens. "Hear that loud noise? Those are the fans sucking the air in to cool the engine," my host enthuses. He invites me to punch the gas. *Woah!* Is this thing street legal? Its top velocity exceeds 220 mph. To clear speed bumps, you have to push a button that raises and lowers the chassis. I'm not certain I have sufficient testosterone to pilot this beast through a residential neighborhood. It's "a little intimidating," Christiansen concurs—a first-timer might opt for the Huracán in the adjacent space. "I mean, this is a *violent* car," he says. "If you're driving this car hard, it's giving you whiplash every time you shift."

I'm definitely not man enough. As if to prove it, I ask about the fuel economy. Driving conservatively, Christiansen says, you might eke out 15 mpg on the highway, 5 to 7 in the city. He loves how these cars drive, he says, but he doesn't like the attention they attract. Lamborghini and McLaren owners are "A-type personalities, definitely image conscious," he says. They are typically men in their fifties and sixties, but he has sold a number of Lambos to the Chinese students who attend nearby Diablo Valley College as a stepping-stone to Berkeley or Stanford. "Their parents will say, 'Oh, here's $200,000, just go get a car,'" he says. "Sometimes they're in the more-money-than-brains club. They don't know how to drive the cars." Some just want to be able to say, "Look what I have and what you don't have."

We enter another showroom to visit the Bentleys. They *drip* wealth: elegant, imposing. In the center of the room is a Mulsanne, base price $360,000, but this customized Mulliner edition is $404,000. Its 6.25-liter twin-turbo engine bears a plaque—"Hand Built in Crewe, England"—with the engine number and the name of the person (Steve Brown) who oversaw the fabrication. The supple dashboard leather is sourced from cows raised in barbwire-free environments to avoid scratches. The floor mats are made from lamb's wool. "The ultimate luxury!" Christiansen says, noting the polished wooden consoles, hand-stitched seats, and door panels fitted with heavy chrome ashtrays "for cigars or whatever." The car has massaging front and rear seats. Another backseat option is an illuminated, handcrafted wooden cocktail cabinet, complete with a pair of handblown crystal decanters "designed for Mulliner by the exquisite glassmaker David Redman of London," Bentley's website notes. Rolls-Royce's equivalent, the Phantom, starts at $450,000. Another $12,000 gets you the Starlight Headliner—thousands of tiny LEDs embedded in the ceiling leather to approximate the night sky. The option is customizable: Rolls will configure the stars as they appeared on the day you were born. Christiansen considers it a gimmick, "but I will tell you, it's really tough to sell a Rolls-Royce now without the Starlight Headliner."

His clients rarely haggle over price. They are comfortable with the notion of fair profit, and profit margins on some of these ultra-luxury brands are surprisingly low, but personal touches help make up the difference. Christiansen has seen customers request alligator skin on the center consoles. "A lot of these brands, Maserati, McLaren, Ferrari, Lamborghini—say your wife has a Hermès bag that is a certain color that no one offers. You can actually send a sample. They'll replicate it and paint the car that color." General Manager Ketan Bhatia, who used to oversee West Coast sales for Rolls-Royce, stops over to say hello. He shows me photos of a Ghost whose buyers had an image of their Yorkshire terrier embroidered on the headrests, with paw prints on the tread plates and an interior color to match the beloved animal's bed—all for $625,000. Another customer ordered his wife a Rolls painted the color of her favorite lipstick. The lipstick sample remains on display at the factory in England, Bhatia says. Any buyer who wants "Elena's Red" has to get the family's permission.

One thing I don't see here today is customers. Luxury-car sales are "more lifestyle than automotive," Christiansen explains. The vehicles follow the money. His team will cosponsor events with private jet manufacturers and fractional ownership services such as NetJets and XOJET, or with San Francisco's St. Francis Yacht Club, to expose affluent people to vehicles "they don't even know they want yet." Customers wander in from time to time, of course. Rocker Sammy

Hagar, a Ferrari collector who sold his Cabo Wabo tequila brand to Campari for $91 million, has been known to stop by the sister dealership in San Francisco "in flip-flops, torn shorts, ratted hair, and a T-shirt. You wouldn't think the guy has two dimes to rub together if you didn't know who he was," Christiansen says. Another guy showed up at the Walnut Creek lot dressed like a plumber and configured a $260,000 Bentley. He was, in fact, a plumber—one who owned a thriving plumbing business. He'd arrived in another Bentley, now on consignment.

The typical auto-sales game of passing hapless customers between sales associates, managers, and finance staffers would never fly here. "It's funny. I hate car salespeople. I really do," Christiansen says. His job is about building long-term relationships and providing personalized service. His clients don't have time to hang around a car dealership for five hours. Some repeat customers have even become friends. They invite Christiansen to weekend golf excursions on their private jets or to parties on their yachts. Once they decide on a car, "they just say, 'You know what I like. Put this together and send it to my accountant.'" The vast majority lease. Up until 2019, thanks to a quirk in the tax code, leasing these super-high-end cars for business use resulted in a much larger tax deduction than buying one would. Should you make your living as a wealth advisor, hedge fund manager, luxury realtor, or corporate lawyer catering to high-end clients, "you can't show up in a Toyota Corolla," my host points out. So you'd lease the Bentley.

Back at home, I joke with my daughter that maybe I, too, should lease a Bentley, since I'm hobnobbing with all these fancy folks for my book. "Noooo!" she exclaims with a vehemence only an aggrieved fourteen-year-old can muster. "If you get a Bentley, I'll disown you! I literally won't be your daughter anymore." Fair enough. Besides, where would I park it? I would *literally* need to move to a neighborhood where having a $400,000 car in the driveway wouldn't make me look like a schmuck. I wouldn't need to travel far, though. As of 2020, there were forty-eight U.S. zip codes, from Miami Beach to Bridge-hampton, New York, where the median single-family home sold for at least $2 million. Thirty-four of those zip codes were right here in California. Thirteen zip codes in three states broke the $4 million barrier. And then there was 94027.

Let's go and have a look around.

CHAPTER 3

THE ONE

*Let there arise next to the little house a palace,
and the little house shrinks to a hut.*

—KARL MARX, *WAGE, LABOR AND CAPITAL*

The "glamorous" residence at 202 Atherton Avenue sits on two acres with two gated entrances, a rose garden, and a large pool. Built circa 1949, it boasts four bedrooms and four and a half baths, private guest quarters, "grand formal rooms," a library, a breakfast room, an elevator, and a caretaker's apartment. The seller wants $17.8 million, but the realtors didn't bother staging the house. They figure the buyer will tear it down. "Ideal for new construction," the listing notes.

Around the corner, on Selby Lane, a one-acre lot is for sale—no house, no pool: $8.5 million. Just down the road is a cul-de-sac with several gated driveways; almost every property around here has a security gate with a call box. A seller wants $12.75 million for one of the properties, featuring an 8,880-square-foot house on just over an acre, with a "deep park-like backyard," pool and pool house, basketball court, and "lush screening." That's code for: You'll never see your neighbors.

Back on Atherton Avenue, number 74 can be had for $12.9 million. From the back corner of its 1.5-acre lot, you could heave a stone into the backyard pool of 69 Tuscaloosa Avenue, where, for $26 million, you get an 11,155-square-foot contemporary home on 1.7 acres with five bedrooms, eight full baths, heated white oak and limestone floors, "disappearing glass walls for indoor/outdoor living," and a kitchen with "rare labradorite countertops." A children's bedroom, painted purple, includes a two-story climbing wall with glass catwalk and play loft. The property is located, the listing boasts, in the "#1 Zip code in the United States."

Atherton, California, is indeed first in one respect. It reliably tops annual lists of the nation's most expensive real estate, outdoing even classic wealth havens such as Aspen, Beverly Hills, Greenwich, Palm Beach, Park City, and Sagaponack—the priciest Hampton. Viewed by satellite, Atherton is distinguishable by its large, lush lots. It's median home listing price exceeded $7 million in 2019. Lacking commercial properties and multifamily housing, Atherton abounds in the privacy and security many ultrawealthy folks covet. Roughly half of its homes have alarms connected directly to the police department, which functions a bit like a private security force. The town's old-school exclusivity, along with close proximity to Stanford and neighboring downtowns, are part of what make the land so valuable, even though much of the action in tech has migrated north. The first wave of Silicon Valley founders liked to purchase big compounds out along Highway 84 in the Woodside Hills, Elizabeth told me. Their wives would then divorce them because they didn't like raising the kids out there by themselves—this phenomenon became known as "the 84 Divorce." Now, she says, all the rich young techies want to live in San Francisco.

James Everingham skipped over the city entirely. He and Karina had planned on building a big modern house in Santa Cruz, where he'd lived for twenty-six years, but construction was going to take forever. Then Karina stumbled upon the Ross listing, which had everything they wanted. Banana tags along as Everingham takes me for a tour. At five thousand square feet, the house is spacious, open, and ultramodern, with seventeen-foot ceilings and high-end details: copper, Venetian plaster, reclaimed redwood. An enormous eat-in kitchen has a built-in Miele coffee machine—very Jetsons; push a button and it produces the perfect cup. Did he ever imagine owning such a kitchen? "One kitchen?" he teases. "I have two!" Indeed, there's a smaller one for caterers.

He shows off a closet packed with programmable Lutron switches and terabytes of data storage. All of the home's features are controlled with a smartphone app, including a high-tech bathroom window that my host turns instantly opaque with a tap. Another bathroom features the most beautiful tub I have ever seen, exquisitely hand-crafted from koa wood to match the kitchen cabinetry. It came with the house. (The tub's Swiss manufacturer quoted me $21,400, including shipping.) The house also boasts tall, modern fireplaces and high-design furnishings inside and out. Floor-to-ceiling glass walls in the main living area slide out of sight to make the room one with the outdoors. In addition to the pool, the bucolic backyard features large decks, a tiled fountain and hot tub (*yes*, he's been in it), and stands of towering redwoods for shade. Even though he has no children to leave messes, Everingham told me he has four house cleaners, a pool guy, and a gardener—there's even a garden on the roof! The house, of course, has the obligatory wine room, though Everingham knows little about the beverage. (He likes the red kind.) But a jackpot winner goes with the flow.

———

Back down in the city, in an elegant, blindingly white apartment, I pop a whole egg into my mouth and regret it immediately. A fleeting, bemused look from my hostess, Malin Giddings, indicates that I have revealed my class. To be fair, it was really half an egg, topped with an anchovy. I devoured it all at once because I wasn't sure how to navigate the anchovy. After that, I studiously avoid the prosciutto-wrapped asparagus pairs Giddings has also made available for snacking, accompanied by flutes of a green vegetal concoction. It's not bad. *"Skål!"* she says, raising a glass.

We are sitting at a polished wooden backgammon table, a family heirloom, in Giddings's glamorous flat in San Francisco's Nob Hill. Having never stepped directly from a wood-paneled elevator into someone's place of residence, I'm already feeling out of my league. Giddings, who speaks with flair in her native Swedish accent, is in her mid-seventies. Her outfit perfectly matches the apartment, which is entirely white, floor to ceiling, with blue accents and gorgeous views.

In 2018, the personal finance site GOBankingRates named San Francisco America's most expensive big city to live in comfortably, requiring a pretax income of at least $123,268. This was based not on owning a designer apartment in Nob Hill, but renting an ordinary one-bedroom flat at going rates. New York City, at $99,667, was a distant second, roughly tied with San Jose. My own city, Oakland, ranked fourth, at $95,611. (DC was fifth.) That three of the nation's five priciest cities are right here in the Bay Area is a result of all the tech wealth that has flooded the region. Should you hit the digital jackpot and be in need of an abode, Giddings is your go-to. A fellow realtor described her as "the queen of San Francisco real estate," and I quickly discovered why. Not only was she raised on the grounds of the Swedish king's royal palace, but in a career spanning more than four decades, Giddings estimates she has sold *$4.5 billion* worth of homes, condos, and apartments in San Francisco, mostly at the very top of the market. The year prior to my visit, she told me, she was responsible for 83 percent of home sales $12 million and up north of California Street. That would include the swanky neighborhoods of Nob Hill, Pacific Heights, Presidio Heights, Russian Hill, Sea Cliff, and Telegraph Hill, where old-money socialites and celebrities rub noses with tech founders, venture capitalists, finance titans, and captains of industry. She won't sell anywhere else—can't relate.

In my (upper) middle-class neighborhood, a house for sale goes up on the multiple listing service (MLS), accessible through any realtor's website. The seller's agent hosts a few open houses. Potential buyers wander through, bids are collected, and a deal is negotiated. In a hot market, deals can be closed within weeks. But luxury properties often take years to sell. "In the Bay Area everyone is used to this idea that if a house doesn't sell in two weeks it gets a stink on it," says Austin Forbord, a San Francisco businessman whose family company, DZINE, is the local pioneer of what one might call "bespoke staging"—outfitting hyper-luxury spec homes with hundreds of thousands of dollars' worth of art and high-design furniture manufactured specifically to match that particular project. Once the listing price exceeds $5 million, Forbord points out, the number of potential buyers drops off dramatically: "North of $10 million, it becomes very thin."

At that price point, open houses evaporate and the MLS listings often go away, too. Wealthy sellers don't want commoners sniffing around their properties, and well-heeled buyers demand a realtor's full attention. Showings are by appointment only, "otherwise it's a petting zoo," says Frank Nolan, co-owner of San Francisco's Vanguard Properties, who does $150 million to $170 million in annual sales. Would-be buyers are often asked to show their money in advance, "because a lot of people would love to see a house like that just to see a house like that."

With Giddings's properties, buyer and seller are brought together via a network of elite realtors who, like brand manager David Christiansen, nurture close bonds with their clients. These are multi-year relationships in which Giddings serves as matchmaker, advisor, friend, and de facto therapist. "I may even go home for Sunday dinners and put their children to bed and all of that," she says. Some clients like her to be involved long after the purchase: "We're thinking about this in *this* color. Can you just come by?"

Money is almost never an issue. Giddings's mission is to find the right fit and manage people's expectations. Given San Francisco's tight building restrictions, its luxury stock tends to be older—mansion-esque—and limited in other ways. The uber-rich want "absolutely stunning bridge-to-bridge views, and there has to be terraces, an outside space and garden," Giddings says. But the way the city's neighborhoods are laid out, one can't combine panoramic bay views with south-facing gardens, she says. "You have to convince this billionaire: 'You have to choose! Do you want a view or do you want a garden?' Then he says, 'Malin, did you hear me? I want a view *and* a garden.'"

San Francisco recently leapfrogged over Moscow and London to third on the list of global cities with the most billionaires. The historical turf of the local old-money elite—the bold-name families one reads about in the *Chronicle*'s society column, regulars at cotillions and debutante balls and opening galas—has been invaded by people who, to borrow from Mark Zuckerberg, prefer to move fast and break things. Indeed, walking around Pacific Heights on a pre-pandemic spring afternoon, one senses a neighborhood under siege. Every fourth or fifth house is under construction and visitors compete for parking with contractors' vehicles. The streets are empty of humanity but thrumming with the clanking of hammers, the shriek of power tools, and the distant chatter of Latino workers who commute from far-flung locales where wage earners can still afford the rent.

One might think a person with humble roots would be hesitant to buy into such extravagance, but Giddings assures me it's the opposite. It's the inheritors who are timid. But the new money doesn't want what the old money wanted: a grand house with a grand entrance and old-fashioned details. "That is not in vogue," Giddings says. The house has to be large, with the mandatory views and terraces, but it must be "more horizontal than vertical," and very plain-looking from the outside.

A growing public resentment, heightened by the pandemic, of economic unfairness, has made the wealthiest among us, if not fearful, then at least wary of drawing attention. High-end home sales are shrouded in secrecy. Realtors sign confidentiality agreements and transactions take place between shell companies. This may sound like a nifty ploy to conceal one's assets from the taxman, but the realtors I interviewed insist it's more about privacy. You could be dealing with Jeff Bezos, a Russian mobster, your second cousin—you'd never know. "Almost everybody does it like that in New York City," Nolan says. The same ethos applies to new construction. At a panel discussion I attended, local architect Matthew Mosey talked about how his affluent clients would like to keep up with the "fancy Joneses," but don't want to do anything that pushes the envelope too far.

That ethos is suitable for the progressive Bay Area, where a million bucks these days barely buys a fixer-upper and the tech-wealthy are blamed for making housing unaffordable for the rest; my daughter's ninth-grade English teacher, a Stanford alum, supplemented his public school salary with weekend shifts at Starbucks. And protestors famously targeted the buses that tech companies chartered to shuttle employees to and from their motherships in the South Bay, where housing prices were even more out of reach. "My doctor in Palo Alto, my gynecologist, she's like, 'This is our last appointment. My husband and I are moving to Portland,'" Elizabeth told me. "And I'm like, 'Why?' And she says, 'We can't afford a house.' Two Stanford-educated doctors with no student debt can't afford a house in Silicon Valley!" So much for technology making the world a better place.

———

A jackpot will buy you some damn fine real estate, but you may miss the sense of community neighbors provide. Absentee ownership is rampant in wealthy enclaves and multimillion-dollar condo developments. Realtor Nolan had recently been in Miami touring luxury condo buildings whose residents told him they rarely saw anyone in the hallways because their neighbors owned "second, third, fourth, fifth homes," he recalls. "We have that here, in Nob Hill—even Pacific Heights. San Francisco is a very desirable place to spend a few weeks out of the year. I know people who have places just to come to the ballet or the opera here from overseas."

Why would anyone do that? Well, because they can. It may even earn them a green card. Under America's EB-5 visa program, which Congress created in 1990, foreigners who invest $900,000 (originally $500,000) in a targeted employment area (TEA) are fast-tracked for permanent residency. In 2017, the family of Donald Trump's son-in-law and top advisor, Jared Kushner, pitched EB-5 visas to investors at a Beijing Ritz-Carlton to bankroll a real estate development in Jersey City. The attendees were urged to act quickly, before Congress changed the rules: "Invest $500,000 and immigrate to the United States," a brochure noted. In Canada, which had a similar program,

Chinese investment in the Vancouver area led to skyrocketing housing prices, Potemkin condo buildings, and an influx of trust-fund princelings peeling around town in Lamborghinis. "They don't work," David Dai, the founder of a local supercar club, told the *New York Times*. "They just spend their parents' money."

The EB-5 program was meant to bring jobs to underserved areas, but it was riddled with fraud and corruption. Estimates of the number of jobs the developments would generate were inflated and TEA maps were gerrymandered to connect poor areas with rich ones, allowing developers to use the money for upscale projects. A similar thing happened with President Trump's "opportunity zones," which were sold to the public as a way to incentivize development in overlooked areas. At Concours d'Elegance, I overheard a finance guy explain to the owner of a 1958 Ferrari cabriolet on the block for $7 million to $8 million how he could more or less legally launder his auction profits by rolling them into a shovel-ready project in an opportunity zone that *wasn't really* an opportunity zone.

The EB-5 rules were tightened in late 2019, but absentee ownership remains rampant. A couple in their thirties paid $27 million for the house next door to Mike Depatie's place in Pacific Heights, but he's never met them: "It's been under construction for three years. They are completely tearing it apart," he told me. Across the street is a sixteen-thousand-square-foot house owned by Harry Potter director Chris Columbus, who resides in Malibu. Depatie has lived here five-plus years, and has never met him, either. "I live in a neighborhood where nobody's home and everybody's working on their house," he says. "They are mostly kind of behind gates, if you will. Nothing but nice people, but you're not going to drop by and borrow sugar from them."

Wealth has certainly changed Bruce Jackson's Seattle neighborhood. His home, like Martha's, is large and elegant, but not what you'd call a mansion. He bought it for less than half a million in the early 1990s, after making his first million off stock options he earned as a

Microsoft product manager. Later, as president and chief financial officer of a pioneering dot-com-era start-up, Jackson, whose surname I changed at his request, was instrumental in taking the company public. Within two years, his shares were worth $80 million on paper—jackpot! "I was like, 'I should sell it all. That's a shitload of money. I don't know what I'm going to do with it, but that sounds great,'" he says over Mexican takeout on his back deck, which has a view of Lake Washington. He couldn't just dump all of his stock and spook the investors, but he did unload "thankfully, a reasonable amount" prior to the dot-com bust—about $30 million worth in today's dollars. He gave 20 to 25 percent of his remaining shares to various charities, in part because he feared having so much money might make him reckless.

When Jackson moved to his current neighborhood, homes still could be had for $200,000. Now the median home value is $2.1 million, and the vibe is less neighborly. The house next door sits empty most of the year because the owners have houses elsewhere. "We still do most of our yard work, but that's starting to be the exception on the street," Jackson says. And "when our kids were growing up, there were, like, fifteen kids at that bus stop to go to the public school. That's not the case anymore."

It's not that moving into a larger house in a nicer neighborhood won't bring us joy. For a 2019 paper, Clément Bellet, a researcher at the London School of Economics, analyzed American Housing Survey data covering three million suburban homes. Families who had recently moved into bigger houses reported greater "house satisfaction" commensurate with the size of the upgrade, but the effect became negligible for houses larger than three thousand square feet. For example, the increase in house satisfaction one gets when moving from one thousand to two thousand square feet is more than 3.5 times the bump one gets when going from three thousand to four thousand, Bellet says.

What's more, when an existing home falls within the top 10 percent of a neighborhood's house-size distribution, the owners grow increasingly less satisfied as newer, bigger homes pop up nearby. Bellet calls this the "McMansion effect." It helps explain why, although the average size of new homes in America increased from 2,100 square feet in 1980 to 3,000 square feet in 2008, the average house satisfaction of recent movers remained the same.

A big house has downsides, too. It requires more water, upkeep, energy to heat and cool, and time and hassle. At some point, you will need to hire gardeners, housekeepers, pool cleaners, and even security consultants. Property taxes are a drain: $236,020 a year for a $20 million home in San Francisco. And with size comes obligation. Significant wealth requires "a certain stature and certain behavior and certain parties that look right to do," Giddings told me. "If you've never entertained on a big scale because you come from a small background, it would bring you a lot of stress." The techies, in particular, would "like to go in the closet and hide." Giddings's father, Nils K. Ståhle, was the longest-serving executive director of the Nobel Foundation, and some of her tech billionaire clients remind her of the laureates she would meet as a girl. "They are usually very, very nerdy people. When they came to Stockholm to receive the Nobel Prize, they almost had to have a week of manners school with my father: 'Walk backwards! Don't turn your back to the king.' They were so nervous. It was just terrible. This is the same thing if you come into extreme wealth and you've never entertained on that level. It's extremely hard."

I concur. If you don't know what you are doing, you might even consume an entire egg in one bite.

San Francisco is pretty nuts, but if you're seeking a real estate experience that's viscerally over the top, you're better off poking around places like Naples, Florida, and the Hamptons, whose 1 percenters bitch about the helicopter noise of the 0.001 percenters. But for an even starker contrast, one need only head down to Los Angeles, home not only to the nation's second-largest homeless population, but also to a series of increasingly ridiculous "giga-mansions." Forget privacy and exclusivity. This is pure, hyper-extrinsic showmanship.

For several years, giga-mansion developer Bruce Makowsky, who made his fortune selling designer handbags on QVC, was trying to unload a thirty-eight-thousand-square-foot contemporary Bel-Air mansion he'd built: twelve bedrooms, twenty-one baths. "The U.S. real-estate market is completely void of homes for the ultra-affluent," he'd lamented to *Forbes*. Makowsky's monstrosity wasn't void of anything but humility. The listing boasted three kitchens, five bars, a full-time staff of seven—*can one sell that?*—a forty-seat theater, four-lane bowling alley, massage studio and wellness spa, fitness center, and an auto gallery stocked with $30 million worth of handpicked luxury cars. There was also an eighty-five-foot infinity pool and seventeen thousand square feet of outdoor decks. One could watch *Succession* on an eighteen-foot outdoor screen whilst enjoying beverages from several pre-stocked champagne and wine rooms. An entertainment area featured translucent foosball tables and a wall of candy dispensers that would give a pediatrician fits. The place was lavishly furnished and adorned with more than 100 art installations, including a blinged-out, five-foot-tall camera sculpture by the main staircase. On the roof was a vintage attack helicopter from the 1980s TV series *Airwolf*, "meticulously refurbished" to match the "luxurious details" of the house. A purchaser would need to have either extraordinarily specific tastes or none at all. Which is perhaps why Makowsky ended up slashing his asking price from $250 million to $150 million, and then $94 million, for which the house finally sold in October 2019—minus the fancy cars and such.

Rival developer Nile Niami is a former Hollywood producer who originally priced his last giga-mansion—"the Opus"—at $100 million. Among other amenities, it came with Damien Hirst paintings, a matching gold Rolls-Royce and Lamborghini, and a Cristal champagne vault. He couldn't find a buyer, and the Opus ultimately ended up in the hands of one of his lenders. But Niami also aimed for the giga-mansion hall of fame with a residence he christened "the One." Calling the One a "residence" is a big stretch. At 105,000 square feet, with an initial asking price of $500 million, Niami's still-unfinished project was like Makowsky on steroids: twenty bedrooms, a private nightclub, a fifty-car garage, five elevators, four infinity pools, an infinity moat, and a room whose walls and ceiling were jellyfish tanks—although that pricey detail never made the cut, because Niami defaulted on his loans, forcing the One into receivership. "Anyone who buys one of my homes is making a statement about who they are," Niami once bragged to a reporter, and of that I have no doubt.

—————

These immense party houses and fast cars and bespoke experiences may all be fun for a while, but even the good life has limits. Say you're ravenous, and I buy you a burrito. You're so happy with the burrito that I order you another one. By the third burrito, you're starting to hate me—and burritos. You have exceeded your "satiation point." This happens with possessions, too. I'm not saying you will hate your fourth house or your fiftieth pair of sneakers, but there's a marginal utility effect: You can only live in one house and wear one pair of Yeezys at a time.

For a 2018 study in the journal *Nature Human Behaviour*, a team of psychologists from Purdue and the University of Virginia crunched Gallup World Poll data covering more than 1.7 million people. They found, in the United States and Canada, that people's self-reported positive emotions improved with rising earnings up to a satiation point at about $65,000 per year. Negative emotions (stress, worry, etc.) declined as earnings increased, reaching an inverse satiation point at $95,000. Life evaluation scores, which measure how well we believe we are faring in our lives to date, maxed out at annual earnings of $105,000. The upshot of these and similar past observations is that we tend to hit peak satisfaction when all of our basic needs are met and we no longer live in fear of our credit card bills.

Intriguingly, the researchers observed, life evaluation scores in the United States and other wealthy nations reverse and begin to decline once people pass the satiation point. While their data on very high earners was too limited to provide a complete picture, they hypothesized that the decline may be related to heavier workloads, greater responsibilities, and time demands that limit high earners' opportunities for enjoyment. Other factors, they wrote, may include increased materialistic values and social comparisons, and unfulfilled material strivings.

Wealth-related social comparisons are particularly toxic, as they bring about feelings of inadequacy. "Most of the search for wealth is not about how good the stuff is. It's about what the stuff says about how valuable of a person you are," says forty-one-year-old Sam Polk, whose memoir, *For the Love of Money*, recalls his days as a hedge fund trader on Wall Street. His moment of revelation, which prompted him to change careers, came when the fund he worked for offered him a $3.6 million year-end bonus and he became *angry*—he felt he deserved $6 million to $8 million. Polk was just seven years out of college. "The guy who was giving me that bonus was literally taking home $400 million that year," he told me over appetizers at a Newport Beach restaurant. "You live in this total myopic cocoon of other people that have this kind of money."

Psychologist Bob Kenny, a founding partner of North Bridge Advisory Group in the Boston area, spends his days helping super-rich clients and their children grapple with their wealth anxieties. If anything, he says, affluent folks are at a small *disadvantage* when it comes to finding happiness, because Americans tend to think that more money would solve their problems. "Wouldn't it make things better if I had that house on the ocean, if I just had *something*? Deep down we believe that," Kenny says. But his clients don't have this fallacy to cling to. "I say to people all the time, 'Look, retail therapy works, but so does cocaine,'" he says. "The problem is, it wears off. When you go out to buy something and it's new and it's pretty, the latest iPhone or the Tesla—God, *this is great!*—it just isn't sustainable. Not that you don't have enough money, but that it'll lose its kick, so you buy another one. I know a guy who bought three."

"iPhones?"

"Teslas," Kenny replies. "His fourth car was a BMW convertible or something. And you wouldn't meet him and think, 'God, that is one happy guy.'"

CHAPTER 4

FROM THE ELITE TO THE IMPOSSIBLE

Being rich is having money; being wealthy is having time.

—HENRY WARD BEECHER

So maybe money can't necessarily buy happiness—or community. But one thing it definitely buys is access: to prominent people, spectacular places, political influence, and even personalized health care, which could be useful, for instance, during a viral pandemic. The trappings are pretty stylish, too. The sitting area at Griffin Concierge Medical in Tampa, Florida, has the vibe of an upscale bed-and-breakfast, with sunlight casting through double-hung windows onto warm hardwood floors. Nashville's Brentwood MD feels more like a wealthy man's living room, with a wide, brown leather sofa and an expensive-looking wooden coffee table with photo books. "You feel like you're in a high-end furniture store, or even a spa, for that matter. Just very stately, appointed, everything is very intentional," says forty-four-year-old Scott Pope.

Pope is the CEO of ROAMD, a network of nearly one hundred membership-based concierge medical practices. He's a pharmacist by training, and a concierge patient in Charlotte, North Carolina, where he lives. Joining ROAMD lets concierge doctors extend their wealthy clients the same level of attention while traveling that they enjoy at home. For annual fees typically ranging from $2,000 to $10,000 per head—some docs charge up to $40,000—a person can expect highly individualized, proactive, and unusually private primary care.

Primary care is a numbers game. The average physician is responsible for 1,200 to 1,900 patients. Under an intermediate model known as direct primary care, for which patients also pay an annual fee in addition to regular insurance, that figure might be five hundred to one thousand, Pope told me. But with concierge medicine, most doctors have three hundred or fewer patients, and he knows of at least one practice that accommodates just twenty-four. "If you have a physician who couldn't pick you out of a lineup, you probably don't have a relationship with them," he says. "We think COVID is going to put even more pressure on consumers, because this is not the time of your life when you want to be number three thousand on your physician's to-see list."

Nobody has solid numbers on this upscale niche. The data he has available, Pope says, suggest that there are roughly ten thousand concierge and direct primary practices in the United States, and the number is growing 10 percent to 15 percent annually. That doesn't count big players such as Duke University Health System in Durham and Atrium Health in Charlotte, which host their own, largely autonomous, concierge practices.

When you walk through a concierge doc's front door, there is no check-in process. The receptionist smiles and greets you by name, offers coffee and fresh fruit, and asks how your spouse and children are faring, or your business. There are no lines, no waiting rooms with buzzing fluorescent lights or coughing patients. Some practices time appointments so one client never encounters another. "The privacy component is one of the better parts," Pope says. You also get your doctor's cell number. Depending on the plan, a patient might have unlimited phone and text access, unlimited personal visits, and, especially now, unlimited televisits. Some docs will even make house calls.

The appointments are never rushed, and they are comprehensive. When you have your annual physical, it's not just "check the box," Pope says. You're getting into pharmacogenomics testing and DNA analysis, metabolic diagnostics, and intensive screenings for risk factors related to cardiovascular disease, cancers, and so on. "I'm at that phase of my life that testosterone levels can start to drop," he says, "and that's something that my concierge physician is working on with me." You can forget Walgreens. Many practices have services that will fill your prescriptions and deliver them right to your home. Others have in-house pharmacies stocked with common drugs—amoxicillin, say—all included in the package.

When the pandemic came along, concierge doctors got busy. Dr. Jordan Shlain, a ROAMD investor and founder of the California-based concierge practice Private Medical, was sourcing viral tests as early as January 2020. "He procured testing supplies and [personal protective equipment] long before the federal government was waving the flag and warning people that this was coming," Pope says. "Jordan is a beacon of light in what is otherwise a complete mess."

In a nation with brutal disparities in access to health care and in which politicians and NBA players and wealthy citizens were able to get COVID tests when nobody else could, I doubt everyone would see things quite that way. Yet Pope insists concierge medicine, at its lower price points, is no longer just for the wealthy and connected—it's the future of medicine. The standards of care we put up with are "completely blasphemous," he says, and the way insurance works makes little sense. Does your auto policy cover fill-ups and oil changes? No, it pays for the big stuff: accidents, vandalism, and theft. But health insurance tries to do it all and "it's wildly inefficient, very expensive." Concierge and direct primary are the solution, Pope says. They decouple the oil changes and fill-ups from the catastrophic accidents— for those, you buy a cheap, high-deductible plan on the side.

And all of this might make sense if every American could afford health insurance and we had enough primary care physicians, but neither of those things is true. The most recent data available suggest more than 27 million Americans were uninsured in 2018, and the Association of American Medical Colleges is predicting a substantial shortage of primary care doctors in the coming decade. I'll take my coffee and croissants elsewhere if it means that all of us can have access to a doctor. On Pope's point that everyone deserves concierge-quality care, we agree completely. Then again, there are all sorts of things people should have that they are unlikely ever to get.

The explosion of wealth at the topmost tiers, combined with the time constraints related to accumulating and managing it, have given rise to another kind of concierge—one that will never be available to the masses because that would defeat the entire purpose. And that purpose is to cater to the needs and desires of a hyper-exclusive crowd.

Writ large, concierge services in the United States are a $3.4 billion industry with 127,000 providers, and growing at 3 to 4 percent annually, according to the market research firm IBISWorld. The broader industry goes after households earning $100,000 and up, and corporations that will enlist firms such as Delegated, which charges $420 to $1,800 per month to act as a virtual personal assistant for up to two employees, taking calls, scheduling meetings, doing research, arranging travel, and otherwise helping harried executives juggle their work and personal lives. But the *luxury* concierge sector, a game of global access with just a handful of key players, takes personal services to the extreme. This niche traces its origins to circa 1929, when the concierges of all the grand hotels of Paris teamed up to create Les Clefs d'Or—the Golden Keys—a network meant to help its members cater to their well-heeled guests. Clefs d'Or now functions as a global fraternity of more than four thousand hotel concierges. To join, a person must have five years of hospitality experience, pass a "comprehensive test," and otherwise prove, "beyond doubt, their ability to deliver highest quality of service." Of the tens of thousands of hotel concierges in the United States, only about 660 have earned the right to wear Les Clefs' crossed-keys emblem.

American Express took luxury concierge services beyond the hotel walls starting in 1984. Platinum cardholders, in addition to a suite of travel- and dining-related points, upgrades, and pampering opportunities, are offered a rotating selection of "By Invitation Only" packages—a prime Wimbledon experience, VIP access to the Venice Biennale (a key destination for art aficionados) and the Monaco Grand Prix, a gastronomic tour of Tokyo with PBS *Lucky Chow* host Danielle Chang, etc. Sprinkled throughout the descriptions are words like "insider," "unique," "exclusive," "private," "prestigious," "premier," and, of course, "luxury." But on a more fundamental level, Platinum membership gets you 24/7 access to Amex concierges, who will do their best to fulfill customers' every desire.

Most requests are run-of-the-mill—book me this sought-after restaurant, send my spouse flowers on our anniversary—but some are much more personal. One former Amex concierge, answering questions about the job on Reddit, recalled a client who phoned in regularly seeking sex-massage recommendations, knowing full well the staffers were not allowed to make such referrals. Another client asked the concierge to call everyone on a list of manufacturers to find out what each would charge to build certain concept vehicles the customer coveted, including an amphibious James Bond–style, all-terrain vehicle that would transform into a Sea-Doo when it hit the water.

There is another credit card so exclusive the mere sight of it will have hotel managers and maîtres d' fawning over you, upgrading you to the best suites and tables and bringing you Dom Pérignon on the house. The Centurion Card, better known as "the black card," began as a myth. In 1999, Amex decided to make it a reality. "There had been rumors going around that we had this ultra-exclusive black card for elite customers," Amex executive Doug Smith told the fact-checking website Snopes. "It wasn't true, but we decided to capitalize on the idea anyway. So far we've had a customer buy a Bentley and another charter a jet."

The no-limit black card, issued by invitation only, instantly identifies its holder as a whale—someone with vast resources. Amex won't say what it takes to get an invite, but word on the street is that you must have been a Platinum cardholder for at least a year, ringing up a minimum of $350,000 in annual charges. If invited, you pay an initiation fee of $10,000 and an annual fee of $5,000. In exchange, you get, in effect, the billionaire express pass. Credit card guru Brian Kelly, aka The Points Guy, has the business version of the black card. He wrote on his website about the time he lost a $2,800 jacket and Amex replaced it, no questions asked. When he checked into a Las Vegas hotel, he was automatically upgraded to an executive suite. He got VIP tickets to Stevie Wonder and early access to *Hamilton* tickets for his employees. Amex even sent him a Tiffany crystal decanter and glasses as a holiday gift. But the biggest benefit, he wrote, was Ray, his favorite concierge. Kelly, who travels extensively, estimates that the services of Ray and his colleagues alone are worth $20,000 a year. They were able, in one case, to get him out of Bali in a hurry after a volcanic eruption closed the airport and left thousands of travelers scrambling for alternatives.

According to Snopes, one Centurion cardholder requested a handful of authentic Dead Sea sand for a child's school project. Amex dispatched an agent via motorcycle to obtain the sand and courier it to London. Another black card holder had Amex plan their entire wedding. A third wanted to purchase the *actual horse* Kevin Costner rode in the film *Dances with Wolves*—the animal was tracked down in Mexico and delivered to the client in Europe. The sky's the limit. In November 2015, when Chinese billionaire Liu Yiqian bought Amedeo Modigliani's *Reclining Nude* at auction for $170 million, he said he intended to put it on his black card. The year before, he'd reportedly used the card to purchase a $36 million Ming dynasty teacup. (Amex won't comment on private transactions.) The travel points from the Modigliani purchase alone would ensure Yiqian's family free first-class travel and accommodations for life—not that they needed them.

Among Amex's rivals in the luxury space is Quintessentially Group, a members-only concierge network with offices in fifty countries. Quintessentially promises incredible access for its global clientele, which includes, its founders have claimed, hundreds of billionaires and thousands of hundred-millionaires. (Virgin Atlantic's Richard Branson, rapper P. Diddy, Madonna, and author J. K. Rowling have reportedly been among its clients.) Want a last-minute table at Noma in Copenhagen on a Saturday night? No problem. A private performance by Elton John? Done that. A safe driver to pick up your kids from boarding school in a clutch and deliver them to your vacation home on Martha's Vineyard? Say the word. Polo lessons from an actual pro? Ask Catherine Mills, head of equestrian services, whose duties have ranged from sourcing a top-notch steed for an international competition to showing up at a children's garden party in central London with a bunch of ponies "and walking them through the front door."

Back in 2017, Wealth-X noted a shift in the consumption habits of ultrawealthy Americans and Canadians toward "experiential luxury." Families were seeking "transformative travel" ranging from "socially engaged trips" to space flights, memorable dining excursions, exclusive entertainment and beauty services, and "in-home indulgences linked to high-quality design, architecture, and fine art"—although this did not preclude acquisition of "a desirable luxury asset, such as a super yacht or private jet." The good life is more than fun and games, however. Quintessentially offers "bespoke" tutoring and placement services that deploy "insider knowledge" and "deep analysis of every student's past studies and future aspirations" to place your kids where they belong, be it a top-notch kindergarten or an elite university. The company can source nannies and dog walkers, get you a callback from a world-renowned cancer specialist, identify the best criminal defense lawyer for a wayward sibling, stock your Menorca compound with top-shelf liquor, schedule your workouts. "No request is too small or too big. It just can't be illegal or immoral," said Jacob Zucker, who at the time of our interview was the company's marketing manager for North America.

Morality is in the eye of the beholder. As COVID-19 compelled middle-class families around the world to cancel vacations, Quintessentially said one of its clients had shelled out one million British pounds to secure a full-service villa on the Côte d'Azur. "It's the birth of the £1 million package holiday," chief marketing officer Fiona Noble told the *Times* of London. To minimize the risk of infection, such arrangements would employ private jets and helicopters to get families to their destinations: yachts, villas, and private islands whose crews and staff would be pre-quarantined.

Quintessentially, which came to the United States in 2003, was founded in London three years earlier by Aaron Simpson, Paul Drummond, and Ben Elliot, a nephew of Duchess Camilla Parker Bowles and self-described "relentless, bossy fucker." Friends were always hitting up the well-connected trio for help getting into this or that event, and they realized there was money to be made helping cash-rich, time-poor families enjoy their leisure. The company's "lifestyle managers" are expected to be familiar with clients' tastes, schedules, hobbies, birthdays and anniversaries, and to proactively recommend exclusive activities family members might enjoy, from art openings to pheasant hunts. There are three levels of service—Dedicated, Elite, and Quintessence—dictated by the experience level of the assigned lifestyle managers and the amount of personal attention a member demands. The most popular tier is Elite, which costs U.S. members $20,000 per year.

One of the company's past slogans was "from the elite to the impossible," so I asked Zucker to describe some of the "impossible" requests, like the time Quintessentially negotiated with Egypt's Ministry of Antiquities to secure one of the pyramids for a Saudi client's engagement bash—the party cost hundreds of thousands of dollars and the bride-to-be arrived in a horse-drawn carriage. "You would think, 'Oh, the pyramids are sacred, no one should be allowed,'" Zucker said. "We were able to make that happen." For just under $10,000, another couple was spirited by helicopter to the base of an iceberg off the coast of Chile, where a chef prepared them a romantic meal. There was also the client who demanded a realistic great white shark that he could drag out onto the beach for pictures—amazingly, after a few misses, the concierges found their cartilaginous predator in a local taxidermy shop. Another guy wanted the Quintessentially crew to find him an uninhabited island in international waters where he might then establish a "micronation."

Most requests are not quite so elaborate: "We can source a pet jellyfish for somebody," Zucker noted helpfully. But then there was the Dubai member who didn't want to shower in tap water: "She wanted to shower in bottled water, so we made that happen."

Tiger Jam is just the sort of event where a Quintessentially member might find himself, a fun-packed Las Vegas weekend where one can mingle with celebrities, play a round of golf at the exclusive Shadow Creek club—with pointers from the most famous golfer on the planet—attend a private concert (Ed Sheeran, Train, etc.), and play some high-stakes poker, all to benefit Tiger Woods's educational foundation.

At the poker portion of one such affair, I met Sam, a thirty-three-year-old partner in a cannabis company that had sold a month or so earlier for a truly extraordinary sum. Not surprisingly, he seemed a little stoned. Very nice guy, in any case, and his wife was equally charming—newlyweds basking in the glow of unfathomable wealth. He'd just been in London, where, apparently unbeknownst to his wife, he bought a hotel. The Golden State Warriors had clinched an NBA finals berth, and at one point Sam (a pseudonym) was telling a group of us how he'd put a block of prime seats up for sale online at $10,000 a pop, never dreaming anyone would pay that much—he'd actually planned to use some of them himself. But then Peter Guber, one of the team's owners, had scooped up the whole batch. Sam couldn't believe it. "I mean, he's a billionaire," chimed in "poker brat" Phil Hellmuth, the evening's emcee, embellishing his friend's net worth. "His house connects to the Hotel Bel-Air, bro. I've never seen anything like it."

Sam, clad in a black Louis Vuitton T-shirt and a stylish red jacket, showed me a photo on his phone from a few years earlier: His wife, then girlfriend, was sitting in the kitchen of a modest apartment pipetting liquid into vape devices Sam had designed, literally on the back of a napkin, after taking apart rival gadgets to see how they worked. He offered me a hit from his own bespoke vape device, a bling-y, double-barrel design with rings fused to the base so you could hold it like brass knuckles. I heard someone say this one-of-a-kind gadget had cost him $100,000.

Less than an hour earlier, Sam had been playing poker at a table with Tiger, NBA superstar Russell Westbrook (who at the time had a $205 million contract with the Oklahoma City Thunder), and others for whom the $11,000 buy-in was like $20 for most people. Nearby tables were populated by company founders, private equity and venture capital dudes, and at least one senior vice president from Merrill Lynch's wealth division. Hellmuth, mic in hand, wandered around doing play-by-plays and razzing players good-naturedly, including one hefty fiftyish gent who had recently sold his own company for hundreds of millions. Watching from the sidelines were well-heeled spouses and golf enthusiasts and a few relative paupers such as myself, wondering what, exactly, we were doing behind the velvet rope with celebrities and an open bar and an ice sculpture.

A number of my affluent informants told me they were struck by the extent to which their newfound money had instantly opened up doors to famous people, exotic places, and events much like this one. "I think that's what rich people get," Watts says. "It's not that they get happiness . . . but they're given incredible access. So anything they want to do they can have. Where you and I can't get front-row seats to Lady Gaga on the last night, that's easy for them." But there are practical benefits as well: Having friends within these rarified social circles might well help you advance your career, bankroll your business, get your kid a high-paying job right out of college, and perhaps burnish your cred. "The thing that is the least obvious and probably the most socially corrosive is just the power that comes along with wealth. The social power. The undeserved access to whatever you want—whoever you want," Hanauer told me. "People return your calls: United States senators, university presidents, everyone."

After hitting his Amazon jackpot, Hanauer resolved to spend just one-third of his non-family time on business matters. Another one-third would be spent "making the world a better place," and the rest he would dedicate to "the life of the mind"—things that interested him. He went through an astronomy phase, he told me, during which his wealth bought him quality time with some of the top researchers in the field—whose projects he then supported. Everybody wins, right? But selling access is a risky proposition for scientists and intellectuals, as some discovered after the criminal perversions of the late Jeffrey Epstein came to the public's attention. The prominent scholars and elite universities Epstein had carefully cultivated with his millions suddenly found themselves in a very uncomfortable spotlight. Investigations followed, and there were a number of high-level academic resignations, including that of Joi Ito, who stepped down as director of MIT's famed Media Lab.

Back at Tiger Jam, I struck up a conversation with Erwin Raphael, a gregarious auto exec who is in his mid-fifties and looks ten years younger. At the time, he was vice president and chief operating officer of Genesis, Hyundai's luxury brand. In a subsequent interview, we get to talking about the issue of access. Raphael is no name-dropper, but he's willing to oblige. Okay, sure, he's played golf with Tiger—"Like, who does that?"—and with former boxing icon Sugar Ray Leonard. He's met Priyanka Chopra and Beyoncé. He's tight with Westbrook. "I had Kenny G come over and serenade my wife for her birthday—at no cost, I might add. So you get these really amazing opportunities. It just goes on and on."

Raphael grew up poor in the Caribbean and dreamed of being wealthy one day. "It was very materialistic," he recalls. "Lots of parties and, you know, the boat and the fancy car and that type of thing." His fantasies had nothing to do with making smart investments or doing business or forging useful relationships. Now it's all about that for him. One interesting aspect of having a lot of money, Raphael has discovered, is he rarely needs to spend it. "If I want to be on a boat tomorrow to Catalina with five friends, I can do that, because I've got friends with assets who would be happy to let me utilize their boat, their resort in Hawaii, their resort in Bimini," he says. Every year, he and his wife get great Super Bowl seats for free because his company sponsors the league. His family takes posh vacations using his work-travel points. "Yesterday I played golf at Riviera Country Club and I hosted three of my friends. I'm not a member. It's $300,000 up front and probably four grand a month on top of that. And not only did I play, I didn't have to pay greens fees," Raphael says. "A poor person couldn't have access to it, much less play it." And because he needn't spend a dime on such excursions, "I'm able to take my cash and invest it."

Which brings us to another sneaky aspect of the wealth fantasy that we'll explore in the chapter to come. Namely, the way that having lots of money inevitably means one spends a good deal of time *thinking* about that money—what to do with it, how to keep it, and how to grow it. The opportunities are astounding, to be sure, but they also can be ethically challenging and necessitate a lot of vexing decisions, which is perhaps not what you thought you were signing up for when you bought that lottery ticket from the five-and-dime.

PART II

CHAPTER 5

ENTOURAGE

The art is not in making money, but in keeping it.

—PROVERB

Work and responsibility are not the first things that come to mind when we fantasize about becoming wildly rich, unless we're dreaming of having *less* of those things. But extreme wealth is like parenting a demanding child. It can bring you pleasure and comfort and pride, but also worry and anxiety. You will spend the rest of your life feeding and nurturing it, fretting over it, and cleaning up its messes. The bigger the fortune, the greater the time and emotional commitment. "I liken it to being told you have to work in the family business, which is making shoes, even if you don't care anything about shoes," says author Martha. "You just have to do it."

Great wealth is a job no matter what you do with it. Giving it away, managing and investing it—even the fun parts can end up being a chore. Yachts require upkeep and paperwork and crews to manage, and that boat has to be where you want it, when you want it. If you buy an expensive boat and rarely use it, that, too, may be a thorn in your side. Vacations and parties need to be planned, properties managed, business opportunities vetted, philanthropic endeavors carefully thought through. Tax season can get exceedingly complicated. One can purchase a racehorse for surprisingly little money, but they are pricey to maintain. An inexperienced owner, cautions the website Thoroughbred OwnerView, may require a team that includes a trainer, a veterinarian, a bloodstock agent, and "possibly an experienced owner you know and trust."

"All you see when you look forward to being rich is that it takes away a lot of your struggle," says attorney Richard Watts. But "no matter how much you delegate all of these responsibilities to a family office, or to a lawyer, to an accountant, to money managers, they have to take direction. There's always daily issues of 'Do you want to go into this equity fund? Do you want to go to this management fund? Do you want a contract with this partnership?' You kind of can't get away from it. And if you do try to get away from it and let someone else completely manage it, which I never recommend, you hazard the possibility of losing your money, because people in those positions— it's just very tempting to filter money out and steal your money."

That temptation may have been too great for Jason Kurland, our lottery lawyer. In August 2020, Kurland was indicted by federal authorities for allegedly conspiring with mob associates to defraud several lottery clients, including the $1.5 billion jackpot winner, out of at least $107 million. Some of the funds, prosecutors alleged, were spent on private jets, fancy vacations, luxury vehicles, and yachts. (Kurland and the others pleaded not guilty.)

Dealing with his family's wealth has proved quite the headache for Michael, a forty-eight-year-old from Southern California whose father, a wealthy businessman, died of cancer without ever putting his affairs in order. Michael's dad had squirreled away $30 million to $40 million in various banks, investment accounts, foreign assets, and real estate, yet he never made his intentions clear to the family. He was a difficult man, whose wealth had already created a lot of problems in Michael's life. Now it fell upon his son to hire expensive lawyers and accountants to iron everything out so the family could be set up properly. Michael was pursuing a PhD when his father passed, but "I've been stalled, I'd say, for eighteen months to two years," he told me. "It's been a full-time job."

For Michael and several other people I interviewed, family wealth has taken an emotional toll. An entrepreneur in his mid-fifties, whom

I'll call Jonathan, cleared about $40 million from the sale of his company, which did online corporate training. He lives in a big house in an upscale suburb and has a fine lifestyle, but hitting the jackpot has affected his worldview pretty profoundly. "You move from this mentality of creating wealth to preserving it," he says. "Fundamentally, something shifts. All of a sudden I get scared to death of losing something that I never had before. And now you're afraid that if you lose it, then you won't know what to do. It's just a weird psychological thing."

To make things weirder, his in-laws were loaded. Not long after he married his high school sweetheart, her father sold his own company and walked away with hundreds of millions of dollars. Much of the money went into a family trust that wound up, after the father-in-law passed, in the hands of Jonathan's wife and her two siblings. All three families were by that time financially independent, so "now you've got this shared asset that no one is sure what to do with." The sheer scale of the family wealth makes Jonathan's concerns about losing it seem pretty irrational. But emotions are emotions. "You put the walls up and you want to guard it and protect it and defend it and heaven forbid somebody should take it from you," he says. "You're fear-based now."

In some ways, being very rich and very poor are strangely similar. Just as having not enough money creates fear and anxiety, so can having more than you know what to do with. At both ends of the spectrum, money tinkers with our notions of self-worth, our egos, our social lives, the stability of our marriages, our relationships with children, parents, and siblings—even our mental health. Raising that difficult child properly requires a network of friends and relatives, teachers and advisors, except in the ultrawealth world those teachers and advisors wear business casual and charge substantial fees. "I'm a lawyer, not a therapist," one estate lawyer who caters to ultra-high-net-worth clients told me. "Although the fact of the matter is, you become one."

This theme came up repeatedly, often unsolicited, in my chats with wealth professionals and, indeed, almost everyone I met who works with superwealthy customers and clients. Our culture, perhaps more than most, uses money as a means for judging a person's value in our society. Almost by osmosis we are conditioned to keep our financial affairs to ourselves. Sociologist Rachel Sherman, who wrote a book called *Uneasy Street* about the anxieties of wealthy Manhattanites, had one woman nearly cancel their interview because Sherman used the word "affluent" in an outreach email.

Sherman struggled to find subjects to interview, even anonymously. I can relate. I found that the wealthier a prospective subject was, the less likely they were to engage with me. One aspect of coming into money is that we grow more cautious in our public interactions and proclamations, to the extent that most people who possess hundreds of millions of dollars (including big lottery winners, who tend to go off the radar entirely) are approachable only through intermediaries. Company founders and rich investors are often happy to chat about their business acumen and charitable activities, but asking questions about their wealth triggers defensive instincts. "I think it just feels so transgressive, even if you have an ironclad feeling that no one is ever going to know who you are," Sherman told me. "Wealthy people are often particularly told, 'Don't talk about it. People will just want to be friends with you for your money or take advantage of you in some way.'"

They also tend to be pretty sensitive about how they come off, and fair enough, because society tends to view the super-rich as a monolith. In fact, rich folks come in a wide variety of flavors. But anyone's cringeworthy move can reflect poorly on the entire demographic. Jeffrey Epstein's pedophile nest. Heiress Leona Helmsley declaring that "only the little people pay taxes." Kim Kardashian, amid the surging pandemic, bragging that she had just "surprised my closest inner circle with a trip to a private island where we could pretend things were normal." Even former Starbucks CEO Howard Schultz objecting to journalists calling him a billionaire—"person of means" or "person of wealth" would be more acceptable, he said, prompting a collective facepalm from the rest of America. I mean, who would want to be associated with such people? One wealthy New Yorker, when Sherman inquired about her family's assets, replied: "No one asks that question. It's up there with, like, 'Do you masturbate?'"

I've asked lots of people that question (the one about net worth), usually prefacing it with "This is going to seem rude, but . . ." Most gave me a ballpark figure, but for others the answer was vague. They couldn't complain. They were comfortable. Fortunate. Doing better than most, not as well as some. "Well, that is a bit of a taboo, isn't it? Everyone exaggerates and no one wants to be benchmarked," Mike Depatie responded. "The real question is, why do you want to know?" (He relented, but swore me to secrecy.)

Our reluctance to speak candidly about our wealth creates misunderstandings and social divisions as we increasingly sort ourselves into socioeconomic tribes. For if we can't even talk to our friends, let alone outsiders, about the problems money brings, then in whom can we confide? Our financial entourage, of course! Apart from me, the only nonrelatives who knew the whole truth about Martha's financial situation were her wealth advisors. And even that can be awkward. My wife and I enlisted an old friend, an estate lawyer named Amy Shelf, to do some work for my late mother, but when it came time to deal with our own affairs, we hired an attorney we didn't know. It was more comfortable to discuss our finances with a complete stranger.

I was actually surprised Shelf chose that career path, given her rebellious youth. Estate planning "had never occurred to me," she concurs. "I went to law school and thought I would be pursuing some form of social justice issue." At UC Hastings College of the Law, she took an employment discrimination course taught by Joe Grodin, a retired California Supreme Court justice. It was inspiring and powerful, she recalls, and then she would go to her next class: federal income tax. "I was shocked to understand how policy-heavy tax is as a part of our society and as an area of legal practice—to see how people's behavior changed immediately when the tax code changed."

But Shelf found tax law intellectually stimulating and so, after passing the bar, she took a job with an upmarket firm, helping high-net-worth clients plan their estates. She later cofounded her own firm, whose clients range from fairly low-income to ultrawealthy, including people in their twenties who "barely graduated from high school and kind of went right into the whole tech founder scene, and now they're worth $30 million, $40 million."

Such wealth, particularly newly acquired, stirs up a hornet's nest of emotions. "There's a lot of therapist-like work that I do," Shelf says. "Money is so loaded, and something that triggers so many complicated thoughts and feelings, as well as a lot of neurotic behavior. I mean, we have clients who have a hard time even admitting to *us* what they're worth and what they own, and we can't give them appropriate advice without that information. People feel a sense of guilt. They feel a sense of responsibility. They feel self-conscious about it. They are worried about their kids being too privileged and not engaged and being trust-fund babies and all of those stereotypical ways that we see people fuck everything up."

At the same time, many wealthy clients find it hard to give money away outside their family. Grown children often feel "a lot of resentment" if they're not the primary beneficiaries, especially if the family hasn't talked things through. "So people have expectations and stereotypes that they impose upon themselves and other people," Shelf says, "and it's difficult to make well-reasoned decisions in the midst of that emotional turmoil." This is why we turn to our money managers, accountants, and estate planners—even salespeople and realtors—for emotional support. It is also why the wealth industry has massively expanded to include specialists in social work, education, psychology, and family dynamics.

Most of us cannot afford this brand of therapy. Economists Saez and Zucman define "middle class" as individuals and households in the 50th through 90th wealth and income percentiles. In 2019, by their calculations, those households had taxable earnings ranging from just over $30,000 to $136,500, but even at the top of that spread, our interactions with legal and financial professionals are one-offs. You might have a lawyer draw you up a will and a living trust, sparing your beneficiaries from dealing with probate court after you die. Or you might enlist an accountant to do your tax returns. But when your net worth hits eight or nine figures, you will need a lot more hand-holding if you want to grasp the opportunities now within your reach—and avoid the pitfalls. And that's how Dennis Covington came into the lives of Jerry Fiddler and Melissa Alden.

When Fiddler hit the jackpot, he didn't rush out and buy a Bentley or a lake house. He bought a guitar. He reveals this tidbit over coffee and pastries at a Berkeley café. He senses my bemusement. "Seriously," he says. "Everybody buys himself an IPO thing."

The IPO in question was that of Wind River Systems, a tech company Fiddler cofounded in the early 1980s in the "very tiny, one-car garage" of a rented house just across town. By 1997, *Forbes* had Fiddler listed as the fifty-first-wealthiest person in tech, with nearly $110 million in assets. That was only on paper, and before the dotcom bust. But in 2009, when Intel bought Wind River for more than $1 billion in today's dollars, he cleared somewhere between $80 and $100 million. To be fair, his IPO present was no Guitar Center special, but a one-of-a-kind instrument built by a renowned classical luthier. It had just come off exhibit at the Smithsonian. "I don't know how I heard about it," Fiddler says. "But I said, 'I've got to have that!'"

The jackpot itself "happened pretty suddenly, but dawned on me gradually." Fiddler was too immersed in his work to pay it much attention. He was raised middle-class in Chicago, where he earned a degree in music and photography from the University of Illinois and stayed around for a master's degree in computer science. He moved to California for a job at Lawrence Berkeley National Laboratory developing "embedded" industrial software, and later partnered with a lab colleague to launch Wind River. The company's first product, a digital tool kit built around a Linux operating system called VxWorks, sold like hotcakes. It was so stable that NASA selected it over Microsoft's products for the Mars Rover. "We grew over 100 percent a year for six straight years. We were 69 on the *Inc.* 500," Fiddler says. "But when you grow that quickly without any finance behind you, you're really stretching your cash." He stopped cashing his paychecks and Melissa, his wife, loaned Wind River money from a modest inheritance to keep the company afloat until it went public.

Fiddler didn't sell any stock until almost two years after the IPO. By then he had stepped down as CEO and transitioned into the role of chairman. Chief financial officer Dale Wilde showed up at his office one day and told him the new CEO wanted to do a secondary public offering, but Fiddler held way too much stock; to make the offering possible, he would need to unload at least a quarter of his shares. "I probably wouldn't have sold any at all," he recalls. But "Dale kind of bludgeoned me. He said, 'You're wealthy, but 100 percent of your eggs are in this one basket that's relatively illiquid. If anything ever happens, you're going to go from wealthy to broke. It's just financially stupid.'" So Fiddler sold off a chunk—$15 million or $20 million—although "that's a wild-ass guess." It was a ton of cash, anyway. And "it's like, holy shit! What do I do with it? Do I put it all in my checking account? I got no place else for it."

These days Fiddler runs Zygote Ventures, a one-man venture capital outfit that funds young start-ups in the tech, biotech, and agriculture sectors. One of them, Bolt Threads, makes sustainable fabrics from mushroom mycelium and spider silk—designer Stella McCartney is a customer. Bolt Threads got a funding infusion just before the pandemic hit. Another is Nanōmix, a diagnostics device-maker that pivoted to develop a ten-minute COVID-19 test. Last we spoke, that company was running on fumes, but even if it were to fail, Fiddler says he will be fine. A progressive Democrat, he admits to feeling some guilt on account of his wealth. He was an early member of the Patriotic Millionaires, a group of well-heeled citizens that advocates for more equitable tax policies. He and Melissa share a five-bedroom house—nothing outrageous—in an upscale neighborhood, and socialize with the same "fairly scruffy" crowd from before they were rich. Other than "too many guitars," a Tesla Model S, and the fact that he will never have to worry about paying his bills, his family lives a fairly normal life. Well, okay, they did use private jets for vacations a few times, but only because Fiddler was insanely busy running the company then, and private travel seemed like the only practical way to bring along his late mother-in-law, who was blind and diabetic. "So my kids knew we can take a private jet and most of their friends can't," he says.

Perhaps the most jarring thing about coming into wealth was having all these professionals in his orbit whom he never needed before. Worth millions on paper, with three kids and another in utero, he and Melissa needed to get their affairs in order. Someone steered them to Myron Sugarman, a San Francisco attorney who specializes in estate and taxation issues. "Myron has got clients who are worth far more than me," Fiddler says. "He's seen this movie over and over again."

Sugarman led the couple to the conclusion that help would be essential. You don't just stick this kind of money in your savings account. "I realized there was going to be a lot of work involved in managing this that I had no interest in and no aptitude for," Fiddler says. "It's *real* work."

The Fiddlers needed an entourage.

————

Enter Dennis Covington, the founder of a boutique wealth firm called Ohana Advisors. He chose the name, a Hawaiian word meaning extended family and community, to remind his clients that the world doesn't revolve around their nuclear families. "We tend to have this perspective that it's *my* money," he says. "There's this dynamic about whether you should give money to your siblings. People get really standoffish about that. And I keep bringing them back to the Thanksgiving dinner table. If you're giving money to your kids, why aren't you giving some money to your siblings and your nieces and nephews, for starters, and other friends, and the people that have taken care of you over the years?"

Ohana is what's known as a "multifamily office," a one-stop shop that not only nurtures its clients' wealth but helps them grapple with the vexing questions that accompany affluence, questions related to how you want to spend and invest and give your money away in life and after death. How much to give your kids and what to tell them—and when. Whether to contribute to existing charities—which ones?—or create a charity of your own. Who should run your family foundation, if you decide to establish one, and what its mission will be. Where you stand on tax shelters. And whether you will sully your legacy, for instance, by structuring your giving according to how much it saves you in taxes. For that matter, is it wrong to take every advantage of a system that is clearly rigged in your favor? These are not the worst dilemmas, to be sure, but hasty decisions may bring about some very unpleasant consequences.

Covington is in his late sixties, tall and avuncular, with wire-frame glasses and whitish hair combed neatly back. At the time I visited Ohana's tasteful office suite in Marin County, his small team of experts was serving just ten longtime clients with investible assets ranging from $20 million to about $300 million. "We would not bring on clients at $20 million now," he says—they were either grandfathered in or the result of an existing client's divorce. "I'm exceedingly proud of the fact that we have a perfect record of retaining both spouses, which you would think would be nearly impossible."

Most of Covington's clients are entrepreneurs and venture capitalists, never hedge funders or real estate moguls. "Real estate guys are addicts for real estate. They just want to take their money and roll it into the next thing," he explains, and "hedge fund managers think they know everything." In his experience, the way people earn their money translates into how they manage it, so you will see regional differences based on the local industries—commodities in Chicago, energy in Texas, aerospace and biotech in Florida, tech in California, real estate and finance in New York. Wall Street produces tons of wealth but "very little social benefit," he says, and Wall Streeters tend to feel very deserving of their money because they "were able to kind of grab it themselves," whereas his clients are more team-oriented.

Most of them have experienced the humility of seeing one or more companies fail, so they "would probably say that there's an element of luck involved in them becoming wealthy. The hedge fund guy says, 'It's all me! I'm a fucking genius.'"

In the mid-1970s, after serving a stint in the military, Covington earned a master's degree in finance from UC Berkeley, followed by four years in Michigan with the Ford Motor Company. By 1985, he found himself back in California, interviewing with a man who represented a type of entity Covington had never heard of: a "family office." Family offices are limited liability companies that extraordinarily wealthy families create to manage their affairs. The first family office came about in 1838, when financier J. P. Morgan's clan established the House of Morgan to oversee their sprawling assets. The Rockefellers followed in 1882 with an office that is still in operation. As of 2016, according to Ernst & Young, there were at least ten thousand such entities worldwide, at least half of which didn't exist before 2000—the typical family was worth $200 million or more.

A multibillionaire's office might have dozens of employees, including real estate experts, estate lawyers, accountants, financiers, aircraft managers, and security personnel. These LLCs often hire a CEO and chief information officer, and have boards of directors consisting of both family members and outsiders. Staffers pay the family's bills and wrangle club memberships; manage properties, yachts and helicopters, and household staff. They book meetings and travel; arrange for medical procedures; plan parties and family reunions; work with architects and security consultants; and see to the educational needs and financial literacy of children and grandchildren. They devise tax-advantaged strategies for philanthropy, insurance, and risk management, disburse trust assets to kin, organize weddings and funerals—the tasks are endless. A full-service office, Ernst & Young estimates, costs $10 million a year or more to operate.

The man interviewing Covington represented the Morrises, whose patriarch founded Mervyn's department stores, and Covington was hired to bring analytical rigor to their family office. It was 1985, the year after the first Mac was introduced, and the technology was "rudimentary," he recalls. The business realm was dominated at the time by clunky IBM boxes with 5¼-inch floppy disks, and the Morris office relied on paper documents that came in the mail. "If someone were to ask us, 'What's my net worth?' you would say, 'I'll get back to you in two weeks.'" The job proved disappointing, in any case. Covington expected the family to invest in new businesses whose operations he might oversee, but that didn't happen, and there were "a lot of family dynamics that ultimately turned sour, and they didn't like me being there and I didn't like being there."

Fortunately, a woman he knew, Sara Hamilton, had just launched something called Family Office Exchange. A spate of leveraged buyouts during the Reagan years had made hundreds of families extraordinarily rich, practically overnight. Family offices were blooming like poppies in April. "People were starving for a frame of reference. Everybody was just sick and tired of reinventing the wheel," Covington says. "The wheel, at that point in time, was very often like a nineteenth-century office. People literally had cabinets full of cards that held their stock positions, and on the cards they would write whenever they bought or sold shares." So Hamilton set out to build a best-practices hub for the financial elite, which now claims 380 member families with average investible assets of $500 million. Prior to launching Ohana, Covington spent four years working for Hamilton as a consultant. "I talked to, like, a hundred families and found out a couple things," he recalls. "One is, I loved the industry. I said, 'This is what I want to do forever.'"

Covington's wealth management strategy relies less on stocks and bonds and more on the accredited investments we talked about earlier that are off-limits to most Americans: private equity, venture capital, hedge funds, real estate development deals, credit vehicles, and even commodities like timber—"things that you couldn't just give notice and you get your money back at the end of the next quarter." Ohana also devises strategies for taxation, charitable giving, estate planning, education—everything, really. "We are, as they say in the

military, asshole to belly button," he says. "It's a very intimate relationship. People share things about their kids, and we're there when they
have major life events and things like that."

———————

With estate planning, the default mode is to stiff the taxman. At a
2017 meeting with Democratic senators, former Goldman Sachs
COO and Trump economic advisor Gary Cohn reportedly joked that
"only morons pay the estate tax." And the tax is indeed easy to circumvent. There's "a whole tool kit," Covington explains, to transfer
assets tax-free from one generation to the next while the parents are
alive. Deploying these tactics, the offspring might end up with up to
half of a family's total investment assets even before their parents kick
the bucket, resulting in a far smaller taxable estate.

Lest you have any qualms about using every trick in the book to
minimize your taxes (and maximize your intergenerational wealth
transfers), attorney Harvey Dale, who has advised many a billionaire and has taught tax law at New York University for decades, offers
his reassurance. Dale points to the legal opinions of the well-known
twentieth-century federal judge Learned Hand. In the case of a businesswoman who tried (and failed) to pass off a blatant tax dodge as a
corporate reorganization, Hand wrote that a citizen "is not bound to
choose that pattern which will best pay the Treasury; there is not even
a patriotic duty to increase one's taxes." Later, in a dissent stemming
from a rich couple's divorce, he wrote: "Over and over again courts
have said that there is nothing sinister in so arranging one's affairs as
to keep taxes as low as possible. Everybody does so, rich or poor; and
all do right, for nobody owes any public duty to pay more than the law
demands; taxes are enforced exactions, not voluntary contributions.
To demand more in the name of morals is mere cant."

Hand wasn't arguing that America's tax policies are moral—
because they arguably are not. He's simply saying that playing by the
rules is not *immoral*. But I'm not convinced. Since when does simply
being legal make something morally and ethically legit? James Ever-

ingham told me he has friends who get together and come up with crazy tax-avoidance schemes, but he won't partake: "I'm a completely irresponsible person," he jokes. "I don't give a shit. I *want* to pay taxes. I probably pay the highest amount of taxes possible."

Ethical questions aside, tax dodges require trade-offs. Notably, when you set up an irrevocable trust for your children, they may end up with a lot more tax-free money, but you have relinquished your control. All investment and disbursement decisions are henceforth made by the trustee you named in the paperwork, and disputes over the trustee's decisions can lead to epic lawsuits and family feuds. Trust is crucial, but hedging one's bets is also a must. Watts told me about a new client with assets of about $500 million who hired him to evaluate the estate and succession plans his entourage had put in place. Turns out the man's advisors had created an out-of-state irrevocable trust as a complicated tax dodge. "That's the wrong directive, and that's what estate planning lawyers mistakenly do—they go hog wild with expensive estate planning to make it tax-free," he says. Watts then called and asked the trustee, an accountant, whether he had fiduciary insurance—in other words, was there anything in place to protect the client if, for example, the trustee were to embezzle his money: "Sure enough, he has nothing. Well, that's horrifying to me that a guy has been in place for ten years, with the best of intentions maybe, but who knows?" So now his client has a $500 million insurance policy.

Most of Watts's clients are worth between $100 million and $1 billion—a level at which it makes more sense to have their own dedicated family office. He is their fixer and right-hand man, keeping watch over their entourages, business strategies, and personal affairs. His Family Business Office has been in operation for more than three decades. "Our clients have a lot of moving parts, and they're buying boats and ships and building homes in other countries, so they really need someone to master lots of different skill sets, and we have law firms all over the world that do that for us," he says. Some clients are aging founders facing the dual dilemmas of inheritance and succession—whether to pass on a business to the offspring, put an outsider in charge, or sell the damn thing. Others are "self-made" guys in their fifties who own "ships with helicopters, and those ships are fully manned with crews of fourteen."

One of Watts's duties is to deal with people's wealth-related tasks that take up "so much of their time that they're just miserable." When someone wants to pitch a client on a partnership or an investment opportunity, first they have to convince Watts of its merits. If a trusted employee is suspected of stealing—"happens all the time"—Watts is tasked with getting to the bottom of the situation. One American client bought a $20 million lot in the British Virgin Islands to build a house without realizing he would need a "Non-Belonger" license and other British legal documents. "That's one of fifty issues," Watts says. The client also had to haggle with a local association over the architectural plans and find a trustworthy contractor in an unfamiliar place. "And can you get a competitive bid when they've all got issues and you're going to spend 50 percent more than you thought because everybody's stealing from you?" His clients get completely overwhelmed by these kinds of things. "But for us it's kind of like a doctor looking at an appendix and saying, 'This might hurt a little bit, but I can anesthetize you, pull it out, and you're going to be fine.'"

His true specialty, though, is dealing with family problems. A wealthy couple with adult children on the dole is feeling used. A succession plan is creating resentment. A patriarch is agonizing over how much money to leave his kids without ruining them. Presumptive heirs are bickering over a beloved vacation property. Prenuptial and divorce contracts, which Watts helps negotiate, always make for interesting tensions. He playacts one common scenario: A superwealthy couple's daughter is marrying a man of modest means and the parents want to give her $1 million to kick-start her new chapter in life. Not to create any consternation, Watts will say to his clients, but do they intend that the money be for both newlyweds?

"No, I really want *her* to have it."

"Well now, have you ever thought about the fact that the husband has got a bank account of $10,000 and you're giving money to your daughter. . . . How do you think that's going to affect the marriage?" He just wants people to think through their choices, because he's seen what results from making bad ones. "I can put a stencil from one family to the next and anticipate what's going to happen," Watts says.

Consider, too, that money managers stand to benefit by convincing clients to keep their wealth in the family. Their compensation, after all, typically depends on the amount of assets they have under management. If a client sets up irrevocable trusts for his kids, that person's wealth advisor keeps collecting fees. This perverse incentive creates a disconnect between the public interest and that of the wealth industry, with the client somewhere in the middle. "I feel like I want to live in a society where I'm taxed so that other people can go to school and have health care," says Michael, our stymied PhD candidate. "And yet, out of the other side of my mouth, I'm having conversations with these estate lawyers about how do you shelter the most money so that it doesn't get taxed. It's weird."

"I've had this conversation with myself many times," says Fiddler, who set up tax-advantaged trusts, including trusts for grandkids who don't yet exist. He feels about taxes the way he feels about software, he explains. When President Bill Clinton's patent chief wanted to make software patentable, Fiddler thought it was a "really lousy idea" and told lawmakers as much during congressional hearings. "We lost that battle, and we were always going to lose that battle," he says. But one of the very first things Wind River then did was to hire a patent attorney and "start patenting everything in sight. It went against everything I wanted, but the rules are the rules. You can fight as hard as you can to change them, but you've got to play by the rules of the game as they exist."

Watts's "stealth ministry" is to nudge clients toward thinking about the greater good and how they can be of service to others. People constantly ask, "How much is too much to leave our kids?" But that's the wrong question, he says. "The right question is, How much is too *little*?" Asking the wrong questions leads to the sorts of horror stories Watts shares in his books *Fables of Fortune* and *Entitlemania*. The latter, which focuses on intergenerational wealth, brought him a host of new clients. They flew in "from all over, saying, 'My God, it's already happening with my kids, and we've got $100 million and I know I don't want to give it to them. So what do we do?' And I said, 'Well, I want you to know that if you left them nothing, they would probably be happy.' And that just terrorizes people, that thought."

As we are soon to learn, what should probably terrorize them even more is the knowledge of what raising highly materialistic kids could mean, not just for the family, but for the health and survival of our society.

CHAPTER 6

THE PSYCHOLOGY OF CONSUMPTION

To be content with little is difficult;
to be content with much, impossible.

—MARIE VON EBNER-ESCHENBACH

A few chapters back, we touched on intrinsic vs. extrinsic pursuits. Intrinsic ones, you may recall, are those that satisfy innate psychological needs. They include such things as volunteering in the community, nurturing true friendships, and striving to be attentive to the needs of others. Extrinsic pursuits are outward-facing and involve appearances, social status, material wealth, and financial success. Coaching your daughter's hockey team is intrinsic. Buying three Teslas is extrinsic. Practicing yoga to stay grounded is intrinsic. Attending yoga classes so that everyone can see how hot you look in yoga pants is extrinsic. Nobody is just one or the other, but a balance that favors intrinsic values is the key to a satisfying existence.

Finding that balance can be difficult in our highly materialistic society. The premise of America's consumer culture, bolstered by an incessant barrage of commercial and economic messaging, is that we should strive to attend the right schools and land the right jobs so we can afford a lifestyle that allows us to fit in with the people we consider our peers. If we cannot afford that lifestyle, we borrow. In a book he co-edited, *Psychology and Consumer Culture*, psychologist

Tim Kasser and his coauthors liken our capitalistic social structure to a religion whose existence hinges on the buy-in of its adherents. Consumeristic aspirations, behavior, and beliefs—aka our "materialistic values orientation"—shape the culture, and the culture shapes us in turn. And as with most religions, there is enormous social pressure to conform.

The tendency to measure our lifestyle against those of others applies whether one is dirt-poor or ridiculously affluent, although the uber-wealthy take such comparisons to the extreme. When I first spoke with Richard Watts, he'd just gotten back from presenting at Mitt Romney's annual E2 Summit at the Deer Valley Resort in Park City, Utah, where "250 of the richest guys in the country" convene each year to discuss business and politics and America's problems and how they can help solve them. JPMorgan Chase CEO Jamie Dimon was on hand, as were former House majority leader Paul Ryan, "two or three U.S. senators, several governors," and many a billionaire. (Economic inequality was not on the agenda.)

After three days spent mingling with people "whose minimum net worth was probably $500 million," he felt desperate to escape. "You can feel in the discussion the measure is how big you are," recalls Watts, who is quite wealthy himself, but a pauper in that room. "When they group together, it's about who's got the biggest boat—and I can say that in a lot of different ways that are nasty, but the biggest boat is pretty quickly identified." He told the group as much during his presentation. "At the end of the day, not only am I invited to walk out of the castle, but I *need* to walk out of the castle," he said, and everyone laughed. But "I was really saying something very true—that getting around all of that, somehow you begin to lose the gratitude for everyday, simple things."

Intrinsic vs. extrinsic isn't just about how much money or popularity or stuff a person has. Rather, it's about how much importance we affix to these things—it's the *love* of money the Bible condemns. "Wall Street doesn't draw people that are interested in doing something specific," Sam Polk points out. "It draws people that are interested in using their talents and their education in order to get the money."

Kasser, an emeritus professor of psychology at Knox College in Illinois, whose scholarship on materialism and other topics includes more than 120 articles and books, writes that a strong materialistic values orientation is one of the ways we compensate for fears and doubts about our self-worth, safety, and ability to counter challenges. But it's not a healthy way to compensate. Highly extrinsic people have fewer positive and more negative moods, lower life satisfaction, and poorer psychological adjustment than intrinsic ones. They exhibit more greed, less spirituality, and more anxiety and depression. They consume more goods and incur more debt. They have lower-quality relationships and shakier marriages. Simply put, they are less happy. "This is completely at odds with what consumer culture tells us," Kasser told me.

In the early 1990s, psychology researchers Patricia and Jacob Cohen asked about 750 young people in upstate New York to rate the importance of various accomplishments, from "getting good grades" to "having expensive possessions," and life priorities from being "a really good person" to "being rich." The same kids were interviewed to determine whether they met the criteria for various mental health diagnoses. The ones who admired materialistic qualities or prioritized being rich were significantly more likely—in some cases more than twice as likely—to exhibit symptoms of paranoia, narcissism, passive-aggressiveness, overdependence on others, separation anxiety, avoidance of social interactions, odd behaviors, and difficulty forming close relationships.

Given such negative associations, one might ask why anyone would espouse extrinsic values, and why they are so integral to American culture. Marketing and media are part of the reason. But there's also a substantial body of research suggesting that we grow increasingly materialistic when our psychological needs are unmet. Economic uncertainty can trigger extrinsic values, which are heightened, Kasser and the University of Missouri's Kennon Sheldon found, when people experience "psychological threat"—threats to our survival, self-esteem, social inclusion, and sense of order, control, and community. "Most really successful people are driven by fear, either economically or validation-wise," says Doug Holladay, whose nonprofit, PathNorth, helps wealthy and powerful men find deeper meaning in their lives through "disruptive" experiences. "You can keep running and building and accumulating, but it's all a pretense."

A number of my subjects, Holladay included, said they didn't think superlative wealth changes people so much as it amplifies their existing tendencies, so if you were well-grounded before, you will probably remain so as a billionaire. Unfortunately, Holladay says, highly accomplished people tend to be pretty poorly grounded. "Their narrative is to create the appearance of great success and happiness—look at social media: 'I'm having the best time. I'm living the life,' which is a total fantasy and totally untrue. They've grown up in the world of shaping a brand. It's not authentic and they hate their lives."

Holladay has a wide-ranging résumé. He attended Princeton and Oxford. He has worked with underprivileged kids and lived in Ethiopia. He was an aide to President Ronald Reagan's chief of staff James Baker and has served as a diplomat in the State Department. He's also a private equity investor, a Georgetown lecturer, and a Goldman Sachs alum. During one long-ago job interview at Morgan Stanley, he recalls a banker marveling over all the things Holladay had already experienced: "He looked at me and said, 'I'm in prison. It's a really nice prison. I have everything anybody could want, but I'm trapped.'"

That's the kind of person Holladay is trying to help. PathNorth's maiden voyage brought several dozen CEOs, senators, and other wealthy and prominent guests on a "magical mystery tour" aboard the *Orient Express*, complete with professional magicians. The "disruptive" part took place each night at black-tie dinners, where Holladay probed the men with questions, prompting them to open up about their "illusions" about life and the "mysteries" they struggle with. Each year, he brings a crop of CEOs to a Trappist monastery for a two-and-a-half-day silent retreat. "It's crazy. I mean these big hedge fund managers, most of them have no faith." The experience will change them, Holladay promises, but being alone with themselves may prove terrifying. On another trip—to Wimbledon with former tennis pro Stan Smith—he surprised the group with a lunch at Dans le Noir?, a restaurant where customers are asked to share the experience of the establishment's sightless owners and servers. "Imagine thirty very control-oriented people for two hours in pitch-black," Holladay says. "You have to trust the waiter." They unpacked the experience later: What did people learn about themselves? During a PathNorth annual meeting in Charleston, South Carolina, some two hundred members wound up at Mother Emanuel, the Black Methodist church where white supremacist Dylann Roof slaughtered nine parishioners in 2015. The church people talked about how they had forgiven Roof. "It was not a happy time. I had people really pissed," Holladay recalls. The CEOs struggled with how anyone could forgive such a monster. After a long and "very animated" conversation, he had them write letters to themselves about a person they needed to forgive. A month later, he mailed them their own letters, prompting at least one participant to rekindle a relationship with his long-estranged mother.

These luxurious attempts at self-realization strike me as a sad substitute for authentic life experiences, but if such excursions can make our business and political leaders more empathetic, then why not? "The ancients nailed it," Holladay says. "They talked about to have a great society you need to have great people. When people become more grounded, fully alive, purposeful, the society changes. It becomes better."

Warren Sapp must have been seeking psychological validation if the assets detailed in his 2012 bankruptcy filing are any indication: Large nude woman painting. Lion skin rug (female, lioness). Lion statue. De Grisogono timepiece. Louis Vuitton suitcase. Flat-screen television—fifty-eight-inch. Boxing glove signed by Muhammad Ali.

Roughly 240 pairs of Jordan brand sneakers and sandals, most still in the original boxes . . .

Sapp, then not yet forty, had risen out of poverty to become one of the NFL's best-paid defensive linemen. In 1998, he signed a $36 million contract with the Tampa Bay Buccaneers before re-upping with the Raiders six years later for another $36 million. Raised by a single mom in a tiny house on an unpaved road in a flyspeck Florida town, he reportedly earned more than $82 million during his football career. Now Sapp was claiming he had about $1,300 in his bank accounts and debts of $6.7 million against $6.45 million in assets. Those assets included a high-rise luxury condo in Hollywood Beach and a fifteen-thousand-square-foot lakefront mansion in Orlando's upscale Windermere neighborhood featuring a boathouse, a lazy-river pool, and an outdoor kitchen. Sapp's ex-wife, to whom he owed $876,000 in alimony and child support, lived in the lake house. Among his other liabilities were unpaid income and property taxes, and more than $75,000 in ongoing monthly support payments to his ex and four other women with whom he had fathered children.

Leigh Steinberg, the legendary sports agent whom director Cameron Crowe followed around as inspiration for the movie *Jerry Maguire*, can attest to the financial challenges athletes face. Steinberg, who has represented a record eight No. 1 NFL draft picks and was said to be worth at least $75 million himself, has spent much of the past decade recovering from his own bout with bankruptcy—the result of alcoholism and a string of personal and professional woes (death, divorce, lawsuits, and children with a rare medical condition). Now seventy-two and sober, Steinberg is regaining his former glory. He scored a major coup in 2017, signing rookie superstar Patrick Mahomes to four years with the Kansas City Chiefs for a guaranteed salary of $16.4 million plus a $10 million signing bonus. Mahomes re-upped in July 2020, inking a ten-year, $450 million contract extension that made him the highest-paid player in NFL history.

Steinberg's headquarters, in a shabby 1980s-era building on Newport Bay, has a somewhat ascetic vibe. His modest office is crowded with nostalgia: civic awards, sports memorabilia and magazine covers, and photos of Steinberg with famous clients (Mahomes, Warren Moon, Steve Young), politicians (Bill Clinton, Ted Kennedy, Barack Obama), and movie stars (Julia Roberts, Tom Cruise, Cuba Gooding Jr.). Steinberg is looking slightly weathered himself. His cheek is marked by a fleck of brown spit from a chewing tobacco habit he never managed to kick. A magnet on his mini-fridge reads: "Falling down is part of life. Getting back up is living."

Steinberg has seen plenty of pro athletes fall down financially, and he does his best to save his own clients from that fate. They face challenges akin to those of lottery winners: the opportunists and hangers-on, thieving advisors, and nonstop solicitations for loans or investments in slam-dunk businesses that turn out not to be—to say nothing of the temptations. In *Broke*, a 2012 ESPN documentary, veteran athletes recalled how they had snapped up houses and cars for relatives and all kinds of crazy things for themselves—mansions, yachts, bling. "We were draped in jewelry: chains, crosses, you name it," said former wide receiver Andre Rison. "I guarantee I spent $1 million on jewelry."

"You're a little reckless when you first get that money," added Leon Searcy, a first-round NFL draft pick at age twenty-two. "Everybody had their suit guy. Everything was tailor-made, from the jackets to the pants to the 'gators' you wore, the hats, the Rolex, and the bracelet on your wrist."

"Probably one of the dumbest things I ever bought was a fox coat," said JaMarcus Russell, another top draft pick, marveling at his bad judgment. "It has a big hood on it with a gray stripe that goes down and it makes me almost look like a silverback. I've probably worn it three times."

All of them were young men at the peak of their talents, finally getting their due amid a hyper-macho culture in which attention—from coaches, teammates, and fans—is a form of currency. And although it's gotten harder over the years for poor kids to make it to the big leagues, a sizable subset of football and basketball players still come from adverse economic conditions and are no strangers to psychological threat. "There's a really good chance that they haven't been exposed to substantial amounts of money," says Hyundai executive Erwin Raphael, who serves with Steinberg on the board of Direct Sports Network, and who has counseled athlete friends on business and finance matters. "You might as well get plutonium or something. You just don't know what you don't know, and unfortunately many of them don't take the time to learn."

Elite Olympians, too, are high-risk, says Steinberg, who has represented several. They train 24/7 and are typically homeschooled rather than attending normal high schools, "where you go out on dates and you have to learn social skills and awareness." And "like the boy in the bubble, they come out into the real world and understand that they can buy a fancy car, they can buy any jewelry they want."

————

Colleges and major sports leagues have embarked on financial literacy efforts. Even so, Steinberg estimates that only maybe one-third of professional athletes manage their money well. Players who don't bother to seek out sound financial advice, or who fail to heed it, end up budgeting according to their latest paycheck—a huge mistake, especially in football, where careers are short, injuries inevitable, and salaries seldom guaranteed. You can live like a god on $5 million a year, but the money won't last. Rookies are often laughably oblivious to Finance 101. Only after Rison noticed a big chunk missing from his first check did he learn about taxes, and the fact that he would be taxed separately by every state in which he played an away game.

These athletes have "no point of reference," says a veteran sports business manager I'll call Frank, whose firm caters to baseball and basketball stars. The NBA and MLB programs that recruit financial advisors to educate the players are "kind of a joke," he says. "Like, what an entrée, right?" The only valuable part, he says, is when the leagues bring in former players to talk about how they lost a fortune. And that's easy to do thanks to youth and ignorance, material striving, and unforeseen expenses. Most players have to maintain at least two residences, one where their team is and one back home. In addition to the various taxes, they have to pay agents, financial planners, accountants, and other members of their professional entourages—which often include personal trainers, masseuses, and nutritionists they hire to help keep their bodies in top form. Some of Frank's longtime clients will hire a person just to open their mail: "You can't imagine— if you're a star, you have thirty boxes delivered to your house a day— earphones, shoes, underwear."

Frank told me his firm had just signed two new athletes making more than $35 million per year. He gets involved in the most intimate details of his clients' lives, enlisting people to clean their homes, do their laundry, cook their meals. "In my world, an old client is thirty-four. That's the old man and the sea," Frank says. "I have numerous clients that are nineteen and some that are twenty. This house cleaner I hired for one player, I need her to clean the house twice a week, wash all of his clothes, fold them, and put 'em in his room. Why? Because he's never done that before! He went straight from high school." The firm tries to help the kids learn some basic life skills, "but we have to make it as easy as possible for them." For instance, a client would be unlikely ever to walk into an auto dealership: "We talk about it. They decide what they want. And I buy the car and have it delivered on a truck."

His athletes aren't *wealthy*, Frank emphasizes, yet they have eye-popping salaries: often $1 million or more *per month*. "You have large cash flow," he says, "and we're trying to create wealth." If a client wants to buy a nice car, or a house for his mom, Frank is all for it. The problems arise when a player tries to support, as Steinberg puts it, "a village"—a crew of old friends and extended family members who assume, when the athlete signs a contract, it's their payday, too. "Basketball especially takes away a normal youth," Steinberg says. "They're spotted at ten, eleven years old, and they're surrounded by [Amateur Athletic Union] coaches and shoe companies. They generally have a large contingent of people around them who all think that somehow they're part of the project." The highest-paid athletes can support this kind of entourage, but "a backup point guard for the Grizzlies can't pay three family members," Frank says. "If you do that over eight years, you're not going to have a lot left."

True superstars have no excuse, Steinberg says. The veterans have been through the wringer already, whereas the hottest young pros can afford top-notch representation and counsel. Given the pyramid structure of incomes in professional sports, guys like Mahomes and Steph Curry can live off their commercial endorsements while investing their huge paychecks. If Curry wants a particular car or brand of designer clothes, he can easily cut a deal. Big names get comped on almost everything—hotels, sunglasses, shoes: "We've done endorsement deals with jet companies, so certain athletes have their whole families flown to games and they can use private jets in return for an endorsement," Steinberg says. "The irony is, the people who make the most money end up paying for the least things."

It's usually back-benchers who get in trouble. Steinberg enlists financial professionals to educate his clients. Then again, this is their moment, and trying to convince them to sock it all away for a rainy day is not going to fly. "They're going to rebel," Steinberg says. "You have to at least allow for some reasonable accoutrements to the fact that they are successful. It's not going to kill them if they buy a car for $20,000 more than another car." That said, he's seen some rookie moves. One former client, a wide receiver, got a "reasonable" bonus and immediately went out and bought a $375,000 Rolls "that the minute you drove off the lot lost $75,000," Steinberg says. "It's homes and the decoration of the homes. I mean, endless expenditures: diamonds and personalized jewelry and clothes. When you walk into an athlete's closet you would think Imelda Marcos was there. They have hundreds of pairs of shoes—you couldn't wear them in a lifetime." Single guys are the most susceptible. "You get addicted to the lifestyle," Steinberg says. "Have to have the best home, the best architect, the best designer, the best clothes, the best car, eat at the best places."

As Sapp discovered, out-of-wedlock children are a drain on re-

sources, and divorce is a killer, between the legal fees and the way assets are sold off at fire-sale prices. Athletes, too, get it in their heads
to open a bar, a restaurant, a limo service, a gym—all businesses that
are likely to fail when you don't know what the hell you're doing. Web
start-ups are another money sink—Steinberg took a bath on tech investments himself—as are companies pushing new types of training
gear, water and sports drinks, and nutraceuticals. One of his clients, Steinberg told me, invested in those plasticine balls that go in
gumball-type vending machines.

———

The materialistic binges of the newly rich are perversely entertaining, but there's an aspect to these extrinsic pursuits that should worry
all of us. Namely, because societal instability and psychological threat
encourage extrinsic behavior, and extrinsic behavior leads to further
insecurity and distrust, a vicious cycle is created that bodes poorly
for our increasingly threadbare social fabric. In 2013, Kasser and psychologist Jean Twenge of San Diego State University reported a notable increase in materialism among high school seniors from 1976 to
2007, a change they attributed to advertising culture but also to rising instability in the adult world. A growing body of research further
suggests that extrinsically oriented people are more likely to behave
selfishly and to engage in antisocial acts. They are more manipulative
and less socially inclined. They compete rather than cooperate. They
don't care as much about environmental problems such as climate
change, and are more likely to harbor environmentally destructive attitudes and behaviors. Over the past few decades, America has witnessed a marked deterioration of civil society, with people showing
less and less willingness to communicate honestly and work together
in good faith to tackle our collective problems. "Materialistic values
not only heighten our vulnerability to serious social and environmental problems, but also undermine our ability to work cooperatively in
finding solutions to these problems," note Kasser and his colleagues.

The good news is that our values and attitudes are not fixed in stone. Even highly materialistic people can be prompted to behave less selfishly, and it is here that Kasser, whose work has made him something of an activist, finds a glimmer of hope. In one study, for example, college students who were asked to write about aspects of the American Dream associated with freedom, family, and helping others made more environmentally sustainable policy recommendations than did members of a control group. "Similarly, in studying a group of highly extrinsic adults, we found that getting them to think about intrinsic values led them to be more interested in helping poor people in other nations and fighting climate change," he told me.

In August 2019, the Business Roundtable released a statement signed by 181 public company CEOs declaring, in essence, that there's more to capitalism than shareholder value—that companies should be committed to "*all* stakeholders," treat their employees right, contribute to their communities, and respect the environment. Many observers panned this as empty rhetoric—yet another cynical attempt by the rich and powerful to stave off the pitchforks. But suppose capitalism *could* be reformed. Suppose Corporate America were to move in the direction of B corporations, a fledgling business movement of fewer than four thousand companies that are *legally bound* to do what the Business Roundtable claims a corporation should do. The executives themselves would stand to benefit psychologically, if not financially. "I mean, there's all kind of data on CEOs that are, oh my gosh, they're just dying emotionally—they're lost and dying," says Holladay, whose nonprofit's website describes PathNorth as "a tribe of leaders trying to become better people."

His clients are mostly men, and most men "are terribly lonely and disconnected, but if you put a couple zeros on that, it just makes it worse," he told me. "The way I frame it in PathNorth is the unintended consequences of great wealth or positioning or notoriety. There's a whole lot of merit badges that isolate you, and it could be the wealth thing. It could be just the fact that you're CEO of a public company and you don't know what the hell you're doing."

CHAPTER 7

LOSING TRUST

*For what shall it profit a man if he shall gain
the whole world, but lose his soul?*

—MARK 8:36

Nobody sets out to be lonely and disconnected, but our financial choices often lead us in that direction. We tend to compare ourselves to those within our socioeconomic orbits. As the philosopher Bertrand Russell once put it, "Beggars don't envy billionaires, just other beggars who are more successful." We take our cues from the people closest to us in education, geography, politics, profession, and (yes) wealth. These are the people we collaborate and socialize with, turn to for counsel, and marry and procreate with. Like clusters with like, and thus we sketch out our social boundaries and amplify our advantages or lack thereof. As we move into increasingly affluent surroundings, our boundaries shift. We calve off from old networks and join new ones. Our points of reference start to change, as do our expectations, our sense of what's normal.

Even modest wealth differences trigger tribal tendencies. Is it such a sin to want to relocate to a place where you have more space and more privacy, better-funded schools and well-maintained parks, superior infrastructure, low crime, and all the rest? No, it's a natural instinct. Yet people also self-segregate for reasons we aren't so eager to talk about. Namely, the awkwardness of being a have among have-nots, of being in the company of people we believe will judge us and feel judged by us in turn. There's research suggesting that the higher a person travels up the socioeconomic food chain, the more likely they are to feel deserving of their lot. And that tendency, combined with a dash of guilt, helps fuel a clustering instinct. We want to be free to enjoy the fruits of our labor without being reminded constantly of our privilege, so we enter the bubble. "These communities step you up and away from the norm," Watts says. "It's kind of a badge a little bit: We're in this private gated community and we got *this* famous guy and *this* famous guy, and we're all rock stars in here. But we're left alone. We understand what it's like having people who always want something from us and here we don't want anyone to get stuff from us. We want you to stay away."

The lifestyle in the bubble is pleasant. The lawns are well-groomed and the pools inviting. The roads lack potholes and there are ample options for tennis and golf. But there are psychological ramifications to living in the bubble. In a 2005 study, Dartmouth College economist Erzo Luttmer found that people's self-reported happiness decreased as the average incomes of their neighbors increased. In fact, when our neighbors bring home $5,000 more per year, he says, the negative effect on our own psychological well-being is about the same as if we had experienced a $5,000 pay cut. The effect is strongest among people who spend the most time socializing with close neighbors as opposed to friends from elsewhere, which further implicates social comparisons as the culprit. Interestingly, as our neighbors get richer, we become more satisfied with the towns we live in—community wealth begets a nicer commons—but less satisfied with the quality of our friendships and our allotment of free time. "People appear to be giving up leisure, to allow their friendships to suffer, and to work more," Luttmer wrote, "perhaps in an attempt to mimic the material living standards of their neighbors."

Over the past four decades, we have become increasingly segregated by wealth. Sociologists Sean Reardon at Stanford and Kendra

Bischoff at Cornell found that the percentage of families in urban areas living in either "poor" or "affluent" neighborhoods more than doubled from 1970 to 2012. Researchers call this "income segregation," and it varies by region. Income segregation in greater Philadelphia more than tripled from 1970 to 2007, at which point 43 percent of families lived either in rich neighborhoods or poor ones. In 2012, in the Dallas-Plano-Irving region of Texas and the Detroit-Livonia-Dearborn region of Michigan, more than 45 percent of families lived at one extreme or the other. In New York–Wayne–White Plains (New York/New Jersey), more than half were thus segregated. Nationally, the proportion of families living in middle-income areas fell from 65 percent in 1970 to 44 percent in 2012.

You've probably heard of white flight. This is *wealth* flight. In 1965, according to the Economic Policy Institute, the CEOs of the 350 largest public companies collected about twenty-one times as much compensation as the typical worker, on average. That's a big difference, but people could still relate to one another. As of 2019, the ratio was 320-to-1.

The equity distribution within companies is even more skewed. Tim O'Reilly discovered as much while flirting with the notion of selling his thriving tech publishing company. It's not that he needed the money. He'd already hit the jackpot back in 1995, when O'Reilly Media sold Global Network Navigator, the very first ad-supported website, to AOL in a deal that netted him the equivalent of about $21 million in today's dollars. But O'Reilly, who is nearing retirement age, felt compelled to consider his company's future, so he sketched out a rough stock plan, calculating each employee's value to the enterprise based on salary and tenure. "It was pretty egalitarian, where the people at the top got maybe ten times the people at the bottom," he says. But when he showed the plan to some compensation consultants, "they're like, 'Oh, no, no, no! This is totally wrong!' " The typical equity arrangement in Silicon Valley is logarithmic. Second-tier employees get about one-tenth what the top tier gets. The third tier gets one-tenth of that. Before long, you might have differences of 10,000-

or 100,000-to-1 between the founder and the low-level workers, O'Reilly says. "And everybody goes, 'Oh, well, that's just fair.' It's not fair at all! It's just the way it works. And if you're in the right place at the right time with the right connections, you get to think that you're really special."

When company founders cash in, they don't tend to stay put. Just as you or I might cross the street to avoid a panhandler, wealthy folks may relocate to avoid awkward economic disparities. From 2007 to 2012, Reardon and Bischoff found, income segregation increased more, on average, in metropolitan areas with larger increases in income inequality—places such as Cape Coral–Ft. Meyers, Florida; Worcester, Massachusetts; and Las Vegas–Paradise, Nevada. In places where inequality changed little, so too, on average, did income segregation. And rich families in high-inequality areas were far less likely to live in mixed-wealth neighborhoods than poor families were. We hit the jackpot and bail. And this has broader consequences, for it turns out that regions characterized by concentrated wealth and concentrated poverty have less economic mobility than those where rich and poor commingle.

Income segregation also affects whom we interact with on a daily basis. Erwin Raphael, who happens to be Black, lives with his wife in a luxury condo development in Southern California—a "like-minded" community where the average income, he estimates, is $500,000 to $700,000 a year. "They're Asian, they're Middle Eastern—and that could be Persian or Jewish or whatnot. They're white, they're Black. . . ." He pauses. "Not very many Black. There's probably 1 percent Black. But one of them happens to be the head coach of the Chargers!"

Everingham doesn't regret moving to Ross. There's a house on sale for $85 million half a mile down the road—"if you're in the market," he jokes. Everyone is rich here, so "there's not awkwardness." Back in Santa Cruz, "your neighbor next door might be worth ten times you or be struggling. A block up, you've got people who got put in jail for robbing banks." His Netscape jackpot was common knowledge in town, and he started feeling like he could be a target.

Perhaps wealth shouldn't matter in our neighborly interactions, but it does. Even if we don't openly discuss our finances, we drop little hints all the time. We talk about pesky landlords and mortgage payments, kitchen remodels and landscaping projects, our modes of transport, careers and alma maters, hobbies and vacation destinations, schools and camps, the sporting events we attend and our children's plans after high school. We glean other information from nonverbal cues, linguistic characteristics, clothing, possessions, and physical traits. We use all of these things to compare—and to judge.

————

Martha doesn't want to be judged. For years, she had the best of both worlds. Her money gave her freedom to pursue a literary career, but apart from owning her own place, her lifestyle was little different from that of her nonwealthy friends. She had "a profound wish not to be separate from everybody else—not to be in some horrible bubble where you can only talk to the guy who has a yacht and is flying around on his private jet," she says. "I don't want to be forced into that life. That's not who I am. On paper I am, but as I live, I don't want to be that person." And yet she can now feel her wealth throwing up walls and straining her sense of belonging within her community of writer friends. "I feel more and more in this little isolation chamber," she says.

One friend told Martha about a health care snafu. She had added her husband to her insurance plan, but thanks to the quirks of Obamacare, the extra income from a part-time teaching job she'd taken on to cover the bills had increased the family's health premiums by more than her job paid. She'd been working for nothing. Martha was sympathetic, but "whatever sympathy I'm expressing isn't going to be like, 'Oh God, I know exactly what you mean, because last week I got hit by this medical bill.' I don't have that thing that every American has, a huge anxiety about their health care costs." Another time, over dinner, one friend was talking about her spouse wanting to retire, and could they really afford that? "Three of the four of us are saying, 'I wonder about that, too.' And I just don't have anything to say."

Succumbing to the bubble can ease such awkwardness. Then again, it can seriously mess with a person's perspective. "It's something I'm explicitly pushing back against," says Bruce Jackson, the former tech executive who, like Everingham, is a big cyclist. "The number of dinners I go to which focus on people talking about their travel plans are legion. Guilty! Not like I'm holier-than-thou, but I don't want to hang out with people talking about how nice it was to bike through the South of France."

The downside to being in Ross, Everingham says, is that it looks like Mayberry: It's safe and clean. Almost entirely white. No homeless people, etc. "Out of sight, out of mind, and that's not necessarily a good thing," he told me. In his profession, you want to be able to connect with the everyman. "I mean, building good software is an act of empathy, you need to see pain and feel pain," he says. "You lose career-useful perspective when you're not around those problems."

At the Concours d'Elegance, the annual auto show and zillionaire fest at Pebble Beach, I introduce myself to a woman in her early fifties whom I'll call Sally. She was raised middle-class in the Midwest and she and her husband now have a small technology consulting firm. They recently signed a prominent new client and saw a big bump in income as a result. "We just went from solidly 'middle class' for the Bay Area (let's say $400–500k/year) to well above that over the last couple of years," Sally wrote me later.

Joining the pair for "car week" were an English couple with ample financial resources. And thank goodness, Sally said, because most of her friends couldn't have afforded this event. Their "club" tickets, which included breakfast and lunch buffets, were $850 a head. If you forgot your sun hat, one vendor was peddling stylish ones from $400 to $4,000. Sally emailed me later from Disneyland, where she and her husband were vacationing with family and "didn't blink" when they were offered a signature suite for a "minor" up-charge. This "isn't a humble brag," she wrote. "It makes me really really really nervous. The cognitive dissonance of privilege gnaws at me."

I don't doubt Sally and her husband embrace their middle-class values, but characterizing a $400,000 to $500,000 income as "middle class" is the bubble talking. A household income of $450,000 would put them within Silicon Valley's top 7 percent. Some of Rachel Sherman's affluent New Yorkers described themselves similarly. "Everyone wants to be middle class," one young inheritor told me. Except they really don't. It's more that they don't want to be stereotyped as *rich people*. They want to be viewed as authentic—which is why wealthy politicians, even including Elizabeth Warren, love to talk about their humble family roots. The upper-class bank balance? They can live with that.

———

According to the calculations of economists Saez and Zucman, actual middle-class income in 2019 ranged from about $30,000 to $136,500 per adult, while middle-class net worth extended from roughly $58,000 to $790,000. Should you manage to scrap your way into the top 1 percent—which required a *minimum* household income of $481,000 or net assets exceeding $5.6 million—your relationships with actual middle-class friends and family members may require extra care and feeding. Because those wealth differentials can create lots of problems.

Mike Depatie, for example, had a relative who fell substantially behind on her bills, so he offered to cover the debt. It would be a gift, he said, but the relative insisted she wanted to pay him back. They came up with a repayment schedule: $100 a month. She never even made the first payment, and then they didn't speak to each other for fifteen years. The whole situation was "unbelievably stupid!" Depatie says.

Jerry Fiddler has had relatives come to him for loans many times. "Almost always I do it, because I can and I'm happy to, and almost always I know it's not going to get paid back." He doesn't care about the money. "It's a rounding error," he says. "My reluctance is I'm afraid of losing this person as a family member that I'm close to and that I can be comfortable with." If he says no, there's going to be resentment. If he says yes, and there's a problem, the borrower is going to feel awkward around him: "It's a lose-lose situation."

Everingham is no longer on speaking terms with one sibling. Their conflict wasn't entirely about money, "but my means definitely exacerbated the situation." For one, he had spent millions of dollars building a compound near Santa Cruz for his immediate family members—"a beautiful place, on fourteen acres." But they didn't like the area (too liberal), and there were other complaints. Tired of dealing with the situation, Everingham eventually signed the property over to his family members. They ended up selling and moving to South Carolina, where they bought a house and "subsequently burned through all that money and mortgaged the house, and now I'm the asshole that won't lend them money again."

Martha's friends can see she's no pauper. But it's not as though she can come crying to them with her wealth problems. I ask her whether she's ever been tempted to bail out struggling peers. "That is a can of worms," she says. "I've only very occasionally found ways of doing that that have not created rifts." One friend messed up her shoulder and was in pain, so Martha treated her to a professional massage, and that was fine. Another had a child accepted to a private school, but the family couldn't afford the tuition and no scholarship money was forthcoming. Martha quietly cut a deal with the school: She would pay the tuition and the administrators would pretend they had come up with a way to make things work.

As these tales suggest, the "helping friends and loved ones" part of the wealth fantasy is trickier than it seems. Even inviting old friends and relatives to join you on your new adventures can be fraught. Assuming the excursion is pricey, you'll have to pick up the tab, and one can do that only so many times before your guests' pride intervenes. Or maybe they don't seem sufficiently grateful, which rubs *you* the wrong way. It might also be that they can't afford three weeks off work to accompany you to Machu Picchu.

Despite our best intentions, big wealth differences are a social minefield that make all involved acutely aware of their position in the pecking order. The problem goes both ways. Not long ago, at a local venue, I ran into a musician I knew from my punk rock days. He used to be good friends with another Bay Area musician who became an international rock star, fabulously wealthy. They still talk, the "poor" musician told me, but things are super awkward now. He's reluctant to reach out to his old friend. "I feel like he'll think I want something from him."

As we sequester ourselves in upscale neighborhoods, pursue new friendships and expensive hobbies, and sink more time into our travels and high-status careers, our old lives and acquaintances can slowly fade away in the rearview. It's not deliberate, Bruce Jackson told me. It's just that your kids and their kids are at different schools now, so there are fewer chance social encounters. (For a time, his attended Lakeside, an exclusive private school where the Ballmers and the Bezoses and the Gateses have all sent their children—"Somebody flew a private plane to one of the soccer games.") And maybe now you get your groceries at Whole Foods, while your old friends still shop at the QFC. Without batting an eye, you can sign up for a fabulous overseas bicycle trip that your old pal who earns $60,000 a year could never afford. Physical proximity is a factor, too. "We stay in touch with some of the same folks, but they're not in the same hood," Jackson says. "That's just a reality. It's not like we've said, 'Okay, let's drop them—they don't have a Mercedes!'" Conversely, "I have never seen somebody go, 'Oh, you're rich. I hate you. I'm not going to be your friend anymore'—maybe it happened and I don't know about it."

One curious thing about wealth is that the differences *within* the 1 percent are just as stark as those between the 1 percent and the rest of us—bubble within bubbles. "If you have only millions, you are not a B person. You don't get invited to the billionaire parties," Watts says. There are events all around the world where the wealthiest of the wealthy connect, and "if you don't have a great big yacht, I mean a *big* yacht, you're just not there. You're kind of segregated from the group."

Playing this game of thrones has a price. The 0.001 percent is such a tiny pool, its inhabitants so protected and bound with so many obligations, that a person in this milieu might wake up one day to realize that all of his relationships are transactional. The billionaires throw their parties and schmooze with celebrities and politicians and the other big fish, Watts says, "and then they come to me and say, 'God, I just didn't realize this would take away my friends. It's like a movie star: I've elevated myself to this place where the people around me all want something. And if they don't want something, then they're grading me for what I've got.'"

CHAPTER 8

THE MARRIAGE PREMIUM

Byrdes of on kynde and color flok and flye allwayes together.

—WILLIAM TURNER, *THE RESCUING OF ROMISH FOX*, 1545

The extent to which our financial status affects our social universe—the places we live and work, the people we befriend, how society perceives us and how we perceive ourselves—has important ramifications for one of our most consequential personal pursuits, that of love, romance, and a life partner.

We tend to couple up before we are fully formed financial human beings. Even so, we tend to seek partners similar to us in education and culture, interests, intelligence, and geography. Doctors marry doctors. Lawyers marry lawyers. Philip Cohen, a sociologist at the University of Maryland, did an informal analysis of the Census Bureau's 2011 American Community Survey data, looking specifically at first marriages of people younger than fifty to partners of the opposite sex. He observed that 71 percent of college graduates had married their like. About half of the female high school dropouts married male dropouts. More than half of the men with professional degrees married women with professional or postgraduate degrees. We also pair according to language, culture, race, religion, etc. Researchers call this "positive assortative mating" or "homogamy." That's just a highfalutin way of saying, "Birds of a feather flock together."

There's evidence, too, suggesting that the wealth of a potential partner's family may factor into our selection criteria. Using data from a survey that tracks families over multiple generations, economist Kerwin Charles and his colleagues at the University of Chicago and Harvard found, after adjusting for age and race, an association between the wealth of husbands' and wives' families similar in magnitude to the wealth correlation between parents and their offspring. Sons and daughters from the highest and lowest quintiles of parental wealth were particularly likely to marry people whose parents were in the same economic brackets. Sorting by wealth and education may exacerbate economic disparities among families with two working partners. But nothing much to be done about that. Birds gonna flock.

Relationships between romantic partners who are intellectually compatible but light-years apart in family wealth are by no means impossible, although we never did find out what happened to Cinderella and her prince. But such pairings require more work, because just as wealth differences can create problems with friends and family, they can monkey-wrench a romantic partnership. Even dating becomes problematic when everyone knows what you're worth. "The very day after the IPO, I became a lot more attractive," James Everingham told me. "The women inside Netscape, especially new ones—they knew who were the Mozillionaires. I remember walking past a cube and this young woman whom I was going out on a date with, I heard her on the phone say, 'Yeah, I met this guy in Santa Cruz and I think he needs some help spending his money.' Shit. You know nobody's motivations, right?"

Michael, the PhD student we met earlier whose wealthy parents subsidized his lifestyle, ended up marrying his girlfriend. She came from a working-class family. They'd met in graduate school and were living together in the condo his parents had paid for, trying to make a go of it as professional photographers. Then his dad insisted he wanted to buy the newlyweds a house. Michael resisted, which angered his father, so he finally caved in. It was a nice house—three bedrooms, 1,800 square feet—but way more expensive to maintain than the condo had been. What's more, living off his parents' largesse made Michael feel emasculated, and he started to be repulsed by changes he perceived in his (now-ex) partner. "The entitlement seemed to blossom," he says. Why couldn't they go on this or that vacation, she would ask, and Michael felt compelled to remind her his parents had *just bought them a house*. "When you buy your own house, as a human, you don't go on a vacation for a few years. We didn't even buy it! So it just became this weird expectation. Subtle little things where it started to make me feel like I'd created a monster, and I had become a monster, too."

————

Richard Watts deals regularly with the havoc that superwealth imposes on the love lives of his clients and their adult children. When a husband hits the jackpot, for example, it's not uncommon for him to feel like Don Juan and go out and cheat on his wife. Watts used to send that client what he called the "cold shower fax"—"I'd circle it: their income. Wife doesn't work. You're going to pay her $40,000 a month forever. I'd ship it to them and say, 'I wish you wouldn't do that. That's what it's going to cost you.'"

For longtime couples, though, one partner's windfall is viewed as a win for both. The spouse doesn't feel like, oh, that's *his* money. (The wealth creator is usually a he.) But pairings that commence when only one partner is super-rich are more problematic. Sometimes "it's the superwealthy daughter marrying the super-good-looking quarterback-y kind of guy that everybody wanted and she can have, and she's not too attractive but she comes with a big purse," Watts says. And when they get divorced, as often happens, "the recognition that the rich daughter is now single makes her a huge target." One of his clients has a thirty-three-year-old daughter who has been married three times: "She wants so badly to be in love, but with a $100 million bank account, she just can't find it."

Martha had difficulty discussing her situation without bringing up her ex, because her wealth anxieties are so intertwined with her failed marriage. She was in her thirties when she and—let's call him Steve—began dating. Martha didn't reveal much about her family finances, but Steve, who was in the process of divorcing his first wife, managed to piece a few things together. She owned her own flat, after all, and didn't appear to require a day job.

They'd been dating about eighteen months when she became pregnant; they decided they would tie the knot after Steve's divorce was finalized. In the meantime, he expressed concern about what would happen should Martha die in childbirth. He began insisting they consult an estate lawyer and put a plan in place. Martha went along—naively, she says. "Somebody in another family might have said the word 'prenup' to me." But nobody did.

She is confident Steve didn't marry her for her money. He was, however, a bit too eager to "help" her get to the bottom of her financial mystery. "He was just like, 'Find out, find out, find out. If you don't want to, I will!'—and he *did*. He pushed for more information." There were aspects of love and respect in their relationship, Martha says, and Steve couldn't understand her wish to keep certain financial details at bay. But his help often felt like scorn. "You don't even know what you have!" he would say, and "If it weren't for me, you wouldn't even know about *that*."

When she and her relatives at last began doing annual phone calls to discuss the family finances, Steve, unlike the other spouses, asked to listen in. That said, he was the only nonrelative, save her advisors, with whom she could talk about her wealth. And though kind and helpful in many ways, he was also contemptuous and shaming, especially when they split up. "To counselors or lawyers he would say, 'She's worth $50 million and doesn't even know it!'—and I wasn't, actually, at that time."

In the end, Martha initiated a divorce. Steve's generous settlement gave him the house they had lived in, assets, and a substantial income, and yet he acted aggrieved. "The kids were dealing with a bitter split, and their dad often, especially at the start, seemed to feel almost broke, and very hard done by. One of his go-to moves was mocking me for my wealth."

Martha is never dating again, she jokes. Since the divorce, she's had one "sort of serious" two-year relationship and another "serious" one-year relationship. Neither was catastrophic. Both were nice people who didn't seem interested in her money. "It's the least attractive thing about you," one told her. But even as Martha grew closer to her partners, she kept the details of her wealth under wraps, to the point that her "sort of serious" partner began jokingly asking whether she was in the mob. Her only friend who knew everything worked for a charitable fund—their relationship had started out professionally. One day, while talking about a man Martha was dating, the friend said something like, "Of *course* he's into you, because you're the whole package—you're smart and nice and pretty and this and that and the other thing, and you're rich, too!" Martha was mortified. "It just made my skin crawl to think that's part of what makes me a good package. It's like, 'Oh my God, I'd rather be no package at all.'"

A person of modest means facing the prospect of marrying a super-rich partner has a different set of questions to navigate. If your pay-check is a rounding error in your partner's portfolio, are you still willing to put in eighty-hour weeks to build your career? "It almost became a cliché to meet hedge funders who were married to women of great intellect and promise" who'd abandoned their careers, says bestselling novelist Gary Shteyngart, whose 2018 book, *Lake Success*, scrutinizes the inner life of one such character, a daughter of immigrants who graduated from Yale Law before marrying an emotionally stunted hedge fund manager and dropping out of the working world. "When did the ambition leave them?" Shteyngart had wondered. "How could they allow their husband's career to become the only one in the family? What would that mean for their daughters and their view of themselves? In the old days, you married your secretary. Now you married an MD-MBA-JD-VP at Goldman Sachs and 'took her off the market.'" (That's actually a thing wealthy people say.)

Elizabeth, our Silicon Valley product executive, learned her lesson the first time around. She had earned an undergraduate degree in industrial design and done research in robotics and artificial intelligence before working in robot design at IBM. She went on to get a master's degree in computer science, followed by stints at the famed R&D lab Xerox PARC, and a PhD program. Amid this intellectual whirlwind, she married a prominent professor thirteen years her senior, a Rhodes scholar with famous friends and a jet-setting lifestyle. It was a giddy time, but she could feel her identity getting subsumed. "I was flying around with the Annenbergs in their plane. I was going to Rhodes scholar reunions and meeting Bill Clinton and Ira Magaziner. It was very high—highest of the high." Until it wasn't. "I finish my dissertation. I get divorced, and I'm sitting in Silicon Valley as a single parent at the absolute kickoff of the wave of the internet."

What saved her were the construction skills she'd learned from her father, which enabled her to buy a fixer-upper as an insurance policy, lest her tech career flopped—which it did not. Elizabeth, always a scrapper, gained traction in the Valley despite the demands of single motherhood. By the mid-1990s, she was helping build a distributed peer-to-peer e-commerce platform—"basically blockchain plus Bitcoin"—decades before its time. Things went uphill from there. Her real estate bets paid off and she invested in new ones. She also landed a series of high-level gigs in product management.

On two subsequent occasions, men far wealthier than Elizabeth have sought her hand in marriage. Both times she got engaged only to call it off later. "I realized I would be entirely living in their world," she says. The first suitor loved going on crazy adventures, and he would always pay her way, but her friends—mostly academics and artists and scientists—couldn't afford to accompany them. "Because of that, it was easier for me to follow him into his life. And if we split up, he would have all the money." The second guy told Elizabeth that if she wanted more kids, she wouldn't have to work anymore. "And I'm like, 'Yeah, but say five years from now we split up. I've compromised my ability to earn and I'd probably stop investing in my own life. But there's no equity in the life we share, because your money is your money.' That was just a bad deal for me." In the end, she married a compatible techie with a good deal less money in the bank than she had. "My husband and I laugh about it, because anytime we're interacting with people, it's just a presumption that *he* made the money—always, always, always," she says. "It's so weird."

———

She's right that it's weird, but statistically that's a pretty reasonable presumption. Wealthy men outnumber wealthy women—vastly so within the ranks of the ultrawealthy—to the extent that a man who hits the jackpot is going to be hard-pressed to meet his financial match. That's where Janis Spindel comes in.

Spindel is the founder of Serious Matchmaking, a Manhattan-based firm whose specialty is finding spouses for (mostly) straight men with Forbes 400–level wealth. "We're the Rolls-Royce or the Bentley of matchmaking," Spindel boasts. Her typical client has from two to nine homes, she says. "They have all their toys: cars up the wazoo, planes up the wazoo, yachts up the wazoo." They are hedge funders, real estate developers, "captains of industries. . . . I have a lot of amazing-beyond-belief celebrities, politicians, entrepreneurs. I mean, clearly we don't deal with teachers or blue-collar or white-collar people. That's not what the women we deal with want."

Spindel, who shares responsibilities with her grown daughter, Carly, has a classic New York vivacity. "If someone would have told me thirty-one years ago that I would be doing this and making a bloody fortune," she says, "I'd look at them like they had another head!" She grew up in New Jersey and inherited the "gift of gab" from her father, who owned nine furniture stores and "could sell ice to an Eskimo in the dead of winter." She spent years as a manufacturers' rep in the garment industry. Wherever she traveled, she found herself schmoozing with "well-educated, good-looking, well-groomed, financially independent people—I just know. I have radar."

One thing led to another. "I was a man magnet, and all my single friends were wealthy men," she says. She kept meeting women—at the beauty parlor or the nail salon—who seemed perfect for this or that guy friend. She began making introductions, and her intros led to wedding vows. "That was when the matchmaker was born. I looked at my husband. I looked at the phone. I said, 'I could do this.'"

She and Carly have since catalyzed nearly four thousand marriages, Spindel says, of which only two that she knows of have ended in divorce—an extraordinary statistic. At any time, they might have 300 to 350 paying male clients, from twenty-somethings to octogenarians, whom they match with some of the more than 57,000 "members" in their database—all well vetted, she insists. "Men don't come to us for dates. They don't come to us for trophy wives. They don't come to us to get laid." Rather, they are busy and powerful types who are accustomed to outsourcing key aspects of their lives, including courtship, to "people who are really good at what they do." These men want a woman with "the entire package: beauty, brains, body, and balance," Spindel told me. "We deliver on a silver platter exactly what he's looking for. The rest is up to chemistry and the universe."

Brains might mean anything from a Harvard degree to self-taught and street-smart. A member needn't be in Mensa, Spindel says, but she has to be witty and well read and up to speed on current affairs. Because suppose your client is schmoozing with the president of JPMorgan Chase at some event and his match is across the room talking with the CEO of Deutsche Bank "and you're freaking out that they're not going to be able to hold their own and you're going to have to run over there to babysit—that's not what you want."

To get into her database, Spindel says, a woman must be beautiful inside and out. "Men fall in love through their eyes. They're superficial and shallow, and I'm the first person to tell them that. The most important thing is 'What does she look like?' They want someone who takes care of her body and who leads a healthy lifestyle, who's thin, because all the men that we deal with definitely have an allergy to fat. They want someone who's intellectually stimulating and intellectually challenging, who they feel is going to bring something to the table, because these men have it all. It's like a pizza. They have every slice, they're just missing one. The one slice is what they pay us to find."

The Spindels' services range from "basic"—$25,000 to $65,000 for a one-year contract, for men in the tristate area (New York, New Jersey, Connecticut) who can be matched easily from the existing database—to "Global VIP/Elite," which runs $1 million or more, depending on the amount of effort involved. A few years ago, an American client who favored the "Nordic" look (blond hair, blue eyes) sent Janis and Carly on a seven-week, nine-country "international love tour" on his private jet. They found his match, a British woman, at the Ushuaïa Hotel in Ibiza. Introductions were made, and two days later the client threw a big party on his 210-foot yacht. The couple has been together three years now, Spindel says.

She won't take just any rich dude. She and Carly run background checks and conduct a site visit to the man's primary residence—like a bespoke social services visit. "We really have to *like* the guys." One was rejected, for example, she says, because he was acting difficult and "there was something about him that gave me the creeps." A client has to be a gentleman. Women members, meanwhile, pay a modest "consultation fee" and an interview fee ranging from $250 for a small-group session to $1,250 for a one-on-one with Janis and Carly both. The fees are intended to eliminate "the riffraff," Spindel says. "We won't do the bimbette thing. I've had gold diggers that have tried to come, and there's not a chance in China, because our process weeds them out."

The women, who might range from schoolteachers to the founders of companies, according to Spindel, are asked "rambunctious questions." The vetting criteria are traditional: Tattoos and body piercings are deal breakers. Ditto "boob jobs"—unless they are "tasteful." Old-school gender roles are emphasized. Men and women alike are asked about their attitudes regarding child-rearing responsibilities, and their answers "tell us what we want to hear," Spindel says. "We deal with women that are very powerful and very busy and run companies," she adds, "but all they want is a great guy to treat them well who is honest and caring and trustworthy. When they meet him, then everything else falls in place, and they take a step back."

But that just seems sexist and kind of demeaning. Why make women the commodity? Why not recruit successful, highly educated women as paying clients?

"Been there, done that. No thank you," Spindel says.

"Oh really?" I ask. "Why?"

"Because they're needy. They're annoying. You can never satisfy them. They think their shit doesn't stink. They have selective reading and selective hearing, and all I do is scream at them. Twenty years ago, my husband looked at me and said, 'You're *done* with women.'"

Serious Matchmaking does, however, cater to wealthy parents desperate to marry off their hapless adult children. One client approached Spindel on behalf of his twenty-nine-year-old son. "Whoa, did he need help!" Spindel says. "We did a major, major, *major* makeover on this dude. He lost fifty pounds. He got hair plugs. He went to a stylist, had his teeth redone, had veneers. We literally started at his head and worked our way down to his toes." He married the first woman they matched him with. She was the daughter of a wealthy jeweler who had offered the Spindels any necklace up to $350,000 in value if they found her a husband—the daughter needed a makeover, too, Spindel says. The jeweler wanted a grandson. If the couple produced a boy, he promised, Janis would get a $10,000 bonus. They ended up having twin boys, "which is hilarious," she says. But Grandad never ponied up.

Super-rich kids may be no more keen on arranged marriages than you or me, but some families get a little nervous when their offspring falls for a commoner. In *Crazy Rich Asians*, when the bridegroom's insanely wealthy parents hire a detective to investigate his fiancée, that isn't just a fictional conceit. "We have a private detective that's capable of a worldwide strike," Richard Watts told me. "I use him all the time. If I want to find out about criminality—I can go to whatever level I want. See where you've been, what jobs you've had."

Most parent-clients want Watts to check out their children's love interests. "They're just being protective," he says. They won't mention it to the kid unless something troubling is revealed. In one case, a young woman's fiancé had an old drunk-driving arrest. The clients took this information to their daughter: Did you know? "She goes, 'No, and I don't care,' and that's the end of that." But Watts's guy has also found undisclosed divorces and secret love children, which could be more significant issues.

If a young heir or heiress won't ask their betrothed for a prenup, Watts's clients will amend their trusts to make sure the family money is "segregated and quarantined." A wealthy daughter may not be allowed to move funds into a joint account with her husband, nor invest in his business ventures, without a trustee's prior approval. "Husbands, when the wife has got a lot of money, have all these ideas how they can start their own companies," Watts says. "They've never done it before. But they have a great idea and they just need a million to start."

Wealthy offspring often fear that a prenup will create tensions in their relationship, and it may well, because then the "poor" fiancé has to lawyer up and negotiate: "'Come on, five years before there's any equity? You should at least allow $250,000 a year. Or there should be a guaranteed payment if they get divorced in the first five years. Give them a million bucks.' And the spouse is going, 'How about half a million?' You get all that kind of stuff, which is pretty surreal," Watts says. When a marriage fails, he works with lawyers for both sides to manage the fallout. "Mom and dad usually are saying, 'Your directive is to avoid damaging my relationship with my grandkids. So go in surgically like a Navy SEAL. Figure it out. Pay them what we've got to pay them, but let's make sure she's not unhappy with us because we want to see our grandkids. That's worth millions to us."

Love never stood a chance.

CHAPTER 9

MY BODYGUARD

The more security you seek, the less freedom you have.

—ROBERT KIYOSAKI

Prenup or no prenup, wealthy marriages beget children who have to be nurtured and kept safe. And so, for the busy couple with everything, Denida Zinxhiria offers nannies who are capable not only of changing diapers and calming unruly toddlers—but of kicking somebody's ass if the need arises.

Zinxhiria, a thirty-eight-year-old Greek woman with dark hair and expressive eyebrows, is the founder of Athena Worldwide, a global security consultancy that specializes in training female bodyguards to protect corporate executives and wealthy families. She came up with the Nannyguard concept while working for high-net-worth clients whose caregivers compromised safety with rookie moves such as revealing the family's location on social media. If nannies (and "mannies") were a security problem, she figured, why not make them part of the solution instead?

Nannyguards are either seasoned security officers who want to add childcare to their quiver of skills or existing nannies whom Zinxhiria's academy trains in security fundamentals, including surveillance, countersurveillance, and physical combat. Zinxhiria, who holds degrees in counseling and psychology, also teaches behavioral intelligence—alertness to body language—and how to size up and circumvent potential threats. A successful Nannyguard can determine the safest routes to school and identify the most tactically secure hotel rooms for a family vacation. She can wrangle children who are unused to being told "No." She is familiar with common security formations, social media dos and don'ts, and how to deal with aggressive reporters—if a paparazzo tries to photograph a prominent client's child, she is trained to photobomb and ruin the picture. And should her preventative tactics fail to thwart a physical threat, a Nannyguard is prepared to fight.

The good life, as we have seen, has trade-offs. A jackpot enables all manner of advantages and access, but it also complicates our friendships and romantic partnerships, creates tensions with family, and sometimes feeds feelings of insecurity and isolation. Managing wealth is a major time suck. Unwanted solicitations are a bother. Business succession is a huge can of worms. And something else happens, too, when we segregate ourselves according to the number of zeros in our bank balances. As Everingham hinted, we begin to lose touch with how normal people live. They become the "other." We become oblivious to their problems, or worried that they wish ill upon us. And sometimes they do.

Andrew Carnegie lamented this very condition around the turn of the twentieth century, the so-called Gilded Age, when economic inequality was at levels similar to what we see today. In "The Gospel of Wealth," he wrote:

We assemble thousands of operatives in the factory, in the mine, and in the countinghouse, of whom the employer can know little or nothing, and to whom the employer is little better than a myth. All intercourse between them is at an end. Rigid Castes are formed, and, as usual, mutual ignorance breeds mutual distrust. Each Caste is without sympathy for the other, and ready to credit anything disparaging in regard to it. Under the law of competi-

tion, the employer of thousands is forced into the strictest econo-
mies, among which the rates paid to labor figure prominently, and
often there is friction between the employer and the employed,
between capital and labor, between rich and poor. Human society
loses homogeneity.

This estrangement—of rich from poor, CEO from worker, upscale
Palo Alto from shabby East Palo Alto—helps explain the prolifera-
tion of fences and cameras and security gates in towns like Ross and
Atherton. This isn't paranoia, Richard Watts insists. People just want
their privacy. But what is privacy, really, if not the ability to keep others at arm's length and thereby ensure the safety of our family and
property? America's elite families erect walls both literal and figura-
tive, and the more affluent the family, the higher the walls. The billionaire who throws a party, as one of Watts's clients did, and invites
only fellow members of the three-comma club: That's a wall. When I
tweeted at sports apparel billionaire Michael Rubin, a member of his
"social team" responded with the email address for a senior communications staffer, who was entirely unresponsive. That's a wall, too.

In fact, with few exceptions, every time I reached out to someone worth more than a couple hundred million dollars, even when I
had a trustworthy introduction, that person's entourage intervened
with pre-interviews and rejections. Hedge funder Ray Dalio's publicity team politely fended off my advances. So did intermediaries for
billionaire businessman David Steward, Craig Newmark of Craigslist,
and Sheila Johnson, the cofounder of Black Entertainment Television.
Sam, the cannabis entrepreneur I met in Vegas, was down to share
his story, but his company's PR folks put the kibosh on it—bad optics,
they decided, given the stark socioeconomic disparities in marijuana
enforcement. An ultrawealthy auto collector who had spent hundreds
of thousands of dollars building a meticulous slot car replica of the
Monaco Grand Prix, complete with buildings and landscapes rendered in exquisite detail, declined to participate because he's "a pri-

vate person" and doesn't want the public (and the tax authorities) to know the details of his insane classic auto collection—which includes one little red sports car worth at least twenty times as much as my house.

Several potential sources declined to participate, citing personal or family safety. One CEO had been stalked previously. Another had experienced a break-in soon after his company went public and he suspected a connection. Nick Hanauer, more open than most, wouldn't say where his son attended college. One high-end architect told me about a super-rich client who demanded a fortified front door in case of "civil unrest" and that his swimming pool be relocated to better shield his home's inhabitants in case of a radiation event.

Such precautions may sound extreme, but given the zeitgeist these days, a bit of upper-class paranoia is understandable. Indeed, amid the economic upheaval, incivility, and political bitterness of the past decade, more and more superwealthy families have felt compelled to enlist security firms—and not just ADT or First Alert, but providers of advanced estate protection technologies; social media monitoring; background checks on business partners, lovers, and employees; GPS trackers and safe rooms; drivers trained in evasive tactics; advance teams to suss out locations; and, of course, close protection—bodyguards. "We got a world-class security system with cameras and everything because why wouldn't we?" Phil Hellmuth told me during my visit to Las Vegas. "I'm a professional poker player. Everybody thinks I have all this cash lying around. I don't, actually. That makes it worse, because if someone did break into my house, now they're just going to beat you up, right? I've heard stories."

At a casino restaurant called Javier's, Hellmuth introduced me to his friend Casey, who, during a brief conversation, informed me he had a covert security escort watching us. Casey looked to be in his late forties. He was nobody I recognized, and I never did find out what industry he was in or what he was worth. But if I were to start acting sketchy, he assured me, his guy would be over in a flash. At what level of wealth does a non-celebrity require this kind of protection? "That depends on your level of paranoia," one lawyer for the wealthy and powerful told me. "The richer you are, the more in danger you are."

———————

Plenty of exceedingly affluent people—even billionaires—will eschew a security detail. But recall Tim Kasser's research associating our desire to accumulate with insecurity, mortality awareness, and psychological threat. And remember how our friend Jonathan, who sold his online education company for $40 million, felt after his liquidity event: "You're fear-based now." Combine these sentiments with an astounding wealth gap, a global pandemic, a mob ransacking of Capitol Hill, and our natural drive to protect family and resources, and it's hardly a surprise that Christian West's business is thriving.

West, fifty-one, is founder and CEO of AS Solution, one of the top global providers of security for Fortune 500 executives, fast-growing start-ups, and families of extraordinary net worth. Headquartered in Bellevue, Washington, AS has about six hundred employees and one hundred major American clients, of whom about forty-five are private individuals, typically billionaires "and up." The firm's revenues—$70 million in 2019—have grown 20 percent annually for five years running. Does this mean rich folks are getting more paranoid? "I don't like the word 'paranoid,'" West says, "because a lot of things come with that kind of wealth." Suddenly you find yourself living in a huge house with gardeners, pool cleaners, and contractors coming and going—and you have other houses, too. To some extent, you need security just to keep track of everything. But often it's "the chatter in the local society that makes them think about it." People will call West after someone in their circles has experienced a break-in or a home invasion.

We don't just wake up one day and decide we need security, in other words. There's usually something that freaks us out—it could be a scary news article, an uncomfortable encounter, or an actual threat. Corporations hire security teams for their executives amid tense acquisitions, layoffs, protests (animal testing created security issues for some of West's European clients), or after some unauthorized person manages to "tailgate" their way into the C-suite. Family clients may have had a stalker or a trespasser, or somebody is sending suspicious packages to their home or attempting to blackmail them. Zinxhiria has been hired to keep a client's disgruntled mistress or a former employee at bay, or because her client has controversial political or religious views they believe put them at risk. Mass shootings and terrorist incidents—like the knife and truck attacks in Europe in recent years—bring new business, too, West says.

But a lot depends on the public temperature. Amid the layoffs, foreclosures, and Occupy protests of the Great Recession, personal and executive protection firms reported revenue spikes of 30 to 50 percent. Pandemic-related economic and political upheaval, the murder of George Floyd, and the exceedingly bitter 2020 election season poured fuel on the fire. Clients are "very, very aware of what is being said about the wealth gap, and about them and their image and their fortune," West told me.

A dedicated security detail is a major undertaking. With shift changes, round-the-clock protection for an individual, including logistical support, may require up to sixteen people, Zinxhiria says. Toss in estate security, strategic planning, logistics and transportation, and you're talking about $1.5 million to $2 million a year to protect a family, West says. In addition to manpower, an advanced home setup might include surveillance cameras, motion sensors, and laser trip wires. The plan may require construction of new walls and fences. For clients who abhor such barriers, cables buried around the periphery of an estate can be used to detect intruders. An emerging security niche, "crime prevention through environmental design," relies on natural barriers such as thornbushes under windows, plantings that clearly demarcate property lines, and pathways and gardens laid out strategically to thwart undetected entries and exits.

When someone gets West on the line, his first step is to assess how much protection they truly need and what they can afford. How real, and how serious, is the threat? In an adrenaline-soaked clip from the Discovery Channel series *Kidnap & Rescue*, Michael Guidry—

whose firm, the Guidry Group, specializes in kidnap and hostage situations—describes how his team rescued a Chinese banker who was seized and buried alive by Malaysian terrorists, who then retaliated by killing one of Guidry's men. That is not going to happen in Lower Manhattan. Stranger abduction, of kids especially, is a classic fear, but it is rare in the United States and almost never related to wealth. Ransom kidnappings here are all but nonexistent, a federal law enforcement source told me. Yet West's clients always seem to know somebody who knows somebody who had a scare of one sort or another. "So I'll say there is definitely a risk to having that kind of money," he says. "It's very hard to hide—and why should you hide it?"

Well, for one, because your security measures might creep out your kids. It's "utterly frightening," wrote a person who claimed to be a child of billionaires, and whose account seems credible, on the question-and-answer site Quora. "You're always afraid of being kidnapped or killed or tortured or whatnot. . . . Our homes are decked with state-of-the-art security devices. Seeing those complex security devices in your house, in the room where you sleep, in the bathroom where you shower, reminds you that you live in danger. It's this constant reminder that you're DIFFERENT."

And you *are*. Few billionaires would ever send their kids to a public school. And if you have a Nannyguard, or a security team following you around and monitoring your social feeds and investigating friends and crushes and their families, that's not a normal childhood. Some patriarchs love their security, West says, because his team will handle all the annoying little details—arranging travel and lodgings, meeting logistics, driving, parking, and hotel check-ins—saving the client time and making him "feel really good and really productive." Young kids, too, are usually fine with a bodyguard, whom they view as a companion and occasional playmate, Zinxhiria says. But spouses and adolescents resent the invasion of privacy: "It's very hard for them to deal with unknown people who come into their lives."

West works with families to strike a balance. When a family member resents a visible security presence, he might deploy covert operatives instead. Sometimes it's enough to equip a wealthy family's teenager with a GPS tracker and panic button, or even just to install a locator app on the kid's phone. It all depends on the threat level and the family's tolerance for risk. West's agents usually get along well with teenagers, he says. "But if they try to, like you see in bad movies, show up at a frat house with suits and sunglasses and earpieces, the other kids would run away in a heartbeat." In such a case, you'd use younger bodyguards and have them dress down in T-shirts and jeans, and "maybe they don't have to go inside the frat house. Maybe they can be right outside so they can hear what's going on."

Teenagers, of course, are famous for being dumbasses. Plenty of adults are, too. Which is why West runs family training sessions: "It's about social media, it's about security awareness, it's about safe driving. It's about protecting your information—don't be an easy target. Don't log on to weird networks," and *never, ever* reveal your location. If you simply must Snap or tweet or Instagram the awesome thing you're doing, at least wait until you leave the venue in question. "A lot of people give themselves away by doing not-so-smart stuff," he says. One client approached Zinxhiria after a person tried to blackmail his family. His teen daughter had sent her boyfriend nude photos, which leaked, of course. "For families that have a specific name and millions behind them, cyber threats can be very serious," she says.

Indeed, social media makes the elites more vulnerable. It's easy enough to figure out where people live and the places they frequent. And now the haters have their choice of digital platforms. If I were to tweet out something highly critical or borderline threatening about one of his clients, West says, his team would see it and ask: Is this Mechanic guy capable of carrying out a threat? Is there any indication he would actually try something? Does he live near our client? Has he done anything like this before? Why is he saying this? If it's just a one-off rant, no problem: "But if you do it ten thousand times a day, maybe we should figure out who you are."

People who are both wealthy and prominent experience their share of awkward stranger encounters. Someone might spot you on the street or at a restaurant and ask for an autograph or a selfie, and that's okay. But someone coming to your house is a different story. In late 2011, an obsessed fan scaled the walls of Halle Berry's estate three times in one week—the second time, the actress had just entered her kitchen from her yard. "I turned to see him less than a foot behind me," she recalled. A few years later, a stalker scaled two formidable gates and forced his way through a patio door and into the Hollywood Hills mansion of Sandra Bullock, Hollywood's best-paid actress that year, with earnings of $51 million. Bullock was alone in her bedroom and heard noises. She came out and spotted the man in a downstairs hallway. It turned out he had a Utah concealed-weapons permit and a cache of illegal weapons at home. He had come unarmed, but carried a delusional letter referring to Bullock and her young son: "I love you and Louie and only want to be a part of your lives [sic]. . . ." He added, "You are my wife by law, the law of God and belong to me."

It's this kind of low-probability, high-stakes scenario—along with vague fears of civil uprising and dirty bombs and things like that—that have a steady stream of billionaires and celebrities beating a path to Tom Gaffney's shop. Gaffney is fifty-nine. Over the years, Gaffco Ballistics, his company in South Londonderry, Vermont, has designed and built hundreds of luxury safe rooms for affluent families, movie stars, famous musicians, and former presidents. These are not sad little Jodie Foster bunkers, but beautifully appointed master bedrooms, walk-in closets, home theaters, and other elegant and livable spaces one would never know are outfitted with bomb-resistant doors, electromagnetic locks, communications gear, redundant power sources, and blast-proof Kevlar plating that can stop a barrage of AK-47 fire.

Gaffney doesn't advertise and he doesn't have to. His business has grown 20 percent a year for more than a decade by word of mouth alone as more and more wealthy elites, security consultants, government officials, and high-end architects embrace him as their go-to guy. He won't name names, of course, but he has done a bunch of work in Hollywood. (Berry and Bullock both sought refuge in special security rooms, news reports noted.)

Gaffney usually gets involved at the design phase of a client's estate. A couple of times, in Mexico City and Lagos, Nigeria, he has made entire homes into fortresses, and often he'll build out a whole wing, because why fortify a master bedroom only to leave your children elsewhere, unprotected? Some families, particularly in remote areas where emergency response times are slow, request escape tunnels. Gaffney has completed projects in Colorado and Vermont—on a mountaintop near the Killington ski resort: "Real estate guy from Florida. He wanted safe rooms in there and he had a corridor behind the bedrooms where he could go grab his kids and make a run."

Safe rooms are pretty commonplace, but the kind he makes are relatively rare, even among billionaires, Gaffney says. The typical build-out costs $200,000 to $500,000, and while that's the price of a house for most Americans, for his clients it's like installing a standard alarm system. Among those clients are hedge funders who drop $50 million to $100 million on their estates and literally hedge bets for a living. "It's all about risk for these guys," Gaffney says. "Do they take it a step further? Yeah. They can afford to. They've got an underground pool, an underground movie theater. There can be basketball courts—some of the stuff in these houses is just truly amazing." One Greenwich client wanted his wine room transformed into a posh stronghold. "I suppose he had about two or three million dollars' worth of wine in there," Gaffney says. "It was a huge cellar. We lined all the walls with ballistic fiberglass, the door as well. His whole thing was, when he went out, he wanted to go out drunk."

For a dirty bomb scenario, you'd fortify the underground theater. Gaffney installs special filtration units that purify the air of radioactive, chemical, or biological agents: "You've got your food, you've got your water, communications—satellite phone, number one. Dedicated phone line, and of course your computers. You've got CNN and everything else. And your backup power—everything is redundant." Terrorism aside, Gaffney believes a lone-wolf intruder is the most realistic of his clients' fears. But lone wolves beware: These billionaires are armed to the teeth. "It's the weaponry they keep in these residences that I found surprising," Gaffney says. "Growing up in Ireland, we didn't have guns. Some of the weaponry I've seen in people's houses matched what I've seen in Iraq."

Some clients hire Gaffney to build safe rooms within safe rooms. They'll create a fortified walk-in closet measuring twenty by twenty feet, and then, "behind the cabinetry, they'll have a door into a small area, and they'll put a gun port in the door so they can return fire." Another client from Greenwich requested a sniper's nest in the attic area of his mansion. "He wanted to get the guys coming up the driveway," Gaffney recalls. "I said to myself, 'You're mad! First of all, you're going to go to jail for life. You just can't be up there in a sniper's nest and shoot people.' But this is an extremely wealthy guy. This is what he wants to do." Somebody talked him down, fortunately. Gaffney rarely meets his clients in person. Instead, he works with their architects and security consultants. I ask him whether any of his safe rooms have been used for their intended purpose. "I would never hear of that," he says, unless one of its systems failed or a damaged safe room needed repairs. "I'm out of that loop. I go in, I build it, walk away."

If his services were in demand when we first spoke, the pandemic and #BlackLivesMatter protests made them more so. "We have seen a spike," Gaffney said in a follow-up email. "Political and civil unrest appear to be the main driving forces." The day before, a crowd had staged a protest in front of billionaire Michael Bloomberg's Southampton place. (Some of the protesters reportedly carried plastic pitchforks.) "We fielded a lot of calls from the Hamptons today," Gaffney said.

He doesn't have a safe room for himself, and why would he? Gaffney has no ultrawealth aspirations. "I'm a boutique shop," he says. "I'm pretty happy, the level I'm at. Thirty years ago I might've gone and tried to take on the world. Not anymore." He relocated from Manhattan to South Londonderry fifteen years ago. They are totally different worlds. The first time we spoke, southern Vermont had just been blanketed by eighteen inches of fresh snow. Gaffney skis now and again, but what he really enjoys is snowshoeing in the woods with his wife and dog, a Samoyed named Murphy. "We do that every morning. It's a nice way to start the day," he told me.

Nobody ever bothers them.

CHAPTER 10

THE OFFSPRING

Super-rich kids with nothing but loose ends /
Super-rich kids with nothing but fake friends
—FRANK OCEAN

We've covered the time and work and responsibility a jackpot often entails, the isolation, trust and security issues, and the reluctance of the superwealthy to engage with outsiders. Well, all of the above was shaping up to be a hurdle for Bob Kenny, who was eager to learn about the inner lives of America's wealthiest citizens.

We met Kenny before. He's a developmental psychologist and cofounder of North Bridge Advisory Group, which helps superwealthy parents and their children "manage the unique opportunities, dilemmas, and challenges that can accompany family money." Back in 2007, though, he was the newly minted associate director of Boston College's Center on Wealth and Philanthropy. The center's data guru, John Havens, had projected that the baby boomers and their successors would leave behind about $59 trillion in private wealth between 2007 and 2061. Some portion of that would go to charity, and so getting a handle on the mindset of America's elite was of big interest to the philanthropic world.

With a $250,000 grant from the Bill & Melinda Gates Foundation, Kenny and Havens set out to survey ultra-high-net-worth families. "If you've got kids and you got more money then you're going to spend in your lifetime, you've got a dilemma," Kenny explains. "And if you don't think about it and plan it out a little bit, you're going to cause a problem. . . . You gonna give it to them now, give it to them later, not going to give it to them at all? How do you talk about it? How do you think about it?"

A decade earlier, Kenny was working at the other end of the wealth spectrum. When he was a teenager, his upper-middle-class family had packed him off to St. Paul's Abbey School in Newton, New Jersey, a boarding school run by Benedictine missionaries bound by vows of poverty. If a monk wanted to go somewhere, the friar would hand over the car keys. The school had its own gas pump and the monks charged all personal purchases to the abbey. "In some ways they were the wealthiest people I ever met," Kenny says. "They didn't worry about where their next meal, their health care, anything was coming from. That definitely had an effect on me."

After college, and a master's program in educational psychology, Kenny took a position at Harvard's Graduate School of Education, where he grew interested in how people approach ethical decision-making. He applied his knowledge during a subsequent long-term gig counseling pregnant adolescents, most of whom were poor. But as he approached fifty, Kenny yearned to do something different. Someone told him that More Than Money—the same inheritors group Jeff Weissglass got involved with—was hiring an executive director. He landed the position and, in short order, discovered that his pregnant teens had at least one thing in common with these young heirs and heiresses: Society defined and stereotyped both groups by how much money they did or didn't have. The foundations that funded adolescent pregnancy care assumed the girls were getting knocked up because they were poor, "which was not necessarily true," Kenny says, whereas the inheritors were pegged as "entitled and spoiled and lazy—and there's no basis for that." The anti-inheritor bias proved so toxic that some of Kenny's former colleagues shunned him after he took the new job. "They're like, 'What a sellout! What a cop-out! Why would you do that?'" he recalls. "What does it say about our culture that everyone wants to win the lottery in some way, shape, or form, and there's a whole segment of our culture that hates people who win the big payout."

This is indeed a paradox. Oscar Mayer heir Chuck Collins gave away his $500,000 inheritance in 1986, when he was a young man. (Invested in the S&P 500, it would be worth about $14 million today.) He has since dedicated himself, through the Institute for Policy Studies, to educating the American public about inequality. His memoir, *Born on Third Base*, includes the following scene: Speaking to a crowd of about 350 people, he asks who among them feels rage toward the wealthiest 1 percent. Almost everyone raises a hand. He then asks, "How many of you wish you were in the wealthiest 1 percent?" They laugh, but again, almost everyone. "People are envious," Kenny says. "And what you end up doing with envy is demeaning whoever it is that you envy, because they have what we think we deserve."

During his time at More Than Money, Kenny grew friendly with Paul Schervish, then the director of the Center on Wealth and Philanthropy, and when Schervish offered him the associate director job, Kenny jumped. He'd seen how inheritors grappled with their unearned fortunes. Now he wanted to better understand their parents. Havens was the numbers guy "and I was in charge of: 'I'd like to know what these people are thinking, and nobody ever asks them.'"

Finding participants proved difficult. Families with $25 million "don't like to tell you too much about themselves, and so they keep themselves pretty isolated." But eventually his research team managed to recruit about 165 households, of which 132 were included in the final analysis. The results were "pretty amazing," he says. Average household wealth, omitting the two billionaires who'd responded, was about $75 million. Seventy percent of the respondents were men. A significant proportion said their greatest aspiration was to be a good parent, which surprised Kenny: "I didn't expect it to get that personal that fast." But in the comfort of their homes at night, cloaked in anonymity, these fortunate citizens proved willing, even eager, to go deep. Their replies offered an unprecedented window into the anxieties of the yachting class.

We fantasize about the freedom riches will bring, but these men and women were far from carefree. They harbored deep anxieties about finances, work, and family. The center's report, "The Joys and Dilemmas of Wealth," was never released, in part because it was deemed insufficiently quantitative. But journalist Graeme Wood was given access to the five-hundred-plus pages of survey responses for a piece in *The Atlantic*. On the whole, Wood wrote, the participants were dissatisfied with their fortunes; most said they wouldn't be secure until they had racked up, on average, one-quarter more assets than they had. One heir to a huge fortune, who wrote that his greatest aspiration was "to love the Lord, my family, and my friends," said he wouldn't feel financially complete until he had $1 billion stashed away.

The subjects offered boilerplate responses, Kenny recalls, when asked how their fortunes helped them achieve their life goals. But when they were asked how wealth adversely affected their parenting ambitions, "we hit pay dirt." The respondents' anxieties about their children were based on their own life experiences: They had felt judged and stereotyped. They didn't know who their friends were. They were distrustful, wary of people's motives, never sure how much information to share. Few, interestingly, cited the classic concern that a big inheritance would result in spoiled, aimless, nihilistic offspring. Rather, they feared their kids would be misunderstood and demonized, as they felt they had been.

The conventional wisdom that wealth destroys children and families is not entirely wrong. There are some kids to whom one could hand all the money in the world and they would do fine. But when it comes to the second and third and fourth generations, wealth creators need to tread carefully lest they cause lasting damage.

Take Michael, the one who put his PhD on ice to sort out his father's $30–$40 million estate, and whose family wealth had caused marital problems. Like Martha, he entered adulthood unprepared to deal with money. His dad, who hailed from a large family and an abusive childhood, was extrinsically oriented, highly competitive with his siblings, and intensely driven to succeed. "He was very mean. He could be very cruel," Michael recalls. An engineer by training, he began selling computer systems to corporations for million-dollar commissions. He wound up running several large telecom firms. Michael's mother worked in the apparel industry.

The superwealth didn't come until late in Michael's adolescence. He grew up in a fairly typical suburban home, but always with the fancy leather sofas and marble-top tables and "that kind of shit," he recalls. They took expensive vacations and Michael's father drove high-end Mercedes and BMWs. Insecure and emotionally abusive, he expressed his love—if "love" is the word—through his wallet: "My parents ran out of gifts for Christmas and birthdays by the time I was, like, sixteen or seventeen, because I had gotten the electric guitar and the stereo, I had gotten the TV, I had gotten a bicycle, and I got a car." He recalls his dad coming home from a casino with tens of thousands of dollars in cash and peeling off a few hundred-dollar bills for him and his sister. "I just remember being a little bit jaded—desensitized— because my parents had spoiled us," he says.

Life after college was problematic, and his dad's abrasive personality made it worse. "We all developed these really weird habits," Michael says. "For me, it was spending." He landed a business job with a six-figure salary, but "I didn't keep a fucking penny of it, because I didn't think about having to save money." His parents also bought him a condo, and would deposit $2,000 every month into his bank account, an allowance they had never discussed. The handouts made Michael even less disciplined. He spent so wantonly—on clothes, gadgets, restaurants, travel—that when he decided, after nearly a decade of working, to go back to school, he had nothing in the bank: "I could probably have had a couple hundred thousand dollars saved up if I had just not been stupid."

Unwilling to face his father's disapproval, he quietly took out student loans, but kept spending as before, maxing out credit cards in a futile attempt to make himself feel better—classic retail therapy. He hid his debt from his parents, and even, to an extent, from his girl-friend. By the time they were married, his financial life "was a wreck. It was a runaway train." He was an emotional wreck, too. His parents had raised the allowance, again without discussion, to $4,000 or $5,000. But despite these payments and a condo owned free and clear, he was dying financially. He also was wracked with guilt because, though he'd always worked hard, "I didn't feel like I earned it." Not just the handouts, but the entitlement—the fact that he could quit a high-paying job to attend art school, then go try his luck as a photog-rapher and quit that, too, as soon as challenges arose. His privilege felt inauthentic. "It just gave me this ability to be like, 'I don't like the way this client is talking to me—I don't have to fucking deal with that bullshit,'" Michael says. "It's not a luxury that people who are trying to make it in any kind of field actually have. So there's an underlying shame."

Over four decades of advising wildly well-off families, Watts has gathered more than enough tales of woe to fill not just one book, but two. The biggest mistake wealthy parents make, he says, is to try and cushion their kids from the pain of failure. With the best of in-tentions they pursue what he calls "drone" parenting: "Okay, strate-gically, how are we going to map the pathway of our kids?" Parents who wear Rolexes tend to have big Rolodexes. They can ask the CEO they play tennis with every Saturday about an entry-level job for their daughter. They can call the member of Congress for whom they held a fundraiser to see about internship opportunities. With money and connections, they strive to protect their kids from hardship and pro-vide every opportunity, every chance of personal enrichment, every "experience" that looks good on a college application. When adversity arises—a conflict with a professor, an encounter with the law, a career or business failure—the parents are there to bail them out.

They do so instinctively, out of love and fear, without recognizing the harm they are causing. The kids "are not gaining the failure that teaches them how to carve their own identity," Watts says. "They're not creating self-value from failure and then recovery. And so they just kind of float along on the top of this giant foam that parents are creating, not knowing where the bottom is until something happens."

That something could be low self-esteem, bad relationships, anxiety and depression, delinquency, addiction, or worse. Working- and middle-class communities have been hard hit by the opioid crisis, but Watts points out that addiction to painkillers and heroin is also hugely problematic among wealthy kids in the Southern California community where he lives and practices. There have been suicide clusters, too, in upmarket towns such as Palo Alto. In early 2018, four teens in affluent Orange County took their lives within a three-week period. One was Patrick Turner, whose father was president of the Santa Ana Country Club, of which Watts is a member. "Patty" was a sixteen-year-old sophomore at Corona del Mar High School who loved football and baseball. On a Friday, the boy played a round of golf at the club with his father. The following night, in the center field of a local baseball diamond, he "disemboweled himself like a Japanese warrior," Watts says. Patty left notes behind. His school was a pressure cooker and he couldn't deal any longer. Perfection was required. His record of As and Bs felt like failure. "One slipup," he wrote, "makes a kid feel like the smallest person in the world."

———————

If our impulse is to associate societal woes with poverty, that's partly because (a) it's where researchers have historically looked, (b) the intensive police presence in poor urban neighborhoods ensures that low-income teens, typically people of color, are arrested and charged at far higher rates than rich kids, and (c) we were all raised on Hollywood tropes. As it turns out, teens from wealthy families are at least as likely, and sometimes even *more likely* than their low-income counterparts, to abuse drugs and booze and engage in antisocial behaviors.

The first hints of this emerged in the early and mid-1990s, at the tail end of the crack epidemic. Suniya Luthar is now sixty-two, with an infectious smile, bright brown eyes, and short snow-white hair. Back then, she was a fledgling psychologist working as an assistant professor and researcher in the department of psychiatry at the Yale School of Medicine. She was studying resiliency among teenagers in low-income urban communities, and one of her early findings was that the most popular kids were also among the most destructive and aggressive at school. Was this a demographic phenomenon, she wondered, or merely an *adolescent* one, this tendency to look up to peers who acted out?

To find out, she needed a comparison group. A research assistant suggested they recruit students from his former high school in an affluent suburb. Luthar's team ultimately enlisted 488 tenth graders— about half from her assistant's high school and half from a scruffy urban high school. The affluent community's median household income was 80 percent higher than the national median, and more than twice that of the low-income community. The rich community also had far fewer families on food stamps (0.3 percent vs. 19 percent) and fewer kids getting free or reduced-price school lunches (1 percent vs. 86 percent). The suburban teens were 82 percent white, while the urban teens were 87 percent nonwhite.

Luthar surveyed the kids, asking a series of questions related to depression and anxiety, drug use ranging from alcohol and nicotine to LSD and cocaine, and participation in delinquent acts at home, at school, and in the community. Also examined were grades, "social competence," and teachers' assessments of each student. After crunching the numbers, she was floored. The affluent teens fared poorly relative to the low-income teens on "all indicators of substance use, including hard drugs." This flipped the conventional wisdom on its head. "I was quite taken aback," Luthar recalls.

Perhaps the results could be explained by cultural differences— contemporaneous studies had found relatively high drug use among whites. But there was evidence to suggest another factor. In a study of Mexican American high schoolers in Texas, Jeffrey Swanson, a behavioral scientist at the Duke University School of Medicine, had found that family wealth was the most important predictor of drug use. More than 30 percent of the richest and poorest kids in his sample of about 1,800 students reported using alcohol, amphetamines, barbiturates, cocaine or crack, inhalants, marijuana, tobacco, tranquilizers, or "other drugs" in the previous thirty days, compared with 18 percent of students from middle-income families.

Luthar has expanded her findings over the years, conducting surveys and one-on-one interviews with students at struggling public institutions and elite private ones—fifteen thousand kids in 2019 alone. What Swanson observed in the Texas teens has held true across the board. Children from the highest levels of community affluence and those from the lowest levels are the most vulnerable, Luthar says, albeit for different reasons. In a cohort of young people her team has followed since middle school, the ones from the richest families were diagnosed with drug and alcohol problems at twice to three times the national rate. "There is a lot of pain. There's a lot of addiction and suicide," she says. And "a lot of these go unreported because parents don't want to broadcast that this kind of tragedy happened in their family. Even with the numbers we have, I think there's quite an underestimation of what's actually going on."

In hindsight, this isn't so surprising. Rich kids, after all, have better access to cars, fake IDs, and their parents' extensive wine and liquor collections. Highly successful parents may be too busy to supervise, and their kids have more discretionary cash to spend on drugs—which are just as available at private schools as public ones. Kids from rich families are also the most likely to report that they self-medicate to ease anxieties associated with the outsized expectations of their teachers and parents. "I wish I could say that this was a brilliant idea I had," Luthar says. "It wasn't. It was fortuitous that I stumbled upon it. It would never have occurred to me to say kids like my kids are at potentially greater risk than those in poverty."

The reason it never occurred to her is that, when she was starting out, few in her field were even considering wealthy families. This lack of attention amounted to "an interesting sort of reverse classism," she says. Like Kenny, she took flak from colleagues when she switched from studying the problems of the poor to those of the privileged. "Why would you want to work with them?" people would ask. "Don't they have everything going? Why are you wasting your time?" The notion seemed to be that the rich people's problems were not as real, or that wealthy people were unworthy of empathy. "There is a lot of judgment," Luthar says. "And now we have the whole thing where the parents are 'helicopter' and 'snowplowing.' It's relatively rare that someone comes along and says, 'Can we talk about this stuff with some kindness?'"

Perhaps the most counterintuitive part of Luthar's work is related to wrongdoing. Despite our preconceived and frankly racist notions of who breaks the rules and commits the crimes in our society, she has found comparable levels of antisocial behavior among disadvantaged teens and their wealthy counterparts. Drugs aside, she writes, rich children are more prone to "widespread cheating and random acts of delinquency such as stealing from parents or classmates," whereas poor teens are more likely to commit crimes related to self-defense, such as carrying a weapon.

Those findings are consistent with data from New York City's controversial "stop and frisk" program. During the 1970s, city officials, desperate to reduce crime, started encouraging police officers to detain and question people on the street—and pat them down if the cop suspected wrongdoing. The stops, predictably, were concentrated in high-crime neighborhoods, which also happened to be the poorest and brownest, and most of the people detained were young men. In 2009, based on the city's data, a person was more than twelve times more likely to be stopped in Brooklyn's Brownsville neighborhood, where nearly 40 percent of families lived in poverty, than on the Upper East Side, which had a 6 percent poverty rate. From 2004 through 2012, the NYPD stopped and frisked more than 4 million people—2.3 million Black, 1.4 million nonwhite Hispanic, 435,000 white, and 348,000 of other races. The whites, who accounted for only 10 percent of the stops, were more than five times as likely as the Black subjects, and almost four times as likely as the nonwhite Hispanics, to be carrying illegal drugs or weapons, though the nonwhite subjects were more likely to have firearms.

———

Virtually every wealthy parent I've interviewed has struggled with the question of how to raise kids with good values. Child rearing in the bubble can turn into a status contest: Who is dressing their children in the coolest outfits, taking them on the most enriching vacations, sending them to the right camps and the right schools? "It's very interestingly competitive," Elizabeth told me. "Wealthy people create such an environment, and such opportunities for their kids, and friends of their kids, that as a parent who's not *that* wealthy, you lose your kids in this way."

Case in point: Her daughter was invited to spend the weekend with a friend who was turning thirteen. A middle-class birthday weekend might consist of group water play at the community pool, pizza for dinner, cake and ice cream, Netflix, and a sleepover with pancakes in the morning. But these parents were Silicon Valley venture capitalists: The girls were flown to Los Angeles on a private jet and put up in the five-star Beverly Hills Hotel. A Hollywood stylist arrived to primp them for a concert that evening by the pop band Tokio Hotel. The next morning, they flew back up to the parents' five-thousand-square-foot house near Lake Tahoe. From there they proceeded to Squaw Valley, where the girls spent the entire day skiing with a private instructor. "When my daughter would get invited to go skiing with them, I wasn't invited, so I'm not skiing with her," Elizabeth says. So "defensively, I bought an old, abandoned 1950s cabin, just to be able to ski with my kid."

Some kids might be mortified by such an over-the-top party. In the late 1970s, when he was six, comedian Maz Jobrani's family fled Iran's Islamic Revolution and settled in Tiburon, California. His father, who owned an electric company under the shah, had managed to get a lot of his money out of the country. It was hard enough for Maz being one of the few Iranian Americans in Marin County, but then his dad goes out and buys a used Rolls-Royce. "Tiburon is affluent, but also very liberal and low-key," he told me. "Rich people there are driving Saabs, maybe Volvos, *maybe* Mercedes. And here comes my dad in a Silver Shadow with me in the back, and I'm like, 'Oh my God!'"

When Nick Hanauer's wife headed a capital campaign for their children's school, Seattle Academy, there was talk of putting the family's name on a new building. "When we mentioned that possibility to our children, my daughter burst into tears and begged—literally. I don't think she'd ever been more upset about anything we suggested, ever," he recalls. "I think the good news is that our children are largely embarrassed by their circumstances. They just don't want to stand out. But to be clear, we don't live in rural Kansas. We live in Seattle fucking Washington. There's a lot of rich people here. And by the way, Bill Gates won. We're not rich compared to them. And Jeff Bezos. Those people are rich people!"

He's being ironic. The fact that hundred-millionaires can point to billionaires to downplay their privilege demonstrates why "inequality is so corrosive and people have a right to push back," he says. "Because the neoliberal view is that no matter how rich I am, that hasn't harmed you. And if you resent it, you're being selfish and envious and immoral. But that is just objectively false. The farther apart you stretch a society economically, the farther apart the rungs of the ladders of opportunity are stretched, and the farther one must travel inside that social construct to feel successful."

———

Ultrawealthy families vary a good deal in how they raise their children, but patterns emerge. The child of billionaires who held forth on Quora could not say with precision how rich the parents were— "I don't think they'd discuss that with me"—but their family circumstances were clearly more *Succession* than *The Middle*. They had "and still have" fifteen homes around the globe, including one on a private island. Childhood was "kind of like a vacation"—traveling on private jets and staying in the best suites. "From the moment I was born, I was able to have nearly anything that I even thought of desiring. . . . Want to get a car? Sure, I'll call the guy." The kid had an Amex black card and could make purchases without checking the price tags: "Looking back as an adult, it's actually kind of repulsive."

The parents were loving but busy, and they traveled often, leaving childcare to the help. A more reliable presence was the pressure to succeed, and to never undermine the family's reputation: "You are constantly reminded how successful and great your parents are. Your parents did this! Your grandparents accomplished this! Now, what are YOU going to do? . . . Today, as a young adult, I'd like to think I'm out of that crazy tunnel."

Security consultant Zinxhiria told me she feels "heartbroken" by the parent-child relationships she observes in her clients' households: "They live in these huge mansions, huge distances one room from another. The children don't get to see their parents very often, and the parents lack—how can I say it? *Love.* I was working for a teenager for two years—I never saw her mother hugging her." Families with hundreds of millions or billions of dollars—not all, of course, but many—outsource most of the childcare, and those kids are desperate for parental attention. A youngster would be burning up with fever, Zinxhiria says, and "we were the ones taking the children to the doctor, not the mother."

Tracy Gary can relate. Her mother and stepfather amassed vast resources—hundreds of millions in today's dollars. They had a private jet, a helicopter, a yellow Rolls-Royce, and estates in Florida, Minnesota, New York, Wisconsin, and Paris, each with its own staff. Gary's mother, a stockbroker-turned-socialite, was financially savvy and taught her daughter valuable lessons about money and investing and how to do business. She and her husband also modeled the importance of charitable work and volunteerism. But love was never part of the bargain.

Although neither parent had a job, both were consumed with travel and fancy clubs and social events, and would be gone half the year. "My mother could spend $200,000, $300,000 a year on dresses," Gary says. "She was really into looking good and being in *Women's Wear Daily* and all this crap that I could care less about." Her mother and stepfather were prolific drinkers. On a typical day, Gary told me, they would put away at least two bottles of scotch. Child rearing was left to Nellie Lorance ("the Black woman who raised me"); Lottie Hines, who was mixed-race; and Otis Stuart, the family's Black butler and driver. "I probably had less than five dinners alone with my parents my entire childhood," she says.

This is not to imply that 0.001 percenters cannot be loving and conscientious parents, because of course they can, but that's not how it was in her family. And such tales are not uncommon among super-rich offspring. Only much later did Gary come to understand that normal families sit down together to eat and interact. Until Nellie died, when Tracy was middle-aged, she had never once seen her mom in their kitchen. "And she didn't want *me* going in the kitchen because she felt that I would eat," Gary recalls. "I gained a lot of weight in boarding school because of all these restrictions. I was supposed to be a debutante, I was supposed to be all these things."

In the summer of 1965, before packing her off to that boarding school in Minnesota, Tracy's parents sat her down for "the talk." Not the talk Black parents give their kids about racism, but the one some ultrawealthy parents deliver to make sure their kids don't squander the inheritance. They announced that they had decided to buy Tracy and her older brother stability in their lives. Each child would receive $1 million, her mother said, "and it will accumulate until you're twenty-one."

This was Gary's jackpot. She was fourteen years old. She didn't know what "accumulate" meant, let alone what $1 million was worth. She certainly didn't know that $1 million invested in the S&P 500 that August would have been worth about $191 million in August 2020. But it wasn't to mess around with, anyway. Her mom and "Poppy" hoped and expected their kids would use the money in the service of others. By age thirty-five, they wanted her to have invested the bequest back into the community somehow, whether by launching a business, supporting nonprofits—or whatever form service might take. They would pay for her schooling, too, including 90 percent of college expenses. She would have to work summers to make up the rest. And so, despite all of the misery it caused, the family wealth gave Gary two things that would prove invaluable: First, the fuel for what was to become her mission in life. Second, a top-notch education, which, as we are about to learn, is all but guaranteed to the progeny of America's jackpot winners, while most Americans depend on the luck of the draw.

CHAPTER 11

GETTING IN

If money go before, all ways do lie open.

—WILLIAM SHAKESPEARE,
THE MERRY WIVES OF WINDSOR

On a sunny, pre-pandemic January morning in the Oakland Hills, I locate my preprinted name tag, grab a complimentary coffee and croissant, and take a seat in an assembly room at Head-Royce, a prestigious local K–12 private school, to hear the sales pitch. Carl Thiermann, head of the upper school, has been here twenty-eight years, fifteen in his current role and before that in the English department. Two of his own kids attended Head-Royce from kindergarten through senior year. "My older son now is in grad school studying biophysics," he tells the assembled parents. "And my younger son is living at home, unemployed."

The parents laugh. Shahana Sarkar, dean of academics and community, makes a face.

"Are you kidding?" a parent asks, hesitantly.

"Yes! Dylan is a math major!" Sarkar exclaims.

Thiermann grins. He had her there for a second. "Yeah, he's in college. Yeah. Sorry, I just—"

"Studying *my* subject!" Sarkar interjects. She teaches multivariable calculus.

The parents laugh again. As if a Head-Royce alum would be unemployed.

It's easy to poke fun at an institution some local parents jokingly call "Rolls-Royce," but Head-Royce is a different world from the urban public high school my kids attend, where, on parents' night, teachers politely beg for basic supplies. The private school's twenty-two-acre campus has a safe, clean, collegiate vibe. A stairway descends from the street onto a stone plaza with wooden benches and newish wood-shingle buildings certified LEED Gold for sustainable construction. The plaza overlooks an outdoor swimming facility and a playground and basketball courts for the lower grades. The upper school has well-maintained tennis courts and fields for baseball, soccer, lacrosse, etc.—football is out of vogue in this demographic—and a large gymnasium with banners celebrating the Jayhawks' championships in numerous sports, including tennis and golf. Across the road, an eight-acre greenbelt with walking trails and outdoor classrooms is taking shape. "Our director of sustainability definitely likes to push people to get them out of the rooms and into the environment," Thiermann says.

A walking tour takes us down quiet, carpeted hallways where students leave backpacks and laptops unattended, confident nobody will steal them. There are about 380 students in the upper school, and the eight-to-one student/faculty ratio ensures small, interactive classes. The teachers have an average of eighteen years of experience—three-quarters hold advanced degrees—and the students we meet seem about as engaged and confident as any parent of adolescents could hope for.

Then there's the course offerings. In addition to the basics, students can take Japanese literature, ethics, astronomy, organic chemistry, robotics, filmmaking, five levels of Latin or Mandarin, and AP music theory. For coders, there's mobile and object-oriented design. More esoteric fare—Arabic, anyone?—can be had through a network called the Global Online Academy. "My son really enjoyed an Intro to Investments course he took over the summer," Sarkar notes. During our tour, in a neurobiology classroom—neurobiology!—we watch a student present her class project. It is titled "Examining a VEGF/CA9

RNAi as a Treatment Option for Patients with Surgically Resected Glioblastomas to Increase Median Survival Time Beyond the Current Standard of Care." I might just faint.

Head-Royce's extracurriculars are similarly rich. The debate team competes in Arizona, Illinois, Kentucky, and Tennessee. A Global Engagement program takes kids farther afield. "It is not 'Hop on a tour bus and go see the sites,'" Sarkar explains, "but rather a chance to immerse students in a problem we see here in Oakland and abroad, as well as experiencing the culture." Admissions director Kathrina Weekes chimes in that her daughter, a junior taking Mandarin, would be spending the winter break in China studying sustainability and trade. Another group was off to Greece to learn about the Syrian refugee crisis. In 2019, students interested in housing and homelessness embedded with an Oakland fair-housing collective before traveling to Prague and Berlin.

Tuition here is $47,300. Not cheap. But it includes extensive nurturing. Our final stop is the college counseling office. Virtually all Head-Royce grads go on to a four-year college. The chatty parents quiet down as codirector Tania Bradt steps out to introduce herself. Each Head-Royce counselor, she tells the group, hails from a college admissions department. This is a private school perk we seldom consider. Bradt worked at Penn and UC Berkeley, and spent seven years as an administrator in Stanford's undergraduate admissions. Codirector Brittany Dávila played a similar role at Barnard and Fordham. Their colleague Kora Shin "actually was our rep from Wesleyan University for eight years before joining our team," Bradt says. Not only does her team have great connections, they know precisely how admissions committees think.

Each of Head-Royce's four counselors is responsible for only thirty students. In ninth and tenth grades, they engage with the students' families and coordinate with grade-level deans and advisors to nudge the kids onto academic and extracurricular paths that will help them "discover their interests, set them up for success, and of course be able to tell their story to the colleges when it is time to apply." Come junior year, the counselors begin meeting with students and parents one-on-one. "It's very individualized," Bradt says. "We take pride in getting to know our families really, really well." Some 120 to 130 respected colleges visit campus each year to present and recruit—a testament to the school's reputation, she adds. The process intensifies during the second half of the year, with weekly or biweekly counseling appointments. The summer before senior year, the focus shifts from self-exploration to churning out applications. "We're drafting essays, we're reviewing applications, we're thinking about helping them with their interviews, we're really going through the checklist of all of their schools and requirements and making sure we help them come up with a work plan that's going to get them there," Bradt says.

Public school kids get this kind of attention only if their families can afford it. The parents of a Massachusetts public high school junior sent me a contract from an independent counseling firm called Campus Bound. The company wanted $7,500 for comprehensive face-to-face advising, timeline management, and essay mentoring, all standard at Head-Royce and Bentley—another local "independent" school comparable to Head-Royce in its academics and the amount of hand-holding kids receive. Any doubt about privilege was dispelled by a walk through Bentley's student parking lot, where I counted five BMWs, seven Mercedes, two Jeeps, a Range Rover, and a Tesla Model S. (No Bentleys.) But who am I to begrudge these kids a clean, safe, well-resourced school, a compelling education, and adult guidance with a difficult and stressful process? If anything, driving home after my tours, there was but one question pinballing around in my head: Why can't every kid have this?

_____

Upward mobility in the United States, to the degree it exists, relies on higher education. A college degree has become a prerequisite for a middle-class life, while a degree from one of the top institutions buys a powerful, lifelong social network, callbacks from sought-after employers, and a crack at very high compensation. As of mid-2020,

Americans twenty-five and older with a bachelor's degree or better were earning 79 percent higher median pay than those with only a high school diploma. Elite colleges deliver a huge bump. In 2015, median income for the top 10 percent of earners ten years after entering college was about $70,000, while their Ivy League counterparts were making $200,000 or more. More than 20 percent of the world's billionaires attended the same ten U.S. colleges—7 percent went to Harvard.

A degree from an elite school can really level the socioeconomic playing field. A 2017 study from the National Bureau of Economic Research found that the poorest students attending the nation's eighty-two most selective colleges (based on *Barron's* ratings) ended up only 7 percentiles behind the richest students in postgraduate earnings. "Ivy-Plus" schools were the most efficient mobility engines. These include the traditional Ivies (Brown, Columbia, Cornell, Dartmouth, Harvard, Princeton, University of Pennsylvania, and Yale) plus the University of Chicago, Duke, MIT, and Stanford. Sixty percent of Ivy-Plus students who came from families in the bottom 20 percent of earners ended up in the top 20 percent. The Ivy-Pluses were also the schools most likely to propel bottom-quintile students into the 1 percent.

But to catch that mobility train, a student has to get in—and through. And that's where wealthy offspring have a big advantage. The Ivy-Pluses enroll more students from top-earning 1 percent families than from the entire bottom 50 percent. That's a *shocking* statistic. Equally shocking, compared with kids from the bottom 20 percent, the children of 1 percenters were seventy-seven times more likely to attend an Ivy-Plus college.

History offers a partial explanation. Back in the day, only young white men from well-to-do families applied to the Ivies and their ilk. Princeton's first nine presidents kept enslaved Black people, and not until 1794 were students (a sizable portion of whom hailed from Southern states) informed they could no longer bring their captive manservants with them to campus. The first Black students to graduate from Princeton weren't admitted until 1945, part of a navy-sponsored program, and women weren't allowed in until 1969. Harvard proved a bit more progressive, graduating its first Black man in 1870 and opening its doors to women in 1879 through a program dubbed "the Annex." But Harvard and Yale later followed Columbia's lead and capped the number of Jewish students admitted. In 2014, an anti-affirmative-action group sued Harvard, so far unsuccessfully, claiming it discriminates against Asian applicants.

Discrimination aside, getting into an elite school was never a cakewalk. Although college enrollment was declining prior to the pandemic, as happens when jobs are plentiful, competition for the top fifty or so schools was more cutthroat than ever. From 2009 to 2019, the average Ivy League acceptance rate fell from 11.4 percent to 6.7 percent. Penn's rate plummeted from 17 percent to 7 and the University of Chicago's from 27 percent to 6. For its class of 2023, Stanford accepted just one in twenty-three applicants—that's 4.3 percent, the lowest admittance rate in the school's 134-year history.

This recent trend has three causes, none related to the quality of the education: First, the adoption of shared technology platforms such as the Common App have made applying to multiple schools much easier. Second, colleges now aggressively solicit less-qualified applicants in the hope that having a lower acceptance rate will boost their stature (and also to ensure that they admit enough students who can afford full tuition). Finally, and most notable for our analysis, an ever-widening chasm between haves and have-nots in America has left parents petrified that their kids will end up on the wrong side of the divide. College admissions has become an arms race. The stakes are high, and those with the most money have the superior weapons.

————

The race begins at birth. An academic achievement gap between rich and poor is already observable by the time children reach kindergarten. That gap has grown over the decades, as household earnings exploded at the top of the income scale and stagnated further down.

Families in the top 10 percent of earners invest heavily in their children's success, spending about five times as much as median-income families do, sociologists Sabino Kornrich and Frank Furstenberg determined. This is partly the result of a "shadow education system" of fancy preschools, private tutors, and test-prep coaches. Kornrich subsequently found that spending on young children (six and under) by the top-earning families had tripled from 1972 to 2010, while spending by lower 20 percent families barely budged. Increasing incomes at the top only accounted for part of the difference. Another possibility, Kornrich suggested, was that changing community norms were pressuring like-minded parents to spend more—the bubble again.

Wealthy parents have additional tools. Shortly after birth, for example, each brand-new American is assigned a social security number. Once that happens, the family can create a taxpayer-subsidized savings account for their future scholar's education. These investment accounts, known as 529s, grow tax-free so long as the money is used for qualified tuition, fees, educational supplies, and room and board for students of accredited colleges, graduate schools, or professional schools. Congress recently changed the rules so parents can also withdraw up to $10,000 a year to cover K–12 private school tuition.

Anyone can open a 529, but these accounts are especially beneficial for wealthy families. Here's why: As of 2021, any person may give any other person up to $15,000 per year as a tax-free gift. The 529 rules allow a parent—or grandparent, or family friend, or crazy-rich uncle—to contribute up to five years' worth of that gift all at once. That's $75,000 per parent, so if both parents contribute the maximum, their newborn starts life with $150,000 in the stock market. On the child's fifth birthday, the parents can contribute another $150,000, tax-free, and so on until the fund grows too big. Contributions are cut off once the account exceeds a certain value—typically $300,000 to $500,000, depending on the state—but the money in the account can keep growing tax-free even after the limit is exceeded.

To see how this favors the wealthy, let's do the math. Ohio, for example, lets families contribute to a child's 529 until the value hits $482,000, and allows those families to deduct up to $4,000 in annual 529 contributions, per beneficiary, from their taxable income. For our calculations, we'll use the "moderate age-based portfolio" administered by Vanguard on the state's behalf. Using Vanguard's published return rates and fees, we can approximate the outcomes for two fictitious kids born to different Ohio families on the same day.

Meet Eleanor. Her father teaches French and Italian at a community college in Marysville. Her mom works for a local nonprofit. With two kids and a mortgage, they can afford to contribute only $6,000 a year to Eleanor's 529 fund, which they created the week she was born. Eleanor attends a high school much like Oakland Tech, the scrappy public school my kids attend, but she's a strong student with her heart set on Stanford. By the time she's college age, her fund will be worth $211,464—almost $97,500 more than her parents put into it. Given her parents' incomes, the IRS would normally charge them 15 percent on these investment gains, and Ohio would take 3 percent. So, by making 529s tax-free, state and federal lawmakers have given her family an educational subsidy of $17,544. Not bad.

Now here comes Nigel. His family lives in New Albany. His dad is a corporate lawyer in Columbus and his mother is a banker. They are 1 percenters. Nigel attends a private K–12 school a lot like Head-Royce, and his parents withdraw $10,000 each year from his 529 to help cover tuition. Nigel favors Stanford, too, and his parents hope he will go on to earn an MBA or law degree. In anticipation, they have made the maximum 529 contribution: $150,000 at birth and $150,000 at age five. On Nigel's tenth birthday, they put in another $52,684, bringing his balance up to the limit. By the time Nigel comes of age, his fund will be worth $688,660. Factoring in the $130,000 his parents took out for private school, that amounts to an investment profit of just under $466,000. Including the state 529 deductions, which Elizabeth's parents cannot take because they don't itemize deductions, they get state and federal subsidies totaling $116,774.

So all told, Nigel's wealthy family gets almost seven times the subsidy that Eleanor's does. In effect, taxpayers are covering two and a half years of his private school tuition, and we've seen the advantages that imparts. He has taken interesting and rigorous courses from high-caliber teachers and traveled abroad for school activities. His close relationship with his counselors will show in the strength of the recommendation letters they write on his behalf.

Eleanor's school has four college counselors serving grades ten through twelve—the same number of counselors as Nigel's school, but her public high school serves about two thousand students. At Oakland Tech, each counselor is responsible for 375 kids, including more than one hundred seniors. The counselors organize classroom presentations and family information nights, and plenty of college reps visit the school in person or via Zoom, but there are no mandatory counseling sessions. The squeaky wheel gets the grease—and counselors just don't have the bandwidth to personally coach kids through the application process, let alone help them conceptualize, shape, and edit multiple admissions essays. Oakland Tech counselor Emily Schoenhofer told me she feels ill-equipped to give individual students the attention they deserve. Some fall through the cracks, she says. "I would love to meet many times with my college-bound students, but a lot of my time is spent with students who are struggling."

Eleanor takes advantage of a drop-in essay mentoring clinic run by parent volunteers, but that doesn't come close to the focused attention Nigel gets. Eleanor's family, unlike his, can't afford private test prep, for which Princeton Review charges up to $280 an hour. Instead, they spring for the company's $900 course consisting of eighteen classroom hours and three proctored practice tests. Her parents pay out of pocket, because 529 funds cannot be used for counselors, essay coaches, tutors, or test prep, even though much of that is baked into Nigel's tuition—to which you and I are contributing.

Now let's suppose, despite all these differences, that Nigel and Eleanor end up with comparable grades and test scores. Both are active in clubs and sports and volunteering. Both write really compelling essays. Who gets into Stanford? The fact that Eleanor is middle-class and attends a big urban high school are points in her favor. Admissions officers are often looking for socioeconomic diversity, and Nigel's privilege is pretty obvious from his application. On the other hand, most colleges—including prestigious ones that lack Stanford's massive endowment—are careful to accept a certain percentage of students who can pay full freight, and those schools can safely assume that most families whose kids come from so-called feeder high schools have ample resources.

Feeder schools like Nigel's are responsible for an inordinate number of admissions to elite colleges. According to an analysis by the *Harvard Crimson*, one in twenty students in Harvard's class of 2017 came from just seven schools—four private, three public. These included Boston Latin, Phillips Academy Andover, Noble and Greenough, and Lexington High in Massachusetts, New Hampshire's Phillips Exeter Academy, and Trinity and Stuyvesant, both in Manhattan. "There's a joke that Harvard was started a year after our school as a place for our students to go," James Montague, a counselor at Boston Latin, told the *Crimson*.

With the exception of Lexington High, even the public schools on this list are insanely hard to get into. Boston Latin accepts about one in three applicants, while Stuyvesant's acceptance rate is 3 percent, lower than any Ivy League college. (In 2019, out of 895 spots, Stuyvesant admitted just seven Black kids.) And one can understand why rich New Yorkers might be desperate to get their kindergarteners into Trinity, which cut off applications in a recent year after getting more than ten for each available slot.

Nigel has another ace in the hole. His father graduated from Stanford. A 2018 survey of admissions directors by *Inside Higher Ed* found that 42 percent of private colleges and 6 percent of public ones gave an admissions boost to the children of alumni, and sometimes to grandchildren and siblings of alumni. Some top institutions have rejected the legacy system, but many cling to it, including most of the Ivy-Pluses and schools such as Notre Dame, the University of Virginia, and the University of Southern California, which calls its legacies "scions."

The freshman classes at legacy schools are typically 10 percent to 20 percent descendants of alumni—rivaling and sometimes exceeding the enrollment of underrepresented ethnic groups. A survey of Harvard's class of 2019 found that 28 percent of incoming freshmen had one or more alumni relatives, and 17 percent had at least one alumnus parent. More than two-thirds of the direct legacies reported that their families earned at least $250,000 a year, and 43 percent said their parents earned at least $500,000. For the classes of 2000 through 2019, Harvard's average legacy acceptance rate was about 34 percent, compared with 6 percent for non-legacies, according to an analysis commissioned by the group that challenged Harvard's admissions policies. At Stanford, the legacy admissions rate is about three times the non-legacy rate.

This, of course, has nothing to do with merit and everything to do with the belief that legacies and their families are likely donors. In *The Price of Admission*, the Pulitzer Prize–winning journalist and author Daniel Golden points out that elite private colleges, as a condition of their tax-exempt status, are prohibited from engaging in racial discrimination, yet the legacies who suck up slots at the expense of other qualified students are overwhelmingly wealthy and white.

If Nigel's parents were rich enough to fund a new building, that would further boost his chances. Children of big donors often end up on the dean's or director's "interest list." That's better than being a legacy. The expert analysis entered into testimony by the group suing Harvard found that 42 percent of dean's listers were let in— seven times the overall acceptance rate. Amid his research, Golden learned that New Jersey real estate mogul Charles Kushner had pledged $2.5 million to Harvard, payable in $250,000 annual installments, right around the time his son Jared was applying. "His GPA did not warrant it, his SAT scores did not warrant it," a former official at Jared's private high school told Golden. "We thought for sure there was no way this was going to happen." But Jared was accepted, graduated from Harvard in 2003, and ended up advising his father-in-law in the White House. (A Kushner company representative denied any relationship between the family contribution and Jared's admission.) The elder Kushner's gift, by the way, was tax-deductible. "Is that really a gift?" Golden asked *Vogue* rhetorically. "Or is that a purchase of a good or service?"

If a billionaire is willing to purchase a building to get his child into a top college, one wealthy acquaintance said to me, what's the problem? Wouldn't the utility of having that building for the benefit of all students, rich and poor, make up for the inequity? There's a logic to that argument, but try telling it to the middle-income kid who sacrificed her childhood in pursuit of an Ivy League education, only to lose out to a less-qualified rich kid. "I was always sent to the best schools," wrote Quora's putative billionaire offspring. "Even if I didn't have the grades. . . . That's something that I didn't understand when I was little. I'm not as smart as these kids, so why am I in the 'smart' school? Well, it turns out that you don't actually belong here. . . . Mom and Dad used their connections! You took a spot from a kid who was smart enough and actually deserved it."

Suppose Nigel and Eleanor both get into Stanford. Tuition, room and board, and related expenses run about $78,200 per year, the school estimates—$313,000 over four years. Eleanor is more than $101,000 short. If Stanford doesn't fill the gap, she will have to take out loans, but Stanford grads do pretty well financially. She'll be okay. Nigel will be a lot more than okay. Not only will he graduate debt-free, he'll have enough left in his 529 to cover business school or law school tuition—maybe both! If he doesn't use that extra money, it will continue growing at taxpayer expense. It can one day be used for the education of Nigel's own children, and we're off to the races again.

None of this is to suggest that legacies are just a bunch of slackers. They did, after all, have access to a top-notch primary and secondary education. With the exception of star athletes and kids whose parents can afford to buy a building wing, most applicants with shabby grades and test scores are going to be hard-pressed to get into an elite university, legacy or not. So what's a wealthy parent to do when their kid fails to live up to expectations? They have three choices. They can accept reality and help the kid find a job. They can send him to a perfectly respectable state school or community college. Or they can go nuclear: they can cheat.

The Operation Varsity Blues scandal ensnared dozens of wealthy and prominent Americans who allegedly paid William "Rick" Singer, a disgraced ex–basketball coach and college advisor, a total of about $25 million to bribe and cheat their children's way into prestigious colleges and universities. A handful of parents decided to risk a federal trial, but as of late 2020, twenty-nine had pleaded guilty. Among the most culpable, prosecutors said, was Doug Hodge, the former CEO of a financial firm called PIMCO. Hodge, sentenced to nine months in prison in early 2020, had come back to Singer again and again. He'd paid huge bribes, including $325,000 to a Georgetown coach to get two of his kids admitted as tennis recruits and $525,000 to get two more of his kids into USC for soccer and football. None were qualified. Some of the parents had engaged in schemes to rig their children's ACT and SAT tests, complete with bogus psychological testing to earn the kids special accommodations that would enable the cheating. These parents embarked on their vile deeds, the prosecutors wrote, "from perches at the apex of money and power," where they lived lives of "extreme, almost unfathomable privilege."

Some of the guilty parties issued public statements professing shame and embarrassment. Hodge felt "the deepest remorse," he told the judge at his sentencing. But "I do not believe that ego or desire for higher social standing drove my decision-making. Rather, I was driven by my own transformative educational experiences and my deep parental love."

The moral: There *is* such a thing as loving your children too much.

_____

As of this writing, the pandemic had thrown the world of education into serious disarray. Teaching, campus life, standardized tests, admissions requirements—nobody knew quite how things would be handled and what to expect. In March 2020, after my children's high school sent students home to quarantine, a district-wide scramble ensued to make sure lower-income families had enough food to eat, since many Oakland Tech students rely on meals distributed at school. Better-off parents donated money, and volunteers helped hand out provisions. Communications from the school were spotty at first. Some teachers got their classes on Zoom promptly. Others went AWOL. And because of the disruptions and unequal access to computers, Wi-Fi, meals, reliable teachers, and even home environments amenable to learning, the district made all spring semester classes credit/no credit.

The transition to pandemic mode proved challenging, too, for private school families, but the difference was tangible. I checked in with a friend whose daughters attend College Prep, an academically rigorous school considered even more prestigious than Head-Royce. He told me he has always been an advocate of public education and felt his kids would do well wherever they went. "But over the years, I have to admit with a modicum of guilt that their experience has been amazing." The small classes, passionate students and teachers, deeply curious nerd mentality, commitment to arts and humanities, engaged parent community, "and yes, ample resources dedicated to a million projects and field trips, etc., have made our kids excited to go to school each day."

Amid the pandemic, the advantages have "multiplied dramatically," he said. The administration kept parents in the loop at every stage of deliberations. Students had all been given laptops anyway, so tech wasn't an issue, and homework was always online. The school's small class sizes made remote teaching manageable, and the low student-to-teacher ratio made it easy for kids to get extra help; College Prep even provided high-quality tutors at no additional cost. His children received letter grades, my friend said, and his daughter's advisor would call to follow up on minor matters—"the personal attention and concern felt remarkable." Prom was canceled but there was

a "senior night," for which each soon-to-be graduate was mailed a
care package "with cute gifts and sentimental items" to open during
a Zoom gathering. Jack Black made a cameo. "The shocking truth is
that if you pay $48,000 for a small, intense high school, the school
makes incredible efforts to meet your needs," my friend said. "I, in
turn, have felt deep gratitude, relief, and guilt—probably in that order.
I'd highly doubt that anyone is asking for their money back. And from
what I've heard, the school has a long waitlist."

CHAPTER 12

LOSING TOUCH

Money throws gas on your values. If you're already kind of an asshole, you're going to be a big asshole, but if you're a pretty good person, it allows you to do great good.

—JAMES EVERINGHAM

Paul Piff just landed on Park Place. I own it. "Shit," he says.

I also own three railroads, a couple of high-rent monopolies, and a smattering of random properties. Piff is low on cash. He's toast.

We're playing Monopoly in his modest office on the fourth floor of the Social and Behavioral Sciences Gateway building at the University of California, Irvine. The thirty-nine-year-old psychology professor is among the leading experts on how differences in wealth and status affect our attitudes, values, and behavior. It seemed clear that wealthy people, like poor people, are influenced by their socioeconomic circumstances, and Piff wanted to find out how. On his desk, accompanying a bare-chested Iggy Pop figurine and a squeeze toy in the shape of a brain, is a framed print of a Campbell's soup can with the slogan "Empathy . . . Have some!" Piff, who inherited his Persian mother's dark eyes, olive skin, and dark hair, projects an empathetic presence himself. But his frustration is showing. He's ready for this "absurd" game to be done so he can go home for dinner.

The game is absurd because it is rigged in my favor. More than a decade ago, as a postdoctoral researcher in the lab of the UC Berkeley psychologist Dacher Keltner, Piff used a similar setup to see how people would respond to being placed randomly into a position of privilege. Roughly two hundred student volunteers were paired off and pitted against one another in rigged Monopoly games, their status determined by coin toss: The "rich" player was given the most popular playing piece, the little car, while the "poor" player received the undesirable boot. ("We actually validated this stuff," Piff says.) The rich player was also allotted twice as much cash as the poor player, collected twice as much when passing GO, and passed GO more often, because the rich player got to roll two dice but the poor player only one. The researchers watched remotely as subjects played for fifteen minutes, and then stopped the game and debriefed the participants.

The observations were amusing. As the games progressed, rich players became increasingly cocksure. They grew condescending, spoke louder, moved their pieces more aggressively, and even consumed more pretzels than the poor players did from bowls the researchers had put out as part of the experiment. "Physical dominance" was also tabulated. "We had little gradients on the table where you could measure how much space a person is taking up from when they began to when they ended," Piff recalled. "The richer players began to take up more room. They got bigger as they got richer."

The whole thing was a bit like a TV nature special featuring these fascinatingly weird human animals. "What I don't talk about is one of the funny, quirky effects, just because it's almost meaningless: They had their money all fanned out. It was just everywhere. You could imagine someone who's got a lot of money would just stack it, but no! Anyway, I'm going to roll. Five. Tennessee. I'm not going to buy it."

He can't afford it.

The Monopoly experiment wasn't the most rigorous science ever, and Piff never published it—although the study was later replicated by others and used in his popular TED Talk, "Does Money Make You Mean?" But his observations were consistent with a large and growing body of work by Piff and various colleagues. Inside and outside the lab, in a host of experiments deploying a multitude of setups, these researchers have found that people of higher socioeconomic status, compared with those lower down the ladder, are more self-oriented and less attuned to the needs of others. They are more willing to behave unethically in their own self-interest: to lie during negotiations, misreport the results of a dice game that results in a prize, or express willingness to steal from an employer—pilfering food from a restaurant where they work, for instance, or taking a ream of office paper for home use. "Lower-class" participants proved equally willing to do such things only when the goal was to help someone else, such as swiping the restaurant food for a hungry friend.

Piff and his colleagues also have found that wealthier people are more prone to entitlement and narcissistic behavior than poorer ones are. Literally narcissistic! In the classic myth, Narcissus falls in love with his own reflection. In a study of 244 undergraduates, Piff observed that "upper-class" individuals were more likely than their "lower-class" counterparts to regard themselves in a mirror before posing for a photo they were assured nobody would ever see. This was the case even after researchers adjusted the results to account for differences in ethnicity, gender, and the participants' previously reported levels of self-consciousness.

In another memorable experiment, Piff's team placed a pedestrian at the edge of a busy crosswalk near the Berkeley campus and watched to see which drivers would stop and let the person cross. They recorded vehicle makes and models and estimated ages and genders of the drivers. It was impossible, of course, to know anyone's true economic circumstances and motivations, but suffice it to say that Fords and Subarus were far more likely to stop than Mercedes and BMWs were. In a related experiment, people driving higher-end cars were more likely to cut off other drivers at a busy intersection.

Our stereotypes about wealthy people, including notions that they are out of touch or culturally tone-deaf, are supported by the social psychology literature. For example, when experimental subjects are shown a drawing of a face with three other faces around it—these faces might be smiling or frowning or crying—and the subject is asked to rate how happy the central face is, wealthier subjects tend to focus on the primary face and ignore the others, whereas less-well-off people will take the surrounding faces into consideration. Numerous experiments of this nature suggest that people of lower socioeconomic status are more attuned to social context.

It follows from these results that wealthy people who are exposed to the suffering of others should exhibit less compassion than their poorer counterparts do, and this has been confirmed in the lab. When we experience compassion, though nobody knows why, our hearts slow down. Piff's colleagues Michael Kraus and Jennifer Stellar hooked volunteers up to EKG devices and showed them two short videos, a "neutral" video of a woman explaining how to construct a patio wall and a "compassion" video of cancer-stricken children undergoing chemotherapy. Relative to the wealthier subjects, the poor ones not only reported higher levels of compassion for the children, they had a significantly larger slowdown in heart rate between the neutral video and the compassion video than their wealthy peers.

If wealthier people are less moved by others' suffering, they also should be less likely to help people in need. Piff teamed up with Kraus and others to test this hypothesis. One experiment employed what's known as the Dictator Game. Participants are given ten points and told that the points will be redeemable for cash later on. They are then given an opportunity to share some or all of their points with a broke participant they will never meet. (Indeed, the person is fictitious.) Lo and behold, people in the highest income bracket gave away 44 percent fewer points, on average, than those in the lowest bracket did. In some ways this was counterintuitive. "You would imagine that the benefit of keeping these ten dollars is going to be minuscule" for the rich subjects, Piff says. And yet, "as wealth goes up, the stinginess seems to increase." This jibes with real-life data. Wealthy individuals and families give more money to charity on average than poor families do, but they give away a smaller proportion of their incomes. What's more, relative to extremely wealthy families, people with modest earnings direct a substantially greater portion of their charitable dollar to fulfilling people's basic needs, such as food, clothing, shelter, and health care.

Piff, Kraus, and others have also measured people's willingness to donate time and effort to a stranger. In one experiment, volunteer subjects are put to work on a list of small tasks to be completed in cooperation with another person yet to arrive. After a while, a woman bursts in. She is an actor posing as the other participant, and she arrives late on purpose. The actress is visibly stressed and upset and apologizes for her lateness. The experimenter escorts her into another room and then offers the first person the option of helping the latecomer by taking over some of her tasks so she can leave on time. In this contrived situation, "lower-class" subjects are significantly more willing than "upper-class" subjects to help out the stranger. This, too, aligns with data on charitable giving, Kraus told me in an email, but because the latter is skewed by people giving and volunteering at church, "it was important to go into the laboratory."

———

As a young researcher, Piff, like Suniya Luthar, discovered that most of the research in his area of interest focused on the plight of the poor. "A lot of that work talked about poverty as a kind of pathology, a set of environmental and life circumstances, neighborhood factors that predisposed you to a whole spectrum of negative consequences: depression, adverse health outcomes, reduced achievement. Those findings get replicated over and over again." But nobody was addressing the questions he wanted to ask. Namely, what are the social and psychological ramifications of being *on top* of the economic food chain, of occupying positions of privilege? "They're not necessarily bad. They could be entirely positive, but it was 'Okay, let's talk about social consequences: How does this impact how you see the world, how you make sense of yourself?'"

Piff, too, had trouble getting wealthy people to participate. "I mean, members of the 1 percent won't sign up for $10 psychology studies," he says. His team could gather data from representative population samples, but "it's hard to get a very sizable sample of billionaires." The upshot is that, when he and his colleagues say "wealthy" or "upper class," these terms are relative—hence the quotation marks. Study volunteers are quite often students whose families might have incomes ranging from less than $15,000 to more than $400,000, but they don't tend to be homeless, nor do their families own private jets and yachts and helicopters. "What does it mean to be rich? I don't know. I'm more interested in the experience of feeling richer, feeling poorer," Piff says.

Indeed, one of the big insights was that there are subjective aspects to wealth beyond measures like wealth and income, the size of one's house, and access to food, education, and health care. One can measure objectively how well a person is doing in life. One can also measure how well a person *thinks* they are doing. "It turns out those two things are different," Piff says. In some experiments, Kraus told me, "we manipulate perceptions of social class and find that the perceptions are what matters for changing behavior. Thus, if you feel rich, you act rich, regardless of your actual wealth." That said, he added, being wealthy is a lot more significant than *feeling* wealthy, largely because being wealthy "puts you in chronic contexts where you are likely to feel wealthy all the time."

———

All of which brings us back to Monopoly, whose precursor, the Landlord's Game, was created as a critique of runaway capitalism. The most interesting part of his experiment, Piff says, came afterward, when players were asked to talk about what they had done to affect the game's outcome. The obvious answer was that the fix was in and the rich player got lucky with the coin toss. But the rich players were almost twice as likely as the poor ones to talk about game strategy—how they'd *earned* their win: "That stuff becomes very, very amplified."

And so it goes in the real world. Some of us are born better off than others, "but that's not how people experience relative privilege or relative disadvantage," Piff says. "What people do is attune to the things they've done: 'I've worked hard. I worked hard in school.' You start plucking out those things. So, yes, systems are rigged, but we're almost equipped, independent of how rigged they are, to think about those things that we did to contribute to our success."

Successful people tend to feel deserving of their lot, research suggests, regardless of whatever advantages they may have enjoyed in life. As a corollary, they tend to view less-fortunate people as having earned their *lack* of success. "So you're more likely to make sense of inequality," Piff explains, "to justify it, make inequality seem equitable."

Numerous experiments have borne this out. In one set of studies, student volunteers who ranked themselves higher on a ladder representing wealth, education, and family status were more likely to cast themselves as more deserving than those who ranked themselves lower. What struck him most about that result, Piff said, was that "upper-class" students exhibited even higher levels of entitlement than psychologists observe in successful adults under similar conditions. "All they've done at this point is graduated high school!" he says. "They don't *have* a socioeconomic status! They only have the SES of their parents."

———

Piff's Monopoly experiment was good fun, but it didn't come close to approximating America's true economic divide. He and a research assistant spent four days testing different variations of the rules. The setup had to be such that the game was obviously rigged, and would leave the rich player in a winning position after fifteen minutes, but it couldn't be *too rigged*. The poor players needed a sliver of hope, otherwise they wouldn't bother trying.

To hew closer to reality, I challenge Piff to a game pitting the 1 percent vs. the middle class. Using Saez and Zucman's 2019 figures, that's a ballpark wealth ratio of 53-to-1. To make the game playable, the poor player would need enough cash to buy property. But if he starts with $500, then the rich player (me!) is due more than $26,000, and now we've got a problem: A Monopoly set contains only $20,580. Giving the poor player only $100 doesn't feel sufficient, so we change our setup. Piff will still represent the middle class, but I'll be a run-of-the-mill 10 percenter. So he gets $500 and I'll start with $4,500.

As we count out our cash, Piff tells me about some of the backlash his work has received over the years. Tons of hate mail. "I used to get a lot more. But I still probably get an email a day. I think most of it is political, because it seems so clearly ideologically driven." Piff considers himself progressive. I ask him whether he thinks his liberal values are reflected in his work. "Probably inherently," he says. They likely affect the questions he chooses to ask. For example, publishing a finding suggesting that poor people are less generous than rich ones might be hard for him. He would do it, absolutely. The question is, if a preliminary experiment pointed toward such a conclusion, would he devote all the time and effort required to unpack the result? "That I don't know," he says. "We're all kind of biased toward counterintuitive findings." As we talk, I realize I've screwed up my math: If Piff is middle-class and I'm an average 10 percenter, I should have ten times as much money as him, not nine. "So I'll just take another $500, okay?" I ask.

He looks at me with a bemused expression: "I love that as I was doing some personally revelatory sharing, probably some large proportion of your mind and attention was devoted to calculating out how much more you should've gotten."

The nerve of the little people.

————

A layperson perusing the literature on wealth and behavior would likely conclude that wealthy people are assholes, but that's not really fair. "When I'm talking about these findings, it can just sound like flat-out rich-bashing, which I'm not interested in doing," Piff says. The picture is more nuanced. One can be extraordinarily rich and not exhibit these patterns, or be quite poor and exhibit them. The effects

he and his colleagues describe are "small to medium" and they are av-
erages. It's the gradient that interests him.

Further complicating our wealth stereotypes is the fact that the
most compassionate choices aren't always the best ones. In one set of
experiments, Piff and Berkeley colleagues Stéphane Côté and Robb
Willer presented experimental subjects with moral quandaries. One
was the so-called footbridge dilemma, a "high-conflict" scenario that
evokes a visceral response: You are standing on a bridge over a railroad track and see that a trolley heading your way is going to run
over five people. You can save their lives by pushing a stranger off the
bridge into the trolley's path. Only about one-third of the participants
deemed this choice acceptable. The second scenario, familiar to fans
of *The Good Place*, was the "trolley problem." You're at the controls
of a trolley zooming down a track toward a group of five workers. If
you do nothing, you will run them over. If you pull a lever, the trolley
switches tracks and you'll run over only one guy. Sixty-nine percent
of participants found this option acceptable.

Both of these are "utilitarian" choices with the same outcome: one
person dies so that five might live. But because pulling the lever is less
direct than pushing the man to his death, the former elicits a weaker
moral aversion. The relative willingness of subjects to pull the lever
in the trolley problem was unaffected by socioeconomic status. But
"upper-class" subjects were far more willing than "lower-class" ones
to push the man off the footbridge. Past research, the authors wrote,
depicts upper-class individuals as "somewhat asocial—cold, aloof,
and uncaring about others in their social environment," but these
findings suggested that a high-status mindset could be valuable in
certain situations because these individuals "more readily make dis-
passionate choices to serve the greater good that others might find
quite difficult."

———————

Other findings portend less-desirable outcomes. Kraus and Dacher
Keltner found, for instance, that people who rank themselves at the

top of the social scale are significantly more likely to endorse essentialist beliefs about class, the notion that group characteristics are stable, immutable, and biologically determined. Such beliefs have been used throughout history to justify the mistreatment of low-status groups, including immigrants and ethnic minorities. During the first Gilded Age, for instance, Social Darwinism, a racist distortion of evolutionary theory that attributes upper-class success to genetic superiority, became all the rage among wealthy whites—and such views persist today.

Countless studies, Kraus writes, point to an upper-class tendency toward "self-preservation." That is, people who view themselves as superior in education, occupation, and assets are inclined to protect the status of their group at the expense of groups they deem less deserving: "These findings should call into question any beliefs in *noblesse oblige*—elevated rank does not appear to obligate wealthy individuals to do good for the benefit of society." In fact, when "high-ranking" people are shown representations of rising income inequality, according to Kraus, they tend to attribute the disparities to gaps between wealthy people and the rest in work ethic, talent, and skills—and to attribute class differences to "biology and genes."

As our socioeconomic bubbles become increasingly self-reinforcing, such attitudes tend to encourage an in-group/out-group, *them vs. us* mentality. And that's more than a little bit problematic when the ultimate in-group holds disproportionate sway precisely where it makes the most difference: the halls of government.

PART III

PART III

CHAPTER 13

CAPITAL HILL

There are two things that are important in politics.
The first is money. I can't remember what the second is.

—SEN. MARK HANNA, 1898

Have you ever actually met your congressperson or senator? Talked to them on the phone? Reached out to them directly? Tell me how much money you have, and I can probably predict your response. So can Benjamin Page. In 2010, political scientists Page and Jason Seawright at Northwestern University, and Larry Bartels at Vanderbilt, set out to study the political engagement and attitudes of wealthy Americans. Finding participants proved challenging: "Even their gatekeepers have gatekeepers," noted a frustrated research assistant. But after months of perseverance, the team managed to pin down eighty-three affluent individuals in the greater Chicago area for interviews.

These 1 percenters were very politically active. Virtually all had voted in the 2008 general election and 68 percent had contributed to a campaign. One in five had bundled other people's contributions, which is not something normal people do—even in Chicago with Barack Obama running for president. (Some respondents referred to Obama staffers Rahm Emanuel and David Axelrod by their first names, but 58 percent identified as Republicans.) Reflecting their expectation of political access, 40 percent of the respondents said they had reached out directly to their senator or representative within the preceding six months. That rose to nearly half when the question was expanded to include out-of-state federal lawmakers, Executive Branch personnel, and top regulatory officials. Their outreach, 44 percent of the time, involved "a fairly narrow economic self-interest"—they were seeking regulatory approval or a development permit. They wanted to be sure Treasury honored a commitment. They were bankers who feared a proposed bill would harm their industry.

Compare all of this with the results of a 2016 survey by the non-profit Kennedy Institute. The institute surveyed 1,025 ordinary Americans of whom 80 percent said they were registered to vote, but only 16 percent recalled reaching out to their senator or congressional representative within the preceding *five years*. Roughly half didn't think contacting their lawmakers would make any difference. Of the registered voters, only about two in five could even name one of their senators.

Money changes everything. In *Billionaires*, a book by political scientist Darrell West, one member of the three-comma club brought up his "get-a-senator" strategy—a handy tactic, given that a lone senator can block objectionable legislation or pull strings on a favored donor's behalf. West recalls how Senator Rand Paul held up Senate action for years on a treaty that would have forced Swiss banks to reveal the names of twenty-two thousand wealthy Americans who had assets stashed in overseas accounts, presumably to evade taxes. (An invasion of privacy, Paul insisted.) In another case, a billionaire hedge fund manager persuaded Democratic senator Edward Markey to write a letter to the SEC calling for an investigation of Herbalife, a multilevel marketing company the financier suspected of fraud, and whose stock he also happened to be short-selling. The effort paid off. After Markey's letter was made public, Herbalife's share price plummeted 14 percent.

One would have to be Forbes 400 rich to "get" a senator, but even if you are just a 1 percenter living and working in the company of other 1 percenters, it's practically inevitable you will one day be invited to a political fundraiser at the home of a friend or colleague. There you may find yourself talking policy over cocktails with a sitting senator or member of Congress and feeling a bit self-important now that there's someone in Washington who might actually return your call. So you write a check. "When I was growing up, in movies you watched characters who could pick up the phone and call a senator," former tech executive Bruce Jackson told me. Now he's that guy. He knows Senator Maria Cantwell of Washington and has hosted a fundraiser for Senator Michael Bennet of Colorado. He's never asked for any favors, but he could get a senator on the phone if he wanted. He also discovered, like Nick Hanauer did, that charitable giving buys access to the big players in a field. "So all of a sudden you're socializing with Will Rogers, who ran Trust for Public Land. I know Peter Seligmann, who ran Conservation International. If I was just a worker bee in those nonprofits I might not know them. And now I have dinner with them." And that's political access, too, because such groups have the ears of elected leaders.

If all politics is personal, then so is political influence—sown with connections and fertilized with cash. Wealthy Americans cultivate relationships with elected leaders and powerful officials (a) because they can, and (b) because it works. Political scientist Martin Gilens, now at UCLA, combed through thousands of public survey responses for a 2005 study. He discovered, on issues where the views of wealthy voters diverged significantly from those of the broader public, that the policies ultimately enacted "strongly" reflected the desires of the affluent, but bore "virtually no relationship" to the preferences of the poor and the middle class.

It took months of pestering his people to schedule a phone call with Representative Tom Malinowski, despite the fact that we were friendly in high school. I wanted to ask him about a video he'd posted to his personal Facebook page in October 2018, a few weeks before he was elected to represent New Jersey's 7th District in the House. (He won a second term in 2020.) Malinowski was among the dozens of progressive Democrats who had taken a campaign pledge to reject corporate PAC money. In the video, he predicted that even before he was sworn in, he'd get a call from one of these political action committees. "Maybe it will be a pharmaceutical company or an insurance company. And they're going to say, 'Tom, we're going to organize a little party for you, bring some checks. You don't have to do anything. It's just to get to know you.' And then they've got you."

I wanted to find out what happened. Had they "gotten" Tom? When he arrived to claim his seat, he told me, there were indeed lots of receptions for new House members (as there are for veteran lawmakers) packed with lobbyists handing out cards "and just trying to get to know you." He attended a few such shindigs, and lobbyists come to visit him in his office pretty regularly. He has nothing against them. He was a lobbyist himself once, albeit for Human Rights Watch. His refusal to take corporate money changes the relationship. He can listen to what the person has to say without any expectations from either side. What's toxic is combining lobbying with fundraising. That's how the public option got stripped from Obamacare, he says, and why the benefits of the unpopular tax cuts Republican leaders jammed through Congress in 2017 flowed so overwhelmingly to the superwealthy.

The tax bill is a good case study, emblematic of the power America's jackpot winners wield in the nation's capital. According to an analysis by Public Citizen, during the first three-quarters of 2017—as Republican lawmakers unilaterally hammered out cuts that would add an estimated $2.3 trillion to the national debt—a brigade of 6,243 lobbyists descended upon Capitol Hill, mainly to pursue the interests of corporations, industry groups, and wealthy business owners. That's more than eleven lobbyists per lawmaker. The securities and investment industry deployed 435. Insurance sent 600. Real estate, 251. Commercial banks, 182. Virtually every industry was represented, along with a who's who of blue-chip companies: Amazon, Anheuser-Busch InBev, Comcast, Verizon, General Electric, Microsoft, Novartis, etc. "My donors are basically saying, 'Get it done or don't ever call me again;'" New York representative Chris Collins told reporters that November.

Not only did Collins and his Republican colleagues deliver, trimming the top individual income tax rate to 37 percent and slashing the top corporate rate from 35 percent to 21 percent, they retained breaks and deductions whose removal might have helped pay for the cuts. The very next year, according to an analysis by the Institute on Taxation and Economic Policy, nearly four hundred of America's largest corporations paid an average income tax of 11 percent—the lowest effective rate the nonprofit had seen in four decades of number crunching. Ninety-one firms, including Amazon, Chevron, Halliburton, and IBM, paid zero or less.

When a company pays little to no taxes, it isn't the rank-and-file workers who stand to benefit. New York University economist Edward N. Wolff calculated that, in 2016, the most affluent 10 percent of Americans owned 84 percent of the value of all public equities held by U.S. households, and the wealthiest 1 percent of the population owned more than 40 percent of the stock. As of late 2019, according to an analysis by Goldman Sachs, 1 percenters owned 56 percent of all equities, public and private, totaling $21.4 trillion.

Tax reform's biggest winners skew even wealthier. That's partly because, rather than investing their tax windfall back into their operations, S&P 500 firms spent a record $806 billion in 2018 buying back their own shares on the public markets. The *Harvard Business Review* notes that senior executives, paid largely in stock and stock options, use buybacks to manipulate share prices "to their own benefit" and the benefit of "investment bankers and hedge-fund managers" who are further enriched "at the expense of employees, as well as continuing shareholders." The biggest winners are those with the biggest portfolios.

To secure the votes required to pass tax reform, Republican leaders cut a deal with a pair of holdout GOP senators—Ron Johnson of Wisconsin and Steven Daines of Montana—who demanded a bigger break for "pass-through" income. Pass-throughs are a category of businesses dominated by S corporations and limited liability partnerships, about 70 percent of whose profits flow to the wealthiest 1 percent of the population. They include hedge funds and real estate partnerships (including the Trump Organization), private equity and venture capital groups, and landlords and professional firms: accounting, consulting, law, medical, dental. Pass-through owners spent hundreds of millions of dollars to get tax reform passed. Hedge funds, for example, more than quadrupled their contributions to federal candidates, lawmakers, and PACs during the 2016 and 2018 election cycles as compared with earlier cycles. Political donations from private equity interests more than doubled, and donations from venture capital and real estate industries nearly did. All stood to benefit immensely from a tax bill that would give ultrawealthy investors more money to play with. That's the bread and butter of "hedge fund kingmakers," says journalist Bradley Saacks, who covers that industry for *Business Insider*. "They accumulate a ton of assets and make hundreds of millions every year on management fees alone."

The stance of the rebel senators, who collected $4.2 million from investment, law, and real estate interests from 2013 to 2018, culminated in a 20 percent pass-through tax deduction that is projected to be worth more than $60 billion a year by 2024. The bipartisan Joint Committee on Taxation calculated that more than half of that break will go to individuals earning at least $1 million per year.

Keeping carried interest alive was another priority for wealthy fund managers because it allows them to report their compensation as low-taxed capital gains instead of wages. Carried interest has long been the poster child of shameful billionaire perks. Even President Trump, whose real estate firm profits from carried interest, had voiced a desire to kill it. But the lobbyists prevailed. In June 2017, twenty-two House Republicans defended carried interest in a letter to the leaders of the Ways and Means Committee, which makes tax policy. Their talking points mirrored those of the American Investment Council, a private equity consortium that, as it happened, had hosted Ways and Means chairman Kevin Brady and House Speaker Paul Ryan as honored guests at its posh annual dinner the September before. Mike Depatie has personally traveled to Washington with a group called the Real Estate Roundtable to do his part for the cause. "The carried interest exemption is completely nutty," he admits. "We lobby every year for 'You gotta keep this tax break, it's important to California.' *Bullshit!* People do what they think is in their perceived best interest."

That they do. And they do so come rain or shine or global pandemic.

The coronavirus outbreak was an ideal time for America's most fortunate to step up and help fellow citizens who were losing jobs and health insurance, haggling with bill collectors and landlords, and struggling, as many do in normal times, to keep the lights on and food on the table. Indeed, during the first two months of the pandemic, several hundred family and corporate foundations and individuals doled out billions to ease people's economic pain, acquire protective gear for medical workers, speed up testing, and jump-start the development of new vaccines and treatments. At least a dozen pledged $100 million or more, among them Bank of America, Cisco, Netflix, Sony, Visa, Wells Fargo, Michael Dell, Jeff Bezos, and Blue Meridian Partners—a consortium that included MacKenzie Scott (Bezos), the Gates Foundation (which had already pledged $111 million), and Microsoft's Steve and Connie Ballmer. Google handed out almost $1 billion in grants during that period and, perhaps most impressive, Twitter cofounder Jack Dorsey pledged $1 billion from his personal fortune, about one-quarter of his net worth.

But despite all this do-goodery, the lobbyists for America's elite were busy, as always, looking out for their clients' bottom lines. With lawmakers socially distancing and rescue legislation moving through Congress at warp speed, they managed to slip two special provisions

into the CARES Act, the $2.2 trillion relief package enacted in early
April 2020. The provisions added up to more than $160 billion in tax
breaks for those Americans who needed them the least.

The first provision reinstated the "carry-back" rule, allowing companies that lost money in 2018, 2019, and 2020 to deduct those losses
from profits they'd reported over the previous five years. To understand why this was such a sweet deal for the uber-wealthy and such
a lousy one for taxpayers, consider Boeing. Normally very profitable,
the aircraft giant lost $636 million in 2019, thanks to its 737 MAX
scandal, a fiasco of Boeing's own making and unrelated to COVID.
Now the company can deduct those losses from profits it banked in
2016, for example, when the company's effective income tax rate was
23 percent. That amounts to a retroactive tax refund of $146 million—
a nice bailout for Boeing investors and executives.

The second break, worth $135 billion, lets pass-through owners—
but only the wealthiest ones—deduct losses incurred in 2018, 2019,
and 2020 from earlier *nonbusiness* income. This income, the nonprofit Americans for Tax Fairness emphasized in a protest letter to
Congress, could include profits from the sale of privately held stocks
and bonds, a famous painting, or a yacht—it might also include a
wealthy family's earnings from, say, renting out their Hamptons
beach house or Vail ski chalet.

The takeaway: In a pandemic relief bill, Congress allocated more
money ($161 billion) to help America's wealthiest than it spent to bol-
ster the social safety net ($42 billion), backstop bleeding state and
local governments ($150 billion), or supplement health care provid-
ers and overwhelmed hospitals ($153 billion). That hospital bailout,
too, skewed toward the affluent. Kaiser Foundation researchers found
that well-endowed health centers catering to wealthier, fully insured
patients got more than twice as much bailout money per hospital bed
in the initial round of $50 billion as did scrappier institutions with
needy clients. "Coronavirus is a great illustration of what happens
when our society faces a major calamity," says tax attorney Steven
Rosenthal, a senior fellow at the Urban-Brookings Tax Policy Center.

"Who is the government stepping in to help? Both rich and poor, but the rich are getting a much bigger share, and they'll be able to count it later. It's quite a phenomenal social intervention."

Rosenthal previously served six years as counsel for the Joint Committee on Taxation, and "I had never seen legislation that large pass that quickly," he says. The business tax provisions, backed by both parties, "zipped right through. And they are mammoth in terms of consequence and expense." The privileged few who could afford to hire lobbyists were "genuinely scared about losing businesses and wiping out a good chunk of their fortune. I understand that," Rosenthal adds. "But their fright is not the same kind of fright as people who are going to be thrown out on the street."

However abysmal the optics, the CARES provisions shouldn't come as a surprise, Rep. Malinowski points out. That's just what lobbyists do. "You find a piece of legislation that's moving and you attach your legislation to it. Everybody on K Street has been trying to use these coronavirus bills to get their pet ideas enacted into law." The good news, he says, is that "99 percent" of these efforts fail, and the few infuriating provisions that get passed only strengthen the case for a campaign finance overhaul to stop the ultrarich from treating the Treasury as their personal ATM.

Former senator Russ Feingold knows that campaign finance reform is doable, because he's done it. Making it last? That's the most challenging part. In 1992, as an underdog Wisconsin state senator running for a U.S. Senate seat held by Republican Bob Kasten, Feingold famously painted on his garage door a pledge that the majority of his campaign funds would come from Wisconsinites. He kept his promise and won. A decade later, he cosponsored a bill with the late Arizona Republican John McCain proposing strict limitations on so-called soft money— the currency of corruption.

Direct ("hard money") contributions to individual candidates had long been restricted—as of this writing, you or I can give a federal candidate no more than $2,800 per two-year election cycle. But *soft* money, contributions from corporations, unions, and individuals for so-called party-building activities, was largely unregulated. In the 1990s, led by Bill Clinton and Al Gore, parties and politicians began raising and spending scads of soft money on "issue advocacy ads" that fell just short of telling viewers how to vote. This quickly became the primary conduit for political influence-peddling: soft money contributions quintupled, from $88 million in 1992 to $458 million in 2002, and nearly half of the cash flowed to the Democrats. This amounted to money laundering, critics said—or, as DC insider Leon Panetta would later put it, "legalized bribery."

The McCain-Feingold bill that Congress enacted was actually the House version from Representatives Marty Meehan (D-Mass.) and Christopher Shays (R-Conn.), but its sentiment was the same. The law forbid candidates and parties from raising and spending soft money in federal elections. PACs could no longer spend soft money on ads mentioning a federal candidate by name within thirty days of a primary or sixty days of a general election. Unions and corporations were barred from running issue ads entirely. Individual donations to candidates and parties were capped, and no single person could dole out more than $95,000 total per cycle. "I'm so-and-so and I approve this message" was another result of McCain-Feingold.

But money is a tough addiction to kick, and Washington suffered a rapid and devastating relapse. Thanks largely to Don McGahn—a Federal Election Commissioner who later served as Donald Trump's White House Counsel—a hyper-partisan FEC seemed to all but abandon its mission of enforcing the campaign laws. Federal courts, meanwhile, handed down a series of decisions that would maul Feingold's baby beyond recognition. The Supreme Court struck down the thirty/sixty-day advertising ban, and then, in *Citizens United v. FEC*, held that corporations, including unions and nonprofits, have free-speech rights and therefore must be allowed to bankroll issue ads. Another federal court ruled that PACs that *only* run issue ads— aka super PACs—could take unlimited contributions. The individual two-year spending caps were struck down as well. For the first time since the 1907 passage of the Tillman Act, the nation's first campaign finance law, corporations and wealthy Americans could spend as much money as they desired to get their way with Congress. Soft money was back!

When I caught up with Feingold, he was weathering the initial coronavirus lockdown at home in Middleton, Wisconsin, a suburb of Madison, and getting up to speed in his new gig as president of the American Constitution Society. Feingold lives a half-hour's drive from the family farm of Robert "Fighting Bob" La Follette, a legendary politician who served as governor and represented Wisconsinites in both the House and the Senate throughout the first quarter of the twentieth century. He was among the first U.S. politicians to take on the trusts—the Gilded Age monopolies. La Follette also helped write the Tillman Act, which banned corporate political contributions: "It's bad enough that the trusts control our economy—they're trying to control our political system," Feingold says, channeling his hero. "We're not going to let them do it!"

Railing against the Timber Men and the Railroad Men, La Follette and his allies built a progressive movement that has lasted the better part of a century. "That's why Wisconsin was the first state to have child labor laws, the first state to have unemployment compensation, the first state to have a public utilities commission," Feingold told me. "All of these were progressive reforms that were about breaking the control of private, wealthy interests over the lives of our citizens. So that is the tradition I was brought up in."

His first in-person glimpse of the corporate dick-swinging came in the early 1980s, after he was elected to represent a mostly rural district in the Wisconsin senate. Dairy farmers were up in arms about a product Monsanto was developing: bovine somatotropin (aka bovine growth hormone). BGH boosts milk production by 20 percent, and small farmers feared overproduction would tank milk prices and drive them out of business. (Wisconsin had some 150,000 dairy farms in the 1950s, Feingold points out, and fewer than 10,000 now.) So he proposed a moratorium on the use and sale of BGH: "It really was about the economic power of a giant like Monsanto to completely alter our traditional Wisconsin economy."

In 1990, state lawmakers agreed to a one-year moratorium, and Minnesota followed suit. In the process, Feingold got to see how Big Ag flexes its muscle. "They were obsessed with trying to prevent this populist movement," he recalls. Monsanto "basically sent planeloads of lobbyists from St. Louis." They also hired state-level operatives, including one of Feingold's friends, a former state senator, in an unsuccessful effort to sway him. ("He kept encouraging me: 'Keep going, Russ, I'm making a fortune off of this!'") After the moratorium passed the state assembly, one industry lobbyist declared a "victory for food terrorists." The victory didn't last. Republican governor Tommy Thompson vetoed a subsequent bill that would have extended the ban through 1993, and the industry thwarted mandatory labeling of BGH dairy products—although some producers adopted "BGH-free" as a selling point.

The power of wealthy interests in the political process has "gotten worse and worse" since he was first elected, Feingold told me. During the Reagan era "they really infected the state governments, too, in a way that had not been done before." And DC became increasingly corrupt. When he arrived in 1993 to claim his Senate seat, the nation's capital "was a relatively quiet, almost Southern town." There were no fancy restaurants like Charlie Palmer steakhouse and Johnny's Half Shell where lawmakers schmoozed with lobbyists and power brokers. One old friend from his hometown, Janesville, grew up to be a successful Chicago businessman, and Feingold's swearing-in ceremony marked his pal's first visit to DC. "That's inconceivable now," he says.

Feingold talks like a seasoned politician, but his frustration feels genuine. That "ridiculous decision"—*Citizens United*—overturned the Tillman Act. The courts have unraveled his proudest accomplishment. The 0.001 percent is back at the helm—if it ever left. "We are now in a robber baron era on steroids. And I think everybody can see it even more obviously now in light of this COVID crisis," he says. America's elite "show no ability to contain themselves in terms of wanting to turn public programs into private moneymaking operations." Health care, education: "It seems to infect everything."

Few lawmakers enjoy their mandatory fundraising calls, Malinowski and Feingold both told me. But things weren't quite so bad before the soft-money abuses began, and during the short time McCain-Feingold was in effect. A politician could call up a person and solicit the maximum donation—now $5,600 per couple—and the giver knew not to expect favors. That's all Malinowski seeks now, and his donors don't pester him, other than to sometimes ask whether he has any internships available. Yet some lawmakers, though the law forbids it, feel pressure to make soft-money pitches: "Hey, can you give $100,000 to our campaign committee? It doesn't go to me, but it goes to the overall fund," Feingold says, acting out such a scenario. "Frankly, it makes me glad I'm not running for office, because there comes a point where it just is not credible that you're not basically promising a quid pro quo."

————

Wealthy people, by and large, are more progressive than the broader public on social issues such as abortion, criminal justice reform, and marriage equality, research has shown, but significantly more conservative on economic issues such as taxation and entitlements and the government's role in helping people who are down-and-out. These differences transcend party affiliation. Fifty-eight percent of Benjamin Page's affluent subjects were Republicans, for example, but 87 percent deemed budget deficits a top priority ("very important") for the nation, and their preferred solution was to cut spending on Medicare and other programs rather than raise taxes. Most viewed unemployment and education as key issues, but climate change came in dead last, with only 16 percent deeming it "very important."

The policy preferences of Page's subjects differed markedly from those of the public. Most Americans wanted environmental protections strengthened; the 1 percenters wanted them slashed. Nearly nine in ten public respondents said the government should spend whatever is necessary to ensure high-quality K–12 public schools, versus just 35 percent of Page's subjects—who, after all, could afford private schools and tutors and coaches. Only about half of the wealthy group felt it was the government's responsibility to make sure minorities and whites had educational parity. They also favored less spending on Social Security, health care, food stamps, and jobs programs. The affluent group "tilted toward cutting all the income-redistributive or social insurance programs we asked about," wrote Page et al., and their access to politicians helped explain why elected officials are willing to push for deep cuts in social welfare programs that most Americans support.

Yale's Michael Kraus, whom we met earlier, along with psychologist Bennett Callaghan at the University of Illinois, wanted to find out whether a politician's personal wealth might affect how he or she votes. Using public disclosure data for 2011, the researchers determined that the median net worth of U.S. House members was $5.7 million—more than one hundred times that of their constituents. Republican members voted as Republicans do—their wealth didn't appear to affect their positions. But wealthy Democrats were significantly *less likely* than nonwealthy Democrats to support bills that would reduce inequality by, for example, raising the minimum wage or raising the tax rate on investment profits. This was true even when the researchers adjusted for each member's race and gender, although white male Democrats were also more likely than average to vote for the unequal status quo.

These findings are a further argument for meaningful campaign finance reform, because not only does wealth impart a huge advantage in terms of enacting one's policy preferences, it also enhances one's ability to run for public office. Had Malinowski been able to finance his own campaign, "it would have been so much easier," he told me. There are lots of Americans who would make excellent leaders but will never serve because they don't come from a background that gives them a ready-made network of affluent and well-connected people they can turn to for money and support.

Despite our nation's bitter divisions, most Americans would agree that everyone deserves a fair shake. Some folks will always be richer, others poorer, but a big opportunity gap is anathema to the ideals on which our nation was founded. Malinowski's mother brought him to New Jersey from Communist Poland when he was six years old, and he has spent time studying the history and politics of Eastern Europe. Soviet-era Poland had little income inequality, he says, but the inequality of opportunity there was profound, significantly worse than here. "That's why I don't rail against corporations, but I am very, very passionate and ambitious in fighting for changes to our campaign finance system. And in support of voting rights." Because while most of us will never get the opportunity to own a superyacht, we should at least have a crack at a decent life that includes a solid education and good health care, clean air and water, a meaningful say in the actions of our elected leaders, and the opportunity to step up as leaders ourselves. Inequality is a given, but "the story of America," Malinowski says, "is about how to get the balance right."

CHAPTER 14

THE SNOW BALL GROWS

Ill fares the land, to hastening ills a prey,
Where wealth accumulates, and men decay.
—OLIVER GOLDSMITH

Most Americans have no problem with people earning more for their unique abilities and superior accomplishments so long as we all are given the chance to go as far in life as our natural gifts will allow. "That all men are born to equal rights is true," wrote John Adams, but the notion that "all men are born with equal powers and faculties and equal influence in society is as gross a fraud as ever was practiced by monks, by Devils, by Brahmins, by priests of the immortal Lama, or by the self-styled philosophers of the French Revolution."

So what's a reasonable balance? How much more should a company pay its CEO vs. the guy who mops the warehouse floor, and what other perks should each enjoy? This is where opinions diverge. If the janitor gets $12 an hour, does the chief executive deserve $120? $1,200? $12,000? A housing allowance? A car and driver? CEOs of large public companies usually make double or triple their base salary in the form of preferred stock and stock options. When our CEO sells that stock, should he be allowed to pay a lower tax rate on his profits than the janitor pays on his wages? And how much tax-free wealth should he be allowed to pass on to his offspring, who did nothing to deserve the money? In short, how should the spoils of capital and labor be distributed in a just society?

Dan Ariely, a professor of psychology and behavioral economics at Duke, and psychologist Michael Norton at the Harvard Business School wanted to see how everyday Americans would answer that question. They recruited a nationally representative sample of more than 5,500 subjects. In the first part of their experiment, subjects were shown pairs of pie charts depicting wealth distributions, by population quintile, of three different societies. If you had to join this society or that one, and you would be randomly assigned a position within its wealth distribution, which would you choose? There were three pie charts. One depicted perfect equality—each wealth quintile had 20 percent of the total assets. The second, unbeknownst to the subjects, represented Sweden, whose ascending wealth quintiles owned 11 percent, 15 percent, 18 percent, 21 percent, and 36 percent of the pot. The final pie chart mirrored the distribution in the United States, where the wealthiest 20 percent owns the overwhelming majority of the assets. Just over half of the participants preferred Sweden's wealth distribution to perfect equality. But perhaps more strikingly, when asked to choose between the Swedish and U.S. scenarios, 92 percent of these American subjects—rich and poor, Democrat and Republican—picked Sweden.

The second round of the experiment consisted of two parts. First, Ariely and Norton asked their subjects to estimate what share of America's wealth is owned by each quintile. Participants were then asked to come up with a wealth distribution they considered fair. The results were striking: People dramatically underestimated their nation's economic inequality. On average, they guessed, the richest 20 percent of the population controlled 59 percent of the total assets—in a fair society, they said, that group should get 32 percent. (At the time of the experiment, the top quintile controlled a staggering 84 percent of the national wealth.)

At the other end of the spectrum, the subjects *overestimated* wildly. The bottom 40 percent of Americans—about 125 million people at the time—owned 9 percent of the wealth, they said, and in a fair society the bottom 40 would own 24 percent. The sad reality was that this group owned just 0.3 percent. That two-fifths of our population is excluded entirely from wealth ownership was apparently too much for people to wrap their heads around.

———

About six months after the Norton-Ariely experiment was published, the American public began talking about the 1 percent vs. the 99 percent. This parlance is so ubiquitous today that it's easy to forget how recently it came about. Inequality is timeless, of course. As Thomas Jefferson wrote to John Adams during an early nineteenth-century correspondence, "Every one takes his side in favor of the many or the few."

Indeed, during the mid-1800s, it became trendy for New Yorkers to throw shade at the "upper ten." Nathaniel Parker Willis, a widely read pundit, had published a commentary about a ritual he'd observed in Paris and London, wherein aristocrats lined up their fancy carriages along the city's promenades each afternoon to socialize, see and be seen, and put their opulence on public display. Willis argued that New York City's upper crust should adopt this custom to distinguish true people of position from the hordes of pretenders. "At present there is no distinction among the *upper ten thousand* of the city," he sniffed. But even rich Manhattanites found the notion distasteful, and "upper ten" soon became a derogatory term. A public-relations tug-of-war later ensued between the Gilded Age industrialists, who fancied themselves "captains of industry," and critics who derided ruthless business leaders as "robber barons."

The 1 percent language was coined amid the Great Recession, in 2011, as Occupy Wall Street raged and the government bailed out "too big to fail" financial institutions that had targeted millions of American families with high-risk home loans and remained busy foreclosing on them. Inequality was a major theme in the 2012 presidential race. Two years later, economist Thomas Piketty's *Capital in the Twenty-First Century*, the kind of book normally read only by academics and policy wonks, became a surprise bestseller. The public, it seemed, was again waking up to what happens when financial self-interest is allowed to propagate freely. Namely, when America's elite get to dictate the conditions under which wealth begets wealth, the gap between rich and poor grows at an accelerated clip, as do disparities in political clout and access to capital. Left unchecked, the cycle spins out of control, with results bordering on the absurd. America's 2019 wealth distribution resembles an early-stage coronavirus growth chart—it's exponential.

AVERAGE WEALTH BY PERCENTILE, 2019 (PER U.S. ADULT)

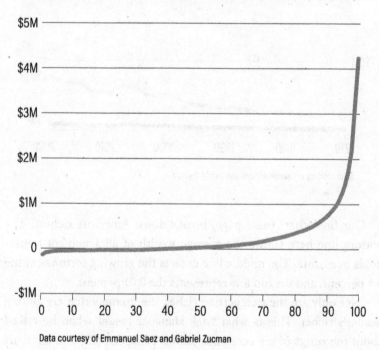

Data courtesy of Emmanuel Saez and Gabriel Zucman

Only two more charts, I promise! Each tracks the growth of family assets over time for selected wealth categories. You've probably seen charts similar to this first one: The bottom line here represents all U.S. households. The middle one depicts the wealthiest 10 percent of Americans, and the top line is for the top 1 percent.

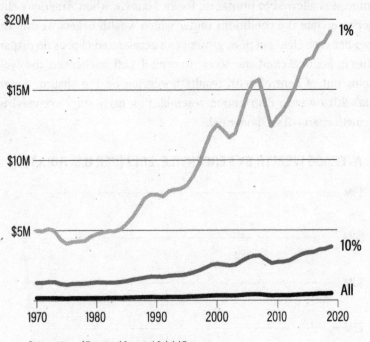

AVERAGE HOUSEHOLD WEALTH (IN 2018 DOLLARS)

Data courtesy of Emmanuel Saez and Gabriel Zucman

Our final chart (next page) breaks down America's richest. The bottom line here shows the average wealth of all 1 percent households over time. The middle line depicts the growing fortunes of the 0.1 percent, and the top line represents the 0.01 percent.

Not only are the rich getting richer, the insanely rich are getting *insanely* richer. This is what Nick Hanauer meant when he talked about the rungs of the economic ladder being stretched so far apart that people can barely contemplate the next rung. "I think the public impression of the 1 percent is really the 0.001 percent," Jerry Fiddler told me. "I mean, they're seeing Kochs and Buffetts and Gates. They're seeing *them* as the 1 percent and they're really not. The gap between me and them is probably larger in a lot of ways than between—I don't know about you—but most people and me." John

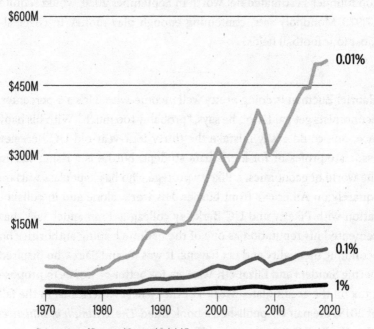

AVERAGE HOUSEHOLD WEALTH (IN 2018 DOLLARS)

Data courtesy of Emmanuel Saez and Gabriel Zucman

Adams saw this coming. "As long as Property exists," he cautioned in one of his letters to Jefferson, "it will accumulate in Individuals and Families . . . the Snow ball will grow as it rolls."

Perhaps it isn't surprising that Norton's and Ariely's subjects were so far off target. The official language of economics is pretty arcane: "annualized," "median," "marginal," "variable." One's eyes glaze over. So let's take a moment to think about our economic differences in a more relatable way. Remember how Piff and I couldn't play a game of Monopoly pitting the middle class against the 1 percent because there wasn't enough money in the game set? Well, suppose we wanted to make it middle class vs. the 0.001 percent, and the middle-class player started with $500. We would need 163 Monopoly sets, and the game would be no fun at all. To take our metaphor to the extreme, a match pitting the middle class against Jeff Bezos, based on the Amazon founder's estimated net worth in September 2020, would require 17,973 Monopoly sets, containing enough play money to cover almost four football fields.

———————

Gabriel Zucman is doing pretty well income-wise. He's a 5 percenter. Economists get paid a lot, he says, "probably too much." With his baby face, one could easily mistake the thirty-four-year-old UC Berkeley associate professor for a graduate student, but he is a rising star in the world of economics, a Piketty protégé who has kept class warfare squarely on America's front burner. His work, alone and in collaboration with Piketty and UC Berkeley colleague Emmanuel Saez, has cemented his reputation as one of the nation's leading authorities on economic inequality and tax havens. It was he and Saez who inspired Bernie Sanders and Elizabeth Warren, for better or worse, to propose a tax on the accumulated wealth of the richest Americans. In the fall of 2019, the pair co-published a book titled *The Triumph of Injustice: How the Rich Dodge Taxes and How to Make Them Pay*.

Back when Adams and Jefferson were debating "the few" vs. "the many," Jefferson argued that, given our young republic's abundance of arable land, and its abandonment of the old English inheritance laws meant to keep *Downton Abbey*–esque estates intact, "rank and birth, and tinsel aristocracy will finally shrink into insignificance." Adams disagreed. "No Romance could be more amusing," he replied, than the notion that the former colonies could escape the fate of every other civilized society known to man. Aristocracy, he wrote, is comprised of five "pillars"—beauty, wealth, birth, genius, and virtues, and "any one of the three first can, at any time, overbear any one or both of the two last."

Asked which man's prediction proved more correct, Zucman replies that what we have in America today is arguably worse than what Adams feared: not a hereditary aristocracy but an economic one "that can present itself as more legitimate than the old-world aristocracy, where you were rich and powerful for totally arbitrary reasons."

Plenty of Americans are still rich and powerful for arbitrary reasons. (Kim Kardashian and Jared Kushner come to mind.) But "there are enough cases of success that look like meritocracy to give an impression of legitimacy to those who are on the top of the income and wealth pyramid," Zucman says.

This is a key point, because economic privilege is to some extent a zero-sum game. Wealth can be "created," true enough, and new industries inevitably pop up that bring prosperity and opportunity to certain groups. But for the few to accumulate mind-boggling wealth and privilege, the many must have little. Consider the equity distribution Tim O'Reilly encountered when he was pondering the sale of his publishing house. The after-the-fact largesse of billionaires cannot change the fact that our economy works for only a fraction of the population. How big a fraction depends on one's perspective. Average wealth per adult (not household) within the wealthiest 10 percent of the population was about $2.8 million in 2019. Move down one decile and average wealth plummets to about $555,000—then $293,600, then $152,000. If you ranked in the twenty-fourth wealth percentile that year, you had $199 to your name—about enough to buy one of the cheaper propane grills at Home Depot. This is how depraved things have become in a republic whose founding document asserted that all people (okay, all white male landowners) were created equal.

The most notable aspect of our economy is not how innovative or resilient it is, Zucman says, but the fact that more than 165 million Americans today live with startlingly little income, a declining life expectancy, and profound stress about their ability to get by. Half of the population of the richest country on the planet "is not prospering," he says. And soaring incomes at the top have left the rest of us fighting for crumbs.

Being wealthy, ironically, makes one's life less expensive in all sorts of ways. Wealthy communities are healthier—rarely are they situated near polluted industrial zones—so well-off families have fewer medical problems. They also have better access to quality medical care and healthy food and outdoor recreation: equipment and fields, parks and playgrounds. There is less crime in wealthy areas, especially violent crime, which takes an extraordinary financial toll. A solid local tax base enables superior municipal services—faster emergency response times, nicer common areas, and better-maintained roads that ensure not only safer driving and cycling conditions, but less wear and tear on vehicles.

Public schools in affluent areas have superior resources, too, because rich parents, aided by tax deductions for charitable giving, organize auctions and funding drives to fill curriculum gaps and pay for enrichment programs, field trips, special projects, and classroom supplies. The town of Ross, where James Everingham lives (population ~2,400) has a tax-exempt private foundation to support its local schools. The 2020 fundraising target was $1.5 million. "The ask amount is $3,800 per student," noted the foundation's website. The money would be used to build a state-of-the-art learning center, fund more than forty electives for middle school students, and retain a teacher-to-student ratio of 1-to-12: "the lowest in Marin County," which would make remote learning a lot more manageable.

Cheap and available capital is another benefit of being wealthy. Rich families can borrow more easily and at lower rates than poor ones. People living on the edge are more likely to lack a substantial credit history and are more likely to have dings in their rating from falling behind on bills or rent at some point. Even with bad credit, a wealthy person is likely to have enough collateral for a loan, and the bigger that loan, the lower the interest rate. If you are borrowing to fund a business or a real estate project, "it's harder to borrow $15,000 than it is to borrow $150,000, and it's easier to borrow $150 million than $150,000," one wealthy investor told me.

The little things add up, too. Affluent Americans just aren't nickeled and dimed to the same extent that their fellow citizens are. They can afford to pay their bills, avoiding late fees and credit card interest, and they aren't subject to penalties for falling below the minimum balance on "low-cost" checking accounts. Banking in poor neighborhoods is particularly pricey, with usurious check-cashing joints, pawnshops, rent-to-own places, and payday lenders serving as the primary financial institutions.

Wealthy drivers, bicyclists, and pedestrians are stopped and ticketed less frequently than poor ones, if not because of their skin color, then because there are fewer police patrolling their relatively safe neighborhoods and eyeing them with suspicion. A *ProPublica* investigation found that residents of the three poorest zip codes in Jacksonville, Florida, were six times as likely to receive a pedestrian citation as people elsewhere in the city. Should one be ticketed for "failing to cross a street at a right angle," a wealthy offender can pay the fine. But someone living paycheck to paycheck may have to contest that ticket in court. If you lose and can't afford the tab, judges in some jurisdictions will put you on probation or even throw you in jail—especially if you're Black.

Affluent people are more likely to have jobs that offer bonuses and good benefits, including health coverage and paid sick leave, and that allow people to work from home if necessary. These are crucial perks at any time, but never more so than during the pandemic. As the virus spread and nonessential workers were ordered home, an analysis of six hundred professions showed that the 24 million workers at highest risk of infection were cashiers and retail clerks, home-care workers, nursing assistants, paramedics, schoolteachers, truckers, etc.—jobs with scant benefits and median annual pay of less than $35,000. Low-wage workers were also among the most likely to see their jobs go away permanently. America's ultrawealthy, including my own subjects, took an initial hit, but by September 2020, according to Wealth-X, their fortunes had bounced back to pre-pandemic levels— the elusive "V-shaped recovery."

———

Wealth and income are distinctive creatures. Given all of the advantages money imparts, breaking into the 1 percent by either measure would come as a relief, but getting there by income is no guarantee you'll get there by wealth. Note that the former requires average household earnings of $481,000 a year, whereas the latter requires north of $5.6 million in assets. It typically takes luck, smarts, privilege, and years of working long hours to accumulate those millions. But preexisting wealth works for itself 24/7, and that is entirely by design.

The performance of Wall Street bears little resemblance to economic realities on Main Street, but things weren't always that way. Economists Daniel Greenwald, Martin Lettau, and Sydney Ludvigson recently calculated that almost the entire increase in the value of public companies from 1952 to 1988 was the result of real economic growth. But from 1989 through 2017, though the markets swelled by $34 trillion, only about one-quarter of the growth was reality-based. Indeed, 43 percent of market growth during that later period came from "a reallocation of rents to shareholders in a decelerating economy." Translation: Wealthy investors and executives stiffed employees and hoarded most of the profit for themselves.

In 1980, before taxes, the average wage earner in the bottom half of the income distribution made $19,198. In 2019, adjusted for inflation, the same worker made $19,105—$93 less! This "didn't happen to us like the weather," Hanauer says. The federal minimum wage was reasonably generous in the late 1960s and early '70s, but Congress left it for dead, and inflation nibbled on the carcass. As of Joe Biden's inauguration, the minimum had been stalled at $7.25 for more than a decade and workers in at least thirty states were still guaranteed less than $10 an hour before taxes. Had Congress raised the wage to $15, McDonald's and Starbucks would be fine, and Howard Schultz would still be rich "and everybody else would have much more," says Hanauer, who in 2013 helped enact a $15 minimum in SeaTac, and later Seattle. Other cities followed, as did the likes of Disney, Facebook, Target, and Amazon. Congress is next on his list, and with the Democrats in charge, there was a chance it could actually happen. Had the minimum wage kept pace with productivity gains, Hanauer emphasizes, it would be $22 today.

Even as half of America's workers scraped by on miserly wages, our most fortunate citizens have enjoyed tax advantages as far as the eye can see. Upper-tier incomes, as the charts on pages 196–97 demonstrate, broke away from the pack starting in the mid-1980s. This was largely thanks to tax cuts signed by President Reagan in 1981 and 1986. Proponents of "supply side" economics, notably New York congressman Jack Kemp, claimed that if we give rich people boatloads more money, their prosperity will magically trickle down to the masses through investments and jobs and economic growth. Taken together, the two bills amounted to the biggest tax break for the wealthy since the Roaring Twenties. Marginal income tax rates— those imposed on the uppermost portions of a high-earner's salary— were slashed dramatically. So was the postmortem tax on big estates, and Congress more than tripled the size of an estate that could be left to one's offspring tax-free. Tax rates on capital gains and corporate profits were also reduced.

Decades later, in 2012, a researcher at the nonpartisan Congressional Research Service sought to determine whether the Reagan cuts and other reductions in marginal income tax rates over the prior sixty-five years had benefited the overall economy. He came up short. The tax cuts did not appear to be correlated with more robust saving, investment, or productivity growth. They did, however, appear to be associated with rich people making a lot more money than before. There was no evidence that the cuts expanded America's economic pie, the report noted, "but there may be a relationship to how the economic pie is sliced."

Tax policy is where America's ultrawealthy truly make out like bandits. Zucman and Saez calculate that people in the bottom half of the wealth distribution pay about 25 percent of their earnings in combined federal, state, and local taxes, while the nation's four hundred richest individuals pay an average of 23 percent. There are several reasons for this. Recall that the ultrawealthy get most of their income not in wages but lower-taxed investment gains. They also pay a smaller percentage of their wages in social security taxes, which as of 2021 max out at annual earnings of $142,800. As of now, the only wealth tax imposed on living Americans—the property tax—hits the middle class hardest. In 2016, according to economist Edward Wolff, a family home accounted for 60 percent of the assets of the average middle-class family, whereas non-investment housing comprised less than 7 percent of the wealth of 1 percenters.

Sales taxes, too, favor the rich. The priciest thing most of us will ever buy is our house, but home sales are generally exempt from sales tax, whether the price is $150,000 or $150 million—though people who buy *mobile* homes in my state, California (not the millionaires, I'm guessing), do have to pay sales tax. At California's Concours d'Elegance, while admiring classic vehicles worth more than my house, I noticed lots of Montana license plates. *Weird.* This is a tax-avoidance play, it turns out. Technically, sales taxes are imposed by the state where an item is delivered, not where the purchase is made. So if Nick Hanauer, to offer a hypothetical example, buys a $3 million Bugatti Chiron, he has two options: He can pay $195,000 in sales tax to the state of Washington. Alternatively, he can pay $1,000 and set up an LLC in neighboring Montana, which has no sales tax, and have that shell company purchase the car tax-free. The Washington tax authorities won't like that. If they catch on, Nick will be charged back taxes and penalties—except that he happens to own a ranch in Montana, so he'll probably be off the hook. On the eighteenth fairway of Pebble Beach, I meet a private equity executive named Peter relaxing with his son alongside the family's cobalt-blue 1966 Ferrari—a $2 million car, more or less. Peter hails from the Boston area. The car has New Hampshire plates. Registering his classic car in New Hampshire instead of Massachusetts would have saved him $125,000 in taxes, and so long as he isn't driving the thing around Beantown . . . well, you get the picture.

Yachters enjoy some phenomenal tax breaks. Buy yourself a little bass boat and you'll pay sales tax in most states. Buy a superyacht and you won't have to. Just helicopter your lawyers out to the vessel as it floats outside state territorial waters and close the deal there. "The signees should record and photograph the latitude and longitude readings of a GPS," advises *Marlin* magazine. "It is then prudent to step back and photograph the GPS unit on the helm with the signers present in the picture." Some states cap sales taxes on luxury yachts, aircraft, and motor vehicles. Boat buyers in Florida pay a maximum $18,000 in sales tax, even on a $50 million yacht. New Jerseyites pay $20,000 tops. If you live in South Carolina, you'll pay no more than $500 in sales tax when you purchase a hundred-foot schooner, a Gulfstream jet, or a Bentley—about the same as you'll pay on a Honda Civic.

All in all, people in the lowest wealth decile pay ten cents in tax on every dollar they earn, Saez and Zucman calculate, while America's wealthiest pay a penny or two. Tax breaks and cheating aside, that's also because most consumer goods are taxed, in contrast to services used disproportionately by affluent families, which include the purchase of theater and opera tickets, luxury boxes at sporting events, country club memberships, and financial and legal counsel. The latter services, too, are employed by wealthy families to further reduce their tax burden by means of tactics that are usually legal but sometimes not—and often fall into the gray areas in between.

America's elite, all told, are doing much better today than during the Reagan years. The inheritance tax—which the Republicans are desperate to repeal—stands at a maximum of 40 percent, and you can give away a great deal of money before it kicks in. What's more, early in the pandemic, conservative politicians and pundits argued that our elders should be willing to sacrifice their lives to protect the economy for their children and grandchildren. That's a rotten take. Then again, in terms of intergenerational wealth transfer, rarely in the last century has there been a better time to meet your maker.

CHAPTER 15

DYNASTY

Our commitment. Your legacy.

If you spend much time poking around the world of wealth management, you will hear the word "legacy" a lot. We touched on one meaning in chapter 11. There are two more: Your legacy is your story—accomplishments, sacrifices, struggles, and failures; relationships with friends, enemies, and loved ones. It's how the world will remember you. The third meaning is literally the assets one accumulates in life, the material wealth you can't take with you to the grave.

Superwealthy folks, unlike the rest of us, spend a fair bit of time pondering their legacies, one version or another. Only a small fraction of the world's billionaires have joined Bill Gates's Giving Pledge, and certainly there's no shortage who are determined to pass the whole kit and kaboodle—companies, properties, stocks, planes, yachts, and connections—to their offspring. We are now in the midst of the biggest intergenerational wealth transfer in the history of the planet. In 2018, the Boston asset management firm Cerulli Associates calculated that, within a quarter century, 45 million American families would pass along $68 trillion.

There was a time when family dynasties protected and expanded their legacies using physical might. "Wealth concentration in a few hands is the single most enduring economic pattern across all polities from Mesopotamia to the present—rarely interrupted, and then only for brief intervals," writes Jeffrey Winters, a Northwestern University political scientist who studies elites in societies from ancient Rome to contemporary America. "For thousands of years, being rich involved being armed, engaging in violence and coercion, extracting resources from broad territories, while also holding positions of direct rule."

Nowadays, America's elite need only muster an army of lawyers, accountants, and lobbyists to achieve the same result: the perpetuation of a new breed of dynasties that will join forces when necessary, like the cells of a slime mold, to create the conditions required for the economic aristocracy to reproduce and thrive. The conditions are three: The wealth must multiply fast enough to maintain an ever-expanding family's power and status. The assets must be easily transferable between generations. And policies must be put in place that enable the family and its businesses to share as little wealth as possible with the government, in life and upon death. Over the past decade, congressional Republicans have introduced no fewer than forty-four bills to repeal the estate tax and the generation-skipping transfer tax, enacted to prevent wealthy families from leaving large fortunes to grandchildren and great-grandchildren so as to bypass a round or two of estate taxes.

America's tax codes are full of provisions that are absurdly beneficial for the dynasties, good for the average 1 percenter, decent for 10 percenters, and problematic for just about everyone else. These flaws (or features, depending on where you sit) are often deliberate—snippets of legalese slipped like malware into must-pass bills at the behest of a wealthy donor or group or industry. Once enacted, they are tough to weed out. Every legislative fix opens up a new swamp of tax avoidance, making for an endless game of Whac-A-Mole between reformist lawmakers and a global industry of wealth managers whose potential market Ernst & Young predicted would be worth nearly $70 trillion by 2021.

With sycophantic politicians and the savviest minds in the business on its payroll, a dynasty can tweak tax policies to its advantage or bankroll candidates willing to help it do so. Barring that, elite families have the means, and the will, to negotiate directly with the IRS or to pursue their interests via a special tax court the public rarely hears about. "The effect," as the *New York Times* put it in 2015, is "a kind of private tax system, catering to only several thousand Americans."

The IRS, by the way, doesn't view things like carried interest or the special tax treatment of offshore insurers—which hedge funders parlayed into an elaborate tax-avoidance scheme—as "loopholes." The law is the law, an agency spokesman told me, and subject to interpretation. If a family or company is audited and found in violation, it can settle up, protest to an IRS appeals board, or take the agency to tax court. If the taxpayer loses in court, they can appeal the case further. If they win, they might stand to save millions of dollars—even billions. And often they win.

That's assuming they are audited in the first place. The water carriers for America's dynasties have done their best to make high-end audits rare. The Republican Party has waged open warfare on the IRS since at least the mid-1990s, with mainstream lawmakers and candidates calling for the agency's abolition. By the end of the Bush years, the IRS was auditing fewer than one in ten of the nation's richest taxpayers (those with adjusted gross incomes of $10 million–plus) and only one in fifteen with incomes from $5 million to $10 million.

These audit rates increased substantially under President Obama, but congressional Republicans, embittered by the passage of Obamacare and the taxes it imposed on the 1 percent, hit back hard. After regaining the House in 2010, they systematically eviscerated the IRS budget and launched a series of dog-and-pony-show hearings based on exaggerated claims that the agency was discriminating against conservative groups. During a contentious 2015 exchange highlighted by *ProPublica*, Representative Mike Kelly, a Pennsylvania Republican, laid into John

Koskinen, Obama's feisty IRS commissioner. Koskinen, in a recent speech, had griped that his overworked employees would have to "do less with less," and referred to the assault on his budget as "a tax cut for tax cheats."

"What in the world were you thinking of?" Kelly demanded. Such talk could crush worker morale and encourage tax evasion, he said. Koskinen countered that the cuts had indeed crippled his agency's ability to enforce the law, and now he was worried his congressional foes were about to make the situation worse. "I don't want you saying later on, you know, you should have told us about this, that it is serious," he told the senators. "It *is* serious."

Koskinen's warnings were ignored, and the cuts continued. From 2010 to 2018, even as the IRS received 9 percent more tax returns, its budget was slashed by $2.9 billion—a 20 percent reduction that cost the agency more than one-fifth of its workforce. Investigations of non-filers plummeted and the amount of outstanding tax debt the IRS formally wrote off (based on the ten-year statute of limitations for collections) more than doubled—from less than $15 billion in 2010 to more than $34 billion in 2019.

Most notably, the bloodbath resulted in an exodus of experienced auditors, people with the expertise required to decode the financial voodoo of the wealthiest taxpayers and their deliberately opaque partnerships. (It can "take months to identify the person who represents the partnership," IRS auditors told the Government Accountability Office in 2014.) Virtually no partnerships were audited in 2018. By then, with Donald Trump in the Oval Office, the kneecapped IRS was scrutinizing the individual returns of just 0.03 percent of $10 million–plus taxpayers, down from a peak of 23 percent in 2010. Audits of $5 million–to–$10 million filers fell from just under 15 percent to 0.04 percent. The Treasury Department's Inspector General for Tax Administration reported in 2020 that nearly 880,000 "high income" non-filers from 2014 through 2016 still owed $46 billion, and the IRS was in no shape to collect. The three hundred biggest delinquents owed about $33 million per head, on average. Fifteen percent of their cases had been closed without any examination by IRS staffers, and another third weren't even in line to be "worked."

The dynasties were safe.

————

Earlier, when I said this would be a great time to die if you're super-rich, I didn't mean any disrespect. It's just a fact. The estate tax exemption is at its highest level in decades—unless you were lucky enough to die in 2010, when the tax was temporarily repealed. Moreover, there are so many work-arounds that former Trump advisor Gary Cohn's reported claim that "only morons pay the estate tax" likely had many a wealth professional nodding in agreement—even though the morons in question are simply wealthy people with a civic conscience.

It's not the 10 percenters who make the rules—or the 5 percenters or even most of the 1 percenters, though they all stand to benefit. Rather, it's the families and business owners whose net worth is measured in ten to twelve figures—or more realistically, their professional entourages—who take pride in coming up with clever new ways to circumvent the spirit, if not the letter, of the law. Tax avoidance (legal) and evasion (illegal) is driven largely by wealth advisors and some of the law firms—people who come up with elaborate new tax dodges and market them to wealthy clients, Gabriel Zucman told me. He's not convinced the superwealthy are any more prone to cheating than the rest of us. "It's really that they have access to more *opportunities* to cheat, because there's an industry that targets them," Zucman says. "So if you want to reduce tax evasion, what's critical is to regulate this industry."

"Families haven't always been pushing back against the kind of planning that's been imposed on them, in part because they don't understand the plans," Patricia Angus, who works with some of the world's most affluent families on wealth and philanthropy matters, commented during a Family Office Association panel discussion. And no wonder they don't understand. That estate tax–avoidance tool kit Dennis Covington mentioned back in chapter 5 contains an alphabet soup of arcane financial instruments, including GRITs, GRATs, GRUTs, CRATs, CRUTs, CLATs, CLUTs, QTIPs, QPRTs, and SLATs.

Grasping how these instruments work will require a quick estate planning primer: As of this writing, the top federal rate for estate and gift taxes, which are linked, is 40 percent, and the IRS allows any individual to give away up to $11.7 million in life or upon death (a married couple can give $23.4 million) before imposing either tax. Charitable contributions don't count toward the limit. You also can give annual gifts of up to $15,000 ($30,000 per couple) to as many individuals as you like. Those gifts needn't be reported to the IRS and they don't count toward your lifetime limit, either. For instance, if I give you $25,000 this year, $15,000 is nontaxable, but I have to report the remaining $10,000 to the IRS, which subtracts it from my lifetime exemption.

So, suppose my wife and I die in a plane crash and leave behind an estate worth $100 million with nothing earmarked for charity. As long as we have never handed out any gifts exceeding the annual limits, the first $23.4 million of our estate goes to our heirs tax-free. After that, the next $1 million is taxed progressively at 18 percent to 39 percent, and the rest of the estate is taxed at 40 percent. All told, our estate will have to pay the government well over $30 million—or more if we live in a state with its own estate tax.

———

But my wife and I are not *morons*. We could have, in this fictional example, reduced our taxable estate by paying the college tuitions of relatives or contributing to 529 college plans for our children and grandchildren, nieces and nephews. We could have created an "irrevocable life insurance trust" or put our primary home into a "qualified personal residence trust," which lets us pass it to our children at far below fair market value—and we would still get to live there! We could have placed our family businesses, real estate, stocks, bonds, and other assets in a "family limited partnership" and granted our children an ownership stake. We also could have directed our $23.4 million tax-free bequest into a dynasty trust, where it would grow for the benefit of our future generations, forever immune from inheritance taxes. These tactics are not always cheap or painless, and they can backfire. But "as you go up in financial strata, you just have more chess pieces," an IRS spokesman told me.

As long as estate taxes have existed, wealthy folks have been coming up with ways to avoid them. Back in 1968, Clifford Crummey beat the IRS on a technicality, enabling what is now called a "Crummey trust." Crummey had created a trust for his children into which he deposited whatever tax-free annual contributions the government allowed at that time. But here's the problem: Federal law allows such gifts to be nontaxable only if the beneficiary has immediate access to the funds. This would rule out gifts to young children. So Crummey stipulated in the trust instructions that, up until the end of each tax year, his minor children or a legal guardian acting on their behalf would be able to request access to that year's gift. (Never mind that he was that guardian.) The IRS objected to this, so Crummey took the agency to tax court. He lost, but prevailed on appeal, even though the appeals court deemed it "highly unlikely" that a minor child would seek access to the money against a parent's wishes. So now you and your spouse can put up to $30,000 per kid per year into a Crummey trust. By the time they are thirty-five, assuming a 5 percent annual market return, each will end up with $3 million free and clear, in addition to whatever you leave them later. You could do the same thing for your grandkids—or great-grandkids, if you live that long.

With interest rates at historic lows, a grantor retained annuity trust (GRAT) is a great tool for depriving the government of a bite of your estate. Suppose Jeff Bezos puts $5 million worth of assets into a GRAT for his son Preston. The assets could be cash, stock, real estate, a Picasso—whatever. Over the trust's lifetime, a duration of Jeff's choosing, the initial $5 million (or its equivalent) is paid back to him in annual installments, or annuities. If the trust assets increase in value, Preston gets to keep whatever remains at the end of the term—and if the assets grow faster than what one source calls the "table rate," a federal interest rate published monthly by the IRS, any excess profit goes to Preston tax-free. It's a wee bit more complicated than I'm telling you, but say Jeff puts $5 million into a ten-year GRAT and the table rate is 3.4 percent. If Jeff's assets instead grow at 8 percent annually, he gets his $5 million back and Preston ends up with $4.3 million—of which $3.3 million is exempt from gift taxes. If Jeff does this with all four of his children, he's just protected $13.2 million from the feds.

GRATs really pay off when you have assets that aren't worth much now but are likely to explode in value—like shares of a pre-IPO stock. In 2008, Facebook cofounders Mark Zuckerberg and Dustin Moskovitz set up what appear to be GRATs, presumably for the benefit of children not yet born. Before the company offered stock to the public at $38 a share, Zuckerberg transferred more than 3.4 million shares (some purchased for as little as six cents apiece) into the Mark Zuckerberg 2008 Annuity Trust. Moskovitz made a similar move with 14.4 million shares and Sheryl Sandberg, Facebook's chief operating officer, socked away 1.9 million shares in her own annuity trust. The executives were thereby able to transfer tens to hundreds of millions of dollars—perhaps even billions in Moskovitz's case—to their beneficiaries while paying almost no gift tax.

You can thank America's wealthiest dynasty for making GRATs even more lucrative. The Walton clan, with combined assets of $215 billion, is renowned for its tax-avoidance prowess. The late Sam Walton liked to be seen as an everyman, salt of the earth, but he was keen on intergenerational wealth planning. In 1953, when the eldest of Sam and Helen Walton's four children was nine, before his stores were incorporated as Walmart, Sam put his family assets into a holding company and granted each child a 20 percent share. "The best way to reduce paying estate taxes is to give your assets away before they appreciate," he observed in his autobiography, *Made in America*.

Sam had a sister-in-law named Audrey Walton. In 1993, Richard Covey, an attorney working on Audrey's behalf, put $200 million worth of Walmart stock into a two-year GRAT for her daughters. Three years earlier, Congress had changed the tax code to curb the abuse of another kind of trust that wealthy people were using to sidestep gift and estate taxes. Covey, who edits a U.S. Trust (now Bank of America) publication called *Practical Drafting*, realized that the changes would enable a new, more lucrative conduit for tax-avoidance: the GRAT. The cure was worse than the disease. "They completely blew it," Covey recalls. "Instead of tightening up on the law, they loosened up on the law, and they didn't know that!"

Covey innovated a GRAT variation that estate planners now call a "Walton GRAT." He structured his client's annuity payments such that, if Walmart's share price increased, she would get back her $200 million along with just enough more to cover the growth predicted by the IRS table rate. Zeroing out the trust in this fashion, Covey realized, would eliminate its value as a taxable gift to Audrey Walton's heirs. There was no downside—just upside if the stock did well.

The plan didn't work. Walmart's stock underperformed during that period. The shares Audrey got back were worth less than they had been, and the kids got nothing. Adding insult to injury, the IRS rejected her claim that the trust's gift value was zero or thereabouts—she owed gift taxes on $7.6 million, the agency claimed. She took the IRS to court and won on appeal. Now everyone uses Walton GRATs. They have saved America's wealthiest untold billions. Churning volatile stocks through a series of short-term Walton GRATs is a no-risk proposition, Covey told me. According to *Bloomberg*, casino magnate Sheldon Adelson used such a strategy to transfer at least $7.9 billion to his heirs, circumventing $2.8 billion in gift taxes.

In September 2015, Alice Walton (Sam and Helen's youngest child) auctioned off her prized collection of cutting horses and embryos—"the culmination of five decades of Walton's selective breeding," according to *Quarter Horse News*. Alice, the world's richest woman as of November 2020, wanted to focus on other priorities, namely her Crystal Bridges Museum of American Art. An avid collector, she had established the museum in Bentonville, Arkansas, in 2011, contributing dozens of paintings from her personal collection. She even purchased a Frank Lloyd Wright house, which was disassembled, shipped, and reassembled on the museum property. Backed by more than $1 billion from the Walton Family Foundation, Crystal Bridges was her gift to the community. But it was also a massive gift, at taxpayer expense, to the Walton progeny.

That's because the Walton Family Foundation was bankrolled by a series of "Jackie O trusts," so named because Jacqueline Kennedy Onassis famously set one up for her heirs. Officially, these are called "charitable lead trusts." A charitable lead annuity trust (CLAT) is just like a GRAT, only instead of the annuities going to the trust's creator, they go to a charity instead—and it can be the creator's personal charity. At the end of the trust term, as with a GRAT, the beneficiary keeps whatever assets remain.

Helen Walton set up her first four Jackie O trusts—one per child—in January 2003, when the table rate was 3.6 percent, its lowest since 1970. A team of *Bloomberg News* reporters obtained the trusts' tax returns for 2007 through 2011 and discovered that they were yielding about 14 percent per year, on average, accumulating money much faster than they doled it out. The combined assets grew from $1.4 billion to $2 billion during that stretch—leaving the offspring with hundreds of millions more dollars that the government could no longer touch.

———

Even as the coronavirus pandemic wreaked economic havoc on the middle class, it offered America's dynasties an unprecedented opportunity to bankroll their future generations. The table rate for the second half of 2020 averaged less than 0.5 percent—which is unheard of. Putting a few hundred million worth of your most battered assets into a long-term Jackie O trust would earn you a big charitable tax deduction, praise from your community, and a massive tax-free gift for your offspring once the economy recovers.

It's not hard to understand why families would employ such strategies. As Mike Depatie pointed out, people act in their economic self-interest. What is perhaps more difficult to understand is why the public puts up with this. Amid the turmoil of the 2020 election season, millions of Americans hit the streets to call for economic justice and an end to police violence. The profound wealth gaps between rich and poor, white and Black, have been growing for decades. And yet the lower 90 percent has been surprisingly tolerant of the 0.001 percent propagating its wealth at everyone else's expense. Why have the masses been so slow to take aim at the anthill?

A lack of political power is one clear reason, and stark partisan divisions another, but the phenomenon also has to do with an entrenched ethos that is peculiarly American. As we will explore in the chapter to come, we are raised on a set of myths that bring about unrealistic dreams and aspirations. U2's Bono summed it up nicely during a 2002 interview with Larry King. "In the United States," said Bono, who is Irish, "you look at the guy that lives in the mansion on the hill and you think, 'You know, one day, if I work really hard, I could live in that mansion.' In Ireland, people look up at the guy in the mansion on the hill and go, 'One day, I'm going to get that bastard.'"

CHAPTER 16

WHO WANTS TO HAVE IT ALL?

No one in this world, so far as I know . . .
has ever lost money by underestimating the intelligence
of the great masses of the plain people.

—H. L. MENCKEN

On a sunny October Saturday, in a cavernous, frigid convention hall in San Mateo, California, several thousand men and women dressed in business casual are up out of their cramped plastic folding chairs, whooping and applauding in anticipation of greatness. These are some of those folks Bono was referring to. The ones who aspire to one day live in that mansion on the hill. They are the marks.

Techno music pulsates from the speakers and an explosion of shiny gold confetti rains down over the front rows as a handsome sixty-one-year-old white dude with salt-and-pepper hair bounds onstage, all confident and mic'd up and dressed in black. He's real estate royalty, filthy rich. And this we know because we just watched his warm-up video: Grant Cardone posing with his private jet, Grant Cardone hanging with Snoop Dogg, etc. Cardone is a celebrity mega-landlord and motivational speaker, the author of self-help books with titles like *The Millionaire Booklet, Be Obsessed or Be Average,* and *If You're Not First, You're Last.* "How's everybody doing?" he gushes. The crowd roars.

"Who wants a better life?" *Roar.*

"Who wants a great life?" *Roar.*

"Who wants to have it all?" *Louder.*

"Who wants to have it *all*?" *Louder.*

"Who Wants To Have It All?" *Loudest.*

As Cardone pumps up the crowd and teases famous names yet to come—Tony Robbins, former NFL star Trent Shelton, Sylvester Stallone—a staffer throws T-shirts into the crowd and a few tired-looking women in tank tops with the word "FUN" printed on them distribute little yellow flags on sticks. Both giveaways are emblazoned with Cardone's slogan: "10X." He orders the T-shirt dude to cease and desist. "You guys need information, you don't need a rag! Who needs information?" *Roar.* "You can get a T-shirt from Walmart. I'm here to share with you how to have it all! Not how to get a little bit. Not how to pay the bills. Not how to pay your house off. I'm not here to talk to you about how to get *enough*."

Here Cardone launches into a humble-origins tale to which this crowd can no doubt relate. "My neighbor, the doctor, they had a boat. We didn't have a boat. The kids knew how to ski. I didn't know how to ski. They had a swimming pool. I had a swimming pool—the *community* swimming pool—and I was the lifeguard," he says. "I grew up watching my mom scared about money every single day. By the time I was fifteen, I swore one day I'm going to make it. One day I'm going to be somebody. And I'm going to give back. . . . I want to share with you how to have everything you've ever dreamed of," Cardone goes on. "If you just want a little bit of success, I'm probably not your guy. If you're one of these people who is like, 'Dude, I don't need money, I don't want money, I don't want financial success,' I'm probably not your guy."

He spots an attendee who has sneaked up front to grab a selfie, as though on cue. "Now, if you are like this man right here—this man's a *greedy* man!" Cardone says. "He crawled up here to get the shot. If you want to get the shot, if you want to get the opportunity, if you want to have it all, you have to be willing to get uncomfortable. Say '10X' if you agree with that!"

"10X!"

"Who would like to have more money? I want more money!"

"Woo-ooo!" answers the crowd.

"A guy told me the other day, 'Grant, money won't buy you happiness.' And I said, 'I know that, bro! But it is the *only* thing Gulfstream takes if you want to fly private.'"

———

Welcome to the Real Estate Wealth Expo, a traveling circus where America's wealth fantasy is alive and well. I paid $69 (regularly $249!) for my VIP ticket—everyone has a VIP ticket, because we're all winners here. The "ultimate VIP" pass, which includes a photo op with the celebs, was listed for $1,495 (a $1,995 value!). And here's an offer you can't refuse: Come back tomorrow and bring all your friends and relatives, Cardone says, and they'll get into this life-changing event for free. Just tell the ticket guys Grant said it was cool.

Cardone's schtick—he calls it "a movement"—is that he'll help you "10X" your life and your bank account. You can be a superwealthy landlord like him. Don't buy a house to live in, he admonishes. That's stupid! *Rent* a place and only buy properties that bring you an income. Take risks, man! Debt is your friend. Saving for a rainy day is "poverty thinking." A penny saved is a missed opportunity. Forget what your mom taught you. Grant is here to reeducate you. He's gonna show you how to turn $100,000 into $1 million, $1 million into $10 million, $10 million into $100 million. Can I get a "10X," people?

I came here today, notebook in hand, to see for myself how some people profit off the dreams of others, and to meet everyday folks who believe so strongly in the wealth fantasy that they will shell out hard-earned cash to spend a fine weekend in this deep freeze. (Tony Robbins likes it cold, one speaker explained.) Because our wealth differences aren't just a matter of rich and powerful people pursuing their self-interest. As Bono suggested, our situation also depends upon a broader cultural ethos that conflates marketplace success with self-worth and insists that, whatever our adverse circumstances, anyone with smarts and moxie can one day drive that Bentley, fly in that

Gulfstream, and live in that mansion. This is the myth that keeps the pitchforks at bay.

The morning's Q&A sessions aren't bad, actually. They don't teach anything practical that you couldn't have found by googling around a little bit, but the guests are engaging and their personal stories highlight the power of perseverance. During a break, I wander outside to talk to some of the Expo attendees. Alex and Elena Delamora, a married couple from Fresno, came here with their pal Noe Ramos to be inspired by the celebrity speakers. The Delamoras want to start flipping houses and Ramos is interested in multifamily units. They don't know how they'll come up with the money to invest, but they're eager to make more than they do now. "Four million dollars a year would be good. That's a number I've thought about before," Ramos says. His friends laugh incredulously. "Net! Not gross!" he insists.

Would having all that money make him happier? "I'm already happy," Ramos says. "I'd just do a lot more things. Travel more. I'd probably be a sugar daddy."

"Oh my God!" Elena says, rolling her eyes.

Shani Harris, thirty-nine this year, recently relocated to Grass Valley, California, from Brooklyn and is now studying real estate, she told me. This is her second Expo—she's also done Robbins's signature event, "Unleash the Power Within." She is here in equal measures for inspiration and to learn things that will help her boost her annual income, currently less than $40,000. "I want to know more about wealth, how to obtain it, manage it, pass it on," she says. Harris aspires to be a philanthropist, to live all over the world, buy land and property, start a holistic retreat center, and set her kids up to fulfill their dreams: "I'd really like them to be entrepreneurs." I ask how much money she has in mind to accomplish all of this.

"Six figures," she replies.

Jay and Samera Harvey, a married couple in their early thirties, traveled four hundred miles from Southern California to attend. They've been flipping mobile homes and want to meet like-minded people, get inspired, and learn to maximize their use of social media.

"With an abundance mindset and limitless potential, we would of course want to be millionaires and help more people, but also live a life of being able to travel and have nice things. Just live in luxury, because that's what we want to manifest and it's what we work so hard for," Samera says. Jay wants to be a billionaire, he says, but only so he could help more people. It's not even about the money: "We're chasing freedom."

According to its website, the Real Estate Wealth Expo has attracted more than 1 million attendees since it launched in 2002. The event was the brainchild of sixty-seven-year-old Bill Zanker, who, in 1980, used his "bar mitzvah money" to launch the Learning Annex. The company's bread and butter was organizing "how-to" courses and seminars ranging from "How to Make Your Own Soap" to "How to Marry the Rich." Zanker told reporters he wanted the Annex to be the McDonald's of the continuing-education industry.

If nothing else, Zanker was a born hype-man. In 1982, to celebrate the enrollment of the Annex's hundred-thousandth customer, he announced that he would throw $10,000 in cash off the Empire State Building. (The police didn't allow it, but the stunt served its publicity purpose.) Zanker created another stir with a course titled "How to Cheat on Your Spouse Without Getting Caught." The Learning Annex catalog also included "The Firewalking Experience," which would become a pillar of Tony Robbins's events. (Robbins and Zanker are longtime business partners.) Somewhere along the way, Zanker figured out that the most surefire way to get filthy rich is to tap into others' desire to do so. And what better pitchman for such a baldly extrinsic pursuit than his fellow New Yorker Donald John Trump?

Roughly a decade before Trump announced his presidential bid, Zanker enlisted him as the keynote attraction for his biggest moneymaker of all, the Wealth Expo. Trump would get $1 million per appearance—the highest rate ever paid for an event speaker. Not long after, the Annex announced that Trump was getting a "raise" to

$1.5 million. These widely reported figures were lies. When asked about the payments during a 2007 deposition, Trump admitted under oath he was getting $400,000 per appearance—the higher figure, he claimed, included the value that the event publicity contributed to his personal brand. Past Expo speakers have included the likes of Rudy Giuliani, Alan Greenspan, Al Gore, Suze Orman, Sir Richard Branson, Magic Johnson, George Foreman, 49ers legend Joe Montana, rapper Pitbull, and ex–Yankees slugger and *Shark Tank* guest host Alex Rodriguez, who was suspended in 2014 by Major League Baseball for taking performance-enhancing drugs, which "cost me over $40 million, and it cost me my reputation."

After doing some back-of-the-napkin math, I'm skeptical that the ticket proceeds alone would cover the considerable cost of putting on such an event, but there's another revenue stream the Expo's promotional campaign doesn't hype all that much. For Zanker, the Wealth Expo and Donald Trump—with whom he coauthored a 2007 book titled *Think Big and Kick Ass*—were a perfect match. For even as Trump headlined Zanker's main stage, he was involved in a sketchy real estate seminar business on the side. In 2018, Trump University, which operated under various names from 2005 to 2010, agreed to pay $25 million to settle class-action lawsuits brought by New York State and "students" who claimed Trump's "instructors" had duped thousands of people into spending millions of dollars on useless seminars and mentoring sessions.

I had read enough about the business model to know that the $997 seminars Wealth Expo salesmen were hawking in between the main attractions—classes the presenters suggested would teach you to use "other people's money" to make a killing in real estate—were very unlikely to make anyone rich, other than the organizers. The unstated goal, if previous industry patterns were any indication, would be to entice attendees to sign up for "advanced" seminars costing tens of thousands of dollars. But these pitchmen covered their behinds: At least twice, I heard one rattle off a legal disclaimer stating that there was no guarantee that people would earn more money as a result of attending the seminars he was selling than it cost them to sign up. In Expo world, as in Trump world, you're either a winner or a loser. The losers, it turns out, are the suckers who shell out for VIP tickets and house-flipping seminars. The winners are the guys who fly around in private jets paid for by the losers' big dreams.

Given our history, it's not surprising that the vague promise of riches can still convince everyday folks to attend such an event, about which even a cursory Google search reveals plenty of red flags. America's first settlers risked a dangerous sea voyage in search of riches that didn't pan out. The gold rush, a metaphor for all economic booms to follow, was the ultimate get-rich-quick frenzy, for which dreamers were willing to drop all else. California wasn't even American turf in January 1848, when gold was discovered at Sutter's Mill—it only became so six months later. But as news of the discovery spread, hundreds of thousands of fortune-seekers embarked on arduous, plague-ridden voyages by land and sea, abandoning their shops and fields to join the hunt. The state's population at the beginning of 1849—estimated at twenty-six thousand, excluding Native Americans—swelled to one hundred and fifteen thousand by year's end.

The very first gold rush millionaire didn't make his fortune from gold. Like Zanker, he got rich by exploiting the wealth fantasies of others. Samuel Brannan was a Mormon merchant and publisher of the *California Star* newspaper. After learning that gold had been discovered, he bought up all the shovels and pickaxes and gold pans he could lay hands on, and then walked the streets of San Francisco waving his hat and holding up a vial of the precious metal, yelling, "Gold! Gold! Gold! From the American River!" In short order, his wares were in such demand that he was getting $15 for gold pans he'd acquired for twenty cents—miners were paying $100 for shovels and picks, and that's in 1850 dollars.

Brannan was just one of many opportunists who "mined the miners." Another was Levi Strauss, a recent immigrant who moved to San

Francisco to peddle clothing and accessories, and ultimately the jeans for which he became known, at exorbitant prices. Edward Gould Buffum, a New York militia lieutenant who traveled west to try his luck, documented price gouging that defies belief. One morning's provisions for Buffum and his companions at Sutter's Fort consisted of a box of sardines ($552 in today's dollars), one pound of hard bread ($69), one pound of butter ($207), a half pound of cheese ($104), and two bottles of ale ($552)—$1,484 all told. "A pretty expensive breakfast, thought we!" he wrote. "If I ever get out of these hills and sit and sip my coffee and eat an omelet, at a more nominal expense, in a marble palace, with a hundred waiters at my back, I shall send back a glance of memory at the breakfast I ate at Culoma saw-mill."

Greed has always been one of the primary drivers of the American story. It fueled the genocide and seizure of land from Native Americans, made slavery a hereditary institution, and gave rise to our system of mass incarceration. It turned Florida from a malarial swampland into a vacation getaway during the 1920s, built the Las Vegas Strip, and compelled Wall Street wonks to invent the collateralized debt obligations and other opaque financial instruments that tanked the U.S. economy in 2008. It transformed western North Dakota from a quiet rural place into an oil-crazed industrial zone complete with "man camps." It gave us Michael Milken and junk bonds, the dot-com boom, the Bitcoin roller coaster, Bernie Madoff, and the college admissions scandal.

———

Our strike-it-rich aspirations might be harmless if not for one inconvenient truth: The wealth fantasy, combined with the peculiarly American notion that anyone can succeed via grit and smarts and hard work, leads us not only to tolerate mind-blowing economic unfairness, but to support the kinds of policies that produced this mess in the first place. Shortly after America declared independence, John Adams recognized that our fledgling nation was a "commercial republic" in which the quest for material rewards would come to define how future generations interpreted his friend's words "the pursuit of happiness." That Adams's warning came to pass is a testament to one of our nation's most entrenched and damaging myths: that of upward mobility.

During the 1830s, Alexis de Tocqueville described America as a place where "there are no longer any classes, or those which still exist are composed of such mobile elements, that their body can never exercise a real control over its members." Even the Gilded Age and the Great Depression failed to overcome this myth. Most of the American communists he knew in the 1930s, John Steinbeck wrote in *Esquire*, were "middle-class, middle-aged people playing a game of dreams. . . . Everyone was a temporarily embarrassed capitalist."

And thus we remain. In a 2018 Gallup poll, 63 percent of American respondents said they were satisfied with their opportunities to get ahead through hard work, even though only 32 percent were satisfied with America's income and wealth distributions. That same year, Harvard economists Alberto Alesina, Stefanie Stantcheva, and Edoardo Teso reported that Americans were significantly more optimistic than their European counterparts about their prospects of moving up in socioeconomic status, even though actual mobility in the United States was significantly worse than in Europe. Americans, they wrote, are "over-optimistic."

The truth is, most Americans are treading water economically and have been for a long time. Absolute upward mobility—doing better than your parents—is no longer assured. A team of economists from the National Bureau of Economic Research compared cohorts of adult children born in either 1940 or 1984, and found that 92 percent of the 1940 group was earning more than their parents had, but only half of the 1984 group was. The decline was even steeper, 95 percent down to 41 percent, when the researchers compared fathers and sons. And because the spoils of economic prosperity have flowed disproportionately to America's top earners since at least the mid-1980s, this situation wasn't going to fix itself.

A good portion of America's misplaced optimism originated with a pair of books written before most of us were born: We'll get to the second one in a moment, but the first was *Ragged Dick*, Horatio Alger's serialized 1868 novel about a homeless shoeshine boy who rises from poverty to upper-middle-class respectability by means of grit, determination, and hard work. *Ragged Dick* was a massive bestseller, and it is hard to overstate its lasting influence on the American psyche.

The tropes of the deserving rich and the lazy poor—makers and takers—are classics, mixing and matching with racist myths to produce toxic stereotypes. President Ronald Reagan weaponized the term "welfare queens" and used it as a justification to slash the social safety net for America's poorest. Twenty years later, 52 percent of respondents in an NPR poll cited "lack of motivation" as a key cause of poverty—about the same proportion as those who felt that "too many jobs being part time or low-wage" was a factor. In 2014, Paul Ryan, another Republican seeking to gut welfare programs, claimed that generations of urban Black men were "not even thinking about working or learning the value and the culture of work." In a reputable 2016 public policy poll, 42 percent of respondents (and 64 percent of Republican respondents) said poverty was caused more by "a lack of individual effort" than by "society's inequality." Sixty-nine percent of respondents in a 2019 RealClearPolitics poll agreed that anyone could achieve the American Dream by working hard—even though only 27 percent said that dream was "alive and well" for them personally.

Some of these views are deeply ingrained. American children as young as four can distinguish "rich" from "poor" people using visual clues, researchers have found, and when psychologist Carol Sigelman described the circumstances of "rich" or "poor" characters to first, fifth, and ninth graders, the children rated the rich characters more favorably in terms of intelligence, motivation, and responsible behavior. In one classic study, psychologist Robert Leahy found that, by the time they reach high school, American kids are beginning to justify our economic differences and attribute poverty to a lack of education and effort.

The "hard work" trope is one that America's wealthiest deploy often. When Bernie Sanders attacked Michael Bloomberg during one of the 2020 Democratic primary debates, declaring the very existence of billionaires immoral, a moderator asked Bloomberg whether he felt he should have been able to earn as much money as he had. Bloomberg, whose holdings were worth more than $65 billion at the time, said, "Yes. I worked very hard for it." Well, sure. Anyone who builds a company works their tail off. But some founders are more clear-eyed than others. Jerry Fiddler worked one-hundred-hour weeks at Wind River Systems, but "anybody who tells you that they're wealthy because they work harder is either lying to you or they're lying to themselves. My cleaning lady works harder than I do and doesn't make as much money," he told me. "The work is necessary, but it's not sufficient."

Our false beliefs about wealth and mobility have real-life consequences. In 2016, sociologists Jeff Manza and Clem Brooks expressed puzzlement about the "tepid public responsiveness to the massive and ongoing increase in inequality." So they investigated and found that a key culprit was "mobility optimism," a measure that correlates closely with whether we think the government should do more to address the wealth gap. "Mobility optimists may simultaneously express hostility to the 'rich' or the '1 percent' and harbor doubts about the 'fairness' of the economy," they wrote. "But they may also retain a belief in the promise of their own (or their children's) economic prospects that insulates them from reacting to historical trends with more vigorous support for policy reform efforts."

The other author who contributed the most to our fanciful mobility narrative was James Truslow Adams, whose 1931 history, *The Epic of America*, introduced the concept of the American Dream: Not "a dream of motor cars and high wages merely," he wrote, but "of a social order in which each man and each woman shall be able to attain to the fullest stature of which they are innately capable, and be recognized by others for what they are, regardless of the fortuitous circumstances of birth or position." Author Timothy Noah noted in *The New*

Republic that both authors came from well-established families that sent their sons to college (Alger attended Harvard) at a time when most Americans did not. Before he became an author, Adams worked on Wall Street and earned enough money to live comfortably.

Their works affected America's self-image in ways neither man would have predicted. The Ragged Dick tale, legal scholar Harlon Dalton writes in his book *Racial Healing*, "conveys three basic messages: (1) each of us is judged solely on her or his own merits; (2) we each have a fair opportunity to develop those merits; and (3) ultimately, merit will out. Each of them is, to be charitable, problematic."

True rags-to-riches tales are pretty rare, but one would never know it from the way these stories are fetishized by businesspeople and politicians. "I came from the projects," boasted former Starbucks CEO Howard Schultz, describing his journey from Brooklyn's Bayview development—"literally on the wrong side of the tracks"—to the helm of the café behemoth as "the American Dream." But others who grew up in the same place at the same time weren't having it. "Bayview was a heavily Jewish, solidly middle-income place. It was an oasis, a sanctuary," a sociologist who spent years studying the area told the *Washington Post*.

For an actual rags-to-riches tale, one might turn to Ford Foundation president Darren Walker, who grew up penniless in rural Texas and went on to become an icon in the world of philanthropy. Throughout his life, white people have used his success to justify the stories they tell themselves: They would say, "'You're an example to me of what happens when you work hard and you sacrifice.' And the implicit message is, the Blacks who aren't successful, it's because they're not working hard and not sacrificing," Walker says.

But those people have it all wrong. The truth, as we will see in the next chapter, is that we live in a nation where the majority has always vigorously protected its own wealth and power, and still does. Throughout American history, if you were the wrong color, the wrong gender, or simply new in town, you had to work a lot harder and sacrifice more than others to have any chance of hitting the jackpot.

CHAPTER 17

THRIVING WHILE BLACK

*I am given to understand that whiteness is the ownership
of the earth forever and ever, Amen!*

—W. E. B. DU BOIS, 1920

It took all of about five seconds for Erwin Raphael to realize that walking into this rural Ohio roadhouse with his college buddy had been a mistake. The Harleys with Confederate flags out front probably should have tipped him off, but Raphael, who is Black, was still pretty green. Born on the former British island of Dominica and raised in St. Croix, he'd heard stories but had never actually experienced *scary* racism. Students at the University of Maryland called him the N-word once or twice, and he thought they were losers, but it wasn't as though he thought he was about to get lynched. This felt different.

He was the fifth of seven boys born into a family that lacked running water, electricity, insurance, or government benefits, but Raphael's father, a work crew foreman with a high school degree, relocated the family to St. Croix soon after to take a refinery labor position that afforded the family a lower-middle-class existence. Raphael remembers his mother, educated through sixth grade and married at seventeen, announcing at dinner one night that she was enrolling in night school because she didn't want to be the only one in the family without a high school diploma. She followed through, earning her GED, and later graduated from college at sixty-five. "Never Too Late," noted a local newspaper headline.

Now fifty-four and married, with kids of his own, Raphael is a wealthy and successful U.S. citizen. He oversees the interplay of Hyundai's numerous North American operations, including its luxury unit, Genesis, which he previously headed. His parents imbued him with a strong work ethic, and the army helped him learn leadership skills, but there's another factor to which Raphael attributes his success. Despite St. Croix's turbulent history of colonialism, slavery, and plantation labor, its Black majority wasn't relegated to permanent underclass status. Even after the United States purchased St. Croix from Denmark in 1917, the island—today 76 percent Black—never adopted the mainland's Jim Crow laws. There were no racial covenants limiting where a Black person could live—no flags, monuments, or statues celebrating slavery days. There was racism, sure, but "St. Croix, like Puerto Rico, was spared the massive transfer of Southern norms," Franklin Knight, an emeritus professor of Caribbean and Latin American history at Johns Hopkins, told me. Whites lacked "the critical mass to dominate the society culturally and economically after the abolition of slavery." Raphael's local heroes included Moses Gottlieb and "Queen Mary" Thomas, who led uprisings against the Danish plantation masters. The Virgin Islands' governors and congressional delegates, St. Croix's teachers and lawmakers, Raphael's family doctor and pastor, the accountant who did his father's taxes, the news anchors on television—most had dark skin like him. He never had any doubt a kid could grow up to be anything he wanted.

The barroom incident, the first of many such encounters, happened in the late 1980s. By this time Raphael had transferred to Ohio State, where he was majoring in chemistry after a stint in the army to cover the expenses his Pell Grant didn't. Eager to better understand the mainland culture, he minored in African American studies. His friends back home were racially diverse, but they shared an island heritage. Here he felt like an outsider even among Blacks: "If I kept my mouth shut and didn't acknowledge that I really didn't know what they were talking about, I might look like I belong." In his technical major, meanwhile, "some of my professors didn't expect me to sit up front and pay attention and be interested in the subject matter. But I did."

The campus was safe and welcoming nonetheless. But on this day he and his friend and their girlfriends had strayed far from the cocoon and embarked on a road trip to a music festival. They lost their way and so, seeking directions, they pulled into a bar in Circleville. "We opened the door and my buddy Dave said, 'Excuse me?' And the guys at the bar almost in unison all turned around, looked at us, two of them got up and started walking towards us, and one said, 'You're at the wrong bar, n—!'"

Dave, a confident Trinidadian, wasn't so easily dissuaded. He tried to explain that they only needed directions. Two more thugs stood up. "We already told you once," one said. "We're not going to tell you again. You're at the wrong effin' bar."

"I was out of there," Raphael says. "Dave came after. We literally ran back to our cars!"

Raphael tells me this story on the terrace of the swanky Balboa Bay Resort on Newport Harbor, steps away from a row of multimillion-dollar yachts. Handsome and fit, with a scar on his face from breaking up a childhood fistfight, he is dressed like a well-to-do islander: pristine white slacks and shirt, light blue seersucker jacket, spotless black low-tops, and a Rolex Yacht-Master II timepiece worth almost as much as my car—a gift, he assures me. Erwin isn't the only Raphael who made good. His late brother LeRoy was a successful physician, a pilot, and a pastor. Another brother, Desmond, was a lieutenant colonel in the U.S. Army, on track to eventually become a general when he died suddenly of a heart attack after returning from Operation Desert Storm. A third brother, Sam, owns a resort in Dominica. Guests regularly ask Sam how he made his money. "The assumption is he must be a drug dealer or something," Raphael says. "His going line is 'I grew up a coconut picker.' People don't walk into hotels and ask a white owner, 'How did you get your money?'"

White Americans tend to resist the notion they enjoy unfair economic advantages, and that's understandable. Researchers have found we all have a tendency to emphasize obstacles and downplay our own luck and privilege. "I run on the beach," Paul Piff told me by way of illustration. "Some days I feel like I'm going particularly fast, and on those very same days, when I'm coming back, I feel like, 'Whoa, that is a heavy wind, and it's making me go slower. I didn't realize when I was going fast that there was wind pushing me.'"

But as we've seen, the luck of our birth—the least fair thing imaginable—has an astonishing impact on family wealth and its propagation. The median net worth of white U.S. households in 2016 was $171,000, according to one widely cited study—ten times the wealth of Black households and eight times that of Latino households. (The Institute for Policy Studies, using a different methodology, reports racial wealth disparities of 50x and 25x, respectively.) Such results cannot—though many a pseudo-scholar has tried—be attributed to differences in natural talent and work ethic and leadership ability. Rather, throughout our history, merchants and politicians, bankers and realtors, restaurants and social clubs, colleges and corporations, landlords and cops, have taken one look at people with darker skin, stood up from their stools, and said, "You're at the wrong bar, n—."

If you can't walk into the proverbial bar, you can't buy a drink, you can't mix with people who enjoy that privilege, and you'll certainly never own the place. That, in a nutshell, is what Raphael, channeling author Shawn Rochester, calls the "Black tax"—a term that can be extrapolated to Native Americans, Latinos, recent immigrants, and other groups whose wealth has been deliberately suppressed by the majority culture. The Black tax goes a long way toward explaining why white families have at least ten times the wealth of Black families, and why COVID-19 kills Black Americans at nearly twice the rate it kills white people. The Black tax is why Raphael—wealthy, veteran, evangelical Christian, and until recently a registered Republican (though never a Trump supporter)—is convinced he's far more likely to be murdered by a local police officer than by a civilian. It furthermore helps to explain why there are just four Black CEOs and not a single majority Black–owned company in the Fortune 500. "This is not a talent issue, but an access issue," noted Skip Spriggs, former CEO of the Executive Leadership Council, a Black business group.

Yet another consequence of the Black tax is that, when we discuss racial disparities in America, we are almost always talking about the bare basics: access to decent housing, clean water, doctors, preschool, college, voting rights, human dignity, etc. But this book is about wealth. If it is unconscionable that some groups experience poverty, homelessness, and incarceration at rates vastly exceeding their share of the population, is it not also problematic that the same groups are dramatically underrepresented within the ranks of wealth and power?

In 2020, according to Wealth-X, the United States had 788 billionaires, a 12 percent increase over 2018. Our population is 13.4 percent Black, so all things equal, we should have at least 105 Black billionaires. We have seven. Five require no introduction: Michael Jordan, Jay-Z, Kanye West, Oprah Winfrey, and the latest addition, Hollywood's Tyler Perry. The sixth, David Steward, is the founder of a St. Louis IT services firm called World Wide Technology. And then there's Robert Smith, the richest Black person in America, with assets exceeding $5 billion. Smith, a former chemical engineer, is the founder, chairman, and CEO of Vista Equity Partners, a tech-focused investment firm. A few years ago, he paid $59 million for a posh three-story Manhattan apartment. But he is still a Black man in America. In a 2018 *Forbes* profile, Smith recalled having dinner with some Wall Street honchos. When he moved to pay the tab, one of the men, a white banker, stopped him: "I can't have a Black guy buy me dinner."

The guy was probably joking, but there's nothing funny about the Black tax, an amalgam of vicious policies and virulent racism that even today results in a steep path to wealth and success for aspiring African Americans. Smith flew largely under the public's radar until 2019, when he dropped a viral bombshell during a commencement address at the historically Black Morehouse College. He pledged to personally wipe out the student debt of the entire graduating class—

about $34 million all told. Students and families were elated, while critics were quick to point out that Smith profits from carried interest and that his gift was a drop in the bucket toward fixing a $1.6 trillion problem. (Smith would later admit to big-time tax evasion.) But for a few news cycles, he sparked a conversation about the crippling impact of debt on young Americans, particularly people of color whose families lack the resources to weather a catastrophe.

———

By March 2020, when the coronavirus hit the economy like a sledgehammer, the scarcity of Black wealth in America was already a national disgrace. Black families were about twenty times more likely to have *negative* wealth than $1 million or more, according to the Institute for Policy Studies, and America's four hundred wealthiest citizens had more combined assets than the entire Black population plus a quarter of the Latino population—including billionaires such as Smith and Florida "condo king" Jorge Pérez. The trend line has been moving in the wrong direction. From 1983 to 2016, the median wealth of Black families, adjusted for inflation, decreased by more than half, even as the number of U.S. households worth north of $10 million increased almost tenfold. "To produce so few rich Black people . . ." says the Ford Foundation's Darren Walker. "I mean, if we're going to have a capitalist system, we should have one where the opportunity to reap the rewards are open to all. And we know our system has never been open. It was designed on the backs of slaves."

Ah, slavery, the 100 percent Black tax. For if taxation is theft, the Southern aristocracy was the most rapacious pack of thieves in our history, stealing the labor, freedom, families, and often the lives of 388,000 enslaved Africans and a dozen generations of their descendants. White prosperity, North and South, would come at the direct expense of well over 4 million brown-skinned people who would receive little in return but scorn, exclusion, and violence.

The subject of reparations came up over drinks not long ago with someone I've known forever—educated, white, liberal. He told me he found it annoying how some African Americans blame their contemporary woes on the horrors of so long ago. I was kind of surprised, but that's a common attitude. Another advantage of whiteness: the freedom to not have to think too deeply about our ugly past—which is also our present. As James Baldwin wrote, in 1959: "Someone once said to me that the people, in general, cannot bear very much reality. . . . They prefer fantasy to a truthful re-creation of their experience. People have quite enough reality to bear by simply getting through their lives, raising their children, dealing with the eternal conundrums of birth and taxes and death."

Slavery in America had but one goal: white wealth. Contemporary economists have calculated that enslaved Black people were the nation's second most valuable capital asset, apart from land. In a 1792 letter to George Washington, Thomas Jefferson noted that he was earning a 4 percent annual profit for each Black child born on his plantation. In another communication, Jefferson stated that a down-on-his-luck acquaintance, if the man's family had any remaining resources, should lay out "every farthing . . . in land and negroes." This was around the same time that Jefferson began backing away from his earlier support of emancipation.

The policies enacted in the South after emancipation had a dual purpose: to maintain white wealth and political power and to prevent free Blacks from attaining any. One needed land to prosper, and the newly liberated were desperate to obtain plots of their own. Toward the end of the Civil War, word went around that each Black family would receive forty acres and a mule in compensation. The harsh reality was that the government had already embarked on the biggest wealth giveaway in U.S. history, and Black people were destined to miss out almost entirely.

The Homestead Acts weren't explicitly racist, but the outcome was. The original act, signed by President Lincoln during the second year of the Civil War, opened up millions of acres of public land in the West. Any adult male, head of household, or Union military veteran could lay claim to a 160-acre parcel. One only had to apply, pay a modest fee, make improvements for five years, and then file for a deed of ownership. It was a once-in-a-lifetime bonanza for white fortune-seekers. "The acquisition of property was the key to moving upward from a low to a higher stratum," wrote author Everett Dick. "The property holder could vote and hold office, but the man with no property was practically on the same political level as the indentured servant or slave." Homesteading was no cakewalk. One needed money up front for travel, fees, and provisions, and homesteaders faced unlucky weather, poor crop yields, and predatory moneylenders. But those who endured were rewarded with acreage that served as a foundation for intergenerational wealth, according to Trina R. Shanks, a scholar of wealth and poverty at the University of Michigan.

The second round, the Southern Homestead Act, took effect shortly after the war. For twelve months, emancipated Black men ("freedmen") and white Union loyalists were given priority claim on 46 million unoccupied acres in five states. In theory, this might have helped fulfill the forty-acre promise (sans mule), but much of the land was unsuitable for farming, and many emancipated Blacks had been roped into long-term labor contracts with their former masters. Breaking a contract got you a year on a prison work gang. Between the two acts, about 270 million acres of farmland—14 percent of the total landmass of the continental United States—was granted to 1.6 million white families, but only four thousand to five thousand Black families. Shanks calculates that more than 48 million living Americans are direct descendants of those Homestead Act beneficiaries. Which means there's a greater than one-in-four chance your forebears benefited directly from the biggest public-to-private wealth transfer in American history—if you're white, that is.

———

Slavery was rough, and so, too, was freedom. This part of the story you know: the widespread violence, harassment, and hostility; the rapes and murders with impunity; the Black Codes that Southern states wrote into their new constitutions in an attempt to preserve conditions much as they were under slavery. For our purposes, suffice it to say the Black Codes and subsequent Jim Crow laws raised a ridiculously high bar for the accumulation of Black wealth.

Fearful of reprisal, and knowing that he who can't play cannot win, white Americans, North and South and West, erected roadblocks to Black prosperity at every turn. In Georgia, a Black barber could not cut a white woman's hair. South Carolina decreed that no person of color could be an artisan, mechanic, or shopkeeper unless they first obtained a (costly) license from the judge of the district court. But the worst were the anti-vagrancy laws, which meant, if you were a Black man who wasn't employed by a white man, you were liable to be arrested, fined, and handed off to a white planter to work off your penalty. The forced labor and arbitrary incarceration of Black Americans were a marriage of racial hatred and economic terrorism. Douglas Blackmon, the Pulitzer Prize–winning author of the book *Slavery by Another Name*, estimates that 50 percent to 70 percent of Black prisoners in the South at any time during the postbellum period "had committed no actual crime or genuinely harmful act against society." Not only were Black men eliminated as economic competition, their labor was being stolen yet again to bolster white wealth.

Reconstruction was a brief, sweet respite from the madness: For a decade or so after the war, with occupying federal troops offering a semblance of protection in the South, emancipated Blacks set out to exercise their newfound right to vote, educate themselves, and acquire what land they could. They launched newspapers, established political organizations, built schools and churches, and took up arms to protect their communities—all previously forbidden. Understanding, too, that political power was a prerequisite for Black prosperity, they sought positions of public leadership. In 1868, South Carolina's House of Representatives was majority Black for the first (and only) time in its history. As Henry Louis Gates Jr. writes in his 2019 book, *Stony the Road*, an estimated two thousand African Americans held public office from the war's end through 1901—twenty became congressmen and two were elected to the Senate. But Lincoln's successor, former vice president Andrew Johnson, was determined that the South be reintegrated into the Union under white leadership. "I believe [Blacks] have less capacity for governing than any race on Earth," he said.

Reconstruction ultimately succumbed to what Southern propagandists labeled the "Redemption," which in fact was nothing more than a successful domestic terror campaign. Republican officeholders were assassinated. States imposed poll taxes and literacy tests on Black voters. Racist white paramilitaries, enraged by Republican victories, slaughtered hundreds of Black citizens in Louisiana and South Carolina and even, at one point, seized control of New Orleans for several days until federal troops restored order. Not only were the militia leaders never convicted, one of them, Benjamin Tillman (of Tillman Act fame), was elected to the Senate and served twenty-four years. After North Carolina representative George Henry White left Congress in 1901, seventy-one years would pass before the South sent another Black representative to Washington.

The "separate but equal" Jim Crow statutes, declared legal by the Supreme Court in 1896, were more severe and more severely enforced in the South, Blackmon told me. But on paper, laws forbidding interracial marriage, housing, education, military service, and so forth "were somewhat indistinguishable" in the North, South, and West. Many of these policies persisted until the mid-1960s, choking off almost every legitimate engine of wealth creation. The few Blacks who managed to attain significant wealth despite the obstacles were often targets—for the white media if not angry mobs.

———

Nothing kneecapped Black wealth, however, like being denied access to capital. Richard Rothstein provides a full accounting in his excellent book, *The Color of Law*. Here's a small taste: By the time the Great Depression came along, Black Americans were already excluded from many American communities by Jim Crow statutes and local racial covenants. In 1890, Rothstein notes, there were Black settlers in all of Montana's fifty-six counties. By 1930, there were few Blacks in any of them and eleven counties were exclusively white. The Black population of Helena, the state capital, plummeted from 3.4 percent in 1910 to less than 0.5 percent in 2010. White communities around the nation forbade Black citizens from even being present after dark. Some rang warning bells at sundown. Others posted signs at town limits. "The sun is never allowed to set on any n—s in Glendive," one local newspaper declared in 1915.

Homeownership was a stretch even for the white middle class in those days. Banks required a 50 percent down payment and imposed mortgage terms of five to seven years with interest to be paid off first. To remedy this, Congress created the Home Owners' Loan Corporation, which bought up bad loans and issued new ones with more reasonable terms. But the realtors hired to do HOLC's appraisals were bound—by their industry's code of ethics, no less—to maintain racial segregation. HOLC famously produced color-coded lending maps with "safe" (white) neighborhoods in green and high-risk ones (Black and mixed) in red—hence "redlining." The middle-class St. Louis suburb of Ladue was green because "not a single foreigner or negro" lived there, one appraiser explained. A comparable suburb was labeled red, having "little to no value . . . due to the colored element now controlling the district."

The National Housing Act of 1934 furthered the social and economic exclusion. A newly created Federal Housing Authority discouraged lending in older or urban areas, instead favoring newer white suburbs that included, according to the agency's official manual, "natural or artificial barriers" (such as highways) to protect against "adverse influences" and prevent "the infiltration" of "lower class occupancy, and inharmonious racial groups."

With the government in their corner, white areas became magnets for commercial development, further boosting home values and ensuring ample funding for education and public services, thereby compounding the advantages of whiteness. More economic terrorism.

Nonwhite families couldn't get loans at reasonable rates, which made
wealth accumulation difficult. The inability to borrow also helped ensure that Black veterans got dramatically less benefit from the GI Bill,
another powerful engine of white mobility. The government's message was as clear as day: You're in the wrong bar, n—.

———

Lest you imagine that these horrors are behind us, remember that
land and property ownership is the historical basis for intergenerational wealth in America, and our legacy of exclusion persists. After
redlining was outlawed, realtors and developers went right on barring
people of color from white neighborhoods and rental properties. (The
Justice Department sued Fred Trump and his son Donald in 1973,
claiming precisely that.) According to census data, white homeownership today is about 76 percent vs. 47 percent for Black Americans,
and that data doesn't consider the *value* of those homes. In 2019, a
team led by Adair Morse at Berkeley's Haas School of Business determined that human lenders and FinTech algorithms alike assigned
higher mortgage interest rates to Blacks and Latinos, to the tune of
$750 million per year in excess payments. Another Haas economist,
Troup Howard, along with Carlos Avenancio-León from Indiana
University, documented a nationwide racial "assessment gap." In almost every state, people living in Black and Hispanic neighborhoods
pay 10 percent to 13 percent more property taxes for "the same bun-
dle of public services" than those living in mostly white areas. A 2019
investigation by New York *Newsday* revealed widespread discrimination by white realtors on Long Island. Agents showed white "test customers" 50 percent more listings, on average, than they showed Black
ones. In roughly one in four instances, white testers were directed
toward largely white neighborhoods, while people of color were offered listings in mixed-race or majority-minority areas.

Raphael has noticed this phenomenon where he lives, in Orange
County—"It's really amazing." One time, he was reading the listings in
the window of a real estate office in Laguna Beach and an agent came

out and talked to a white person who also happened to be looking, ignoring him completely: "The assumption is I can't afford it."

White people make a lot of assumptions about wealthy Black people, Raphael says. They must have gotten lucky somehow, or they made their money in sports or entertainment—possibly drugs—never business. Just yesterday, at the Riviera Country Club, a white member approached Raphael and asked him whether he used to be an athlete. He gets this all the time. "Now, there's a better than even chance that my physical appearance would justify this question," he admits. But "the stereotype is that wealthy Black people are not creators of wealth."

This myopia is further evidence of the Black tax. The Black community has its share of entrepreneurs and businesspeople, academics and inventors, diplomats and judges—people who could be viewed as role models. But successful people of color are "under-indexed," Walker says. And our society's misguided racial narratives contribute "to the lack of achievement and the collective sense of limitations."

To be wealthy and Black in America is to learn to let the little things slide, because they happen most every day, but some slights are hard to overlook. One November, while working for Toyota, Raphael was promoted to assistant general manager at a fabrication plant in Princeton, Indiana, near Evansville. The following month, his new boss invited the entire management team to his home for a Christmas party—all except Raphael, the only Black team member. He was "really hurt," not because he thought the boss was a racist, but because he expected better: "If getting invited to your boss's Christmas gathering is such a big deal, then why would I think I will have the support that I need to grow and develop within the company?" During Raphael's exit interview, the boss expressed regrets—he'd assumed Raphael would have wanted to celebrate the year's achievements with his former team. But the snub played a decisive role in Raphael's decision to jump ship to Chrysler.

The frequency of small misunderstandings, to say nothing of threatening run-ins, begets a kind of hyperawareness. All told, Raphael estimates he's had ten or twelve encounters similar to that long-ago barroom incident in Circleville. It got to where he had to plan his road trips carefully, "because I definitely wasn't comfortable stopping in certain areas." Like Evansville. After accepting the Toyota promotion, he learned that Evansville was once headquarters for Indiana's powerful Ku Klux Klan, whose 250,000 members may have included the governor and a sizable contingent of state legislators: "I thought, 'What have I done? Great opportunity to make money, but I'm certainly going to be lynched.'" An expert marksman from his military days, Raphael went out and purchased a small arsenal. "I was so paranoid, I literally taped—it was like a TV movie—I taped guns strategically to different places around the house, just in case. I was expecting the worst. I would've been terrified, but not surprised, if I woke up at two in the morning and there are crosses burning in my front yard."

The people of Evansville, it turned out, were wonderful. His first night in town, Raphael was eating at a restaurant, and a white family, seeing he was alone, invited him to join them. "I think they were legitimately oblivious to the fact that I was Black. . . . I thought, 'This is weird. This must be a setup!'" He became a member of the local country club and was even elected its president, but couldn't serve because the club's bylaws required its president be thirty-five. (He was six months shy.) Raphael ran, he told me, because everywhere he goes these country clubs have a History Wall with portraits of past presidents, and they are always older white guys. "I thought, I could actually change the face of this club in perpetuity by having this young, Black male picture on the wall. People are going to ask, 'Who *was* that guy?'"

Raphael is that guy. Wealthy. Powerful. A boss. Yet still, as with the protagonist in Ralph Ellison's *Invisible Man*, some white people refuse to see him—or they see him as a threat. Like the Dana Point cop who pulled him over a while back after a long day's work as Hyundai's head of engineering and quality. Raphael knew the drill—every Black parent teaches it to their teens. Hands at 10 and 2 on the wheel, where the officer can see them. Always be respectful. No quick movements, etc. The white officer knocks on the car window, "notices that it's me, draws his gun," Raphael recalls, and that's when he realized he had neglected to get his wallet out and ready in advance: "Oh shit. Now I'm thinking anything could happen, I'm going to end up . . . [*mimes a throat slit*]. I gotta remove my hand to lower the window. I make sure he sees my hand is empty."

"Whose car is this, anyway?" the cop asks.

"It's a company car."

"What company?"

"Hyundai."

"Smart-ass, I didn't ask you what kind of car it is."

Raphael explains that he's a Hyundai executive, but the cop is still skeptical that a Black guy would have such a nice company car. "He also asked, 'Are you on parole or work release?' And I looked at him like, *What are you talking about?* I guess my eyes by this time were glazed over from disappointment and sadness and, holy shit, I can't believe this is happening here in my backyard."

Being invisible is not so scary, but it is equally troubling insofar as the broader implications for Black wealth and advancement. At Genesis, "nobody who comes in and has a meeting with me should not know who I am. It's simply inexcusable," Raphael says. But "I can't tell you how many times people come in and they're *shocked* that I am who I am." One day his marketing chief, Kate Fabian, invited him to a meeting where vendors were making their pitches. Raphael arrived a few minutes late. The seat at the head of the table was reserved for him. "I walked in and everybody stopped. My team and I sat down, and I said, 'Please continue.' That should have been a pretty big hint. Apparently it wasn't." Three separate times, the vendors brushed him off. In one instance, after Fabian outlined the team's priorities and Raphael chimed in with an additional priority, the vendor only addressed Fabian's concerns. When Raphael spoke up, "the response was, 'Well, that's not what Kate said was one of her priorities.' Kate,

God bless her, responded with 'Hey, let's be clear: Whatever is his priority is *my* priority.' You could see their faces turn."

Darren Walker regularly encounters extraordinarily wealthy white men who are unwilling to acknowledge their advantages. They were raised middle-class. Had the paper route. Worked their way through college. Climbed the ladder. Nobody ever gave *them* a handout. "How many times do we hear, 'I started with nothing!'" Walker says. "When in fact, your grandfather bought a little house with his GI Bill and that little house made it possible for your father—I mean, you can see how it all plays out in terms of the wealth gap. It becomes this narrative of 'Well, *these people today* are looking for a handout, a giveaway. They haven't done what I've done.'"

Wealthy whites are "not only oblivious," Raphael concurs. "They would argue very strongly that they don't have any privilege." If anyone is self-made, it's probably guys like him and Walker, but both see "self-made" for what it is—a narcissistic conceit. So, for that matter, do Hanauer and Fiddler and Everingham and other "woke" rich folks I met. They understand that successful people rely deeply on the efforts of others, and that one needn't be a racist to benefit from racist policies, for rare is the white bloodline that hasn't. Yet when Walker challenges billionaires on their self-made narratives or brings up aspects of the Black tax, they will say, "But that's not *my* problem" or "Why are you stuck in these historical things? We should be looking at the future."

"It's very frustrating," he adds.

As it happens, he and Raphael are both very much focused on the future. Raphael recently created a nonprofit network of successful Black men and women—some white, too—that he named the Lantern Network, after the lanterns people once used to indicate safe houses along the Underground Railroad. His goal is to provide a resource for talented Black professionals who lack the high-powered social networks white men take for granted—the family friends and relatives and neighbors one can turn to for mentorship, financial counsel, introductions, and access to capital.

As of summer 2020, the future looked more promising. The COVID crisis had left economic inequality nowhere to hide. Then came the police lynching that broke the camel's back. An exceedingly bitter election season contributed a third element to what was shaping up to be a perfect storm. The pandemic and "the high-resolution video of the George Floyd murder by someone who was confident that he would NOT be brought to justice" were the catalysts we needed, Raphael said in an email. Overt racism has crawled out of its hole these past four years, but "there are even more nonracists and a growing number of anti-racists who will actively engage in the fight."

The fight is no longer just about racist policing and poverty and mass incarceration. It's about Black wealth, too—Joe Biden was even talking about this on the campaign trail. At the height of the George Floyd protests, Omar Johnson, a former Apple marketing VP and chief marketing officer for Beats by Dr. Dre, took out a full-page ad in the *New York Times*. "Dear White corporate America," he began, ...

> I get it. I know you have the best intentions. . . . You want to do the right thing. But you just don't know how.
>
> Is that about right?
>
> I know it is, because you've been calling me. For the past two weeks, several times a day. It's been the same question: What can I do?

He went on to upbraid corporate leaders for failing to nurture Black talent, for failing to include Black people in decision-making, for failing to listen, and ultimately, for failing as *businesspeople*: "This is a business problem, too. And you fix business problems all the time. So, you got this." He laid out a game plan. Most notably, "You need to hire more Black people. Period." Identify, recruit, develop, and elevate talented Black employees. Partner with Black-owned businesses. Believe in the people you hire. *Mentor* them. "No doubt, it's daunting," Johnson writes. "But lean into the discomfort." And "before you call me again—before you ask me what you should say, or what you should change—I'll tell you my answer right now: Absolutely everything . . . See you in the room."

Walker would love to see more Black and Latino and female faces in the room. That would sure help with Big Philanthropy's silo problem—the problem that the priorities of less-wealthy groups are dominated by those of rich white donors who would love to see a New York hospital wing or a science building at Stanford with their name on it. "I think this is the risk. That philanthropy can serve first and foremost the needs of the already privileged," he says. Wealthy whites, for example, have created dozens of foundations dedicated to treating diseases that have affected their families directly, but "I don't know of one foundation that's been created to focus on sickle cell anemia, which basically affects only Black people." There is so much need, Walker adds, that Black America's most fortunate feel "just overwhelmed."

Having a lot more super-rich Black people won't save us, of course. Their existence would at least indicate that we are addressing the racial opportunity gap. But as we'll see in the following chapter, there are other opportunity gaps that need tackling, too, and the derigging of our economic ground rules will be the greatest challenge of all. "My concern now is that we have successful Black people who are also privileged," Walker told me. "So when I say something like, 'I think we should end legacy admissions into elite schools,' they say, 'No way! We just finally got access to these, and you want to take it away?'"

A Black friend who, like Walker, grew up poor and became very well-off financially, said as much to him recently. "I'm not worried about your kid," was Walker's reply. "I'm worried about the kid who you *used* to be."

CHAPTER 18

WOMEN ON TOP

Women with money and women in power are
two uncomfortable ideas in our society.

—CANDACE BUSHNELL

In May 2020, amid the early gloom of the COVID recession, *Fortune* had at least one bit of positive news to report. The number of female CEOs in the Fortune 500 was at an all-time high. Women now ran thirty-seven of the nation's five hundred most valuable corporations. They held 7.4 percent of the top jobs. This was an improvement.

Not only are women more likely than men to be poor, they are far less likely to be very rich. In 2019, 24 percent of U.S. households headed by single women were living in poverty—more than twice the poverty rate of male single-parent households, and the pandemic has worsened that divide. At the high end, meanwhile, among the global population of people worth $30 million or more, men outnumber women by more than nine to one.

To fully explain these wild disparities would require several books. But it's the usual suspects: outdated attitudes at home, at work, in higher education, corporate boardrooms, banks, and statehouses. Wealthy white men defending their turf like tomcats. My recently departed mother was one of only three women in her medical school cohort at the University of Vermont. She graduated third in the class and was subsequently paid far less than her male colleagues. Few of her early patients had met a woman doctor. Some men refused to be treated by her. Others would ask, ten minutes in, when the doctor was due to arrive. When she asked her male bosses whether she could work half-time for a while to care for my brother and me, they said half-time was forty hours a week.

The story of women in America resembles the Black story in that every step on the road to prosperity has been met with bitter opposition: the right to attend college and professional school alongside men, to work outside the home, to be paid and promoted fairly, to not have the boss grab your ass with impunity, to get a bank loan or launch a business, to run for office, and even simply to vote.

When I was a child, working women were still largely limited to jobs men deemed suitable: assistants, caregivers, clerks, librarians, nurses, teachers, secretaries. They were (and still are) paid less than men for similar work. Pregnant employees were sent packing. Like Black men, women of all ethnicities were denied access to the engines of power and wealth—a woman had to marry rich or be born into it. As of 2017, ultrawealthy women were more than three times as likely as men to have gotten their fortunes entirely by inheritance.

Every new gold rush in our history has left women on the sidelines. Consider the excessively lucrative realm of "alternative" investments— hedge funds, private equity, venture capital, real estate, private debt, infrastructure, and commodities. As of 2020, women accounted for just one in five employees of alternatives firms (the same proportion one finds at the equity-partner level of corporate law firms) and 12 percent of the senior positions. A minuscule 3 percent of the total assets held by U.S. hedge funds launched from 2013 through 2017 were managed by women-led firms—there were more funds initiated by men named David than by women.

This is not because women can't compete with the silverbacks. A 2015 study from Northeastern University found that hedge funds managed entirely by women were no less profitable than those managed by men. But the funds with at least one female manager were more likely to fail because they attracted fewer investors. To reach the same level of investment, a female fund manager has to outperform her male rivals by a significant margin, and "that's saying something is wrong with the capital allocation process," noted Jane Buchan, who left the helm of a firm called PAAMCO Prisma to launch her own hedge fund.

What's wrong is that the men who control the money spigot don't trust women with their cash. That's a big problem for women trying to launch their own businesses, says Kim Polese, a technology executive who belongs to a women's investing group called Broadway Angels. Men, especially white men, have bigger financial networks than women do. And unless you have close allies in the finance or venture capital worlds, or have a good friend who does, "you're out in the cold, and that's just a fact," Polese says. "It's the way the industry works."

When a woman manages to get into the room, she has a higher bar to clear, because "the room" is a bunch of white guys sitting around a conference table. "Women don't fit the mold of the typical rock star/founder/entrepreneur," Polese says, so they have to do more to dispel people's doubts. In her experience, some male venture capitalists will make a point of declaring themselves unbiased. They have a daughter, they will say, and they want her to succeed. "I believe them. They're genuine," she says, but the biases are ingrained and unconscious, which makes them harder to counter. This, in fact, is among the raisons d'être of her current venture. CrowdSmart, which Polese cofounded in 2015, uses "human-powered AI" to help investors choose which young companies to bankroll. In 2016, to test its platform, CrowdSmart raised a small fund and invested in nearly thirty start-ups that its algorithm had rated highly. Within eighteen months, 80 percent of the companies went on to attract outside follow-up funding at an increased valuation—a substantially better result than most venture funds achieve, Polese says—and 40 percent were founded or led by women. That's what happens when you de-bias the process.

It is indeed curious how every potentially lucrative new niche becomes a bro culture. Consider cryptocurrencies and their companion technology, blockchain. One crypto fund's 2019 survey of the one hundred most recent blockchain start-ups found that more than 85 percent of their employees—and 93 percent of the executives—were men. Another crypto firm had promotional materials featuring bikini-clad young women. The program for the 2018 North American Bitcoin Conference included eighty-six male presenters and one woman. (After somebody complained, the organizer, investor Moe Levin, replaced two of the men.) The after-party was held at a Miami strip club. "Women, consider crypto," venture capital investor Alexia Bonatsos tweeted that month. "Otherwise the men are going to get all the wealth, again."

Crypto bros defend the imbalance by noting that women are more risk-averse than men. That's actually true. According to a study from Berkeley's Haas School of Business and UC Davis, female investors performed better in the long term because they traded less often, whereas men, overconfident in their ability to beat the market, harmed their profitability with excessive trading. But the gender imbalance may also have to do with the fact that crypto is the love child of two lucrative industries—finance and tech—that have long kept women at arm's length.

Back in chapter 11, we touched on the role of the Ivy Leagues as stepping-stones to high-paying careers. So it is worth noting that those schools were among the last to go coed. Public universities, led by the University of Iowa, began coeducating men and women as early as 1856, but the Ivies, with the notable exception of Cornell, waited until the 1960s and '70s to fully embrace coeducation. My mother-in-law graduated in 1962 from Radcliffe, Harvard's sister college, and though the schooling was the same—Harvard profs used to teach classes twice, once for the men, once for the women—a Radcliffe degree opened fewer doors. By the time my mother-in-law arrived on campus, men and women attended class together, but women were still barred from the main library. They were viewed as a distraction for the male scholars.

Nancy Weiss Malkiel, an emeritus professor of history at Princeton, was hired in 1969, the same year the university finally went coed. Her 2016 book, *Keep the Damned Women Out*, chronicles some of the pushback administrators received from aggrieved male alumni: "If Princeton goes coeducational, my alma mater will have been taken away from me, and PRINCETON IS DEAD," one exclaimed. Another objected to diluting "Princeton's sturdy masculinity with disconcerting, mini-skirted young things cavorting on its playing fields." A member of the Class of '55 argued that allowing female students would harm Princeton's contribution to the nation, because women wouldn't use their "education and talents in public service to the same extent as a male who spends full time at his profession." For every woman admitted, he suggested, a man—perhaps a future leader—"would be denied that opportunity."

The incrementalism of the Ivies, Malkiel says, may have contributed to the scarcity of superwealthy women today, but it's hard to be sure, given the broader cultural assumptions and expectations determining "what women could or could not achieve in terms of wealth accumulation and access to high-ranking positions." Even students at many prestigious women's colleges, she says, "were told explicitly that they were being educated to be good wives."

In the last chapter, we talked about the denial of capital to Black Americans. All women faced similar obstacles. Until 1974, when Congress forced their hand, banks refused to loan money to single women, widows, or divorcees without a male cosigner, regardless of how much money they made. And very few women were admitted to the business schools and law schools that led to high-paying careers. Even now, the higher a woman aims in her profession, the less money she makes relative to the men. In 2019, overall, women who worked full-time, year-round jobs earned eighty-two cents on the male dollar. But female Ivy League graduates, by age thirty-four, make only seventy cents per dollar compared with Ivy League men. Some studies suggest that these wage-gap figures are misleading because they don't account for the fact that more men than women enter high-paying industries and rise to senior positions. Fair enough, but why is that? Are women valued in those industries? Are they recruited and promoted at the same rate? Are they afforded ample flexibility, given what sociologist Arlie Hochschild calls the Second Shift—the fact that working women take on the lion's share of domestic work and household management? Are women encouraged to consider lucrative professions in the first place?

When Polese discovered computers back in the 1970s, she didn't see them as a boy thing. It was just "sort of like, this is magic and I want to learn how to create magic." By 1983, when she was a junior at UC Berkeley, 37 percent of computer science degrees nationwide were going to women. But that was the peak. By 2006, the proportion of women earning CS degrees was down to about one in five, and has remained so since. Polese, who often addresses high school groups, doesn't sense that girls are deliberately avoiding computer science because it's a bro culture. Rather, they don't even seem aware that one can make a career in computing.

It is true that being a high-status woman in a male-dominated realm requires remarkable patience and grit, as you are held to a higher level of scrutiny and a different set of standards than your male colleagues. Polese was reminded of this one day in 2012, when her inbox and text stream started filling up with messages, many from women she didn't know, saying things like "Don't listen to that guy; you're a hero to me and you inspired me." She was surprised, but not *that* surprised: "I figured, 'Oh, okay, there's another one of those snarky, nasty, fact-free pieces out there.'"

The snarky post in question was titled "Sheryl Sandberg is the Valley's 'It' Girl—Just like Kim Polese once was." *Forbes* contributor Eric Jackson had taken aim at her past leadership at Marimba, a dot-com-era company of which Polese was cofounder and CEO. She was a "cautionary tale," Jackson wrote, "buzz-worthy" for the wrong reasons. Rather than focusing on business fundamentals, Polese spent too much time on outward-facing activities. She—and now Sandberg!—"both like[d] magazine covers and editorial spreads" and delivering "public speeches imparting their views of tech, business, work-life balance, and being a woman dealing with power." Both execs were admired by young women and both were regulars in the business media's "arbitrarily created rankings of important people/power." No way did she deserve her spot on *Time* magazine's 1997 list of the 25 Most Influential Americans: "What was *Time* thinking?" Jackson wrote. Polese was clearly in the right place at the right time, "but it also helped that she was young, pretty, and a good speaker."

Polese, now fifty-nine, is still pretty and a good speaker. She's also smart, savvy, and forward-thinking, with a biophysics degree from Berkeley and post-baccalaureate training in computer science at the University of Washington. IntelliCorp, an early AI pioneer, hired her right out of school to work with its customers—she spent her first year on site with aerospace engineers at McDonnell Douglas. At Sun Microsystems in the early 1990s, she was part of the team that created Java, "the programming language that brought interactivity to the Web and Polese to public attention as the engaging human face of what to most was an incomprehensible software product," *Time* noted. She even named Java, on which the internet still depends. (If not for her, it would be called Oak.) When Polese and three fellow engineers left Sun to launch Marimba, it was the first start-up out of the gate with a Java-based platform. That alone made it a promising player amid a host of dot-coms with nothing to offer but hyperbole.

Polese had received a similar treatment in *Fortune* magazine thirteen years earlier. That piece, "The Beauty of Hype: A Cautionary Tale of Silicon Valley," suggested that Marimba was building a cult of personality around its attractive young CEO rather than educating the public about its wonky technology. Polese, the article noted, had been heralded as "'the diva of push,' and 'the Madonna of Silicon Valley,' a geek sex symbol who's more famous than her company." She hated such descriptions, and she certainly didn't feel she should be criticized for giving speeches and doing interviews, which male CEOs did all the time. *Fortune*'s piece appeared in 1999, when dot-com marketers were literally running around city streets in Cupid costumes, posing as street preachers, and otherwise engaging in stupid stunts to generate "buzz" for their start-ups. What made Marimba a true outlier were its growing revenues, a viable product, and a woman on top. "I was always promoting the company and frustrated that the focus in the piece, whatever was written, would always be about me," Polese says.

She had held her tongue in the past, but when *Forbes* called to ask whether she wanted to reply to Jackson's post, she accepted. She pulled her Prius to the side of the road and banged out a response then and there. What inspired her to do so was her surprise that all these women she didn't even know had come to her defense. That was a first: "I realized there are a lot more women who are actually reading this stuff, and that's a good thing, because it means there are more women in the industry." She was also fed up. Polese had a reputation to maintain, and that reputation was being messed with yet again. "My reaction was 'This is just the same old recycled crap,'" she says. Male CEOs also have to be their company's public face, but "they don't get accused of being PR shills, or content-free, or promoting themselves."

In a subsequent apology post, Jackson acknowledged he'd gotten key facts wrong. He had also implied that Marimba, and, by extension, Polese, were failures. In fact, the company's software management platform, Castanet, is widely used by Fortune 500 companies today. It's what quietly updates the software on your computer at work, your smartphone, your electric car, and possibly your fridge—because Castanet is the foundation of Samsung's entire "internet of things."

But the hits kept coming. In the 2019 book *Don't Be Evil*, author Rana Foroohar repeated the "Madonna of Silicon Valley" reference and wrote that Polese had appeared on the cover of *Fortune*—which was incorrect. Those were minor annoyances. What really upset "the mistress of Java," as Foroohar called her, was the claim that Marimba had "flamed out" a couple of years after Polese appeared on *Time*'s Top 25 list. What really happened at that time was that Marimba went public, and its stock price tripled on the first day of trading to make it a $1.4 billion company. Even a year later, with the tech sector going down the toilet, Marimba was trading at its initial asking price. The stock eventually tanked with the rest of them, but Marimba's tech remained solid. In the wake of the bust, in 2004, the company was taken private in a deal worth $239 million, earning its VC investors fifteen times what they had put in—a "home run," Polese says. She'd actually resisted the sale. She wanted to keep building Marimba for the long haul. Had she prevailed, who knows? The company might be worth billions. Her all-male board of directors lacked the patience to find out.

———————

When women break through the glass ceiling of superwealth, by their own hand or otherwise, they often find that being ultrarich and female comes with a unique set of challenges. "There's very much a code of conduct," says Tracy Gary, our would-be heiress. "You're supposed to be thin and play the part and look beautiful, and there's much more of 'Do you look like the trimmings of wealth?' Men don't get that. A suit's a suit. There's much more of a stereotype of the way women are supposed to behave, and it depends a lot on whether the wealth is hers or whether it's her husband's."

"There's an automatic presumption that you did not earn the money," says a source I'll call Annika. And women who do achieve very high salaries "are perceived as angry bulldogs instead of just smart women who chose a path that happened to be financially rewarding." Annika was raised in what was once an extraordinarily wealthy family, and her relatives' incessant nostalgia for the glory days made her feel "lesser than." She ended up working as a university fundraiser, spending a lot of time around ultrawealthy donors. It was no big deal, she told me, "to meet with five men in a day who were multimillionaires-slash-billionaires." But whenever a woman was on the schedule, the team would do lots of extra strategizing around, well, how did she get her wealth and how should they approach her. "We live in a patriarchy. Men are supposed to have the money. Women aren't," Annika says. "Women are supposed to need men to survive."

The male-dominated world of wealth management has been famously dismissive of affluent women who seek an active role in their finances. "Women don't come with the confidence, and they're used to working collaboratively, so they pay more attention to what other people tell them," Gary says. "And they weigh things in a different way, whereas guys are sort of like, 'I'm making this decision, I'm just going to do it.'"

She knows what she's talking about. Since her parents handed her that $1 million at age fourteen, she has founded or helped launch nearly two dozen nonprofits, charitable foundations, and donor networks including Changemakers, OutGiving (Gary is a lesbian), the Women Donors Network, the Women's Foundation of California, Resourceful Women, and Women Moving Millions. As the cofounder and executive director, since 2003, of a nonprofit called Inspired Legacies, she has advised thousands of women, and hundreds of men and families and nonprofits, on philanthropic and financial matters. Her clients include several billionaires, and most have assets ranging from $10 million to $500 million. "Women are more intimidated by what they don't know," she says, "and doubt is cast on them: Are they crazy, or are they actually doing the right thing?"

If a wealthy woman decides, for example, that she doesn't want her advisors doing anything elaborate to shelter her assets from the tax authorities, "you have to be pretty assertive to say that to your accountant who's trained to do everything they can to strip down your taxes," Gary says. Wealthy men have to be assertive, too, as noted earlier, because wealth managers are typically compensated according to the amount of assets under their control. But women are especially vulnerable to being second-guessed. "When you have multimillions of dollars there's this pressure to keep you dependent," Gary says. If, for instance, you have $200 million under management by a firm and decide you want to give half of it away, "the resistance from that advisor, as though they were your father, is unbelievable. They'll do anything they can, they've got to put the brakes on it. So the average person of wealth—women particularly, unless she's very astute—feels like she has to get permission from her financial advisor when she makes big decisions, and it's very patriarchal."

One ultrawealthy woman who requested anonymity told me she is in the process of shifting her assets away from her old-school Wall Street advisors over to an independent female advisor, who is "more simpatico" with her financial worldview. With the men, "I didn't feel fully heard or respected. There was an arrogance and a cowboy culture," she recalls. "There's also motivation to make money based on transactions or vehicles that the bank has developed that don't necessarily have to do with where I want to deploy my capital."

At least she had a choice. When Susan Davis first got into banking, most wealthy women had no say at all in their family's financial affairs. The patriarchs were asked to sign agreements saying the bankers would work with the husband only. "Literally, the wives were often told nothing about the wealth, or they weren't tutored to understand how to deal with the wealth when the husband died," she says.

During the 1960s, Davis, whose father, Theophilus Anthony Davis, purchased the bankrupt Bancroft Racket Company and built it into one of the leading brands in tennis, dropped out of a Harvard master's program to work for a Black newspaper in Boston's Roxbury district. (Davis is white.) "Everyone I knew was apoplectic. I was insane!" She went on to help launch a successful Chicago publishing company and was later recruited as an executive at the nation's first neighborhood development bank, ShoreBank, which some friends of hers had started. In 1980, she got a call from Chicago's Harris Bank, which the federal government had sued for race and sex discrimination. The bank needed to diversify its lily-white, all-male management team, and Davis was one of the few women to be found with executive credentials. "So, I got a very high position at Harris," she says, "and made a lot of money and was able to have a high impact because they needed my kind of thinking."

Her first innovation was a no-brainer that the male bankers apparently had never considered: Stop ignoring female clients. Whenever a patriarch died, his widow was at the mercy of her late husband's male bankers and attorneys. These women "didn't have a clue," Davis recalls. "It was very dysfunctional and they were very unhappy." Without telling her higher-ups, she began meeting with the wives to find out what they wanted—and what they wanted was a financial education. So Davis recruited a professor to come in and teach them all about investments and interest rates and tax law, and how to make sound money decisions. The women were delighted. They told all of their wealthy friends, "and they all came trooping to Harris Bank," Davis recalls. "We were the talk of the town and I won the bank's top award, which was really funny because the bank didn't know what I had done."

Harris Bank's female execs were "the cream of the crop," and they outperformed the men, Davis told me, not only by improving the bank's profitability but also by "increasing happiness with the employees and all kinds of other things." There was, however, a hitch. The bank's senior-most leaders, including its president, were still men, and they all had hand-picked and nurtured male successors. They weren't about to turn around and give those rarified positions to any of the women. ("Why would they?" Davis says.) But when the female bankers saw how things were going to be, they pulled up stakes: "We all left at the same time because there was no position for us to advance to."

Her larger point is that possessing wealth without financial knowledge makes people miserable, and that women, because they view the world so differently from men, actually make superior stewards. "It's tragic the way women have been sidelined in the financial sector—*tragic*. Because women have a philosophy of good for all and men have a philosophy of 'better than,'" Davis says. "Women tend to make decisions based on whether a deal is good for all concerned. And men tend to make financial decisions based on what will make me more money. Those two things are at great odds and the proof is all in the pudding—if we're destroying the Earth that supports us and the evidence is absolutely certain, what kind of crazy is that?"

CHAPTER 19

GIVING IT AWAY

*To give away money or to spend it . . . is an easy matter and
in any man's power; . . . but to decide to whom to give it and
how large a sum, and when, and for what purpose, and how, is
neither in every man's power, nor an easy matter.*

—ARISTOTLE

Andrew Carnegie had some simple-yet-challenging advice for the
well-to-do: Don't die with your wealth intact. Use your fortune for
the betterment of humankind while you're alive. Let your children
fend for themselves. "There are instances of millionaires' sons un-
spoiled by wealth, who, being rich, still perform great services in the
community," he wrote. But these were such rare exceptions that "the
thoughtful man must shortly say, 'I would as soon leave to my son a
curse as the almighty dollar,' and admit to himself that it is not the
welfare of the children, but family pride, which inspires these enormous legacies."

Richard Watts's clients struggle with this. To agree with Carnegie
in theory is one thing. To sever that umbilical cord is quite another.
Watts tries to nudge his families to where they'll just give their kids
$5 million apiece and call it good. "Parents are so reluctant to do that!
'We've got all this money. How can we just get rid of it?' And I say,
'Well, it's going to be rid of in three generations anyway. So the future
generations are going to take care of your problem, and in the process
you're going to destroy some of them.'"

Watts would know. His superwealthy maternal grandfather had a pair of auto dealerships in the Detroit area, rental properties in Florida, and a general partnership in a horse-racing track. His father worked in the patriarch's auto business. The family wealth afforded his parents a very comfortable lifestyle. But one winter day, their three-year-old, Richard's eldest sister, wandered out of their mansion's rear gate and drowned in an icy pond out back. His mother bore three more children but never forgave herself. She became unstable and suicidal, and in the end was institutionalized.

Watts's father wanted a fresh start in California with the kids, so the patriarch issued an ultimatum: If his son-in-law left Michigan, he would have to return all the couple's shared assets and relinquish any claim to the family wealth. So that's what he did—he walked away. Watts's dad thrived in California, where he remarried and eventually acquired an auto dealership of his own. But he always cautioned his children there would be no inheritance, and that was "the greatest gift" he ever gave them, Watts told me. "It's not about leaving nothing. It's about, can you stomach the idea of your kids having to find their own way in life?"

After decades of estrangement from the Michigan clan, Watts received a call from an aunt he'd always liked. She was eighty now, and she just wanted to say how much she had always admired his father's bold move. She'd been following the children's successes from afar and marveled at their independence. The Detroit family, meanwhile, had become a cesspool. "Everything's destroyed," she told him. There had been several suicides—"I mean prominent, wealthy, mature adults," Watts says. His aunt now lived in "a little nothing home" with her son and grandson, who couldn't afford their own places. "She said, 'All the money has just caused sickness and everybody is destitute.'"

Tracy Gary, like Watts, encourages her clients to give away as much of their money as they can stomach, but not to Stanford or Yale or other institutions with massive endowments: "Please diversify," she says, and give to social justice organizations. She is regularly summoned to her clients' deathbeds "because the family is fighting over money and they're worried, so they want me to be there as a buffer." In dozens of such cases, Gary told me, people have wanted last-minute changes to their wills. A client's estate plan directing 25 percent to charity and 75 percent to the offspring might have been written fifteen years earlier, when each kid would have received $5 million. Now 75 percent meant $25 million each, and the client felt that was too much. "The legacy piece," Gary says, "is the last time people can right that wrong."

But there are other wrongs worthy of consideration. Namely, the wrongs that come from our efforts to accumulate and protect wealth during our lifetimes, to segregate ourselves on its basis, and to cling tightly to the advantages it brings. Carnegie's conceit, that giving away great fortunes alleviates the woes that result from their creation, is problematic. For the way philanthropy is practiced in our country not only favors the rich, it can actually exacerbate the estrangement between rich America and poor America.

Between half and two-thirds of U.S. households donate money to charity each year, and three in five volunteer time and effort. Individuals and their estates handed out $353 billion in 2019, according to Giving USA. My wife and I aim to give about 10 percent of our after-tax earnings to groups that assist desperate families and/or work toward racial equity. Before COVID, my teens and I volunteered at a residential facility in Oakland for mothers with young children who have faced poverty, homelessness, addiction, and/or domestic abuse.

I got to talking with one of the moms a while back, a tattooed music and video producer—thirtyish, Black. She and her baby and adorable toddler, King, were living with her sister in a rental house in Stockton. The sister stopped paying rent, everyone got evicted, and her crew ended up here. She was feeling stir-crazy, she told me, because she couldn't do her production work at the shelter. She was trying to save enough money so her little trio could find a place of their own. She had $1,500 so far.

The average rent for a one-bedroom apartment in Oakland at that time was around $2,500, or $30,000 annually. If you worked forty hours a week, fifty weeks a year, earning $15 an hour, that's your entire pretax income. My wife and I have never had this problem, thanks in part to supportive parents, who thrived as a result not only of hard work but also free college and scholarships and government-backed home loans. Our families paid our public university tuitions, helped us buy our first cars, and contributed to the down payment on our first home. We were very privileged that way. And now, every June, my dad sends me a birthday card with a $10,000 check.

I'm grateful. The extra cash is nice to have, but it's not make-or-break. I think about what it would mean for someone like King's mom to have ten grand suddenly appear in her mailbox. That might be enough money to establish a household or cover a year of health insurance or childcare so she could work or attend school. Shouldn't I be giving my birthday money to someone who needs it more than I do? And if $10,000 presents an ethical dilemma for me, imagine a windfall of $100 million—or more. How much should a billionaire give? "Everything!" Carnegie would say: Sell your businesses, leave your kids a pittance, and spend the rest of your days on Earth dispersing your fortune for the common good, else die disgraced.

But it's not enough just to give back after the fact. The four hundred richest Americans pay only pay 23 percent of their annual income in total taxes, Emmanuel Saez and Gabriel Zucman calculate, whereas the rest of us pay between 25 and 35 percent. Their companies, notably Amazon, pay far less. Many billionaires use their family offices and expensive attorneys and lobbyists to avoid paying their share, and often underpay their workers to boot, and then try to make up for it—or simply distract us—with grand philanthropic gestures. Bill Gates is widely admired, and rightly so, for his charitable work, but people my age can remember how he was once a target of congressional hearings and public scorn. We even look back kindly on Carnegie, a businessman whose union-busting efforts resulted in deadly violence—after all, he inspired the Big Philanthropy juggernaut, bankrolled universities, seeded Pell Grants, and built thousands of free public libraries.

So how should we view the generosity of our *robber bar*—er, captains of industry? Is the billionaire who gives away half his wealth more laudable than the guy with $200 million who gives nothing? What are these people's lobbyists doing behind the scenes? Why is a donor giving, and whom does it serve? Has the giver treated workers and local communities with respect? Have they gone to extraordinary lengths to circumvent taxes? Was the money inherited or earned? If earned at the expense of others, was it really theirs to give?

These are complex questions. Turning back to our Bezos example, from 2009 to 2018, Amazon paid just $791 million in federal taxes on $26.5 billion in profits—an effective tax rate of 3 percent, and Bezos himself spent $100,000 to help kill a middle-class relief initiative that would have raised taxes on high-income Washingtonians. In 2018, officials in Seattle, whose booming tech sector drove local housing prices through the roof, proposed a $275-per-head tax on the city's largest employers to help pay for homeless services. Amazon played hardball, halting work on a high-rise tower under construction. The city council's "hostile approach," warned spokesman Drew Herdener, "forces us to question our growth here." It took less than six weeks for city leaders to capitulate.

That September, Senator Bernie Sanders introduced a bill that proposed taxing big employers such as Amazon and Walmart to recoup the costs of federal antipoverty entitlements (food stamps, reduced-price school lunches, Medicaid, and housing subsidies) their underpaid employees were collecting. The bill was ill-advised, as it would have discouraged companies from hiring impoverished people, but it had an amusing title: the Stop Bad Employers by Zeroing Out Subsidies Act—Stop BEZOS. Soon after, Bezos announced that he and his wife, MacKenzie, were launching a $2 billion charitable initiative to fund homeless services and free preschools in low-income communities nationwide. The pledge elicited thousands of Twitter comments, many expressing gratitude, but perhaps more tak-

ing aim at Bezos's business practices. "PAY YOUR WORKERS PROP-
ERLY, YOU MELT," one person responded. Two weeks later, Amazon
announced it would raise its minimum wage to $15 and lobby for a
$15 federal minimum. "We listened to our critics," Bezos said. *New
York* magazine's Eric Levitz was skeptical. Based on its founder's past
behavior, he wrote, the more plausible explanation was that Amazon
hoped to reap positive press even as it crippled its rivals by driving up
labor costs.

January 2019 brought more Bezos news: Jeff and MacKenzie
were divorcing. The split was amicable, they claimed. (The following
month, Jeff published a Medium post claiming the *National Enquirer*
had tried to blackmail him over leaked intimate photos—including
a "dick pic"—that he'd sent to another woman.) The divorce settlement made MacKenzie, a Princeton-educated novelist who now goes
by MacKenzie Scott, one of the world's richest women. She got one-
quarter of Bezos's Amazon shares, worth almost $68 billion as of Oc-
tober 13, 2020. She promptly turned around and did something her
ex never had: She signed the Giving Pledge.

In 2010, Bill and Melinda Gates, their pal Warren Buffett, and thirty-
seven fellow billionaires publicly vowed they would follow Carnegie's
lead and dedicate the majority of their wealth to charitable ventures,
preferably during their lifetimes. As of mid-January 2021, from Bill
Ackman to Mark Zuckerberg, 216 billionaires and would-be billionaires from around the globe had signed on. Paris Hilton's late grandfather, Barron Hilton, is on the list. So is Spanx founder Sara Blakely,
Oracle's Larry Ellison, Elon Musk, Robert Smith, Ted Turner, and others you would probably recognize. The Hanauers, too. Notably absent:
Jeff Bezos, the Waltons, and the Trumps.

The pledge, though praiseworthy, requires a few caveats. Only
about 1 in 13 of the world's 2,825 billionaires (and America's 788
billionaires) are participating. And because the pledge is a "moral
commitment . . . not a legal contract," there is no mechanism to hold

the signatories to their promise. The pledge, in some ways, can be viewed as a consolidation of plutocratic power. Perhaps most notably, a "majority" of one's fortune is not 96 percent or even 69 percent, but half plus one penny. Most of these people could give away half their assets and barely feel the difference. More than 80 percent of the surviving American billionaires on the list had more assets in August 2020 than they did when the pledge was created a decade earlier.

Some signatories have pledged to give away much more than half. In 2015, Zuckerberg and his wife, pediatrician Priscilla Chan, announced they would hand out 99 percent of their Facebook stake during their lifetimes to advance "progress and equality." This impressive gift also requires context. On January 1, 2020, according to SEC filings, Zuckerberg owned 400,468,692 shares of Facebook worth $82.2 billion. This meant the couple would retain $822 million worth. Chan is thirty-six, Zuckerberg thirty-seven—they may well live another fifty years or more. Their shares will be doled out slowly, and at the rate wealth compounds, they will almost certainly remain multibillionaires for life. Facebook isn't all they own, either. Zuckerberg has substantial investments in Asana, MasteryConnect, Panorama Education, and Vicarious. He and Chan own a superlative house in San Francisco, multi-lot compounds in Palo Alto and Lake Tahoe, and more than seven hundred acres of prime waterfront land in Kauai, all acquired for a total of $219 million. (Those are just the properties we know about.) And let's not forget those 3.4 million pre-IPO shares Zuckerberg put into his annuity trust back in '08. If that trust, or series of trusts, remains in effect, by now it would have shielded more than $1 billion of Zuckerberg family assets from gift and inheritance taxes.

And King's mom couldn't afford a one-bedroom apartment.

The selfless billionaire is a rare creature indeed. The best example would probably be Chuck Feeney, who helped inspire the Giving Pledge. He is "my hero and Bill Gates' hero," Buffett remarked. "He should be everybody's hero." By the time the pledge came into being,

Feeney was reluctant to join. After all, he was no longer a billionaire. Feeney had long since heeded Carnegie's advice. His charitable foundation pledged the last sliver of his fortune to Cornell in 2016, capping an epic three-decade giving streak. All told, starting in the early 1980s, Feeney dedicated nearly $9 billion to his philanthropic pursuits, setting aside just $2 million for himself and his second wife, Helga, to retire on. For every $100,000 he gave away in grants, he kept about $25.

Feeney grew up in a working-class family in Elizabeth, New Jersey, during the Great Depression. He was entrepreneurial from the get-go. After serving a noncombat stint in the air force, he was admitted to the School of Hotel Administration at Cornell on the GI Bill, earning extra cash by selling homemade sandwiches at night on fraternity row. He later hustled his way into a graduate program in France, where he teamed up with a former Cornell classmate, Robert Miller, to sell tax-free liquor, and later cars, to American troops overseas. Their partnership would evolve into a business decidedly more lucrative. Feeney, Miller, and their mates basically invented the duty-free industry, those stores that sell tax-free liquor and perfume and cigarettes and accessories in airports and tourist destinations worldwide. "They were making literally hundreds of millions of dollars a year," says attorney Harvey Dale, another Cornell alum, whom the partners brought on as their counsel. "Because of the structure that I had helped put in place, almost none of that was being taxed."

For a time, Feeney and his French wife, Danielle, lived the high life in Hong Kong. They had an apartment in New York City and homes in Connecticut, Hawaii, Cap Ferret on the coast of France, and just outside Paris. They had a luxury car and a driver and threw fancy parties. To this day, Miller hosts bird hunts at his own 32,000-acre Gunnerside Estate in North Yorkshire—"the holy grail of grouse moors"—and two of his daughters married princes. But over time, Feeney, who viewed wealth primarily as a scorecard of his business prowess, grew increasingly uncomfortable with its trappings. He discussed his reservations with Dale, by then a close friend, who introduced him to Carnegie's writings. Feeney was particularly smitten with the "Wealth" essay. He began to eschew material extravagances, dressing plainly, driving a regular car, and wearing a $15 watch. He traveled constantly and could have afforded a fleet of private jets, but insisted on flying coach. "He famously said, 'I don't need more than one pair of shoes. I can only wear one pair at a time,'" Dale told me.

Feeney hatched a plan to give all his money away. Duty Free Shoppers, as the business was called, was obsessed with secrecy. Its profitability depended on governments and rivals undervaluing the company's right to sell tax-free concessions, so the partners held their cards close. Feeney, who didn't want people hounding him for money, applied the same ethos to philanthropy. His stake in DFS and other businesses was consolidated in a holding company called General Atlantic Group, incorporated in Danielle's name to sidestep U.S. taxes and keep Feeney's name off the paperwork—even photographing him was verboten. One day in 1984, without informing his partners, he transferred ownership of General Atlantic Group over to the Atlantic Foundation, a charitable entity he'd set up in Bermuda with Dale as president and CEO. He and Dale also created an intermediary firm to manage charitable gifts and interview would-be grantees. Those grantees, who were forbidden from acknowledging their gifts publicly, had no idea where the money was coming from. When Chris Oechsli, Chuck and Helga's personal attorney and CEO of Atlantic Philanthropies (the now-defunct umbrella entity that included Feeney's Atlantic Foundation), first interviewed for a position at General Atlantic in 1990, he was unaware who Feeney was or the role he played in the organization. Before meeting his future boss, Oechsli told me, he had to sign a confidentiality agreement. He worked at General Atlantic Group almost two years before realizing the whole thing was a philanthropic venture. "We operated on a need-to-know basis," Dale explains.

Feeney used his riches over the years to broker a peace agreement in Northern Ireland, finance a public health system in Vietnam, expand access to AIDS drugs in Southern Africa, and support young leaders around the world—the so-called Atlantic Fellows—who are working to improve their societies. He bankrolled Ireland's public university system and donated billions to American universities—including about $1 billion to Cornell—never allowing the schools to affix his name, or Atlantic's, to the buildings he funded. He lobbied, too, to stay off the *Forbes* list, and managed to dispense with vast sums before the *New York Times* finally outed him in 1997. His stealthy exploits earned him a nickname: "the James Bond of philanthropy."

—————

If anyone can match Feeney in spirit, if not scope, it would be Zell Kravinsky. Now sixty-six, Kravinsky amassed a $45 million real estate fortune, gave almost all of it away, and then went on to give of himself in a way few of us would seriously consider. Like Feeney, he is famously frugal. In late 2019, a few days before Christmas, I turn onto Kravinsky's street in Jenkintown, Pennsylvania, half expecting to find him living by himself in a woodshed. It turns out he and his wife, Emily, have upgraded from the shabby little house they lived in seventeen years ago, when Ian Parker profiled him for the *New Yorker.*

Kravinksy greets me, shoeless, at the front door of his new abode, a brick-and-stucco residence built in 1900. The three-story house—four thousand square feet with five bedrooms, a modest yard, and blue-striped awnings—cost him $590,000 in 2006, though it is worth less now. Kravinsky has a winter pallor and is wearing thick wool socks, a dark blue work shirt, a frumpy cardigan, and jeans that hang loose on his slight frame. "I never buy clothes," he tells me. "I wear stuff out until my wife says I'm an embarrassment, and then she goes and buys something from Lands' End." He owns one suit for meetings with the investment bankers. He got it for $40 at a secondhand store: "It fits! It just has, unfortunately, this mark I can't get out," he says. "I always look like a slob. I don't care. After a point they do business with you or they don't."

He bought the house to appease Emily, a psychiatrist, who is off working today—she doesn't like him talking to journalists, he says.

Personally, he can't stand living in a house this big. But they have four kids "and she wanted to have all these cats. In a small house, that would've been like bedlam." I don't see any cats, but my host assures me there used to be eight and now there are two.

Part of me expected Kravinsky to be cat lady–esque, a bit crazy, but he isn't at all. He is personable, rational, philosophical, and adept with numbers, which is one reason he has excelled as a real estate investor. He knows he's put Emily through hell. She's from an affluent family. Her grandfather was wealthy, and her mother, an editor, cofounded *Ms.* magazine alongside Gloria Steinem. "She grew up on the Upper East Side. She had riding lessons. They had a summer home—they summered in Venice—and she went to a Columbia prep school, whatever the heck it's called." His own family was working-class. His dad was a gruff, disapproving Soviet émigré, a literal communist who was highly critical of his children and found little to admire in American culture. Though Kravinsky shares his father's socialistic tendencies, he declares himself a capitalist, and he is one to the extent that he borrows and leverages tens of millions of dollars to generate tens of millions more. But this is all a game to him. He doesn't care about the money. If he could push a button right now that would make everybody equal and eliminate private property ownership entirely, he would do it, he says. His biggest ambition is to lead a moral, ethical life. And in that he considers himself a failure—though most people would probably disagree.

Given all of the above, I am startled when Kravinsky informs me he is richer now than he ever was. He won't name a figure, but he allows that he would be subject to the wealth tax Elizabeth Warren proposed, which had a $50 million cutoff. I was surprised by this because I'd been under the impression he was no longer even a millionaire, having dispensed with his earlier fortune. But that wasn't why the *New Yorker* was interested, or why *Law & Order* and *House* based episodes on his story, or why Brad Pitt's company, Plan B, wanted to make a film about him. Actor Ralph Fiennes even came to Jenkintown to shadow Kravinsky and learn his mannerisms, and Naomi

Watts was set to play Emily. But too late did the producers realize that Emily, a key character, hadn't signed off on the project—and she refused. Pitt offered to come to Jenkintown to convince her, but Kravinsky told the producers not to bother. "I said, 'She doesn't care how handsome he is or how rich or famous. She's going to slam the door in his face.'" The reason everyone was so fascinated with Kravinsky is that he committed an act of altruism few could imagine. When giving away all his assets wasn't enough, he resolved to give away one of his kidneys—to a complete stranger.

This is known informally as a "nondirected" donation. At the time (summer 2003) fewer than 150 such operations had ever been performed. Since 2016, there have been almost twice that many annually, on average, thanks in part to the stories of Kravinsky and others like him. But two decades ago, anyone who volunteered to give a kidney to a stranger was assumed to be depressed or otherwise mentally unfit. Kravinsky was subjected to a battery of psychological tests, and when he told the vetting surgeon what he'd been up to—giving his millions away—the doc concluded he had delusions of grandeur. Kravinsky does suffer from periodic depression, he told me, "but I don't think that my most charitable moments are my saddest, my most depressed moments. I think it's the opposite."

He didn't want just anyone to have his kidney. He wanted the recipient to be Black. He'd read that African Americans on the organ waiting list were dying at four times the rate of whites. Not only did Black people have a higher incidence of diseases that led to kidney failure, they often weren't told by doctors and dialysis centers that they needed to get on the list. By the time they finally did, it was too late. "My recipient didn't know that she was at death's door," he says. "They hadn't explained to her what her creatine clearance results indicated or that they'd run out of places to stick the dialysis." An organ donor can't specify the race of the recipient, so Kravinsky accomplished his goal by donating at a hospital in North Philadelphia that catered primarily to Black patients.

His friends, and his wife, had tried to dissuade him: *You're being selfish. Think of your family—your children—the hell it would put them through if you were to die.* Kravinsky was unmoved. He considers himself a utilitarian. Utilitarians aim to make decisions that result in the greatest overall good or the least harm. Viewed through that lens, donating a kidney is a no-brainer. The odds of him dying under the knife were about one in four thousand, he had read, whereas the recipient would certainly die without a kidney. It would be selfish not to do it! There wasn't any evidence suggesting that kidney donors lead shorter lives. The only reasonable argument against donation, in his opinion, was that a family member might one day need the kidney, but that seemed pretty far-fetched. Saving this woman's life wasn't heroic. If anything, it probably *was* a selfish act: "I thought of the kidney as my present to myself. I had hoped it would be the beginning of my ethical life. I didn't think of it as a noble life, but a life of decency, of average moral performance."

His wife and friends couldn't compete with his utilitarian logic. Emily told him she was on board, Kravinsky says, but only because she thought he was bluffing. When he snuck off on a pretense one Tuesday and went through with it, she was livid. She wouldn't come see him in the hospital, and "her anger was still red-hot" during his recovery. To this day Emily hasn't gotten over it, Kravinsky says, nor have the kids. The couple has three sons and a daughter, all in their twenties. They get along well with their dad—one of his sons is now his business partner. But when they were small, their mom got in their heads that Daddy had done a bad thing, so there's emotional baggage to contend with.

As for the readers of the *New Yorker* and other outlets that reported on what Kravinsky had done, many thought he was a saint, others a monster. Kravinsky insists he is neither. Just an average, flawed human being. A truly moral performance might involve a thankless, undesirable task such as caring for a relative with dementia. All he ever did was give away some money—look, he made it all back!—and a kidney he didn't need. But "nobody gets articles written about them and nobody makes a movie about somebody's life because they did something they didn't even enjoy for thirty years."

————

The story of Zell Kravinsky raises enough philosophical questions to fill another book. For the moment, though, let's consider just one of them. Namely, if a superwealthy person donates large sums to charity but sacrifices nothing in the process, and perhaps even benefits financially, what sort of deed is that, exactly?

The word "philanthropy" comes from the Greek *philanthrōpos*, an amalgam of *phil* (love) and *anthrōpos* (human). Loosely translated, it means "humane," or "kindly." Given the right incentives and motivations, philanthropy can be exactly that. When the public learned of his generosity, Feeney was hailed, feted, and awarded honorary degrees. He is the subject of a bestselling book. In September 2020, I met Feeney briefly at General Atlantic Group's San Francisco offices. It was a momentous occasion: the signing of the foundation's dissolution papers. House Speaker Nancy Pelosi had sent a personal note to mark the occasion, and Feeney, whose ensemble included a navy blue COVID mask, just viewed a laudatory video message from former governor Jerry Brown, with Bill Gates on deck. Harvey Dale told me he has been advising several "very wealthy people" who intend to follow in Feeney's footsteps. While one could fault Feeney and his partners for using every trick in the book to avoid paying taxes, it would be absurd, given his extreme philanthropy and frugality, to call him self-serving.

Yet as we learned from the Waltons' charitable trusts, giving can be far from selfless. Often, it is ethically neutral. Everingham gave away his entire Netscape jackpot in the end—all but $50,000 or so—to family members and a few charities. He did this not out of a sense of altruism, he willingly admits, but because the money was creating problems for him. He also wanted to prove to himself that he could make it all back again—which he has, and much more. But plenty of what passes for philanthropy in the United States is downright *misanthropic*. In her book *Dark Money*, investigative reporter Jane Mayer writes about how dynasties including the Kochs, the Scaifes, the Coorses, the Olins, and the DeVoses "weaponized" philanthropy to serve their own ideological and business interests.

For these and other ultrawealthy families, philanthropy can serve as what Rob Reich, a Stanford political science professor and author of the 2018 book *Just Giving*, calls a "legitimation project." To put it more bluntly, "it's a reputation-laundering exercise to construct an aura of altruistic do-gooding and distracting people from attending to the source of the moneymaking." Then there's the Big Philanthropy scene, with its glamorous symphony openings and star-studded events such as the Robin Hood Foundation's Annual Benefit and the Met Gala, "which is in principle a charitable fundraiser but more than anything else a status-signaling occasion that being philanthropic is the price of admission to," Reich says.

In the 2018 bestseller *Winners Take All*, author Anand Giridharadas took aim at Big Philanthropy as a tool America's wealthiest use to advance twisted priorities and cement access and influence. We mentioned Jeffrey Epstein earlier, but no less of a stain on society is the Sackler family, whose reckless marketing of OxyContin and other potent opioids contributed to the deaths of hundreds of thousands of Americans. The Sacklers made billions peddling Oxy through their company, Purdue Pharma, and seeded access and goodwill along the way by giving at least $60 million to universities and millions more to cultural institutions including the Louvre, the Met, and the Guggenheim. These institutions pledged to take no more gifts—Tufts University even stripped the family name off one of its buildings—after state and federal authorities sued Purdue and members of the Sackler clan, claiming they knowingly misled the public about the addictiveness of their products, even as people overdosed in droves. In October 2020, Purdue announced it would plead guilty to criminal federal conspiracy charges involving kickbacks and fraudulent marketing, a settlement that includes penalties of about $8.3 billion—much of which the company, having declared bankruptcy, may never pay. In a separate civil settlement that didn't release the Sacklers from civil and criminal complaints pending at the state level, five family members agreed to pay the federal government $225 million. As part of the settlement, the Sacklers admitted they approved a Purdue campaign to pump up OxyContin sales to "extreme, high-volume prescribers" who were already writing twenty-five times as many prescriptions as their peers—reckless behavior that "often led to abuse and diversion." According to the resolution, Purdue also fraudulently transferred assets into family holding companies and trusts in a bid to thwart would-be creditors.

Less egregious but nonetheless notable, Walmart's low prices and high shareholder returns were attained partly by paying miserly wages and shortchanging employees on overtime benefits, among other labor violations, even as Walmart dedicated a foundation to "hunger relief and healthy eating" and "health and human service." And let's not forget Facebook. The platform may help people around the world stay connected, but it has also helped authoritarian regimes consolidate power and foment genocidal campaigns—as Myanmar's military junta did against the Rohingya minority. Facebook established a $15 minimum wage in 2015, earlier than most companies, for contract workers such as cooks, cleaners, drivers, guards, and content reviewers. But has Zuckerberg's baby been a net positive for American society? Arguably not. Its algorithms capitalize on the darkest of human instincts, monetizing our innate tendency to click on the extreme and the outrageous. It profits at the expense of our privacy and until quite recently gave advertisers, including political campaigns, the means to explicitly target, for example, "Jew haters," or to recruit job seekers by race and gender.

Zuckerberg may well have given us President Trump. "Russian actors created 80,000 posts that reached around 126 million people in the U.S. over a two-year period" prior to the 2016 election, Samidh Chakrabarti, the company's product manager for civic engagement, acknowledged in a post. And while Chakrabarti lamented the amplification of "fake news" on social media, Facebook has long resisted meaningful countermeasures. Only in mid-2020, amid public pressure and an exodus of advertisers, did Zuckerberg make a few concessions, but too little, too late to rein in rampant election conspiracy theories or prevent the pillaging of the U.S. Capitol.

America's upper crust has taken much flak from the likes of Bernie Sanders and Elizabeth Warren, who question the morality of a society that allows billionaires to exist. I think these politicians are more or less on point. Philosophically, apart from some nihilistic notion equating "freedom" with unfettered resource accumulation, how can a supposedly egalitarian society justify letting an individual amass hundreds of millions or billions of dollars if not for the good of the society? When I pressed my wealthy sources on the ethics of billionaire-dom, they generally acknowledged that there has to be some number at which making another penny is unethical. The number itself is arbitrary. "In a society where 45 percent of the citizens are hanging on by their fingernails, should a few of us have all this dough?" Hanauer says. "I think the answer is no."

Our adulation of superwealthy givers is a reasonably recent historical development. Consider how the American public reacted when Standard Oil's John D. Rockefeller sought permission from Congress to charter one of the nation's first, and certainly largest, general-purpose charitable foundations. In 1906, by Reich's account, Rockefeller's trusted advisor, Frederick Gates, delivered him a warning: "Your fortune is rolling up, rolling up like an avalanche! You must keep up with it! You must distribute it faster than it grows! If you do not, it will crush you, and your children, and your children's children!"

When Rockefeller approached lawmakers a few years later with a bill that would establish his foundation, he was derided and rebuffed. President William Taft attacked the proposal as "a bill to incorporate Mr. Rockefeller." Taft's predecessor, Theodore Roosevelt, declared that "no amount of charities in spending such fortunes can compensate in any way for the misconduct in acquiring them." Unitarian minister John Haynes Holmes, a cofounder of the ACLU and the NAACP, testified that he presumed Rockefeller and his agents had the best of motives, but "it seems to me this foundation, the very character, must be repugnant to the whole idea of a democratic society."

The notion of a wealthy individual expending vast sums on the public's behalf, based on his own priorities, was widely viewed as an undemocratic power grab. To appease the critics, Rockefeller and Gates amended their proposal with provisions that would cap the foundation's assets at $100 million, subject it to public oversight, and compel it to spend down its entire endowment within fifty years. That won over the House, but the Senate balked. Rockefeller promptly turned to his home state New York Legislature, which approved his foundation in 1913, minus those pesky provisions.

In short, federal lawmakers had the chance to make charitable foundations at least somewhat accountable to the public, and they blew it. We are now living with the result: an exploding network of private entities, beholden to nobody, that can amass unlimited assets and exist in perpetuity. Foundations needn't have a website, physical office, or phone number. They don't have to publish annual reports or reveal their giving strategies to the public, either, though the big ones typically do. In exchange for federal tax-exempt status, a foundation need only file an informational tax return listing assets and expenditures, and spend 5 percent of those assets annually to avoid penalties. The 5 percent includes overhead, so if a foundation treats its board members and salaried executives—which can be members of the donor's family—to an all-inclusive junket in Paris or Ibiza, the expense comes out of the mandatory payout. Some foundations can't even manage 5 percent. Dollar-wise, Michael Bloomberg is among the nation's top donors, but until recently his Bloomberg Philanthropies had among the worst giving rates for foundations of its size, averaging just 4.2 percent from 2010 to 2016, according to the Institute for Policy Studies. (Only in 2018, when Bloomberg was exploring a presidential bid, did his foundation double that dismal payout.) All told, America's private foundations expended 6 percent of their assets in 2019—a year in which the S&P 500 clocked a 29 percent gain.

Candid, which tracks U.S. charitable data, counted about 1.25 million 501(c)(3) charities and nearly 108,000 independent grantmaking foundations as of December 2019, almost double the number that existed two decades earlier. These private foundations are sitting on close to $1 trillion in assets, all publicly subsidized via charitable deductions and tax breaks. Wealthy families have also taken deductions on an estimated $120 billion now stashed in donor-advised funds, alternative charity vehicles with no payout requirement whatsoever. Between these funds and the private foundations, hundreds of billions of tax dollars remain sequestered in the charitable portfolios of our wealthiest citizens at a time of dire need for poor and middle-class families, and state and local governments.

We tend to associate philanthropy with helping society's neediest, but at best about one-third of charitable giving serves that purpose. In his book, Reich cites data showing that families earning less than $100,000 spent about 10 percent of their charitable dollar on "basic needs" giving, while those making $1 million or more dedicated less than 4 percent. Carnegie argued that generous giving would narrow the chasm that inevitably emerges between wealthy capitalists like himself and the workers who toil in their factories, but that outcome is by no means a given. As Reich writes, "Philanthropy is not often a friend of equality, can be indifferent to equality, and can even be a cause of *in*equality."

Consider the tax treatment of charitable institutions and donations. Public charities and foundations are exempt from income, property, and capital gains taxes, and U.S. donors can deduct charitable gifts totaling up to 60 percent of their taxable income. (The CARES Act temporarily raised that limit to 100 percent.) These are extraordinary breaks, especially given the common view of philanthropy as a vehicle to right society's wrongs. In fact, not only are taxpayers subsidizing activities they may very well loathe, but the way the subsidies work is, to quote Reich, "deeply inegalitarian." Namely, if you don't itemize deductions on your tax return, you can't take a charitable deduction, but fewer than 14 percent of taxpayers itemize, and most of them fall within the top-earning 10 percent. If I make $75,000 this year, take the standard deduction, and donate $1,000 to Feeding America, that gift costs me $1,000. If a billionaire with a 25 percent effective tax rate makes the same gift, he pays just $750. In effect, the bottom 90 percent is subsidizing the philanthropic preferences of our highest earners—the higher the tax bracket, the bigger the subsidy. That's a *regressive* policy. If government's aim is to encourage philanthropy as a way to ease structural economic differences, as Carnegie suggested should be its purpose, why subsidize only the wealthiest givers?

Big Philanthropy remains profoundly undemocratic, yet the public and our elected leaders rarely complain anymore. Reich attributes this shift in attitude to the rise of a "marketplace mentality" that also contributes to our tolerance of inequality. "The efforts to provide some legitimacy for the outsized earnings of a small number of people yielded, as they did in the first Gilded Age, an effort to distribute some of these outsized earnings back to society," he says. "And in an era that celebrated business leadership and small government, that meant putting Bill Gates and Bono on the cover of *Time* as the person of the year, and thinking about social entrepreneurs as the way to improve the world."

One could point to Bill and Melinda Gates to argue that we *should* have policies encouraging billionaires to give back. It makes the world a better place, right? But "better" is in the eye of the beholder. In 2016, for Stanford's *Social Innovation Review*, a team of philanthropy professionals conducted an analysis of where the "big bets"—donations of $10 million or more—ended up. Sixty percent of a large sample of major philanthropists (including Giving Pledge signatories) had publicly cited as their top priority "a powerful social change goal" such as eliminating disparities in health care or improving educational opportunities for people in need. That's not quite how things worked out. From 2000 to 2012, excluding the Gates Foundation (an outlier), only 20 percent of the $8 billion in annual big bets went to "social change" giving. The remainder went to universities, hospitals, and cultural institutions that were "often already richly funded, with ample capacity to continue securing major gifts."

The other big asterisk is that just about anything can pass for a tax-exempt public charity. A 501(c)(3) corporation is broadly defined as an organization with religious, charitable, scientific, literary, or educational purposes. There are charities dedicated to "fostering appreciation" for camellias and "promoting the medium of American mime." (The latter, last I checked, had more than $6 million in assets.) In 2017, according to one investigative outlet, the National Christian Foundation—one of the largest faith-based donor-advised funds—distributed more than $19 million of its donors' money to tax-exempt charities that were anti-LGBTQ, anti-Muslim, and anti-immigrant. Among the NCF's leading recipients is Alliance Defending Freedom, a network of Christian lawyers that the Southern Poverty Law Center has designated a hate group for its antigay activities. The Alliance collects tens of millions in tax-exempt donations each year. It has expressed support for foreign laws criminalizing sodomy, represented business owners in court who refuse to serve LGBTQ customers, opposed transgender troops, and even disputed that the 1998 murder of Matthew Shepard, a young gay man, in Laramie, Wyoming, was a hate crime.

We even subsidize public charities that promote racial animus and white nationalism. In his purported "manifesto," Dylann Roof, the white supremacist who slaughtered those Black parishioners in Charleston, wrote that he was motivated by "black on white" crime propaganda he discovered on the website of the nonprofit Council of Conservative Citizens, one of whose former board members, a self-described "race realist" named Jared Taylor, runs the like-minded New Century Foundation, another tax-exempt nonprofit. VDARE Foundation, a vehemently anti-immigrant journalism nonprofit, has collected more than $5 million over the past decade. Its website features headlines such as "Milwaukee Shooting: Six Out of Eleven Mass

Shootings in 86% White Wisconsin Are by Minorities or Immigrants" and "NYPD Releases Pic of Suspect in Tessa Majors Killing. Guess What? He's Black."

The fact that donations to churches and religious groups comprise almost one-third of all tax-exempt giving means that nonreligious Americans are subsidizing religious practice, and members of minority religions (Mormons, Muslims, Jews) are subsidizing majority ones (Catholics, evangelical Christians, etc.). Whether or not you appreciate charter schools, you are helping Sam and Helen Walton's family foundation launch thousands of new ones. You are also subsidizing Hobby Lobby founder David Green, a Giving Pledge signatory who supports right-wing religious causes. Hobby Lobby was represented by Alliance Defending Freedom in a Supreme Court case that allowed the company to deny contraceptive coverage to female employees under the Affordable Care Act.

All told, Reich calculates, the federal charitable deduction costs American taxpayers more than $50 billion per year. He proposes a straightforward solution: Kill it. Replace the deduction with a tax credit, which would render the subsidy more democratic, and cap it at a modest sum. If the wealthy parents of Woodside and Ross want to spend millions of dollars so their public schools can resemble fancy private ones—the perfect example of a well-intended charitable act that perpetuates economic inequality—should parents in poor communities have to pay for that? Should everyday Americans have to shell out $10 million every time a billionaire with a 20 percent effective tax rate pledges $50 million to Harvard? Maybe it's time we rethink this whole sordid business. And while we're at it, maybe it's about time we—rich and poor alike—take a hard look at what it means to be a responsible citizen, an *actual* patriot, in this uniquely troubled age.

CHAPTER 20

PERFECT STORM

In a rebellion, as in a novel, the most difficult
part to invent is the end.
—ALEXIS DE TOCQUEVILLE

Darren Walker gets it. He has heard the criticisms of Big Philanthropy and added some of his own, most notably that the seemingly endless cycle of hoarding wealth and giving back has done little to fix the plumbing that routes society's resources directly to the top and makes the Ford Foundation necessary.

Walker wants to repair that plumbing. His position makes him one of New York City's hottest appointments, but he agreed to meet with me to talk about race and wealth and giving and capitalism and how we all can do better—*have to* do better. He greets me warmly in his spacious office one mid-December Monday clad in a comfy-looking tan outfit. We sit at a conference table stacked with books about art, politics, and famous Black people that he will never get the chance to read: "It's impossible!" The shelves on one wall are crowded with more books, tchotchkes, and photos—Walker shaking hands with Pope Francis; posing with his late husband, David Beitzel, and their bulldog, Mary Lou; a vintage black-and-white of young Darren and his kid sister, shirtless and squinting into the sun, on the porch of their tiny shotgun house on a dirt road in Ames, Texas.

Walker's humble background gives him an instinctive understanding, unique among his peers, of the ways powerful foundations can put their resources to socially valuable use. When I ask whether his family owned the little shotgun house, he laughs as though it were the silliest question in the world. "I'm sorry, I don't mean it like that," he says, "but the Blacks in these neighborhoods *never* owned homes." Walker was born in a charity hospital in Louisiana. His mom was a nurse, single—his father never a part of his life. When he was four, they moved to Ames, where his great-aunt could mind the children while his mother worked. They scraped by without entitlements, but barely. Darren got hand-me-downs from Danny Crane, an older boy from a prominent Houston family for whom "Big," his grandmother, worked. The Cranes were rich. The father was a Princeton man and they were friends with the Bushes. Danny's clothes "were *really nice*," Walker says. "I remember the first time I wore a *Real. Wool. Sweater.* I'd never had—I had acrylic cheap sweaters. To this day, I know why I love nice things: Danny Crane!"

When his mom fell behind on rent or utility payments, white strangers showed up and yelled at her. It was "humiliating," Walker says. "We were always on the precipice." But things were far worse for his aunt and her kids back in Louisiana. They were destitute, visibly impoverished and dependent on food stamps. His cousins went in and out of prison—they still struggle, though Walker gives his mother money to help them stay afloat. In middle-class white communities, college is just that thing you do after high school to enable your dreams. For Walker, it was an escape hatch—from being poor, the indignity of the bill collectors, "all those things that I grew up with, I didn't want to have that happen to me ever again."

He did well enough to get into the University of Texas in Austin with Pell Grants and scholarships. Deft at social navigation, a necessary survival skill for a gay Black man in the South—"I was code-switching before 'code-switching' was a word"—he found his way into the Friar Society, an elite campus group with wealthy and powerful alumni: judges, governors, members of Congress. He even became the head guy: the abbot. As a rare Black face in a bastion of white privilege, he felt the imposter syndrome acutely, and not just because he lacked the money to go out on the town with friends, or because his roommate's parents would treat them to brunch when his mom didn't know it was parents weekend and couldn't have come anyway. Walker recalls introducing himself to a woman at a Friars reception at the governor's mansion. "I extend my hand as I often do, 'Hello, I'm Darren Walker, I'm the abbot.' And before I could say, 'abbot,' she said, 'I'd like a gin and tonic, please.'"

This happened all the time. He would resort to humor—*Can you believe this happened to me?*—when telling friends his war stories. "When you look like me in those rooms," he explains, "people ask you to get them a drink or to tell them what's on the menu for dinner because they mistakenly, out of social conditioning, see me and think there's only one reason I would be there. Not as a peer, and *so* not the person who's being honored or chosen for the award or whatever."

Walker kept straddling the worlds of wealth and poverty after college. He attended law school at UT Austin, worked at a corporate law firm and as an investment banker at Union Bank of Switzerland (UBS), and then spent a year as a volunteer teacher in Harlem, where he was later hired as chief operating officer for a community development organization. Prior to Ford, he served nine years as a vice president at the Rockefeller Foundation. Along the way, he has witnessed profound need and generosity, kindness and ulterior motives, acknowledgment and denial. He meets well-heeled men and women who care deeply about creating opportunities for those who lack them, and also people who show up at charity events mainly to affirm their status as leaders, philanthropists, *charitable people*. And he's okay with that, so long as they are willing to remove their blinders and acknowledge their complicity in the profound unfairness that afflicts our society.

The complicity paradox has long nagged at Walker; that a businessman might, for example, deny his workers a living wage and later seek praise for giving $1 million to a group that feeds the hungry. And so, after he was named Ford's president in 2013, he put his mind to figuring out how he, a poor kid from rural Texas, might encourage

America's elite to connect the dots between their privilege and others' poverty—not to *disparage*, but to help people see how their resources could be better applied toward a more permanent solution to our vicious cycles of wealth and poverty and racism.

For too long, philanthropists had congratulated themselves for applying Band-Aids to wounds they helped inflict, when what the patient—the system—needed was major surgery, an operation that might not go easy on the surgeon. He was troubled, too, by the fact that many foundations—including Ford, with its $13 billion endowment—were invested in companies and deals that ran directly counter to their goals. A family foundation dedicated to fighting climate change, for instance, might have a high-yielding portfolio that includes fossil fuel investments. Or it might hold neutral investments that deliver solid returns but do nothing to advance its causes.

Walker secured permission from his board to move $1 billion from Ford's endowment into "mission-related" investments. This was a pilot project, a proof of concept in "impact" investing—putting cash into organizations that have a so-called double bottom line: "Can you get a financial *and* a social return, environmental return, on your investment?" He couldn't simply reinvest the whole $13 billion. "We're in a war of ideas," Walker says. The war is about who we want to be as a people, and what capitalism should look like going forward. Our perfect storm of Gilded Age inequality, global plague, and racial reckoning have left America at a crossroads. Walker knows which way he wants to go. But because we are socialized to put profits first, he had to demonstrate to his peers in the Big Philanthropy world that one *really can* do well by doing good. Whether he succeeds, and America does, will depend on whether enough people choose to embrace the notion that the value of an enterprise isn't only about how many units it sells, or how quickly it grows, but whether its actions are consistent with society's interests. That is, whether we choose to believe that social value *is* market value. Wealth managers fear "these cockamamie ideas of investments—we're going to lose our shirts and as fiduciaries not fulfill our responsibility. And we've got to disprove that," Walker says. We need to say, "*This* is capitalism. What is not capitalism is the distorted cronyism that we are now getting."

With these ideas in mind, Walker composed an open letter to the philanthropy community. In his letter, titled "Toward a New Gospel of Wealth," he praised the juggernaut that Andrew Carnegie launched— "this vast ledger of undeniable public good"—but went on to say it was time to reconsider Carnegie's vision of philanthropy as a salve for capitalism's worst side effects. "Philanthropy is commendable," he wrote, quoting Dr. Martin Luther King Jr., "but it must not cause the philanthropist to overlook the circumstances of economic injustice which make philanthropy necessary."

Big donors needed to reject "inherited, assumed, paternalist instincts" and dedicate more thought to how they might give the "excluded" people the tools and opportunities to lift themselves up, Walker wrote, a task that would require soul-searching about the true causes of economic inequality—"even, and especially, when it means that we ourselves will be implicated. . . .

> We should ask, How does our privilege insulate us . . . ? How does our work . . . reinforce structural inequality in our society? Why *are* we still necessary, and what can we do to build a world where we no longer are *as* necessary?

When he wrote this, Walker was thinking about the evisceration of the middle class, the inability of regular, hardworking Americans to make a life in which their basic needs were met and their children were guaranteed a decent education and a fair shake. Because, though it sounds cliché, the middle class is truly the soul of the nation. It's what holds us together, represents our best common values. We know this deeply and instinctively. It is why politicians stress their humble roots, and why even unambiguously wealthy people describe themselves as middle class. We claim we revere these values, and yet those among us who were dealt the best cards—not all of them, but the majority—have long stood by, quietly benefiting from the same policies that have left the families that embody those all-American values without a pot to piss in. "Most Americans don't expect that they're going to be in your book. I mean, they're not going to have a huge liquidity event," Walker tells me. "But most hope and wish to have a good life in the middle class, and maybe aspire to the upper middle class. You can always fantasize that you're going to be Warren Buffett, but *that's* the American Dream, and that's what has been diminished and harmed by the promiscuous inequality that's designed right into our economy, our capitalist system, our social structures. What we're getting is actually what we've designed for."

The only likely way to solve this problem short of a bloody revolution is to convince the privileged among us—not just the 0.001 percent, but the 1 percent and the 10 percent, too—that giving back, like hard work, is necessary but not sufficient. If society's "winners" are patriots who truly love their country and care about their fellow citizens, they can prove that by doing more than writing some checks. Because that isn't sacrifice. Sacrifice is giving up your position at the front of the line, and for some people, that will be harder than giving away a kidney.

There's a subset of superwealthy Americans, some of whom we've met, who have joined or helped launch groups such as Patriotic Millionaires, Resource Generation, and Solidaire Network, working to change the rules that stand in the way of a fair and decent society. These fortunate folks are but a small minority, as are the dynasties that aim to twist our system even further to their own advantage. The majority of rich people, I think, are little different from the rest of us—from the people James Baldwin's acquaintance described. They go about their busy lives, loving their children and putting out small fires and trying not to think too much about the advantages they have and the realities of our system and how those realities implicate them.

We stand divided, yet the dire events of 2020 have jarred some wealthy folks into action. Erwin Raphael and his wife created a new foundation to help "level the playing field." MacKenzie Scott unveiled, in July 2020, nearly $1.7 billion in unrestricted gifts to social justice, climate, and civics causes. Banking heiress Susan Sandler pledged $200 million to racial equity groups. Tech executive Elizabeth told me she and her husband are downsizing, shedding properties and possessions, and pondering how to be allies in a social revolution led by voices long ignored. A survey of major foundations found that about 60 percent were giving more than planned in 2020–17 percent more, on average. And Scott made headlines again in December 2020. Calling the pandemic a "wrecking ball," she wrote on Medium that she'd spent the previous four months doling out another $4.2 billion to 384 organizations, from food banks to civil rights groups. But greed and complacency remain formidable adversaries. In a pre-COVID *New York Times* op-ed, Walker wrote of attending a black-tie gala "where guests pay $100,000 for a table." Schmoozing with some of New York's richest philanthropists in an opulent ballroom, "I had the ominous sense that we were eating lobster on the *Titanic*. . . .

> That evening, a billionaire who made his money in private equity delivered a soliloquy to me about America's dazzling economic growth and record low unemployment among African-Americans in particular. I reminded him that many of these jobs are low-wage and dead-end, and that the proliferation of these very jobs is one reason that inequality is growing worse. He simply looked past me, over my shoulder.
>
> No chief executive, investor or rich person wakes up in the morning, looks in the mirror, and says, "Today, I want to go out and create more inequality in America." And yet, all too often, that is exactly what happens.

> It is well past time for the self-styled masters of the universe to awaken from their foie gras stupor, open the castle gates, and get to work on the complex and politically fraught task of remaking the American economy. For how satisfying can it be, really, to win at the same old game of Monopoly in which the other guy never has a chance?

As for the pitchforks, they're not coming. They're here. "Trumpism is pitchforks," Nick Hanauer says. "The dissolution of democratic norms. Increase in racism, xenophobia. The fundamental destabilization of society. The erosion of social cohesion. You're experiencing it!"

Among "the boardroom elite," Walker writes, "I see an evolving understanding that our twisted economy is an existential threat that has pushed our republic to a breaking point." That's a diplomatic way of putting it. Wealth bubbles notwithstanding, America's elite tend to be well educated and well informed. Those who cannot see that our current path leads to a dead end are the ones who have chosen not to see. They will not be moved. But those people of power and privilege who claim that they care need to ask themselves the following, honest question: What am I, personally, willing to give up in order to make things better?

I first met Tracy Gary before COVID shut everything down. We sat on her sofas, maskless, and talked about her work and upbringing, about race and gender and economic inequality. We talked about incredibly wealthy people who actually want to make America great, about those who haven't got a clue, and about how she is doing her best to convert the latter into the former—to convince our bubble-dwellers to let go of what they think they value the most. For though self-sacrifice may not be instinctive, it is the only path to something truly priceless.

I caught up with Gary again in early 2020, by phone, amid the lockdown. She was spending eight hours a day on Zoom, strategizing with social justice activists and tracking down wealthy donors who had fled the big cities for their country retreats, imploring them to smash their piggy banks and come to the rescue of their fellow Americans. She seemed cautiously hopeful. The virus had shined a harsh light on the brutality of the system. Perhaps the scales would finally fall from the eyes of the 0.001 percenters—and the 10 percenters, too. All are welcome.

As the situation grew more dire, Gary sounded increasingly optimistic. The last time we spoke, military troops were firing tear-gas canisters into diverse and largely peaceful crowds of Americans who had risked a potentially fatal illness to express their displeasure over the murder of George Floyd and the centuries of racist brutality that preceded it. The protests had spread around the globe. Cracks were forming in the bubble, and perhaps in the mindsets of some of the people who used to say Black Americans should "just get over" the past—the past that was never really the past. America's grotesquely warped playing field was no longer an abstraction to be pondered over a good Sancerre. It was in your face: disease and death, political and social decay, police violence, anarchist types and armed Trump supporters facing off in the streets, all adding to a status quo of mind-boggling economic unfairness. For Gary, the public outcry felt like a once-in-a-lifetime opportunity. "I'm happier than anything. I'm so excited," she told me. "It's a global social movement. I mean, it's at great cost, but Jesus, we know the cost! There's a lot of stuff for people to look at—including class and arrogance and white supremacy. Everybody's going to have to check their behavior. This is a lifetime dream for me, because I'm still learning, too."

Gary turns seventy this year. She could be retired and living in a mansion, eating truffles and sipping Lafite Rothschild from a Tiffany goblet. She chose to give away her wealth instead. Her miserable upbringing quashed any desire she might have had for such a life. It wasn't just her parents' neglect, or their alcoholism, but the fact that she had witnessed injustice up close and didn't want to grow up to be part of the problem. That was one of the silver linings to an unhappy childhood. Nellie and her other caretakers took her outside the family fortresses and into their own communities and churches. Tracy saw how the other half lived—how white grown-ups treated the brown-skinned women she loved. How, when they ventured out in Florida, Nellie always wore her domestic uniform for fear people would accuse her of kidnapping a white girl. And how, in pale Minnesota, caretaker Lottie, mixed-race and proud, confronted parents whose children stared and commented on her color, saying they shouldn't be raising little bigots. Lottie quit abruptly one day after Tracy's stepdad offhandedly uttered the N-word in her vicinity. Young Tracy took notice of all of it. She felt a stronger bond to these women than to her own family.

It's not as though she took a vow of poverty. Gary has a nice life, enjoys herself, eats well, and lives in a comfortable condo in upscale Tiburon, California, with a delightful view of the San Francisco Bay. The wealth she received from her family has fueled her quest to change the rules—on behalf of women, people of color, LGBTQ people, and anyone else who didn't grow up with a silver spoon. Starting in her twenties, she took her parents' original gift—$1.2 million with interest—and doled out about $100,000 a year until it was gone. She kept going. Her goal now is to earn $140,000 a year from her consulting work, give away $40,000, and live off the rest. Her mother died a few years ago, leaving an inheritance she hadn't anticipated because her mom cut her off financially after Gary came out. So now she gets an allowance of about $40,000 a year, and gives that away, too. Apart from her condo, which is "mortgaged to the max," she has burned her safety net. She prefers it that way. "Keeps me on my toes," she says.

But the superwealthy are still, in many ways, her people. She doesn't hate or disparage them, but recognizes them as fallible, and, like anyone else, deserving of empathy. She tells me about one family who called on her for help with philanthropic planning. The adult children had inherited and sold off a company for a massive jackpot. She got a call from one of the siblings. He was about sixty and had recently gone through a tough divorce. As a consolation present, he'd bought himself a Ferrari. But he felt self-conscious driving it around, so he reached out to other Ferrari owners. They began getting together for drives. As membership expanded, he incorporated the group as a nonprofit and began staging rallies and events that have raised a couple million dollars for local charities. Gary has helped the group with strategic planning. "This is the irony in my life," she says.

"I want them all to give up their Ferraris. But you have to work with them first."

The modest charitable efforts of a bunch of Ferrari dudes won't bring about systemic change, of course. "People go, 'Don't you go crazy working with all these rich people who take so goddamn long to do what you did by the time you were thirty-five years old?' I say, 'No. Everybody's different. Some people really need to enjoy their wealth for a long time, because they have nothing else.'"

Which is sad when you think about it: that we would sacrifice some of the best things, really, that life has to offer in our quest to have it all. For those good-hearted super-rich folks who are unable to see themselves clearly, Gary feels no contempt. She would like to coax and inspire them into leading a more meaningful and ethical life, to help them free themselves from the unquenchable thirst for status, power, and stuff. To rejoin the world of the living and engage with the broader community. To feel the pleasure and kinship that come with giving up some of one's privilege so that others might enjoy a little more. Her true desire, ultimately, is not incremental change but a complete reimagining of what our money-obsessed nation could be, given the collective will: a place where everyone, *truly*, has the chance to prosper, to be educated, to get honest pay for honest work, and to never be tossed aside because of traits beyond one's control.

This needn't be a French-style revolution, one the wealthy must fear, but rather a revolution in which they can play a constructive role, picking up a pitchfork with the rest and using it to bale a neighbor's hay in exchange for camaraderie and a hearty meal. And the rest of us need to be willing to invite these fortunate individuals to dinner and hand them that pitchfork. Because there's too much anger in our society right now. And yes, much of it is justified. There are plenty of people, from billionaires to elected officials on down, who absolutely deserve to feel the wrath of the common people. But anger won't win over the privileged classes, or get them to accept their complicity and embrace the right path. If anger motivates us to get off our behinds and fight—hard—for a better way of being, great. But if anger is the spark, the revolution will only be won with empathy, education, understanding, and personal commitment.

At one point, I tell Gary I like talking with her because she's so quotable. "I don't want to be *quoted*," she replies. "I want the world to change in my lifetime. I saw what alcohol, six houses, a helicopter, and a plane can bring you—arrogance and isolation. You don't know how to connect to people. You don't know how to feel. You don't know how to be empathetic. You're too busy managing the circumstances of your wealth.

"You want to be happier?" she asks. "Redistribute your wealth and your power is what I've done. I'm blissfully happy. I don't have any cash. I don't care. I care about having community. It's like, 'Look, make a living like the rest of the world.'"

We yearn to strike it rich because we believe money will solve our problems. It will solve some of them, and create new ones. The jackpot will be thrilling and fun, for a time. It will make life easier, and more complicated. It will challenge our ethical values and create psychological and social complexities we never imagined when we set out to launch that company, make that investment, purchase that lottery ticket. We will come to see, as did Sam Polk and James Everingham and Bruce Jackson, Jonathan, Michael, Martha, Elizabeth, and Richard Watts's clients, to name a few, that money is a blessing and a curse. We yearn for freedom, but money alone can't set us free, and our collective desire to hoard it—to leave others behind and escape to society's safe pinnacle—will only make us less free. For Doug Holladay's lonely CEOs, wealth and status became a cage with gilded bars. For Gary, wealth was the problem *and* the solution. To be truly free, she needed to rid herself of it and dedicate her life to helping others to do the same.

Rarely have I met a person more at peace with herself.

ACKNOWLEDGMENTS

Writing a nonfiction book is like being superwealthy—except for the lifestyle. It is similar in that it is not as easy as it sounds. Doing it properly requires intention and focus. It's an enormous responsibility that can feel, in turn, joyful, thrilling, isolating, and imbued with anxiety. Often one feels like an imposter. To make peace with the process requires pacing and rhythm, good coffee and better wine, and trustworthy folks on your side. People who have dealt with this before, and whom you can turn to for counsel and mentorship. People who will rub your shoulders when you've been formatting endnotes for ten hours. (Thanks, Ruby!) And who understand the difference between "who" and "whom."

No superwealthy American, or successful author, is truly "self-made." If this book does well, it will be thanks not to the few, but the many. I hereby raise a magnum of Chateau Latour to my father, who has always had my back, and whose comments on my drafts were on point. To my late mother, who gave me my love of music and oddball sense of humor. To my big brother, Rob, who taught me to fight back. To Laura, my lovely wife, who reminded me I could do this when I felt like I couldn't, and who put up with me when I was so deep in Book Land that I admit I was not the best husband and parent. Likewise, to Nikko and Ruby, who tolerated my self-absorption—I love you both more than anything! To Aunt Gladys, the first person other than my editor to read my first draft and claim she couldn't put it down. A toast, also, to my *Mother Jones* editors, Clara Jeffery and Monika Bauerlein, who granted me the flexibility to complete this project, and who have helped me become a better writer and editor over the past dozen years. To Eric Lupfer, my agent at Fletcher & Associates, a savvy editor in his own right who took an interest in my work and called me, out of the blue, to ask whether I'd ever thought about writing a book. (As a matter of fact, I had.) To the inimitable Eamon Dolan, my rock star editor at Simon & Schuster, who understood immediately what I was trying to accomplish, and was masterful at making comments that prompted me to make smart editorial choices on my own—he's damn good with a scalpel, too, I might add. To legal eagle Carolyn Levin, and the rest of my editorial, design, production, and publicity crew members at S&S: Tzipora Baitch, Pete Garceau, Yvette Grant, Anne Tate Pearce, Jackie Seow, Leila Siddiqui, and Rob Sternitzky.

I am moreover indebted to my journalistic colleagues and others who have been so generous with advice, contacts, encouragement, endorsements, introductions, promotion, and/or valuable feedback: Shane Bauer, Marc Benioff, Alex Busansky, Kiera Butler, David Corn, Matthew Delmont, David Dobbs, Kerry Dolan, Jesse Eisinger, Barak Engel, Jason Fagone, Josh Foer, Dave Gilson, Ian Gordon, Ariela Gross, Miguel Helft, Stephen Hinshaw, Adam Hochschild, Jamilah King, Andy Kroll, David Kutzman, Noel Lindsay, Ryan Mac, Jane Mayer, Zach Mider, the entire *Mother Jones* crew, Peggy Orenstein (thanks for the toy Lamborghini!), Alexi Oreskovic, Ian Parker, Brandon Patterson, Edwin Rios, Gary Rivlin, Adam Rogers, Bradley Saacks, Eric Schlosser, Gary Shteyngart, Michael Sokolove, Clive Thompson, and Jen Vogel.

Here's also to Ella Rosenthal, who helped format the endnotes (fun!), Jen Werner for the author photo, Jenny Summers for making it pop, and designer extraordinaire Carolyn Perot for making my charts look nice. I would have made lots of dumb mistakes if not for my intrepid fact-checkers: Graham Hacia, Caitlin Harrington, Beatrice Hogan, Fergus McIntosh, Adam Przbyl, and Sam Stecklow. To Tim Choate and Elizabeth McKoy, Joe Donnelly, Cory Johnson, Warren Lilien, Adam Nelson, Bryan Reynolds, Paul Roesler, and other friends who offered a sounding board, a sofa to crash on, and/or help with introductions. And of course, to my fellow "enemies of the people"—

the hardworking reporters without whose work this book, and our democracy, for that matter, would never have been possible.

A writer of creative nonfiction is lost, of course, without great characters. I am deeply grateful to the fortunate Americans who were willing to set aside society's taboos and share their personal stories and insights: Susan Davis, Mike Depatie, Ramses Erdtmann, James Everingham, Jerry Fiddler, Tracy Gary, Malin Giddings, Nick Hanauer, Phil Hellmuth, Doug Holladay, Bruce "Jackson," Zell Kravinsky, Tim O'Reilly, Kim Polese, Sam Polk, Erwin Raphael, Leigh Steinberg, Darren Walker, Jeff Weissglass, Tal Zlotnitsky, Annika, Elizabeth, Jonathan, Martha, Michael, Sally, and others who shall remain nameless.

I am likewise grateful to all the busy academics, authors, businesspeople, college counselors, educators, lawyers, politicians, and wealth and philanthropy professionals who were generous with their time, and whose own work proved invaluable. Extra-special shout-outs to Doug Blackmon, Jerry Fiddler, Austin Forbord, Phil Hellmuth, Tim Kasser, Bob Kenny, Michael Kraus, Michael Norton, Chris Oechsli, Tim O'Reilly, Paul Piff, Erwin Raphael, Emmanuel Saez, Trina Shanks, Amy Shelf, Darren Walker, Richard Watts, Gabriel Zucman, and others who went beyond the call of duty in one way or another.

To anyone who slipped my addled mind, thank you, too! And please forgive me.

My own wealth fantasy is that *Jackpot* will add something meaningful to our ongoing conversation around wealth and opportunity in America, and inspire readers to question our deeply held cultural myths and socioeconomic patterns so that we might emerge from this unsustainable era as a more united people, and a better nation.

RESOURCES

A few organizations trying to build a better society.

FOR WEALTHY INDIVIDUALS

Class Action. Working to combat classism and class biases. (Classism.org)

Justice Funders. A Bay Area network whose members aim to transform philanthropy-as-usual so as to redistribute opportunity, power, and, ultimately, wealth. (JusticeFunders.org)

Patriotic Millionaires/Wealth for the Common Good. High-net-worth individuals pushing for more fairness in taxation, wages, and political influence. (PatrioticMillionaires.org)

Resource Generation. A group of fortunate young people exploring how to use their family wealth to advance social justice. (ResourceGeneration.org)

Solidaire Network. Promoting the funding of social change movements. (SolidaireNetwork.org)

Women Donors Network: Leverages members' wealth and expertise to pursue systemic change and access to economic opportunities for those who lack them. (WomenDonors.org)

Women's Foundation of California. Calling its members "feminists for racial, economic, and gender justice," the group has a "Funders Policy Institute" that teaches women to fund and advocate effectively for progressive social policies. (WomensFoundCA.org)

FOR EVERYONE

Americans for Tax Fairness. A coalition of national and regional groups fighting for more equitable taxation. (AmericansforTaxFairness.org)

Bioneers. "A fertile hub of social and scientific innovators with practical and visionary solutions for the world's most pressing environmental and social challenges." (Bioneers.org)

Center for Community Change. Helps low-income people get involved in improving their own communities. (CommunityChange.org)

Financial Accountability and Corporate Transparency Coalition. A nonpartisan alliance dedicated to opposing tax-haven abuses and corporate chicanery. (TheFactCoalition.org)

Hedgeclippers. Brings attention to the outsized influence of hedge funds and billionaires in the political process. (Hedgeclippers.org)

Inequality.org. A portal for data, analysis, and commentary on wealth and income inequality.

Institute for Policy Studies. A group of scholars and activists working with social movements to promote democratic ideals and challenge the concentration of wealth, corporate influence, and military power. (IPS-DC.org)

Jobs with Justice. Fighting for workers' rights and an economy that works for all. (jwj.org)

National Domestic Workers Alliance and **Caring Across Generations.** A coalition seeking recognition and labor protections for domestic workers. (DomesticWorkers.org)

National People's Action. A grassroots network advancing economic and racial justice. (PeoplesAction.org)

Other 98 Percent. A progressive grassroots network that uses social media to reshape America's prevailing economic narratives. (Other98.com)

Public Citizen. A consumer-rights group and think tank aiming to ensure all citizens are well-represented in the halls of power. (Citizen.org)

Racial Wealth Divide Project. A Prosperity Now initiative that harnesses the group's partner network to "aggressively address racial economic inequality." (www.prosperitynow.org/racial-wealth-divide-initiative)

RESULTS. Promotes civic engagement and advocacy on hunger/poverty issues. (Results.org)

Unidos US. Part of a national network advocating for the civic engagement, prosperity, and civil rights of Latinos in the United States. (UnidosUS.org)

United for a Fair Economy. Educates the public on economic inequality. (FairEconomy.org)

For more resources (and author blog), see ReadJackpot.com.

NOTES

INTRODUCTION

1 *significant stakes in nearly three dozen companies:* Nick Hanauer's partner page, Second Avenue Partners, http://www.secondave.com/nick-hanauer.

1 *Microsoft purchased in 2007 for $6.3 billion:* "Microsoft to Acquire aQuantive, Inc.," Microsoft press release, May 18, 2007, https://news.microsoft.com/2007/05/18/microsoft-to-acquire-aquantive-inc/.

1 *a sleek private jet:* "Dassault Falcon 900LX," GlobalAir.com, https://www.globalair.com/aircraft-for-sale/Specifications?specid=1349.

1 *prestigious private high school:* Seattle Academy, https://www.seattleacademy.org/.

1 *"a beautiful house":* All quotes from author interview with Nick Hanauer, June 10, 2019.

2 *referring to himself as a "plutocrat":* Nick Hanauer, "The Pitchforks Are Coming . . . For Us Plutocrats," *Politico*, July/August 2014, https://www.politico.com/magazine/story/2014/06/the-pitchforks-are-coming-for-us-plutocrats-108014.

2 *hopes to persuade government officials:* See: https://nickhanauer.com/about/.

2 *helped convince Jeff Bezos:* Author email with Nick Hanauer, July 20, 2020.

2 *1 percent of the company:* Ibid.

3 *Amazon went public:* Alex Wilhelm, "A Loopback in IPO: Amazon's 1997 Move," *TechCrunch*, June 28, 2017, https://techcrunch.com/2017/06/28/a-look-back-at-amazons-1997-ipo/.

3 *split-adjusted share price:* "Amazon—23 Year Stock Split History," Macrotrends, https://www.macrotrends.net/stocks/charts/AMZN/amazon/stock-splits.

3 *spiking north of $1,200:* Amazon share prices in late April 1999 (x12): Yahoo Finance, https://finance.yahoo.com/quote/AMZN/history?period

1=859852800&period2=928195200&interval=1d&filter=history& frequency=1d.

3 *In the late 1800s:* Nick Hanauer confirmed the details in a follow-up email. "Pacific Coast Feather Company History," FundingUniverse, http://www.fundinguniverse.com/company-histories/pacific-coast -feather-company-history/.

3 *sales exceeded $100 million:* Ibid.

4 *nearly half of American adults:* Zac Auter, "About Half of Americans Play State Lotteries," Gallup, July 22, 2016, https://news.gallup.com/poll /193874/half-americans-play-state-lotteries.aspx.

4 *$81 billion on lottery tickets:* "La Fleur's Fiscal 2019 Report," https://la fleurs.com/magazine-feature/2019/09/09/la-fleurs-fiscal-2019-report/.

4 *more than the GDPs of two-thirds of the world's nations:* "GDP Ranked by Country 2020," http://worldpopulationreview.com/countries/countries -by-gdp/.

4 *amount we spend each year on books:* Adult, young adult, and children's fiction and nonfiction. Jim Milliot, "Industry Sales Posted Small Gain in 2019," *Publishers Weekly*, March 14, 2020, https://www.publishersweekly .com/pw/by-topic/industry-news/financial-reporting/article/82693 -industry-sales-posted-small-gain-in-2019.html.

4 *in search of gold and silver:* "The Change in Character from 1606 to 1609," *The Records of the Virginia Company of London*, Library of Congress, 1906, http://www.virtualjamestown.org/exist/cocoon/jamestown /virgco/b000451042.

4 *famine and misery:* "Jamestown Settlement," from *Africans in America: The Terrible Transformation, Part I: 1450–1750*, WGBH, October 1998, https://www.pbs.org/wgbh/aia/part1/1p261.html.

4 *"Men are here nearly crazed":* H. W. Brands, *The Age of Gold* (New York: Anchor Books, 2002), 125.

4 *on a scale from "not important" to "essential":* "The American Freshman: National Norms 2017," Cooperative Institutional Research Program, UCLA, p. 45, https://www.heri.ucla.edu/monographs/TheAmericanFreshman2017 -Expanded.pdf.

5 *consigliere for some of America's richest families:* "Meet the Founder: Richard Watts," Family Business Office, https://www.fbo.com/founder .html.

6 *your odds of being a millionaire:* Victoria Stillwell, "What Are Your Odds of Becoming a Millionaire?," *Bloomberg*, January 21, 2016, https://www .bloomberg.com/features/2016-millionaire-odds/.

6 *at least $1.1 million in net assets:* 2019 threshold numbers from Thomas Piketty, Emmanuel Saez, and Gabriel Zucman, "Distributional National Accounts: Methods and Estimates for the United States," *Quarterly Journal of Economics* 133, no. 2 (2018): 553–609 (updated series, September 2020).

6 *You will be among 18.3 million U.S. households:* Author email with Emmanuel Saez, September 4, 2020.

6 *net investible assets:* "EY Wealth Management Outlook 2018," footnote, p. 7, https://www.ey.com/Publication/vwLUAssets/ey-wealth -management-outlook-2018/$file/ey-wealth-management-outlook -2018.pdf.

6 *$1 million makes you an "accredited investor":* Securities and Exchange Commission, "Guide to Definitions of Terms Used in Form D," Legal Information Institute, Cornell Law School, undated, https://www.law .cornell.edu/cfr/text/17/230.501.

6 *at least $300,000 for two years running:* Eric R. Smith, "Investor Qualifications: A Primer," Venable LLP Fund Forum, January 2016, https:// www.venable.com/insights/publications/2016/01/investor-qualification -a-primer.

7 *a businessman we'll meet:* Author interview with Jerry Fiddler, August 18, 2015.

7 *nearly $29 trillion . . . by 2021:* "EY Wealth Management Outlook 2018," 9.

8 *more than $23.4 million:* "Estate Tax," Internal Revenue Service, https:// www.irs.gov/businesses/small-businesses-self-employed/estate-tax.

8 *$805 million and up:* Author email with Emmanuel Saez, September 4, 2020.

9 *your child's chances of getting in:* "Applicants and Admit Rate by Preferred Group" in "Expert Report of Peter S. Arcidiacono," *Students for Fair Admissions, Inc. v. Harvard*, p. 88, table A.2, http:// samv91khoyt2i553a2t1s05i-wpengine.netdna-ssl.com/wp-content/up loads/2018/06/Doc-415-1-Arcidiacono-Expert-Report.pdf.

9 *a company whose sole purpose:* A "family office." See chapter 5.

9 *If you're worried about the IRS, don't be:* See chapter 15.

9 *You can just call your senator:* See chapter 13.

9 *mad with hubris:* Personal observations. Also see: Mark Jurkowitz, "'Starving to Death on $200 Million' by James Ledbetter," *San Francisco Chronicle*, February 23, 2003, https://www.chron.com/life/article /Starving-to-Death-on-200-Million-by-James-2098124.php.

9 *odds ... were 1 in 41 million:* "California SuperLotto Plus Prizes," Lotto .net, https://www.lotto.net/california-super-lotto-plus/prizes.

9 *least likely to play:* Zac Auter, "About Half of Americans Play State Lotteries," Gallup, July 22, 2016, https://news.gallup.com/poll/193874/half -americans-play-state-lotteries.aspx.

10 *almost one hundred English expressions:* "95 Slang Words for Money and Their Meanings," Online-Spellcheck.com, https://blog.online-spell check.com/english/95-slang-words-money-meanings/.

10 *the four hundred biggest winners end up with more than the 150 million biggest losers:* Christopher Ingraham, "Wealth Concentration Returning to 'Levels Last Seen During the Roaring Twenties,' According to New Research," *Washington Post,* February 8, 2019, https://www.washington post.com/us-policy/2019/02/08/wealth-concentration-returning-levels -last-seen-during-roaring-twenties-according-new-research/.

10 *bribe and cheat:* Google "Operation Varsity Blues."

CHAPTER 1: JACKPOT

15 *Everingham has never been in his swimming pool:* All details and quotes, unless indicated, are from author interview with James Everingham, January 13, 2020, and follow-up emails.

15 *fourth-priciest zip code:* "Most Expensive U.S. Zip Codes in 2020: Medians on the Rise in Country's 100 Priciest Zips," Property Shark, https://www.propertyshark.com/Real-Estate-Reports/most-expensive -zip-codes-in-the-us.

15 *the Mozilla project:* Jamie Zawinski, "They Live and the Secret History of the Mozilla Logo," unnamed blog, October 2016, https://www.jwz.org /blog/2016/10/they-live-and-the-secret-history-of-the-mozilla-logo/.

16 *voted overwhelmingly for Donald Trump:* Clearfield County election results, 2016: https://clearfieldco.org/Election_Files/Archive/16GEES .HTM. Election results, 2020: https://clearfieldco.org/election_files/20GE /2020ES-Official.pdf.

16 *He never dreamed he would one day get paid to program computers:* When Everingham was a teen, he spent a summer working for his contractor brother-in-law, mixing mortar for bricks. Everingham is left -handed, and at the time, he says, left-handed bricklayers, because of some quirk of the trade that allowed them to work more efficiently, were paid an extra dollar an hour. "So I'm like, 'I'm going to be a bricklayer.' That was sort of my aspiration," he says.

16 *Even the receptionist became an overnight millionaire:* Joshua Prager, "Secretaries Get Rich in the Internet Age," ZDNet, April 21,1999, https://www.zdnet.com/article/secretaries-get-rich-in-the-internet-age/.

16 *sixteen-month-old company:* Matt Blitz, "Later, Navigator: How Netscape Won and Then Lost the World Wide Web," *Popular Mechanics,* April 4, 2019, https://www.popularmechanics.com/culture/web/a27033147/netscape-navigator-history/.

16 *$3 billion on paper:* Alice Truong, "Netscape Changed the Internet—and the World—When It Went Public 20 Years Ago," *Quartz,* August 19, 2015, https://qz.com/475279/netscape-changed-the-internet-and-the-world-when-it-went-public-20-years-ago-today/.

16 *in today's currency, was about $8.5 million:* Everingham's share was $5 million and peaked at $12 million; converted to June 2020 dollars with BLS inflation calculator: https://www.bls.gov/data/inflation_calculator.htm.

17 *he created Wardial:* Commodore Software, https://commodore.software/downloads/category/18-hack-phreak-war-dial?start=35.

18 *one of the web's first live cams:* Actually the second, according to Montulli, and the oldest still in existence: https://www.fishcam.com/.

18 *and went snorkeling:* Author email with Lou Montulli, July 21, 2020.

20 *choices are complicated:* Author interview with Nick Hanauer, June 10, 2019.

20 *1 in 292 million:* Powerball odds chart, https://www.powerball.com/games/powerball.

20 *Winning Mega Millions is even less likely:* "How to Play," Mega Millions, https://www.megamillions.com/how-to-play.

20 *incomprehensible odds:* It's roughly the same odds as for jumping into a 270,000-gallon tank filled with orange jelly beans and randomly picking out the lone yellow one. Here's what a 270,000-gallon tank looks like: https://westernlandgroup.com/index.php/2016/12/21/water-authority-brings-new-water-storage-tank-online/.

21 *"It was all gone in five years":* Author interview with Richard Watts, June 13, 2019.

21 *The last time Gallup inquired:* Zac Auter, "About Half of Americans Play State Lotteries," Gallup, July 22, 2016, https://news.gallup.com/poll/193874/half-americans-play-state-lotteries.aspx.

21 *Jason Kurland, forty-seven, represented them all:* Most details and quotes in this section are from author interviews with Kurland on February 22, 2019, and March 29, 2019.

21 *just won a $254 million Powerball jackpot:* Kevin Roose, "3 Asset Man-

agers Win $254 Million Powerball Lottery," *New York Times*, November 28, 2011, https://dealbook.nytimes.com/2011/11/28/connecticut-asset -managers-win-254-million-powerball-lottery/.

21 *quintuple the national median price:* Sydney Maki, "Greenwich Home Prices and Sales Fall," *Bloomberg*, January 16, 2019, https://www.bloomberg .com/news/articles/2019-01-17/greenwich-homes-get-cheaper-as-buyers -from-nyc-cut-their-budgets; "Median Sales Price of Houses Sold for the United States," St. Louis Fed, https://fred.stlouisfed.org/series/MSPUS.

22 *ceremonial check for $254.2 million:* Roose, "3 Asset Managers Win $254 Million Powerball Lottery."

22 *a front for the* actual *winner:* Ibid.

22 *Louise White, an eighty-one-year-old:* Suzanna Kim, "$336 Million Powerball Winner, Louise White, Rhode Island Woman, Claims Prize," ABC News, https://abcnews.go.com/Business/louise-white-rhode-island-336 -million-powerball-winner/story?id=15852662.

23 *biggest individual prize in lottery history:* Daniel Victor, "Winner of $1.5 Billion Lottery Comes Forward (Well, Sort of. Through a Lawyer)," *New York Times*, March 4, 2019, https://www.nytimes.com/2019/03 /04/us/mega-millions-lottery-winner.html.

23 *"a really easy fish to catch":* Author interview with Richard Watts, June 11, 2019.

24 *the lottery handbook:* "You Just Won Big!," California Lottery, *Winner's Handbook*, https://static.www.calottery.com/-/media/Project/calottery /PWS/PDFs/Winners-Handbook-2020.pdf?.

24 *Rockefeller used to get hundreds of letters:* Rob Reich, *Just Giving* (Princeton, NJ: Princeton University Press, 2018), 1–2.

24 *keep them off the Forbes 400:* Trump's commerce secretary, Wilbur Ross, actually lied his way *onto* it. Dan Alexander, "The Case of Wilbur Ross' Phantom $2 Billion," *Forbes*, November 7, 2017, https://www.forbes .com/sites/danalexander/2017/11/07/the-case-of-wilbur-ross-phantom -2-billion/#4a8687a97515.

24 *because of the unwanted attention:* Author interview with editor Kerry Dolan, January 25, 2019.

24 *insured for only $250,000:* "Deposit Insurance at a Glance," FDIC, https://www.fdic.gov/resources/deposit-insurance/brochures/deposits -at-a-glance/.

24 *investment accounts for $500,000:* "What SIPC Protects," SIPC, https:// www.sipc.org/for-investors/what-sipc-protects.

24 *Americans owed more than $14 trillion:* Federal Reserve Bank of New

York press release, May 5, 2020, https://www.newyorkfed.org/news events/news/research/2020/20200505.

25 *Weissglass took a career hiatus:* Author interview with Jeff Weissglass, December 3, 2019.

26 *Depatie invested in hotels:* Details and quotes from author interview with Mike Depatie, April 11, 2019, and emails.

26 *up to the helm of Kimpton Hotels:* David Eisen, "KHP Capital Partners' Mike Depatie: The Boutique Maestro," *Hotel Management,* June 16, 2016, https://www.hotelmanagement.net/own/khp-capital-partners -mike-depatie-his-move-from-kimpton-and-how-he-s-a-value-add-guy.

27 *plus a premium:* This is the "hurdle rate," the return a manager has to beat before the profit sharing kicks in.

27 *fear for his livelihood:* "My business as I have known it could be bankrupt." Author email with Mike Depatie, April 18, 2020.

28 *"That will translate to roughly $900 million":* Author email with Mike Depatie, August 1, 2020.

28 *He doesn't feel America's economic system is unfair:* Depatie did, however, say the advantages wealthy people enjoy in education are "morally corrupt."

28 *hedge fund titan Ray Dalio:* Ray Dalio, "Why and How Capitalism Needs to Be Reformed (Parts 1 & 2)," LinkedIn, April 5, 2019, https://www .linkedin.com/pulse/why-how-capitalism-needs-reformed-parts-1-2 -ray-dalio/.

29 *She fears she's becoming one of* those *people:* Author interviews with "Martha," February 2, 2019; February 11, 2019; and phone/email followups.

29 *"The Gospel of Wealth":* The original title was simply "Wealth." See *North American Review,* No. CCCXCI, June 1889: Swarthmore College, https://www.swarthmore.edu/SocSci/rbannis1/AIH19th/Carnegie .html.

31 *"so that I can actually write my books":* Martha included an expletive that I have omitted here.

CHAPTER 2: RETAIL THERAPY

33 *Being highly extrinsic doesn't presage good outcomes:* Kennon Sheldon and Tim Kasser, "Psychological Threat and Extrinsic Goal Striving," *Motivation and Emotion* 32 (March 4, 2008): 37–45, https://selfdetermina tiontheory.org/SDT/documents/2008_SheldonKasser_MOEM.pdf.

33 *a 16-ounce Japanese A5 Kobe rib eye:* Prime 112 dinner menu, https://mymlesrestaurantgroup.com/wp-content/uploads/2019/09/PRIMEDINNER.pdf.

33 *"each act of slicing, shaving, and sprinkling":* "Masa is Shibui," Masanyc.com (via Wayback Machine), https://web.archive.org/web/20170612054359/http://www.masanyc.com/experience/.

33 *Greenberg knowingly sold him:* Andy Young, "Koch vs. Greenberg Trial Begins," Drinks Business, March 28, 2013, https://www.thedrinksbusiness.com/2015/10/koch-wins-back-damages-from-wine-dealer/.

34 *a $12 million settlement:* Rupert Millar, "Koch Wins Back Damages from Wine Dealer," Drinks Business, October 1, 2015, https://www.thedrinksbusiness.com/2015/10/koch-wins-back-damages-from-wine-dealer/.

34 *"the story behind it, the critical scores":* Karen Hua, "How to Drink Like a Billionaire: A Guide to Wine, Champagne, and Spirits for the 99%," *Forbes*, November 10, 2016, https://www.forbes.com/sites/karenhua/2016/11/10/mark-oldman-how-to-drink-like-a-billionaire-be-a-rule-breaker/#2263b5612159.

34 *a $1,500 cocktail called the ARIA Sazerac:* Aly Walansky, "$1,000 on a Drink? Here Are the Most Over-the-Top Cocktails Around the Country," Today, February 8, 2018, https://www.today.com/food/most-expensive-over-top-cocktails-america-t118661.

34 *at the tender age of twenty-four:* "Phil Hellmuth Wins 1989 World Series of Poker Main Event," PokerGo, August 14, 2020, https://www.youtube.com/watch?v=Q7GAH0bnIGI.

34 *"greatest poker player of all time":* Author interviews with Phil Hellmuth, May 22–24, 2019.

34 *lifetime tournament winnings of more than $23 million:* Phil Hellmuth profile and results, CardPlayer.com, https://www.cardplayer.com/poker-players/1356-phil-hellmuth.

35 *retails for $150 to $400 a bottle:* "Dom Perignon Champagne Price Guide," Wine & Liquor Prices and Guides, BottledPrices.com, https://www.bottledprices.com/champagne/dom-perignon/.

35 *a truly bespoke item:* Jim Farver, "Bespoke This, Bespoke That, Enough Already," *New York Times*, August 8, 2016, https://www.nytimes.com/2016/08/12/fashion/mens-style/bespoke-word-meaning-usage-language.html.

35 *Vacheron Constantin Overseas:* https://www.vacheron-constantin.com/en/watches/overseas.html#filters=from-70000.0-to-90000.0&tab=0.

35 *Les Cabinotiers division:* https://www.vacheron-constantin.com/en/manu facture/craftsmanship/bespoke.html.

35 *don't bother asking what it costs:* In 2019, however, one bespoke VC timepiece fetched $435,000 at Christie's Important Watches auction in Dubai: Robin Swithinbank, "Vacheron Constantin's New, Unique Les Cabinotiers Watches Put the Focus on Minute Repeaters," *Robb Report*, May 2, 2020.

35 *priced at $3,442:* Author communication with Mobiado.

35 *"a celebration of life":* "PRO3 VG—FLEUR," Mobiado.com, https://www .mobiado.com/pro3vg-fleur.

35 *Gresso's Hamilton line:* https://gressodesign.com/smartphone-collection /hamilton.

36 *"the highest quality leather of the Nile crocodile":* They've also got a gold MacBook, if you're looking. "24ct Gold iPhone 12 Max Diamond & Sapphire Dragon Edition," Goldstriker, https://www.goldstriker.co.uk/prod uct/24ct-gold-iphone-12-pro-max-diamond-sapphire-dragon-edition/.

36 *she felt like a mark:* Author interview with "Elizabeth," September 28, 2018.

36 *"Oh, why not!":* This is what my friend Matt says when he calls someone's bet in our weekly pandemic poker game—right before he loses.

37 *the shirt Kurt Cobain wore:* "From Kurt Cobain to Janis Joplin, Listen to Tales Behind Legendary Rock Photos," *Rolling Stone*, undated post, https://www.rollingstone.com/music/music-news/from-kurt-cobain-to -janis-joplin-listen-to-tales-behind-legendary-rock-photos-123067/.

37 *"our Anglo-Saxon clients":* A careless translation, no doubt. Galeries Lafayette Paris Haussmann "Services" page, https://haussmann.galeriesla fayette.com/en/galeries-lafayette-contact-2/.

37 *"the heart of the temple of fashion":* "Enjoy a Parisian Shopping Experience," Galeries Lafayette Paris Haussmann, https://haussmann.galeries lafayette.com/en/events/enjoy-a-parisian-shopping-experience/.

37 *she sent a stylist right:* Her services, now online, have become less pricey: http://www.breejacoby.com.

37 *tailoring jargon:* "Bespoke Suits: Best Guide to Buying a Suit Including Cost, Process & Benefits," Bespoke Unit, https://bespokeunit.com/suits /guides/bespoke/.

38 *four in-person appointments:* "An Experience in Bespoke: A Year in the Making," The Armoury, undated post, https://thearmoury.com/journal /an-experience-in-bespoke-a-year-in-the-making.

38 *billionaires, kings, celebrities:* Kavita Daswani, "Nicolas Bijan Pakzad

Focuses on a New Generation of Super-Wealthy Shoppers with His Boutique at the Waldorf Astoria," *Los Angeles Times*, November 3, 2017, https://www.latimes.com/fashion/la-ig-nicolas-bijan-pakzad-20171130 -htmlstory.html.

38 *pleaded guilty in 2018 to conspiracy charges:* Special Counsel's Office plea agreement, *U.S. v. Paul J. Manafort, Jr.*, Department of Justice, https://www.justice.gov/file/1094151/download.

38 *spent more than $520,000:* Maer Roshan, "In Beverly Hills and Beyond, Bijan Carries on a Tradition of Excess and Exclusivity," *Town & Country*, October 22, 2018, https://www.townandcountrymag.com/style/fashion -trends/a23941829/nicolas-bijan-interview-paul-manafort/.

38 *Trump's sidekick had spent nearly $1.4 million on his wardrobe: USA v. Paul J. Manafort Jr. and Richard W. Gates III* (see p. 7, item 16, vendors E and H), October 27, 2017, https://assets.documentcloud.org/docu ments/4163372/Paul-Manafort-Rick-Gates-Indictment.pdf.

38 *"Really, it's normal":* Cam Wolf, "Paul Manafort's Suit Dealer Doesn't Want to Talk About It," *GQ*, August 21, 2018, https://www.gq.com/story /maximilian-katzman-paul-manafort-suit-dealer-interview.

38 *"The heart of our business is $12,000 per suit":* "You've Never Met a Tailor Like This Before," *Leaders*, July 3, 2012, http://www.leadersmag.com /issues/2012.3_Jul/Lifestyle/LEADERS-Alan-Katzman-Alan-Couture .html.

39 *The rustic three-hundred-acre resort:* This and many other property details can be found on the resort's website, TwinFarms.com.

39 *household names and billionaires:* Locals reference Madonna. Also rumored: Oprah, Ivanka Trump, and Jared Kushner—Twin Farms won't confirm. See Christopher Muther, "A $2,000 Night at New England's Top Resort. Is It Worth It?," *Boston Globe*, August 24, 2017, https://www .bostonglobe.com/lifestyle/travel/2017/08/24/night-new-england-top -resort-worth/Fc5QN4Jlt0dCXSHUsHzxzN/story.html.

39 *young apes dressed in period clothing:* "Donald Roller Wilson," ArtNet, http://www.artnet.com/artists/donald-roller-wilson/.

39 *A bee tour:* https://www.twinfarms.com/activities-and-events/.

39 *A morel-hunting expedition:* Hillary Rowland, "Twin Farms Is the Height of Luxury in Vermont," *Urbanette*, undated sponsored post, https:// urbanette.com/review-twin-farms-vermont/.

39 *a $100,000 BMW:* Muther, "A $2,000 Night at New England's Top Resort. Is It Worth It?"

39 *not a salesman but a "brand manager":* Author interview with David

Christiansen, May 14, 2019. As of late 2020, neither Christiansen nor Ketan Bahia, then general manager, still worked at the dealership.

40 *the first-ever Maserati priced under $100,000:* Associated Press, "Fiat Launches Lower-Cost Maserati at $68,000," CNBC, June 4, 2014, https://www.cnbc.com/2014/06/04/fiat-launches-lower-cost-maserati -at-68000.html.

40 *their numbers increased by 29 percent, to 93,790:* Wealth-X World Ultra Wealth Reports 2017 (p. 22) and 2020 (p. 12). America's ultrawealthy enjoyed a V-shaped COVID recovery, too. The UHNW population of North America plummeted 23 percent by the end of March 2020, but bounced back almost entirely by the end of August.

41 *a Mulsanne, base price $360,000:* "Base Ext WB Sedan," Autoblog .com, https://www.autoblog.com/buy/2019-Bentley-Mulsanne-Base__ Ext_WB_Sedan/pricing/.

43 *sold his Cabo Wabo tequila brand to Campari:* Liz Welch, "How I Did It," *Inc.*, November 2013, https://www.inc.com/magazine/201311/liz-welch /sammy-hagar.html.

43 *a much larger tax deduction:* Philip Colman, "The Tax Code Practically Subsidizes Luxury Car Leases," *Business Insider*, November 14, 2012, https://www.businessinsider.com/tax-loophole-on-luxury-cars-2012-11.

43 *there were forty-eight U.S. zip codes:* "Most Expensive U.S. Zip Codes in 2020: Medians on the Rise in Country's 100 Priciest Zips," Property Shark, November 18, 2020, https://www.propertyshark.com/Real -Estate-Reports/most-expensive-zip-codes-in-the-us.

CHAPTER 3: THE ONE

46 *nation's most expensive real estate:* Kathleen Pender, "Here's How Atherton Became the Bay Area's Most Expensive City for Housing—By Far," *San Francisco Chronicle*, July 27, 2019, https://www.sfchronicle.com /business/networth/article/Here-s-how-Atherton-became-the-Bay -Area-s-14188989.php.

46 *listing price exceeded $7 million in 2019:* "Top Most Expensive U.S. Zip Codes in 2019," Property Shark, November 18, 2019, https://www .propertyshark.com/Real-Estate-Reports/most-expensive-zip-codes-in -the-us.

46 *alarms connected directly to the police department:* Pender, "Here's How Atherton Became the Bay Area's Most Expensive City for Housing— By Far."

46 *"the 84 Divorce"*: Author interview with "Elizabeth," September 28, 2018.

46 *skipped over the city entirely:* Author interview with James Everingham, January 13, 2020, and emails.

48 *"the queen of San Francisco real estate"*: Author interview with Frank Nolan, April 11, 2019.

48 *my (upper) middle-class neighborhood:* Soaring housing prices have rendered traditionally middle-class neighborhoods unaffordable to many middle-class Oaklanders.

48 *"if a house doesn't sell in two weeks it gets a stink on it"*: Author interview with Austin Forbord, March 14, 2019. (Full disclosure: He's a friend.)

49 *leapfrogged over Moscow and London:* "Billionaire Census 2018," Wealth -X, p. 18.

50 *High-end home sales are shrouded in secrecy:* Robert Frank, "Secret Mansion Buyers Hide Behind LLCs," CNBC, October 24, 2014, https://www .cnbc.com/2014/10/24/secret-mansion-buyers-hide-behind-llcs.html.

50 *the "fancy Joneses"*: The words of Austin Forbord, who moderated this 2019 architecture and design panel at the DZINE Gallery in San Francisco.

51 *famously targeted the buses:* Ellen Hunt, "Protesters Block, Vomit on Yahoo Bus in Oakland," SFGate, April 2, 2014, https://blog.sfgate .com/techchron/2014/04/02/protesters-block-vomit-on-yahoo-bus-in -oakland/.

51 *"my gynecologist"*: Author interview with "Elizabeth," September 28, 2018.

51 *America's EB-5 visa program:* "EB-5 Visa," Wikipedia, July 31, 2020, https://en.wikipedia.org/wiki/EB-5_visa.

51 *the family of Donald Trump's son-in-law:* Emily Rauhala and William Wan, "In a Beijing Ballroom, Kushner Family Pushes $500,000 'Investor Visa' to Wealthy Chinese," *Washington Post*, May 6, 2017, https://www .washingtonpost.com/world/in-a-beijing-ballroom-kushner-family -flogs-500000-investor-visa-to-wealthy-chinese/2017/05/06/cf711e53 -eb49-4f9a-8dea-3cd836fcf287_story.html. The family's lawyers have not publicly disputed this report.

52 *Chinese investment in the Vancouver area:* Paul Roberts, "Is Your City Being Sold Off to Global Elites?," *Mother Jones*, May 8, 2017, https://www .motherjones.com/politics/2017/05/hedge-city-vancouver-chinese -foreign-capital/.

52 *Potemkin condo buildings:* Graeme Wood, "Ghost City: Realtor Finds Large Number of City Centre Condos Vacant," *Richmond News*, De-

cember 2, 2016, https://www.richmond-news.com/news/weekly-feature
/ghost-city-realtor-finds-large-number-of-city-centre-condos-vacant
-1.3640322.

52 *"They just spend their parents' money"*: Dan Levin, "Chinese Scions' Song: My Daddy's Rich and My Lamborghini's Good-Looking,"
New York Times, April 12, 2016, https://www.nytimes.com/2016/04/13
/world/americas/canada-vancouver-chinese-immigrant-wealth.html.

52 *riddled with fraud and corruption*: "EB-5 Investment Fraud SEC Whis-
tleblower Lawyers," Zuckerman Law, August 21, 2020, https://www
.zuckermanlaw.com/rewards-and-bounties-for-whistleblowers/eb-5
-investment-fraud-sec-whistleblower-lawyers/.

52 *Trump's "opportunity zones"*: Jesse Drucker and Eric Lipton, "How a
Trump Tax Break to Help Poor Communities Became a Windfall for the
Rich," *New York Times*, August 31, 2019, https://www.nytimes.com/2019
/08/31/business/tax-opportunity-zones.html.

52 *EB-5 rules were tightened:* "New Rulemaking Brings Significant Changes
of EB-5 Program," U.S. Citizenship and Immigration Services, July
23, 2019, https://www.uscis.gov/news/news-releases/new-rulemaking
-brings-significant-changes-eb-5-program.

52 *Wealth has certainly changed Bruce Jackson's Seattle neighborhood:* Author interview with Bruce "Jackson," June 10, 2019.

53 *he feared having so much money might make him reckless:* One big chunk
went to a conservation land trust that was buying up ten thousand acres
of forest land, threatened lynx habitat in Washington State. "We were
basically the primary donors to not have that turn into toilet paper," Jackson told me. He and his wife also gave stock to Seattle's Woodland Park
Zoo. "I was like, 'I'm dumb enough that I'll probably spend all this. So I
should give away this stuff before I get tempted to go buy whatever the
hell I would buy,'" he says.

53 *reported greater "house satisfaction":* Clement Bellet, "The McMansion
Effect: Top House Size and Positional Externalities in U.S. Suburbs,"
SSRN, May 15, 2019, https://papers.ssrn.com/sol3/papers.cfm?abstract
_id=3378131.

53 *increase in house satisfaction one gets when moving:* Author email with
Clément Bellet, September 16, 2019.

54 *$236,020 a year for a $20 million home:* "Understanding Property Tax,"
Treasurer and Tax Collector: City and County of San Francisco, https://
sftreasurer.org/property/understanding-property-tax.

54 *longest-serving executive director of the Nobel Foundation:* Nils Ståhle

was executive director from 1948 to 1972, per the foundation's press representative.

54 *1 percenters bitch about the helicopter noise of the 0.001 percenters:* Josh Harkinson, "Upper-Class Warfare in the Hamptons," *Mother Jones,* July 9, 2012, https://www.motherjones.com/politics/2012/07/hamptons-ira -rennert-mansion-helicopter/.

55 *the nation's second-largest homeless population:* Niall McCarthy, "The U.S. Cities with the Most Homeless People in 2018," *Forbes,* December 20, 2018, https://www.forbes.com/sites/niallmccarthy/2018/12/20 /the-u-s-cities-with-the-most-homeless-people-in-2018-infographic /#721b47671178.

55 *a series of increasingly ridiculous "giga-mansions":* Steve Chiotakis, "Is LA in a Giga-Mansion Glut?," KCRW, May 28, 2019, https://www.kcrw .com/news/shows/greater-la/from-giga-mansions-to-city-lots-housing -for-cas-richest-and-poorest/is-la-in-a-giga-mansion-glut.

55 *"completely void of homes for the ultra-affluent":* Troy McMullen, "America's Most Expensive Home? Bel Air Mansion Lists for Record $250m," *Forbes,* January 18, 2017, https://www.forbes.com/sites/troymcmullen /2017/01/18/bel-air-home-lists-for-record-250m/#399e9a6c4f04.

55 *more than 100 art installations:* Laura, "The Art and Details About the Most Expensive Home Ever Built in the U.S." (photos), *If It's Hip It's Here,* undated post, http://www.ifitshipitshere.com/the-bruce-makowsky-bil lionaire-estate-and-its-art/.

55 *the house finally sold in October 2019:* Jack Flemming, "12 Bedrooms and 21 Bathrooms: Bel-Air Mega-Mansion Sells for $94 Million," *Los Angeles Times,* October 24, 2019, https://www.latimes.com/business/real-estate /story/2019-10-24/12-bedrooms-21-bathrooms-bel-air-mega-mansion -sells-for-94-million.

55 *in the hands of one of his lenders:* Katherine Clark, "Lender Grabs Ownership of Beverly Hills Spec Home Once Listed for $100 Million," *Wall Street Journal,* February 14, 2020, https://www.wsj.com/articles/lender -grabs-ownership-of-beverly-hills-spec-home-once-listed-for-100m -11581716719.

56 *a residence he christened "the One":* Christopher Bagley, "The Making of the Most Expensive Mansion in History," *GQ,* November 11, 2015, https://www.gq.com/story/most-expensive-mansion-500-million-nile -niami.

56 *"Anyone who buys one of my homes is making a statement":* Roy Carroll, "America's Costliest House: Developer Takes $500M Gamble on

Bel Air Eyrie," *Guardian*, March 4, 2018, https://www.theguardian
.com/us-news/2018/mar/04/most-expensive-house-los-angeles-niles
-niami.

56 *positive emotions improved with rising earnings:* Andrew T. Jebb, Louis
Tay, Ed Diener, and Shigehiro Oishi, "Happiness, Income Satiation and
Turning Points Around the World," *Nature Human Behaviour* 2 (January 2018): 33–38.

57 *"It's about what the stuff says about how valuable of a person you are":*
Author interview with Sam Polk, March 5, 2019.

57 *which prompted him to change careers:* Polk now runs Everytable, a "social enterprise" aimed at making healthy food affordable and accessible
to all: "It's basically like True Food Kitchen but done in a way that costs
$5 in Compton—profitably. It's good, man."

57 *affluent folks are at a small* disadvantage: Author interview with Bob
Kenny, March 27, 2018.

CHAPTER 4: FROM THE ELITE TO THE IMPOSSIBLE

59 *"Being rich is having money; being wealthy is having time":* This quote is
sometimes attributed to author Margaret Bonanno or businessman Stephen Swid, but Beecher came first.

59 *"You feel like you're in a high-end furniture store":* Author interview with
Scott Pope, May 6, 2020.

60 *Some docs will even make house calls:* Brentwood MD primary care services, https://brentwoodmd.com/primary-care/.

61 *brutal disparities in access to health care:* This is a dicey problem, because less-advantaged citizens may benefit more from medical advancements and policies that improve overall population health than
from policies specifically aimed at reducing health disparities between
rich and poor. See David Mechanic, "Disadvantage, Inequality, and Social Policy," *Health Affairs* 21, no. 2, March/April 2002, https://www
.healthaffairs.org/doi/full/10.1377/hlthaff.21.2.48. (Yes, that's my dad.)

61 *NBA players and wealthy citizens:* Eric Levenson and Wayne Sterling,
"Why NBA Players Can Get Coronavirus Tests but Regular Americans
Are Struggling To," CNN, March 18, 2020, https://www.cnn.com/2020
/03/18/us/coronavirus-test-nba-celebrity/index.html.

61 *27 million Americans were uninsured in 2018:* Jennifer Tolbert, Kendal Orgera, Natalie Singer, and Anthony Damico, "Key Facts About the
Uninsured Population," Kaiser Family Foundation, December 13, 2019,

https://www.kff.org/uninsured/issue-brief/key-facts-about-the-un insured-population/.

61 *predicting a substantial shortage of primary care doctors:* "New AAMC Report Confirms Growing Physician Shortage," Association of American Medical Colleges, June 26, 2020, https://www.aamc.org/news-insights /press-releases/new-aamc-report-confirms-growing-physicia n-shortage.

62 *time constraints related to accumulating and managing it:* Ashley V. Whillans, Elizabeth W. Dunn, Paul Smeets, Rene Bekkers, and Michael I. Norton, "Buying Time Promotes Happiness," *PNAS* 114, no. 32 (August 8, 2017): 8523–27, https://www.pnas.org/content/114/32/8523.full.

62 *a $3.4 billion industry:* Anna Miller, "Business Concierge Services in the US," IBISWorld, August 18, 2018, p. 4. The report is proprietary, but here are some updated stats: https://www.ibisworld.com/industry-statistics /market-size/business-concierge-services-united-states.

62 *such as Delegated:* "Plans," Delegated, https://www.delegated.com /pricing.

62 *Les Clefs d'Or:* Roberto García, "Legendary Concierges, Unlocking the History of Les Clefs d'Or," Hosco, April 14, 2016, https://www.hosco .com/en/advice/article/unlocking-history-of-les-clefs-dor.

62 *more than four thousand hotel concierges:* Le Clefs d'Or USA, https:// www.lcdusa.org/interesting-facts-figures/.

62 *only about 660:* Ibid.

63 *"By Invitation Only":* "By Invitation Only," American Express, https:// global.americanexpress.com/card-benefits/detail/by-invitation-only /platinum.

63 *One former Amex concierge:* "r/IAmA—I Was a Concierge for American Express Platinum and Black Cards, AMA," Reddit, 2013, https://www .reddit.com/r/IAmA/comments/1gutp0/i_was_a_concierge_for_amer ican_express_platinum/.

63 *would transform into a Sea-Doo:* Another client called in, mortified, from the restroom of a hotel where he'd been participating in a business conference. He had gastrointestinal issues and, long story short, had pooped his pants during a panel presentation. The poor fellow managed to excuse himself, but now he was stranded. The Amex concierge called and explained this delicate situation to the hotel concierge, who ran out and bought the client new pants, underwear, and socks. (His were soiled in transit.) She also had the concierge draw him a hot bath and leave a bottle of Pepto-Bismol in his room. So yes, total lifesaver.

63 *"the black card," began as a myth:* David Mikkelson, "Black American Ex-

press Card," Snopes.com, April 18, 2011, https://www.snopes.com/fact
-check/black-american-express-card/.

64 *minimum of $350,000:* Ethan Steinberg, "The Inside Scoop on the Amex
Centurion (Black) Card," The Points Guy, May 2, 2020, https://thepoints-
guy.com/guide/amex-centurion-black-card/.

64 *the billionaire express pass:* I have a pal whose cousins, ski industry investors, have black cards. Because of it, he says, they will go helicopter
skiing and get to cut to the front of the copter line when they reach the
bottom, in front of the 1 percenters who lack black cards.

64 *the time he lost a $2,800 jacket:* The Points Guy, "Is the Amex Busi-
ness Centurion Card Worth It?," ThePointsGuy.com (via Wayback Machine), January 19, 2018, https://web.archive.org/web/20180119180623
/https://thepointsguy.com/2018/01/is-amex-centurion-worth-it/.

64 *a handful of authentic Dead Sea sand:* David Mikkelson, "Black American Express Card."

64 *Chinese billionaire Liu Yiqian:* Associated Press, "Family Will Fly Free
for Life After $170M Purchase on American Express Black Card," *Mer-
cury News,* November 23, 2015, https://www.mercurynews.com/2015
/11/23/family-will-fly-free-for-life-after-170m-purchase-on-american
-express-black-card/.

64 *hundreds of billionaires and thousands of hundred-millionaires:* Mark
Potter, "Quintessentially Goes Upmarket to Beat Recession," Reuters, June 3, 2010, https://www.reuters.com/article/us-luxury-summit
-quintessentially/quintessentially-goes-upmarket-to-beat-recession
-idUSTRE6522YN20100603.

65 *Richard Branson, rapper P. Diddy, Madonna, and author J. K. Rowling:*
Will Smale, "Mr. Fixer: The Man Who Can Arrange Anything for You,"
BBC News, May 1, 2017, https://www.bbc.com/news/business-39691931.
In a November 6, 2020, email, a spokeswoman describes the company's
members as "a fascinating, inspiring and ambitious group of individuals, including global CEOs, entrepreneurs, and small and large business
owners, as well as influencers, actors, sporting stars and musicians."

65 *with a bunch of ponies:* "Catherine Mills: All in a Day's Work," The Gait-
post, December 3, 2016, https://www.thegaitpost.com/catherine-mills/.

65 *the consumption habits of ultrawealthy Americans and Canadians:*
"World Ultra Wealth Report 2017," Wealth-X, p. 17.

65 *"deep analysis of every student's past studies and future aspirations":*
Quintessentially Facebook post, August 15, 2019, https://www.facebook
.com/QuintessentiallyLondon/posts/10162058673905109.

65 *"No request is too small or too big"*: Author interview with Jacob Zucker, September 23, 2015.

65 *one million British pounds*: Hope Coke, "From Private Jets to Superyachts: How the Super Rich Are Doing Socially Distanced Holidays," *Tatler*, June 29, 2020, https://www.tatler.com/article/super-rich-socially -distanced-holidays-1-million-package-private-jets-superyachts.

66 *"relentless, bossy fucker"*: Charlotte Edwardes and Susannah Butter, "Don't Be Such a Waster: London's Food Waste Czar Ben Elliot," *Evening Standard*, May 14, 2019, https://www.standard.co.uk/news/london/don -t-be-such-a-waster-londons-food-waste-czar-a4141441.html.

66 *Dedicated, Elite, and Quintessence:* Author communications with Quintessentially, November 2020. The company gave pricing for the middle tier only, noting that prices are customized somewhat to the needs and demands of individual members.

67 *a fun-packed Las Vegas weekend:* Tiger Jam, https://tigerjam.com/.

67 *Sam (a pseudonym):* Sam was willing to talk on the record, but his PR team advised against it, and as I was at Tiger Jam as Hellmuth's guest, I will respect this request.

67 *"I mean, he's a billionaire":* Not according to *Forbes,* and by my factchecker's calculations, Guber's Los Angeles compound, which Hellmuth said was worth $200 million, is worth less than $50 million.

68 *a $205 million contract with the Oklahoma City Thunder:* Adrian Wojnarowski, "Russell Westbrook Signs 5-Year, $205M Extension with Thunder," ESPN, September 29, 2017, https://www.espn.com/nba/story/_/id /20862559/oklahoma-city-thunder-star-russell-westbrook-agrees-5 -year-205m-extension.

68 *"they're given incredible access":* Author interview with Richard Watts, June 11, 2019.

68 *"The undeserved access to whatever you want":* Author interview with Nick Hanauer, June 10, 2019.

69 *selling access is a risky proposition for scientists:* It may be risky for the public, too. See Stephanie M. Lee, "JetBlue's Founder Helped Fund a Stanford Study That Said the Coronavirus Wasn't That Deadly," *Buzz-Feed News,* May 15, 2020, https://www.buzzfeednews.com/article/ste phaniemlee/stanford-coronavirus-neeleman-ioannidis-whistleblower.

69 *including that of Joi Ito:* Marc Tracy and Tiffany Hsu, "Director of M.I.T.'s Media Lab Resigns After Taking Money from Jeffrey Epstein," *New York Times,* September 7, 2019, https://www.nytimes.com/2019/09/07/busi ness/mit-media-lab-jeffrey-epstein-joichi-ito.html.

69 *he's played golf with Tiger:* Author interview with Erwin Raphael, July 14, 2019.

69 *He's tight with Westbrook:* Indeed, Russell came over and greeted Raphael warmly that evening.

70 *"$300,000 up front":* This is in the ballpark of what I've seen mentioned online, but I can't verify it because the Riviera Country Club informed me they don't reveal their rates to outsiders.

CHAPTER 5: ENTOURAGE

73 *"You just have to do it":* Author interview with "Martha," February 12, 2019.

73 *a racehorse . . . pricey to maintain:* Paul Sullivan, "Investing in a Racehorse Without Breaking the Bank," *New York Times*, May 4, 2012, https://www.nytimes.com/2012/05/05/your-money/investing-in-a-racehorse-without-losing-yourshirt.html.

73 *a trainer, a veterinarian, a bloodstock agent:* "Select your Advisors," Owner View, https://www.ownerview.com/getting-started/select-your-advisors.

74 *"All you see when you look forward to being rich":* Author interview with Richard Watts, June 11, 2019.

74 *Kurland was indicted by federal authorities:* Jaclyn Peiser, "The 'Lottery Lawyer' Promised Winners He'd Protect Their Money. Then He Stole Millions, Feds Say," *Washington Post*, August 19, 2020, https://www.washingtonpost.com/nation/2020/08/19/lottery-lawyer-kurland-fraud-mafia/.

74 *Dealing with his family's wealth has proved quite the headache:* Author interview with Michael (last name withheld), May 16, 2019.

74 *family wealth has taken an emotional toll:* Author interview with "Jonathan," November 27, 2018.

75 *"I'm a lawyer, not a therapist":* Author interview with an estate lawyer who spoke on condition of anonymity, March 6, 2019.

76 *Sherman . . . had one woman nearly cancel their interview:* Rachel Sherman, "What the Rich Won't Tell You," *New York Times Magazine*, September 8, 2017, https://www.nytimes.com/2017/09/08/opinion/sunday/what-the-rich-wont-tell-you.html.

76 *Sherman struggled to find subjects:* Rachel Sherman, *Uneasy Street* (Princeton, NJ: Princeton University Press, 2017), 18–20.

76 *"I think it just feels so transgressive":* Author interview with Rachel Sherman, June 12, 2019.

76 *Epstein's pedophile nest:* Holly Aguirre, " 'The Girls Were Just So Young: The Horrors of Jeffrey Epstein's Private Island,' " *Vanity Fair*, July 20, 2019, https://www.vanityfair.com/news/2019/07/horrors-of-jeffrey-epstein -private-island.

76 *"only the little people pay taxes":* Enid Nemy, "Leona Helmsley, Hotel Queen, Dies at 87," *New York Times*, August 20, 2007, https://www.ny times.com/2007/08/20/nyregion/20cnd-helmsley.html.

76 *Howard Schultz objecting:* Arwa Mahdawi, "Don't Call Howard Schultz a Billionaire. He's a 'Person of Means,' " *The Guardian*, February 6, 2019, https://www.theguardian.com/commentisfree/2019/feb/06/dont-call -howard-schultz-billionairewealth-washing.

77 *"No one asks that question":* Rachel Sherman, "What the Rich Won't Tell You."

77 *"Well, that is a bit of a taboo":* Author interview with Mike Depatie, April 11, 2019.

77 *Estate planning "had never occurred to me":* All quotes and details from author interview with Amy Shelf, February 1, 2019—and follow-up emails.

78 *the 50th through 90th wealth and income percentiles:* Author email with Gabriel Zucman, September 14, 2020. Income threshold figures (which I've translated into 2019 dollars) are from Thomas Piketty, Emmanuel Saez, and Gabriel Zucman, "Distributional National Accounts: Methods and Estimates for the United States," *Quarterly Journal of Economics* 133 no. 2 (2018): 553–609 (updated series, September 2020).

79 *"Everybody buys himself an IPO thing":* Fiddler quotes and details from author interviews with Jerry Fiddler, August 18, 2015, and April 29, 2020, and follow-up emails.

79 *the fifty-first-wealthiest person in tech:* Associated Press, "Technology's Richest: 12 at Microsoft," *Seattle Times*, September 22, 1997, http://community.seattletimes.nwsource.com/archive/?date=1997 0922&slug=2561899.

79 *when Intel bought Wind River:* "Intel to Acquire Wind River Systems for Approximately $884 Million," Wind River Systems, https://www.win driver.com/news/press/pr.html?ID=6921.

79 *partnered with a lab colleague to launch Wind River:* It began as a micro-consulting firm with just one employee (Fiddler) and a single client. Then Fiddler's landlord announced he was evicting him on the very day that Melissa, then his girlfriend, was laid off from her job as a schoolteacher. They decided to go traveling for a year. Fiddler called his

LBNL colleague David Wilner to see if he would be willing to take over his consulting contract, not expecting a yes, as his friend had a steady paycheck and a young daughter to support. But Wilner had just had a huge fight with his boss. "He said, 'Sure, I'm in,'" Fiddler recalls. When he and Melissa returned from their travels, he officially made Wilner his partner and the two men set about building a consulting firm. Five years later, at 100 employees, they decided to pivot to making products instead. "I wanted to have something to sell other than my hours," Fiddler explains.

79 *NASA selected it over Microsoft's products for the Mars Rover:* "Wind River Powers NASA's Space Exploration—Mars Rovers Lands Safely, Stardust Spacecraft Completes Its Journey to the Comet," Wind River press release, https://www.windriver.com/news/press/pr.html?ID=82.

81 *specializes in estate and taxation issues:* Myron Sugarman, partner, Loeb & Loeb LP, https://www.loeb.com/en/people/s/sugarman-myron.

81 *a boutique wealth firm called Ohana Advisors:* https://www.ohanaadvisors.com.

81 *"We tend to have this perspective that it's my money":* This and other quotes and details from author interview with Dennis Covington, January 31, 2019.

83 *The first family office came about in 1838:* "EY Family Office Guide," EY Global Family Business Center of Excellence, 2016, https://assets.ey.com/content/dam/ey-sites/ey-com/en_us/topics/tax/ey-family-office-guide-2016.pdf.

83 *costs $10 million a year or more to operate:* Ibid., 20.

84 *made hundreds of families extraordinarily rich, practically overnight:* "Our History," Family Office Exchange, https://www.familyoffice.com/about-fox/our-history; also see: Gregg A. Jarrell, "Takeovers and Leveraged Buyouts," *The Concise Encyclopedia of Economics*, Library of Economics and Liberty, undated, https://www.econlib.org/library/Enc1/TakeoversandLeveragedBuyouts.html.

84 *380 member families with average investible assets of $500 million:* "Kristi Kuechler: Managing Director, Investor Market, Family Office Exchange," Middle Market Growth, http://lp.familyoffice.com/rs/974-HBC-453/images/ACG-Kuechler-QA-2018NovDec-article.pdf.

85 *"only morons pay the estate tax":* Julie Hirschfeld Davis and Kate Kelly, "Two Bankers Are Selling Trump's Tax Plan. Is Congress Buying?," *New York Times*, August 28, 2017, https://www.nytimes.com/2017/08/28/us/politics/trump-tax-plan-cohn-mnuchin.html.

85 *Harvey Dale . . . offers his reassurance:* Author interview with Harvey Dale, March 5, 2019.

85 *judge Learned Hand:* "Learned Hand," Wikipedia, August 20, 2020, https://en.wikipedia.org/wiki/Learned_Hand.

85 *a businesswoman who tried (and failed):* Helvering v. Gregory, 69 F.2d 809 (2d Cir. 1934), Justia Law, https://law.justia.com/cases/federal/appellate -courts/F2/69/809/1562063/.

85 *a dissent stemming from a rich couple's divorce: Commissioner of Internal Revenue v. Newman,* 159 F.2d 848 (2d Cir. 1947), Justia Law, https://law .justia.com/cases/federal/appellate-courts/F2/159/848/1565902/.

86 *"I'm a completely irresponsible person":* Author interview with James Everingham, January 13, 2020.

86 *you have relinquished your control:* Julia Kagan, "Irrevocable Trust," Investopedia, April 5, 2020, https://www.investopedia.com/terms/i/irre vocabletrust.asp.

86 *epic lawsuits and family feuds:* Amy Feldman, "When Trusts Go Bad," *Barron's,* March 1, 2014, https://www.barrons.com/articles/lessons-from -trusts-gone-bad-1393663878.

87 *need a "Non-Belonger" license:* "Purchasing Property in the BVI," Sotheby's International Realty, https://www.bvisothebysrealty.com/eng /purchasing-property-in-the-bvi.

88 *depends on the amount of assets they have under management:* Seth Corkin, "The AUM Model Can Be a 'Corrosive Conflict of Interest,'" *Financial Planning,* https://www.financial-planning.com/opinion/financial-advisor -compensation-flat-fee-aum-model.

88 *"I feel like I want to live in a society where I'm taxed":* Author interview with Michael (last name withheld), May 16, 2019.

88 *"The right question is, How much is too little?":* Author interview with Richard Watts, June 11, 2019.

88 *horror stories Watts shares in his books:* See Entitlemania.com.

CHAPTER 6: THE PSYCHOLOGY OF CONSUMPTION

91 *liken our capitalistic social structure to a religion:* Tim Kasser and Allen D. Kanner, eds., *Psychology and Consumer Culture* (Washington, DC: American Psychological Association, 2003), 12 (scroll past the PowerPoint), https://www.yutorah.org/_cdn/_materials/PDF-503648.pdf.

91 *"materialistic values orientation":* Ibid., 13.

91 *"250 of the richest guys in the country"*: Author interview with Richard Watts, June 11, 2019.

91 *"Wall Street doesn't draw people that are interested in doing something specific"*: Author interview with Sam Polk, March 5, 2019.

92 *"This is completely at odds with what consumer culture tells us"*: Author email with Tim Kasser, November 27, 2013.

92 *psychology researchers Patricia and Jacob Cohen*: Tim Kasser, *The High Price of Materialism* (Cambridge, MA: MIT Press, 2002), 14–17.

92 *Marketing and media are part of the reason*: Kasser and Kanner, *Psychology and Consumer Culture*, 11–12.

92 *when people experience "psychological threat"*: Kennon Sheldon and Tim Kasser, "Psychological Threat and Extrinsic Goal Striving," *Motivation and Emotion* 32 (March 4, 2008): 37–45, https://selfdeterminationthe ory.org/SDT/documents/2008_SheldonKasser_MOEM.pdf.

93 *"Most really successful people are driven by fear"*: Author interview with Doug Holladay, May 9, 2019.

93 *A number of my subjects . . . didn't think superlative wealth changes people*: James Everingham and Mike Depatie, among others.

94 *Lion skin rug (female, lioness)*: "I'm DEAD BROKE. And I Lost My Super Bowl Ring," TMZ, April 6, 2012, https://www.tmz.com/2012/04/06 /warren-sapp-broke-super-bowl-ring/.

95 *he signed a $36 million contract with the Tampa Bay Buccaneers*: This and most of the Sapp details are from "The Play-by-Play of Warren Sapp's 59-Page Bankruptcy Filing," *Tampa Bay Times*, April 14, 2012, https://www.tampabay.com/sports/football/bucs/the-play-by-play-of -warren-sapps-59-page-bankruptcy-filing/1225135/.

95 *a boathouse, a lazy-river pool, and an outdoor kitchen*: "Warren Sapp's House Is Up for Sale in 'The New York Times,'" *USA Today*, September 30, 2012, https://www.usatoday.com/story/gameon/2012/09/30/warren -sapp-house-new-york-times/1604095/.

95 *director Cameron Crowe followed around as inspiration*: Larry Getlen, "Leigh Steinberg, the Real-Life Jerry Maguire," *New York Post*, January 11, 2014, https://nypost.com/2014/01/11/leigh-steinberg-the-real-life-jerry -maguire/.

95 *eight No. 1 NFL draft picks*: James Vlahos, "Show Leigh Steinberg the Money (Again)," *New York Times Magazine*, January 15, 2015, https:// www.nytimes.com/2015/01/18/magazine/show-leigh-steinberg-the -money-again-.html.

95 *Mahomes re-upped:* Mark Maske, "Patrick Mahomes Agrees to 10-Year Contract Extension with Chiefs Worth $450 Million," *Washington Post*, July 6, 2020, https://www.washingtonpost.com/sports/2020/07/06/patrick-mahomes-contract-extension-chiefs-10-years/.

96 *"I guarantee I spent $1 million on jewelry":* Raison, Searcy, and Russell quotes from *Broke* (clip 2), *ESPN 30 for 30*, https://criticalcommons.org/Members/JJWooten/clips/espn-30-for-30-broke-clip-2/view.

97 *"a really good chance that they haven't been exposed to substantial amounts of money":* Author interview with Erwin Raphael, July 14, 2019.

97 *These athletes have "no point of reference":* Author interview with "Frank," October 11, 2019.

100 *get it in their heads to open a bar:* Per Leigh Steinberg.

100 *a notable increase in materialism among high school seniors:* Jean M. Twenge and Tim Kasser, "Generational Changes in Materialism and Work Centrality, 1976–2007: Associations with Temporal Changes in Societal Insecurity and Materialistic Role Modeling," *Personality and Social Psychology Bulletin*, May 1, 2013, https://journals.sagepub.com/doi/abs/10.1177/0146167213484586.

100 *"undermine our ability to work cooperatively":* Kasser and Kanner, *Psychology and Consumer Culture*, 20.

100 *our values and attitudes are not fixed in stone:* Tim Kasser, "Materialistic Values and Goals," *Annual Review of Psychology* 67 (January 2016): 489–514, https://www.annualreviews.org/doi/pdf/10.1146/annurev-psych-122414-033344.

101 *"Similarly, in studying a group of highly extrinsic adults":* Author email with Tim Kasser, November 27, 2013.

101 *released a statement:* "Business Roundtable Redefines the Purpose of a Corporation to Promote 'An Economy That Serves All Americans,'" Business Roundtable statement, August 19, 2019, https://www.businessroundtable.org/business-roundtable-redefines-the-purpose-of-a-corporation-to-promote-an-economy-that-serves-all-americans.

101 *observers panned this as empty rhetoric:* Kevin Dugan, "Critics Cast Doubt on CEO Pledge to Downgrade Shareholders," *New York Post*, August 19, 2019, https://nypost.com/2019/08/19/ceos-say-corporations-should-no-longer-put-shareholders-first/; also: Andrew Winston, "Is the Business Roundtable Statement Just Empty Rhetoric?," *Harvard Business Review*, August 30, 2019, https://hbr.org/2019/08/is-the-business-roundtable-statement-just-empty-rhetoric.

101 *B corporations, a fledgling business movement:* https://bcorporation.net/.

101 *"a tribe of leaders trying to become better people"*: "What Is PathNorth?," https://www.pathnorth.com/what-is-pathnorth.

101 *"terribly lonely and disconnected"*: Thomas J. Saporito, "It's Time to Acknowledge CEO Loneliness," *Harvard Business Review*, February 15, 2012, https://hbr.org/2012/02/its-time-to-acknowledge-ceo-lo.

CHAPTER 7: LOSING TRUST

102 *"Beggars don't envy billionaires"*: Michael Kraus, "Beggars Do Not Envy Millionaires: Social Comparison, Socioeconomic Status, and Subjective Well-Being," in E. Diener, S. Oishi, & L. Tay, eds., *Handbook of Well-Being*, Noba Scholar Handbook Series: Subjective Well-Being (Salt Lake City: DEF, 2018), 3–5, https://static1.squarespace.com/static/5432c0d8e4b0fc3eccdb0500/t/5a620f1dc83025e142af134b/1516375837501/KrausSWB2018.pdf.

103 *people's self-reported happiness decreased*: Erzo Luttmer, "Neighbors as Negatives: Relative Earnings and Well-Being," https://users.nber.org/~luttmer/relative.pdf.

103 *we have become increasingly segregated by wealth*: Sean F. Reardon and Kendra Bischoff, "Growth in the Residential Segregation of Families by Income, 1970–2009," US2010 Project, November 2011, https://s4.ad.brown.edu/projects/diversity/Data/Report/report111111.pdf.

104 *45 percent of families lived at one extreme or the other*: Sean F. Reardon and Kendra Bischoff, "The Continuing Income Segregation, 2007–2012," Stanford Center for Education Policy Analysis, March 2016, https://cepa.stanford.edu/sites/default/files/the%20continuing%20increase%20in%20income%20segregation%20march2016.pdf.

104 *the CEOs of the 350 largest public companies*: Lawrence Mishel and Jori Kandra, "CEO Compensation Surged 14% in 2019 to $21.3 Million," Economic Policy Institute, August 18, 2020, https://www.epi.org/publication/ceo-compensation-surged-14-in-2019-to-21-3-million-ceos-now-earn-320-times-as-much-as-a-typical-worker/.

104 *Tim O'Reilly discovered as much*: Author interview with Tim O'Reilly, April 26, 2019.

104 *the very first ad-supported website*: Ibid. Also see: "Global Network Navigator," Wikipedia, https://en.wikipedia.org/wiki/Global_Network_Navigator.

104 *about $21 million*: $9 million in stock, $2 million in cash, and a $3 million investment in O'Reilly's Songbird Studios; $14 million total. I

converted from June 1995 dollars to August 2020 with this calculator: https://www.bls.gov/data/inflation_calculator.htm.

105 *income segregation increased more . . . in metropolitan areas with larger increases in income inequality:* Reardon and Bischoff, "Continuing Income Segregation."

105 *less economic mobility than those where rich and poor commingle:* Patrick Sharkey and Bryan Graham, "Mobility and the Metropolis," Pew Charitable Trusts, December 4, 2013. https://www.pewtrusts.org/en/research -and-analysis/reports/0001/01/01/mobility-and-the-metropolis.

105 *lives with his wife in a luxury condo:* Author interview with Erwin Raphael, July 14, 2019.

105 *Everingham doesn't regret moving to Ross:* Author interview with James Everingham, January 13, 2020.

106 *She had "a profound wish not to be separate from everybody else":* Author interview with "Martha," February 1, 2019.

107 *"Not like I'm holier-than-thou":* Author interview with Bruce Jackson, June 10, 2019.

107 *"We just went from solidly 'middle class'":* Author email with "Sally," September 17, 2019.

108 *within Silicon Valley's top 7 percent:* PK, "Average, Median, Top 1%, and Income Percentile by City in 2020," *DQYDJ*, https://dqydj.com/income -percentile-by-city-calculator/. Even if they earned half as much, Pew's income calculator (based on 2018 numbers) puts them in the "upper income" category (top 30 percent) for a family of four: Jesse Bennett, Richard Fry, and Rakesh Kachhar, "Are You in the American Middle Class? Find Out with Our Income Calculator," Pew Research Center, July 23, 2020, https://www.pewresearch.org/fact-tank/2020/07/23/are-you-in-the -american-middle-class/.

108 *Some of Rachel Sherman's affluent New Yorkers described themselves similarly:* Rachel Sherman, "What the Rich Won't Tell You," *New York Times Magazine*, September 8, 2017, https://www.nytimes.com/2017 /09/08/opinion/sunday/what-the-rich-wont-tell-you.html.

108 *ranged from about $30,000 to $136,500:* Data expressed in 2019 dollars. The researchers define "middle class" as 50th through 90th income percentiles, per author email with Zucman, September 14, 2020. *Average* middle-class net worth per adult was roughly $265,000, Saez and Zucman found. Other researchers, using 2016 numbers and defining "middle class" as two-thirds to double the national median income, found that the median middle-class family of three earned $48,500 to $145,500:

Bennett, Fry, and Kachhar, "Are You in the American Middle Class?";
Samuel Stebbins and Evan Comen, "How much do you need to be in the
top 1% for every state? Here's the list," *USA Today*, July 1, 2020, https://
www.usatoday.com/story/money/2020/07/01/how-much-you-need-to
-make-to-be-in-the-1-in-every-state/112002276/.

108 *required a* minimum *household income of $481,000:* These are Saez and
Zucman's national 2019 figures, but 1 percent income varies by region.
An analysis based on earlier data found that a household needs from
$319,000 (West Virginia) to $827,000 (Connecticut) to make the cut:
Ibid.

108 *a relative who fell substantially behind on her bills:* Author interview
with Mike Depatie, April 11, 2019.

108 *"I know it's not going to get paid back":* Author interview with Jerry Fiddler, August 18, 2015.

109 *Everingham is no longer on speaking terms with one sibling:* Author interview with James Everingham, January 13, 2020, and follow-up emails.

110 *"'Okay, let's drop them—they don't have a Mercedes!'":* Jackson drives a
used Toyota pickup and a Mini Cooper. He does, however, splurge on
fancy bikes.

110 *"If you have only millions, you are not a B person":* Author interview with
Richard Watts, July 15, 2019.

CHAPTER 8: THE MARRIAGE PREMIUM

112 *71 percent of college graduates had married their like:* Philip N. Cohen,
"Educational endogamy," Family Inequality (blog), April 4, 2013, https://
familyinequality.wordpress.com/2013/04/04/educational-endogamy/.

112 *Researchers call this "positive assortative mating":* Jeremy Greenwood,
Nezih Guner, Georgi Korcharkov, Cezar Santos, "Marry Your Like: As-
sortative Mating and Income Inequality," National Bureau of Economic
Research, January 2014, https://www.nber.org/papers/w19829.pdf.

112 *the wealth of a potential partner's family may factor into our selection criteria:* Kerwin Kofi Charles, Erik Hurst, and Alexandra Killewald, "Marital Sorting and Parental Wealth," Population Association of America,
September 22, 2012, https://scholar.harvard.edu/files/akillewald/files
/marital_sorting_and_parental_wealth.pdf.

113 *Sorting by wealth and education may exacerbate economic disparities:*
Greenwood et al., "Marry Your Like: Assortative Mating and Income Inequality." Not all researchers are on the same page about this. See Chris-

tine R. Schwartz, "Trends and Variation in Assortative Mating: Causes and Consequences," *Annual Review of Sociology* 39:451–70, July 2013, https://www.annualreviews.org/doi/pdf/10.1146/annurev-soc-071312-145544.

113 *Relationships . . . are by no means impossible:* Jessi Streib, "Marrying Out of Your Social Class Will Be Hard, but Not Doomed," Quartz, April 19, 2015, https://qz.com/386314/marrying-out-of-your-social-class-will-be-hard-but-not-doomed/.

113 *"The very day after the IPO, I became a lot more attractive":* Author interview with James Everingham, January 13, 2020.

113 *Michael . . . whose wealthy parents subsidized his lifestyle:* Author interview with Michael (last name withheld), May 16, 2019.

114 *the "cold shower fax":* Author interview with Richard Watts, July 15, 2019.

114 *without bringing up her ex:* Author interviews with "Martha," February 1, 2019, and February 11, 2019, and follow-up emails.

116 *"hedge funders who were married to women of great intellect and promise":* Michael Mechanic, "Gary Shteyngart Wants You to Invest in His Hedge Fund," *Mother Jones*, September 3, 2018, https://www.motherjones.com/media/2018/09/gary-shteyngart-new-novel-lake-success-invest-hedge-fund-wealth-rich-1/.

116 *Elizabeth . . . learned her lesson the first time around:* Author interview with "Elizabeth," September 28, 2018.

118 *Wealthy men outnumber wealthy women:* Men were 90.1 percent of the global $30 million-plus bracket in 2019, per Wealth-X, "World Ultra Wealth Report 2020," p. 28.

118 *the founder of Serious Matchmaking:* "Luxury Matchmaking Service," Janis and Carly Spindel: Serious Matchmaking, July 29, 2020, https://janisspindelmatchmaker.com/.

119 *an extraordinary statistic:* And one I have no way of confirming.

119 *"allergy to fat":* This may not be entirely wealth-related: David M. Buss, "Sex Differences in Human Mate Preferences: Evolutionary Hypotheses Tested in 37 Cultures," *Behavioral and Brain Sciences* 12 (1989): 1–49, http://philipperushton.net/wp-content/uploads/2015/02/iq-race-sex-gender-survey-mate-buss-nyborg-rushton-buss-behavioral-brain-sciences-19891.pdf; also see: Quentin Fontrell, "Rich Women Like Rich Men, and Rich Men Like Slender Women," *MarketWatch*, May 23, 2016, https://www.marketwatch.com/story/rich-women-like-rich-men-and-rich-men-like-slender-women-2015-09-28.

121 *insanely wealthy parents hire a detective:* IMDB, "Crazy Rich Asians (2018)," undated plot summary, https://www.imdb.com/title/tt3104988/plotsummary.

CHAPTER 9: MY BODYGUARD

123 *dark hair and expressive eyebrows:* "Female Bodyguards Training and Services, Nannyguards in USA," Athena Academy, https://www.athenaworldwide.com/about-us.

123 *the Nannyguard concept:* "Nannyguards—Female Bodyguards Who Integrate with Personal Security," https://www.nannyguards.com/.

123 *why not make them part of the solution instead?:* Relevant information and quotes from author interview with Denida Zinxhiria, November 19, 2019.

124 *lose touch with how normal people live:* Author interview with James Everingham, January 13, 2020.

124 *"We assemble thousands of operatives":* Andrew Carnegie, "Wealth," *North American Review*, June 1889: Swarthmore College, https://www.swarthmore.edu/SocSci/rbannis1/AIH19th/Carnegie.html.

125 *People just want their privacy:* Author interview with Richard Watts, July 13, 2020.

126 *have felt compelled to enlist security firms:* Author interviews with Denida Zinxhiria, Christian West, and Tom Gaffney; also Josh Harkinson, "These Guys Will Stop You from Killing Your Boss," *Mother Jones*, August 8, 2011, https://www.motherjones.com/politics/2011/08/ceo-bodyguard-executive-protection/.

126 *"We got a world-class security system":* Author interview with Phil Hellmuth, May 23, 2019.

126 *"That depends on your level of paranoia":* Author interview with a high-level attorney who spoke on the condition of anonymity, March 6, 2019.

127 *Christian West's business:* "About Us," AS Solution, August 21, 2020, https://assolution.com/about-us/.

127 *"I don't like the word 'paranoid'":* This and other quotes and company details from author interview with Christian West, November 19, 2019.

128 *reported revenue spikes of 30 to 50 percent:* Josh Harkinson, "These Guys Will Stop You from Killing Your Boss."

128 *"crime prevention through environmental design":* "Protect Your Home with CPTED," Pura, April 14, 2019, http://puraglobal.com/protect-home-cpted/.

128 *an adrenaline-soaked clip:* "Portrait of an Operator," *Kidnap & Rescue*, Discovery Channel, https://www.dailymotion.com/video/x2p9ac6.

129 *is rare in the United States and almost never related to wealth:* "A 10-Year Analysis of Attempted Abductions and Related Incidents," National Center for Missing and Exploited Children, June 2016, https://www.missingkids.org/content/dam/missingkids/pdfs/ncmec-analysis/attemptedabductions10yearanalysisjune2016.pdf.

129 *"You're always afraid of being kidnapped or killed or tortured":* Anonymous, "What Is It Like to Be the Child of a Billionaire?," Quora, October 3, 2015, https://www.quora.com/What-is-it-like-to-be-the-child-of-a-billionaire; also see David Sparazynski's response to "Security: What Does It Feel Like to Have a Full-Time Bodyguard?," Quora, January 9, 2017, https://www.quora.com/Security-What-does-it-feel-like-to-have-a-full-time-bodyguard.

131 *scaled the walls of Halle Berry's estate:* Nancy Dillon, "Halle Berry Stalker, Richard Franco, Sentenced to 386 Days in Jail and Five Years Probation," New York *Daily News*, January 19, 2012, https://www.nydailynews.com/entertainment/gossip/halle-berry-stalker-richard-franco-sentenced-386-days-jail-years-probation-article-1.1008885.

131 *into the Hollywood Hills mansion of Sandra Bullock:* Richard Winton and Kate Mather, "Sandra Bullock Came Face-to-Face with Stalker Outside Her Bedroom, Documents Show," *Los Angeles Times*, July 15, 2014, https://www.latimes.com/local/lanow/la-me-ln-sandra-bullock-stalker-bedroom-20140715-story.html.

131 *Hollywood's best-paid actress that year:* Rebecca Hawkes, "Sandra Bullock Is Hollywood's Highest Paid Actress," *The Telegraph*, August 4, 2014, https://www.telegraph.co.uk/culture/film/film-news/11012632/Sandra-Bullock-is-Hollywoods-highest-paid-actress.html.

131 *Gaffco Ballistics:* "Residential Safe Rooms," Gaffco Ballistics, http://www.gaffco.com/safe-rooms/residential.

131 *designed and built hundreds of luxury safe rooms:* Gaffney got his start building urban check-cashing outlets, which were basically steel boxes, primitive safe rooms: author interview with Tom Gaffney, December 3, 2019.

133 *"Some of the weaponry I've seen":* Ibid. Gaffney has scored federal contracts armoring convoy trucks and building safe rooms in embassies and consulates abroad.

133 *Some of the protesters reportedly carried plastic pitchforks:* Mark Harrington, "Southampton Protesters Demand Higher Taxes for Bloomberg,

Other Billionaires," *Newsday*, July 2, 2020, https://www.newsday.com /long-island/suffolk/pitchfork-caravan-protesters-east-end-1.46279202.

CHAPTER 10: THE OFFSPRING

135 *"challenges that can accompany family money"*: "Our Team," North Bridge Advisory Group, LLC, http://www.northbridgeag.com/our-team.html.

135 *leave behind about $59 trillion:* This is Havens's 2011 calculation; his original forecast, in 1998, was $52 trillion from 1998–2052. See: John J. Havens and Paul G. Schervish, "A Golden Age of Philanthropy Still Beckons: National Wealth Transfer and Potential for Philanthropy," Center on Wealth and Philanthropy, Boston College, estimates compiled December 2011, report released May 28, 2014, https://www.bc.edu/con tent/dam/files/research_sites/cwp/pdf/A%20Golden%20Age%20of%20 Philanthropy%20Still%20Bekons.pdf.

135 *set out to survey ultra-high-net-worth families:* "Wealth and Commonwealth Newsletter Volume 13," Center on Wealth and Philanthropy, February 2008, https://www.bc.edu/content/dam/files/research_sites/cwp /ssi/vol13.html.

135 *"you've got a dilemma":* Author interview with Bob Kenny, March 27, 2018.

136 *inheritors group Jeff Weissglass got involved with:* Jeff is the inheritor/ attorney we met in our chapter 1.

137 *It would be worth about $14 million today:* About $6 million in 1986 dollars. This assumes all dividends were reinvested. I used this calculator: https://dqydj.com/sp-500-return-calculator/.

137 *includes the following scene:* Chuck Collins, *Born on Third Base* (White River Junction, VT: Chelsea Green, 2016), 9.

138 *for a piece in* The Atlantic: Graeme Wood, "Secret Fears of the Super-Rich," *The Atlantic*, April 2011, https://www.theatlantic.com/magazine /archive/2011/04/secret-fears-of-the-super-rich/308419/.

138 *lest they cause lasting damage:* On the whole, my wealthy subjects feel their kids are doing well, although one was concerned one of his sons had become "aimless." But parental wealth was very much a double-edged sword for subjects born into it—Tracy Gary went through much therapy to get to where she is now.

139 *"He could be very cruel":* Author interview with Michael (last name withheld), May 16, 2019.

140 *not just one book, but two:* http://www.entitlemania.com/.

140 *"They're not creating self-value from failure and then recovery"*: Author interview with Richard Watts, June 11, 2019.

141 *suicide clusters, too, in . . . Palo Alto*: Kyle Spencer, "It Takes a Suburb: A Town Struggles to Ease Student Stress," *New York Times*, April 5, 2017, https://www.nytimes.com/2017/04/05/education/edlife/overachievers -student-stress-in-high-school-.html; also see: Yanan Wang, "CDC Investigates Why So Many Students in Wealthy Palo Alto, Calif., Commit Suicide," *Washington Post*, March 30, 2019, https://www.washington-post.com/news/morning-mix/wp/2016/02/16/cdc-investigates-why -so-many-high-school-students-in-wealthy-palo-alto-have-committed -suicide/.

141 *Patty left notes*: David Whiting, "This 16-Year-Old's Suicide Letters Are a Cry for Help and a National Call for Change," *Orange County Register*, March 19, 2018, https://www.ocregister.com/2018/03/19/this-16-year -olds-suicide-letters-are-a-cry-for-help-and-a-national-call-for-change.

142 *Back then, she was a fledgling psychologist*: Luthar's CV: http://www .suniyaluthar.org/#curriculum-vitae.

142 *Luthar's team . . . enlisted 488 tenth graders*: Suniya S. Luthar and Karen D'Avanzo, "Contextual Factors in Substance Use: A Study of Suburban and Inner-City Adolescents," *Developmental Psychopathology* 11, no. 4 (1999): 845–67, https://www.ncbi.nlm.nih.gov/pmc/articles /PMC3535189/pdf/nihms425738.pdf.

142 *a study of Mexican American high schoolers in Texas*: J. W. Swanson, A. O. Linskey, R. Quintero-Salinas, A. J. Pumariega, and C. E. Holzer III, "A Binational School Survey of Depressive Symptoms, Drug Use, and Suicidal Ideation," *Journal of the American Academy of Child and Adolescent Psychiatry*, July 1992, https://pubmed.ncbi.nlm.nih.gov/1644730/.

144 *"widespread cheating and random acts of delinquency"*: Suniya Luthar, "The Problem With Rich Kids," *Psychology Today*, November 5, 2013, https://www.psychologytoday.com/us/articles/201311/the-problem -rich-kids.

144 *more than twelve times more likely to be stopped*: Mathew Bloch, Ford Fessenden, and Janet Roberts, "Stop, Question and Frisk in New York Neighborhoods," *New York Times* Archive, July 11, 2010, https:// archive.nytimes.com/www.nytimes.com/interactive/2010/07/11/nyre gion/20100711-stop-and-frisk.html.

144 *where nearly 40 percent of families lived in poverty*: "Brownsville Neighborhood Profile," NYU Furman Center, 2019, https://furmancenter.org /neighborhoods/view/brownsville.

144 *the NYPD stopped and frisked more than 4 million:* Jaeah Lee and Adam Serwer, "Charts: Are the NYPD's Stop-and-Frisks Violating the Constitution?," *Mother Jones*, April 29, 2013, https://www.motherjones.com /politics/2013/04/new-york-nypd-stop-frisk-lawsuit-trial-charts/.

145 *more than five times as likely as the Black subjects:* My father, a retired sociology professor, points out that there is bias baked into this result, because white subjects would need to be a lot more "suspicious"-looking before police would stop them. One could also argue that Black people, knowing they are more likely to be randomly stopped, would be more careful about carrying contraband.

145 *"Wealthy people create such an environment":* Author interview with "Elizabeth," September 28, 2018.

146 *"Rich people there are driving Saabs":* Michael Mechanic, "Bombs Sometimes, Kills Often, but Maz Jobrani Swears He Isn't a Terrorist," *Mother Jones*, February 3, 2015, https://www.motherjones.com/media/2015/02 /interview-maz-jobrani-iranian-comedian-not-terrorist-memoir/.

146 *"my daughter burst into tears":* Author interview with Nick Hanauer, June 10, 2019.

146 *The child of billionaires who held forth:* Anonymous, "What Is It Like to Be the Child of a Billionaire?," Quora, October 3, 2015, https://www .quora.com/What-is-it-like-to-be-the-child-of-a-billionaire.

147 *Zinxhiria told me she feels "heartbroken":* Author interview with Denida Zinxhiria, November 19, 2019.

147 *hundreds of millions in today's dollars:* Author interview with Tracy Gary, January 15, 2020. When her mom married her stepfather in the mid-1950s, they had the equivalent of about $98 million, and tripled it in time. For inflation adjustments, I used this calculator: https://www.bls .gov/data/inflation_calculator.htm.

148 *such tales are not uncommon among super-rich offspring:* Author Adam Hochschild, the only child of a rich and powerful mining executive, writes in his memoir, *Half the Way Home*, about the loneliness of his childhood and his distant relationship with his father, Harold Hochschild, whose voice "had in it not the sound of money, as Gatsby said of Daisy, but of wealth, which is something different: more enduring, more secure, inextricably connected with land, stretching forward and backward in time." Harold had left to serve in World War II when Adam was an infant, leaving him in the care of an anxious mother and a "chain of nurses and governesses." Returning from Europe to a boy he barely knew, the father's first move was to spirit his wife away for a long weekend, sans young Adam.

After he was named to run what everyone referred to simply as "the Company," Harold worked long hours: "Except for a few minutes at breakfast and bedtime, I saw him only on weekends." The family summered at Eagle's Nest, a sprawling estate in the Adirondacks, where Adam's father hosted a steady procession of prominent guests: businessmen, celebrities, dignitaries, and intellectuals. It was a stimulating environment, but father-son time was by appointment—awkward bonding attempts planned in advance "with the same relentless, methodical determination he applied to everything in life."

148 *would have been worth about $191 million in August 2020:* This assumes dividends are reinvested. I used this calculator: https://dqydj.com/sp -500-return-calculator/.

CHAPTER 11: GETTING IN

150 *a prestigious local K–12 private school:* Elizabeth Schainbaum, "Private Schools Rank Among the Finest in U.S.," *East Bay Times*, February 1, 2008, https://www.eastbaytimes.com/2008/02/01/private-schools-rank -among-the-finest-in-u-s/.

150 *to hear the sales pitch:* I signed up not only because I was writing a book, but because I wanted to see how Head-Royce compared with my kids' current school. I told an organizer I was recording the proceedings, although I didn't say I might write about it. That's because I wanted to experience the tour as a prospective parent would, not as a PR adventure. Information cited about the school is from the tour/presentation and https://www.headroyce.org/.

151 *some local parents jokingly call "Rolls-Royce":* Myself included.

152 *Virtually all Head-Royce grads go on to a four-year college:* https://www .headroyce.org/schools/college-counseling.

153 *comparable to Head-Royce in its academics:* Bentley has similarly high-caliber teachers and college advising.

154 *were earning 79 percent higher median pay:* The workers in question had entered college 10 years earlier. The Economics Daily, "Median weekly earnings by education, second quarter 2020," Bureau of Labor Statistics, July 23, 2020, https://www.bls.gov/opub/ted/2020/median-weekly -earnings-by-education-second-quarter-2020.htm.

154 *were making $200,000 or more:* Christopher Ingraham, "This Chart Shows How Much More Ivy League Grads Make Than You," *Washington Post*, September 14, 2015, https://www.washingtonpost.com/news

/wonk/wp/2015/09/14/this-chart-shows-why-parents-push-their-kids -so-hard-to-get-into-ivy-league-schools/. According to data from Pay-Scale, the median 2020 starting salary for college grads with three years' work experience was $52,201, but graduates of the ten schools at the top of the income scale had median starting salaries between $70,000 and $84,000: Delece Smith-Barrow and Emma Kerr, "10 National Universities Where Grads Are Paid Well," *U.S. News*, January 23, 2020, https:// www.usnews.com/education/best-colleges/slideshows/10-national -universities-where-grads-make-highest-starting-salaries.

154 *7 percent went to Harvard:* Wealth-X, "Billionaire Census 2018" (proprietary report), p. 28.

154 *the nation's eighty-two most selective colleges:* "2009 *Barron's* Profiles of American Colleges," *Barron's* Educational Series, 2008, https://cew .georgetown.edu/wpcontent/uploads/Selective-Institution-List-Selective -Institution-List.csv.pdf.

154 *only 7 percentiles behind:* Raj Chetty, John N. Friedman, Emmanuel Saez, Nicholas Turner, and Danny Yagan, "Mobility Report Cards: The Role of Colleges in Intergenerational Mobility," Opportunity Insights, July 2017, https://opportunityinsights.org/wp-content/uploads/2018/03/coll_mrc _paper.pdf.

154 *seventy-seven times more likely to attend an Ivy-Plus college:* Ibid.

154 *Princeton's first nine presidents kept enslaved Black people:* Martha A. Sandweiss and Craig Hollander, "Princeton and Slavery: Holding the Center," Princeton University, https://slavery.princeton.edu/stories /princeton-and-slavery-holding-the-center.

155 *women weren't allowed in until 1969:* Nancy Weiss Malkiel, "When Women Were Admitted to Ivy League Schools, the Complaints Sounded a Lot Like a Trump Tweet," *Los Angeles Times*, October 21, 2016, https:// www.latimes.com/opinion/op-ed/la-oe-malziel-when-women-claim -male-roles-20161021-snap-story.html.

155 *graduating its first Black man in 1870:* "Richard Theodore Greener," Wikipedia, https://en.wikipedia.org/wiki/Richard_Theodore_Greener.

155 *through a program dubbed "the Annex":* The female scholars were not so much from elite families, and they had no access to campus buildings, but were taught by Harvard professors in "rented rooms on Appian Way." The Annex evolved into sister school Radcliffe, but Harvard itself didn't admit women until 1963. Pat Harrison, "The Complicated History of Women at Harvard," *Radcliffe Magazine*, 2012, https://www .radcliffe.harvard.edu/news/radcliffe-magazine/complicated-history

-women-harvard; also see Radcliffe's history timeline: https://www.rad cliffe.harvard.edu/our-history.

155 *capped the number of Jewish students:* Jason L. Riley, "Harvard's Asian Quotas Repeat an Ugly History," *Wall Street Journal*, October 8, 2019, https://www.wsj.com/articles/harvards-asian-quotas-repeat-an-ugly -history-11570575962.

155 *sued Harvard, so far unsuccessfully:* The group, Students for Fair Admissions, is now eyeing the nation's top court. Anemona Hartocollis, "Harvard Victory Pushes Admissions Case Toward a More Conservative Supreme Court," *New York Times*, November 12, 2020. https://www.ny times.com/2020/11/12/us/harvard-affirmative-action.html.

155 *discriminates against Asian applicants:* President Donald Trump's Justice Department similarly accused Yale of discriminating against Asian and white students. See: Anemona Hartocollis, "Justice Dept. Accuses Yale of Discrimination in Application Process," *New York Times*, August 2020, https://www.nytimes.com/2020/08/13/us/yale-discrimination .html.

155 *Ivy League acceptance rate fell from 11.4 percent to 6.7 percent:* Compare "2013 Ivy League Admissions Statistics," Ivy Coach, April 16, 2019, https://www.ivycoach.com/2013-ivy-league-admissions-statistics/, and "2023 Ivy League Admissions Statistics," Ivy Coach, October 15, 2019, https://www.ivycoach.com/2023-ivy-league-admissions-statistics/.

155 *University of Chicago's from 27 percent to 6:* Justin Smith, "Acceptance Rate Drops to Record Low 5.9 Percent for Class of 2023," *Chicago Maroon*, April 1, 2019, https://www.chicagomaroon.com/article/2019/4/1 /uchicago-acceptance-rate-drops-record-low/.

155 *Stanford accepted just one in twenty-three applicants:* "Stanford University Admissions Statistics Class of 2023," Ivyleagueprep.com, https:// ivyleagueprep.com/stanford-university/; also see: Camryn Pak, "Stanford Admit Rate Falls to Record-Low 4.34% for Class of 2023," *Stanford Daily*, December 17, 2019, https://www.stanforddaily.com/2019/12/17 /stanford-admit-rate-falls-to-record-low-4-34-for-class-of-2023/.

155 *by the time children reach kindergarten:* Anthony P. Carnevale, Megan L. Fasules, Michael C. Quinn, and Kathryn Peltier Campbell, "Born to Win, Schooled to Lose," Georgetown University Center on Education and the Workforce, 2019, https://cew.georgetown.edu/cew-reports/schooled 2lose/.

156 *spending about five times as much as median-income families:* This was in 2006–2007: Sabino Kornrich and Frank Furstenberg, "Investing in

Children: Changes in Spending on Children, 1972 to 2007," *Demography* 50, no. 1 (February 2013): 1–23, https://pubmed.ncbi.nlm.nih .gov/22987208/. See also: Daniel Schneider, Orestes P. Hastings, and Joe LaBriola, "Income Inequity and Classes Divides in Parental Investments," *American Sociological Review* 83, no. 3 (2018): 475–507, https:// journals.sagepub.com/doi/pdf/10.1177/0003122418772034.

156 *spending on young children (six and under):* Sabino Kornrich, "Inequalities in Parental Spending on Young Children: 1972 to 2010," *AERA Open*, April 2016, https://journals.sagepub.com/doi/pdf/10.1177 /2332858416644180.

156 *so long as the money is used for qualified tuition:* IRS Publication 970, "Tax Benefits for Education," p. 57, https://www.irs.gov/pub/irs-pdf /p970.pdf.

156 *especially beneficial for wealthy families:* "Tax Break for the Wealthy— The 529 Account," Physician on Fire, May 24, 2019, https://www.physi cianonfire.com/tax-break-wealthy-529-account/.

156 *up to $15,000 per year as a tax-free gift:* The number is adjusted periodically for inflation.

156 *$300,000 to $500,000, depending on the state:* "Compare 529 Plans," Savingforcollege.com, https://www.savingforcollege.com/compare_529 _plans/.

157 *deduct up to $4,000 in annual 529 contributions:* Ohio generously lets these deductions carry forward into future tax years, until the total deducted matches the total contributed.

157 *"moderate age-based portfolio":* Age-based portfolios invest aggressively at first and then transition to less-volatile investments as the child approaches college age. I used the "since inception" fund yields to approximate real-world returns: College Advantage, "Vanguard Moderate Age -Based Portfolio," https://www.collegeadvantage.com/fundperformance.

157 *the scrappy public school my kids attend:* "Oakland Technical High School, 2018–2019 School Profile," https://oaklandtech.com/staff/files /2018/10/Final.2018.19-School-Profile.10.22.18.pdf.

157 *state and federal subsidies totaling $116,774:* High earners normally pay a 20 percent federal capital gains tax, and Ohio takes 3 percent, so his family's cap-gains subsidy is $93,195 + $13,979 = $107,174. Assuming his parents live until Nigel turns fifty, they get to deduct $200,000 in 529 contributions ($4,000 annually for fifty years) from their state income. Ohio's top marginal tax rate is 4.8 percent, so that adds another $9,600 to Nigel's family subsidy, for a total of $116,774. Eleanor's parents, like

most middle-class families, use the state's standard deduction (same as federal: $25,100 in 2021), so they don't get that extra tax benefit.

158 *two and a half years of his private school tuition:* If we divide Nigel's subsidy by his tuition (same as Head-Royce), we get: $116,774/$47,300 = 2.47.

158 *Some fall through the cracks:* Author interview with Emily Schoenhofer, February 6, 2020.

159 *are careful to accept a certain percentage of students:* Author interview with independent college counselor Wendy Morrison, February 12, 2020.

159 *an analysis by the* Harvard Crimson: Meg P. Bernhard, "The Making of a Harvard Feeder School," *The Crimson*, December 13, 2013, https://www .thecrimson.com/article/2013/12/13/making-harvard-feeder-schools/.

159 *Lexington High:* This is a high-achieving school, but the reason it sends so many kids to Harvard is probably because a lot of Harvard faculty live in Lexington, and nearly half of faculty/staff offspring are admitted in an average year, according to the expert report by Peter S. Arcidiacono in the Harvard admissions lawsuit (see note "*Harvard's average legacy acceptance rate . . .*").

159 *Stuyvesant's acceptance rate is 3 percent:* Eliza Shapiro, "Only 7 Black Students Got into Stuyvesant, N.Y.'s Most Selective High School, Out of 895 Spots," *New York Times*, March 18, 2019, https://www.nytimes.com /2019/03/18/nyregion/black-students-nyc-high-schools.html.

159 *desperate to get their kindergarteners into Trinity:* Suzanne Woolley and Katya Kazakina, "At $50,000 a Year, the Road to Yale Starts at Age 5," *Bloomberg*, March 27, 2019, https://www.bloomberg.com/news/articles /2019-03-27/at-50-000-a-year-baby-ivies-road-to-yale-starts-at-age-5.

159 *42 percent of private colleges and 6 percent of public ones:* Scott Jaschick, "The 2018 Surveys of Admissions Leaders: The Pressure Grows," *Inside Higher Ed*, September 2018, https://www.insidehighered.com/news /survey/2018-surveys-admissions-leaders-pressure-grows.

159 *Some top institutions have rejected the legacy system:* Max Larkin and Mayowa Aina, "Legacy Admissions Offer an Advantage—And Not Just at Schools Like Harvard," NPR, November 4, 2018, https://www.npr.org /2018/11/04/663629750/legacy-admissions-offer-an-advantage-and -not-just-at-schools-like-harvard.

159 *many cling to it:* Jaschick, "The 2018 Surveys of Admissions Leaders: The Pressure Grows."

160 *which calls its legacies "scions":* Brandon Kochkodin, "Notre Dame and Baylor Admit More Legacies Than Harvard and Yale," *Bloomberg*, March

21, 2019, https://www.bloomberg.com/news/articles/2019-03-21/notre
-dame-baylor-top-harvard-yale-for-most-legacies-admitted.

160 *A survey of Harvard's class of 2019:* David Freed and Idrees Kahloon,
"Class of 2019 by the Numbers: Makeup of the Class," *The Harvard Crimson,* https://features.thecrimson.com/2015/freshman-survey
/makeup/. *The Crimson* and Yale's student newspaper compare their incoming classes here: Meg P. Bernhard, "Class of 2019 by the Numbers:
Meet the Yalies," *The Harvard Crimson,* https://features.thecrimson
.com/2015/freshman-survey/makeup-yale/.

160 *Harvard's average legacy acceptance rate was about 34 percent:* Peter
S. Arcidiacono, "Expert Report of Peter S. Arcidiacono on *Students for
Fair Admissions, Inc. v. Harvard,*" p. 88, table A.2, June 15, 2018, http://
samv91khoyt2i553a2t1s05i-wpengine.netdna-ssl.com/wp-content/up
loads/2018/06/Doc-415-1-Arcidiacono-Expert-Report.pdf.

160 *Stanford . . . three times the non-legacy rate:* Ivan Maisel, "What It Takes,"
Stanford magazine, November 2013, https://stanfordmag.org/contents
/what-it-takes.

160 *legacies . . . are overwhelmingly wealthy and white:* Daniel Golden, *The
Price of Admission* (New York: Penguin Random House, 2019), 121–22.

160 *42 percent of dean's listers:* "Expert Report of Peter S. Arcidiacono,"
Students for Fair Admissions, Inc. v. Harvard, Table A.2, 88, http://
samv91khoyt2i553a2t1s05i-wpengine.netdna-ssl.com/wp-content/up
loads/2018/06/Doc-415-1-Arcidiacono-Expert-Report.pdf.

160 *"His GPA did not warrant it, his SAT scores did not warrant it":* Daniel
Golden, "The Story Behind Jared Kushner's Curious Acceptance Into
Harvard," *ProPublica,* November 18, 2016, https://www.propublica
.org/article/the-story-behind-jared-kushners-curious-acceptance-into
-harvard.

161 *"Is that really a gift?":* Bridget Read, "People Are Talking (Again) About
How Jared Kushner Got into Harvard," *Vogue,* March 13, 2019, https://
www.vogue.com/article/jared-kushner-harvard-admission-college
-cheating-scandal.

161 *Quora's putative billionaire offspring:* Anonymous, "What Is It Like to
Be the Child of a Billionaire?"

161 *expenses run about $78,200 per year:* "The Student Budget," Stanford
University Office of Financial Aid, https://financialaid.stanford.edu/un
dergrad/budget/index.html.

162 *Operation Varsity Blues:* "Arrests Made in Nationwide College Admissions Scam: Alleged Exam Cheating & Athletic Recruitment Scheme,"

United States Attorney's Office District of Massachusetts, March 12, 2019, https://www.justice.gov/usao-ma/pr/arrests-made-nationwide-college-admissions-scam-alleged-exam-cheating-athletic.

162 *dozens of wealthy and prominent Americans:* Jacob Shamsian and Kelly McLaughlin, "Here's the Full List of People Charged in the College Admissions Cheating Scandal, and Who has Pleaded Guilty So Far," Insider .com, September 2, 2020, https://www.insider.com/college-admissions-cheating-scandal-full-list-people-charged-2019-3.

162 *Among the most culpable:* Matthew Ormseth, "Admissions Scandal: Prosecutors Seek Longest Sentences Yet for Four California Parents," *Los Angeles Times*, February 4, 2020, https://ktla.com/2020/02/04/prosecutors-seek-longest-sentences-yet-for-4-ca-parents-most-culpable-in-college-admissions-scam.

162 *Hodge, sentenced to nine months:* Kate Taylor, "Former Pimco C.E.O. Gets 9 Months in Prison in College Admissions Case," *New York Times*, February 7, 2020, https://www.nytimes.com/2020/02/07/us/douglas-hodge-college-admissions-scandal.html.

162 *guilty parties issued public statements professing shame:* Shelley Murphy and Travis Andersen, "Felicity Huffman Among 13 Parents to Plead Guilty in Admissions Scandal," *Boston Globe*, April 8, 2019, https://www.bostonglobe.com/metro/2019/04/08/felicity-huffman-others-plead-guilty-college-admissions-bribery-scam/huKhxEGxpc1LcAym5b2ZlL/story.html.

163 *even more prestigious:* No. 6 in the nation vs. No. 29, according to the *Wall Street Journal*, although that was in 2008.

CHAPTER 12: LOSING TOUCH

166 *"Does Money Make You Mean?":* Ted.com, https://www.ted.com/talks/paul_piff_does_money_make_you_mean?language=en.

167 *more willing to behave unethically:* Paul Piff, Daniel Stancato, Stéphane Côté, Rodolfo Mendoza-Denton, and Dacher Keltner, "Higher Social Class Predicts Increased Unethical Behavior," *PNAS* 109, no. 11 (March 13, 2012), http://www-2.rotman.utoronto.ca/facbios/file/PredictionOfIncreasedUnethicalBehavior.pdf.

167 *prone to entitlement and narcissistic behavior:* Paul Piff, "Wealth and the Inflated Self: Class, Entitlement, and Narcissism," *Personality and Social Psychology Bulletin* 40, no. 1 (2014): 34–43, http://media.wix.com/ugd/80ea24_69eafdc5d036419e93600d80c6d5be33.pdf.

167 *Fords and Subarus were far more likely to stop:* Piff et al., "Higher Social Class Predicts Increased Unethical Behavior."

168 *Numerous experiments of this nature:* One example would be Study 4 in Michael Kraus, Paul Piff, and Dacher Keltner, "Social Class, Sense of Control, and Social Explanation," *Journal of Personality and Social Psychology* 97, no. 6 (December 2009): 992–1004, https://doi.org/10.1037/a0016367.

168 *hooked volunteers up to EKG devices:* Jennifer Stellar, Vida Manzo, Michael Kraus, and Dacher Keltner, "Class and Compassion: Socioeconomic Factors Predict Responses to Suffering," *Emotion* 12, no. 3 (June 2012), https://pubmed.ncbi.nlm.nih.gov/22148992/.

168 *the Dictator Game:* Paul Piff, Michael Kraus, Stéphane Côté, Bonnie Hayden Cheng, and Dacher Keltner, "Having Less, Giving More: The Influence of Social Class on Prosocial Behavior," *Journal of Personality and Social Psychology* 99, no. 5 (November 2010): 771–84, https://pubmed.ncbi.nlm.nih.gov/20649364/.

168 *a smaller proportion of their incomes:* "How America Gives 2014," *The Chronicle of Philanthropy*, October 5, 2014, https://www.philanthropy.com/specialreport/how-america-gives-2014/1.

169 *people's willingness to donate time and effort:* Piff et al., "Having Less, Giving More: The Influence of Social Class on Prosocial Behavior."

170 *a critique of runaway capitalism:* The Landlord's Game was patented in 1904 (circa the Gilded Age), by Elizabeth Magie. A stenographer and typist by trade, she was smitten with the ideas of Henry George, whose 1879 bestseller, *Progress and Poverty*, sold millions of copies. Among other things, George advocated a "land value tax" to curb the power of greedy landlords, and Magie hoped her game would help to educate the public about his beliefs. In her version, the square we know as "GO" contained a world map and the phrase "Labor Upon Mother Earth Produces Wages." Her "go to jail" square was a jab at class disparities, reading "Owner, Lord Blueblood, London England, No Trespassing, Go to Jail." See: Monica M. Smith, "The Woman Inventor Behind 'Monopoly,'" Lemelson Center for the Study of Invention and Innovation, July 7, 2016, https://invention.si.edu/woman-inventor-behind-monopoly.

171 *Successful people tend to feel deserving:* Stéphane Côté, Jennifer Stellar, Robb Willer, Rachel Forbes, Stephanie Martin, and Emily Bianchi, "The Psychology of Entrenched Privilege: High Socioeconomic Status Individuals From Affluent Backgrounds Are Uniquely High in Entitlement," *Personality and Social Psychology Bulletin*, May 18, 2020, https://scholar.google.ca/citations?user=-8JQArwAAAAJ&hl=en&oi=sra.

171 *ballpark wealth ratio of 53-to-1:* Using the Piketty-Saez-Zucman dataset, I calculated that average 1 percent wealth was ~$14.2 million per adult in 2019, and average middle-class wealth was a bit over $270,000.

172 *A Monopoly set contains only $20,580:* "How much money comes in a Monopoly game?", Hasbro Customer Service, https://hasbro-new.cus thelp.com/app/answers/detail/a_id/69/~/how-much-money-comes-in -a-monopoly-game.

172 *a run-of-the-mill 10 percenter:* Average 10 percent wealth per adult in 2019 was ~$2.8 million. (That's larger than threshold or median net worth because of the way wealth skews upward within each category.) The ratio is about 10-to-1, so I should have taken $5,000 to his $500.

173 *presented experimental subjects with moral quandaries:* Stéphane Côté, Paul Piff, and Robb Willer, "For Whom Do the Ends Justify the Means? Social Class and Utilitarian Moral Judgement," *Journal of Personality and Social Psychology* 104 (2013): 490–503, https://pacscenter.stan ford.edu/publication/for-whom-do-the-ends-justify-the-means-social -class-and-utilitarian-moral-judgment/.

173 *Both of these are "utilitarian" choices:* See Julia Driver, "The History of Utilitarianism," Stanford Encyclopedia of Philosophy, March 27, 2009, https://plato.stanford.edu/entries/utilitarianism-history/.

174 *likely to endorse essentialist beliefs about class:* Michael Kraus and Dacher Keltner, "Social Class Rank, Essentialism, and Punitive Judgment," *Journal of Personality and Social Psychology* 105, no. 2 (May 27, 2013), https://www.researchgate.net/publication/236955977_Social _Class_Rank_Essentialism_and_Punitive_Judgment.

174 *"These findings should call into question any beliefs in* noblesse oblige*":* Michael Kraus, "Why the Wealthiest 1 Percent Are So Much Richer Than You," *LiveScience* via Yahoo News, April 10, 2014, https://yhoo.it /2V7ozzo.

CHAPTER 13: CAPITAL HILL

177 *"Even their gatekeepers have gatekeepers":* Benjamin Page, Larry Bartels, and Jason Seawright, "Democracy and the Policy Preferences of Wealthy Americans," *Perspectives on Politics* 11, no. 1 (March 2013): 51–73, http://faculty.wcas.northwestern.edu/~jnd260/cab/CAB2012%20-%20 Page1.pdf.

178 *survey by the nonprofit Kennedy Institute:* "2016 National Civics Survey Results," Edward M. Kennedy Institute for the United States Senate,

https://emki-production.s3.amazonaws.com/downloads/64/files/EMK
_Institute_Nat._Civic_Survey_Results.pdf?1458221724.

178 *his "get-a-senator" strategy:* Darrell West, *Billionaires* (Washington, DC:
Brookings Institution, 2014), 11–13.

178 *Rand Paul held up Senate action for years:* Rachel Bade, "Paul in cross
hairs of tax evasion war," *Politico*, March 2, 2014, https://www.politico
.com/story/2014/03/rand-paul-tax-swiss-banks-104148.

178 *a multilevel marketing company the financier suspected of fraud:* See
FTC press release, "Herbalife Will Restructure Its Multi-level Marketing
Operations and Pay $200 Million For Consumer Redress to Settle FTC
Charges," FTC, July 15, 2016, https://www.ftc.gov/news-events/press
-releases/2016/07/herbalife-will-restructure-its-multi-level-marketing
-operations.

179 *Now he's that guy:* Author interview with Bruce "Jackson," June 10, 2019.

179 *charitable giving buys access to the big players:* See chapter 4.

179 *"strongly" reflected the desires of the affluent:* One ultrawealthy art collector, at her superlative hilltop residence in one of San Francisco's most
exclusive neighborhoods—complete with wood-paneled elevator and a
small fortune in artwork on the walls—attempted to convince me that
poor people should not be allowed to vote because, she insisted, they
were ignorant on matters of public importance. This was precisely the
argument, I chided her, that people once used to deny voting rights to
African Americans—and women, for that matter.

179 *"virtually no relationship" to the preferences of the poor and the middle class:* Martin Gilens, "Inequality and Democratic Responsiveness," *Public Opinion Quarterly* 69, no. 5 (2005): 778–96, https://
scholar.princeton.edu/sites/default/files/mgilens/files/inequality_and
_democratic_responsiveness.pdf; see also: Martin Gilens and Benjamin
Page, "Testing Theories of American Politics: Elites, Interest Groups,
and Average Citizens," *Perspectives on Politics* 12, no. 3 (September
2014): 564–81, https://scholar.princeton.edu/sites/default/files/mgilens
/files/gilens_and_page_2014_-testing_theories_of_american_politics
.doc.pdf.

179 *a campaign pledge to reject corporate PAC money:* Karl Evers-Hillstrom,
"Democrats Are Rejecting Corporate PACs: Does It Mean Anything?,"
OpenSecrets.org, December 7, 2018, https://www.opensecrets.org/news
/2018/12/democrats-say-no-pacs/.

180 *add an estimated $2.3 trillion to the national debt:* "The Budget and
Economic Outlook: 2018 to 2028," appendix B: "The Effects of the 2017

Tax Act on CBO's Economic and Budget Projections," 128–29, Congressional Budget Office, April 2018, http://www.cbo.gov/sites/default/files/115th-congress-2017-2018/reports/53651-outlook-appendixb.pdf.

180 *a brigade of 6,243 lobbyists descended:* Taylor Lincoln, "Swamped," *Public Citizen*, December 1, 2017, https://www.citizen.org/wp-content/uploads/migration/swamped-tax-lobbying-report.pdf.

181 *Chris Collins told reporters:* Cristina Marcos, "GOP Lawmaker: Donors Are Pushing Me to Get Tax Reform Done," *The Hill*, November 7, 2017, https://thehill.com/homenews/house/359110-gop-lawmaker-donors-are-pushing-me-to-get-tax-reform-done.

181 *corporations paid an average income tax of 11 percent:* Matthew Gardner, Lorena Roque, and Steve Wamhoff, "Corporate Tax Avoidance in the First Year of the Trump Tax Law," Institute on Taxation and Economic Policy, December 16, 2019, https://itep.org/corporate-tax-avoidance-in-the-first-year-of-the-trump-tax-law/.

181 *the most affluent 10 percent of Americans owned 84 percent:* Edward N. Wolff, "Household Wealth Trends in the United States, 1962 to 2016: Has Middle Class Wealth Recovered?" (Table 10), National Bureau of Economic Research, November 2017, https://www.nber.org/papers/w24085.pdf.

181 *1 percenters owned 56 percent of all equities:* Arjun Menon, David Kostin, Ben Snider, Ryan Hammond, Cole Hunter, Nicholas Mulford, and Jamie Yang, "Wealth and Equity Flows: How the Top 1% of Households Compares with the Rest," Goldman-Sachs, Portfolio Strategy Research, January 29, 2020, p. 29.

181 *use buybacks to manipulate share prices:* William Lazonick, Mustafa Erdem Sakinç, and Matt Hopkins, "Why Stock Buybacks Are Dangerous for the Economy," *Harvard Business Review*, January 7, 2020, https://hbr.org/2020/01/why-stock-buybacks-are-dangerous-for-the-economy.

181 *cut a deal with a pair of holdout GOP senators:* Alexander Bolton, "How Four GOP Senators Guided a Tax-Bill Victory Behind the Scenes," *The Hill*, December 2, 2017, https://thehill.com/homenews/senate/362924-how-four-gop-senators-guided-a-tax-bill-victory-behind-the-scenes.

182 *dominated by S corporations and limited liability partnerships:* Kyle Pomerleau, "An Overview of Pass-Through Businesses in the United States," Tax Foundation, January 21, 2015, https://taxfoundation.org/overview-pass-through-businesses-united-states/.

182 *about 70 percent of whose profits flow to the wealthiest 1 percent:* Aaron Krupkin and Adam Looney, "9 Facts About Pass-Through Businesses,"

Brookings, May 15, 2017, https://www.brookings.edu/research/9-facts
-about-pass-through-businesses/#fact8.

182 *hedge funds and real estate partnerships:* Johnson's own pass-through
business, a plastics manufacturer, also stood to gain—he earned well
over $2 million in pass-through income in 2016. See Jim Tankersley,
"Why a Firm Believer in Tax Cuts Could Derail the Senate Tax Cut Plan,"
New York Times, November 18, 2017, https://www.nytimes.com/2017
/11/18/us/politics/ron-johnson-senate-tax-cut.html.

182 *more than doubled:* From $51 million to $113 million.

182 *venture capital and real estate industries nearly did:* VC giving jumped
from $19 million to $36 million, real estate from $136 million to
$229 million.

182 *"hedge fund kingmakers":* Author communications with Bradley Saacks,
July 11, 2020.

182 *$4.2 million from investment, law, and real estate interests:* "Sen. Ste-
ven Daines Campaign Finance Summary," Opensecrets.org, https://
www.opensecrets.org/members-of-congress/summary?cid=N000330
54&cycle=2018&type=I and "Sen. Ron Johnson Campaign Finance
Summary," Opensecrets.org, https://www.opensecrets.org/members-of
-congress/summary?cid=N00032546&cycle=2018&type=I.

182 *a 20 percent pass-through tax deduction:* Emily Stewart, "Trump Said
This Tax Break Was for Small Businesses. It's Giving $17 Billion to Mil-
lionaires This Year," *Vox*, April 24, 2018, https://www.vox.com/policy
-and-politics/2018/4/24/17275720/pass-throughs-tax-cut-bill; Robb
Mandelbaum, "What the GOP's Final Pass-Through Tax Cut Means for
Business Owners," *Forbes*, December 22, 2017, https://www.forbes.com
/sites/robbmandelbaum/2017/12/22/what-the-gops-final-pass-through
-tax-cut-means-for-business-owners/#6738c95152b2.

182 *the poster child of shameful billionaire perks:* James B. Stewart, "A Tax
Loophole for the Rich That Just Won't Die," *New York Times*, November 9, 2017, https://www.nytimes.com/2017/11/09/business/carried
-interest-tax-loophole.html.

182 *had voiced a desire to kill it:* Alan Rappeport, "Trump Promised to Kill
Carried Interest. Lobbyists Kept It Alive," *New York Times*, December 22, 2017, https://www.nytimes.com/2017/12/22/business/trump
-carried-interest-lobbyists.html.

182 *twenty-two House Republicans defended carried interest:* Letter from
members of Congress to Representatives Kevin Brady and Richard
Neal regarding Carried Interest, Congress of the United States, June 13,

2017, https://www.investmentcouncil.org/wp-content/uploads/carried
-interest-letter-to-chairman-brady-final.pdf.

182 *talking points mirrored those of the American Investment Council:* Jason
Mulvihill, letter to Senators Orrin Hatch and Ron Wyden, "RE: Current
Treatment of Carried Interest Capital Gains Is Appropriate and Should
Be Retained," American Investment Council, July 17, 2017, https://www
.investmentcouncil.org/wp-content/uploads/2017-07-17-aic-comment
-letter-to-the-senate-finance-committee-on-carried-interest-capital
-gains.pdf.

183 *had hosted Ways and Means chairman Kevin Brady:* "2016 Annual
Meeting and Member Dinner," American Investment Council, September 15, 2016, https://www.investmentcouncil.org/2016-aic-annual
-meeting/.

183 *"The carried interest exemption is completely nutty":* Author interview
with Mike Depatie, April 11, 2019.

183 *an ideal time for America's most fortunate to step up and help:* "Philanthropic response to coronavirus (COVID-19)," Candid, https://candid
.org/explore-issues/coronavirus.

183 *foundations and individuals doled out billions:* Alex Daniels, "Foundations and Donors Step Up Grants to Help Workers Hurt by the Pandemic," *The Chronicle of Philanthropy*, April 14, 2020, https://www
.philanthropy.com/article/FoundationsDonors-Step-Up/248510.

183 *speed up testing:* Paul Sullivan, "How Philanthropists Are Helping
During the Crisis," *New York Times*, March 27, 2020, https://www.ny
times.com/2020/03/27/your-money/philanthropy-coronavirus.html.

183 *slip two special provisions into the CARES Act:* Jeff Stein, "Tax Change
in Coronavirus Package Overwhelmingly Benefits Millionaires, Congressional Body Finds," *Washington Post*, April 14, 2020, https://www
.washingtonpost.com/business/2020/04/14/coronavirus-law-congress
-tax-change/; also see: Jesse Drucker, "The Tax-Break Bonanza Inside
the Economic Rescue Package," *New York Times*, April 24, 2020, https://
www.nytimes.com/2020/04/24/business/tax-breaks-wealthy-virus
.html.

184 *more than $160 billion:* The JCT's revised scores for the two provisions
are $25.5 billion and $135 billion (see Title II, section C, items 3 and 5 in
the document "x-11R-20-5255.pdf"), https://www.jct.gov/publications
.html?func=startdown&id=5091.

184 *a sweet deal for the uber-wealthy:* The Joint Taxation Committee calculated that only 7 percent would go to people earning $100,000 or less.

In this doc, produced in 2016, Treasury analysts projected the results of a theoretical break of this nature and to whom the tax savings would accrue: Lucas Goodman, Katherine Lim, Bruce Sacerdote, and Andrew Whitten, "Simulating the 199A Deduction for Pass-Through Owners," Department of Treasury Office of Tax Analysis, May 2019, https://www .treasury.gov/resource-center/tax-policy/tax-analysis/Documents/WP -118.pdf.

184 *the aircraft giant lost $636 million in 2019:* "Boeing Reports Fourth-Quarter Results," Boeing Company, January 29, 2020, https://inves tors.boeing.com/investors/investor-news/press-release-details/2020 /Boeing-Reports-Fourth-Quarter-Results/default.aspx.

184 *a nice bailout for Boeing investors and executives:* The same folks had already saved $1 billion when the company deferred a large portion of its 2017 income to future years to take advantage of the reduced tax rates to come. See table 7 and footnotes here: "Boeing Reports Record 2017 Results and Provides 2018 Guidance," Boeing Company, January 31, 2018, https://investors.boeing.com/investors/investor-news /press-release-details/2018/Boeing-Reports-Record-2017-Results-and -Provides-2018-Guidance/default.aspx.

184 *only the wealthiest ones:* Those reporting previous nonbusiness income of at least $250,000 per person or $500,000 per couple.

184 *Americans for Tax Fairness emphasized in a protest letter:* Frank Clemente, Open Letter to Members of Congress, regarding objections to the CARES Act on the basis of tax handouts to wealthy businesses, Americans for Tax Fairness, April 9, 2020, https://americansfortaxfair ness.org/wp-content/uploads/ATF-Letter-Opposing-NOLs-Provision -FINAL-4-9-20.pdf.

184 *That hospital bailout, too, skewed toward the affluent:* Jesse Drucker, Jessica Silver-Greenberg, and Sarah Kliff, "Wealthiest Hospitals Got Billions in Bailout for Struggling Health Providers," *New York Times*, May 25, 2020, https://www.nytimes.com/2020/05/25/business/coronavirus -hospitals-bailout.html.

184 *health centers catering to wealthier, fully insured patients got more than twice as much bailout money:* Karyn Schwartz and Anthony Damico, "Distribution of CARES Act Funding Among Hospitals," Kaiser Family Foundation, May 13, 2020, https://www.kff.org/health-costs/issue-brief /distribution-of-cares-act-funding-among-hospitals/.

184 *"great illustration of what happens when our society faces a major calamity":* Author interview with Steven Rosenthal, July 24, 2020.

185 *the majority of his campaign funds would come from Wisconsinites:* Andrea Drusch and National Journal, "Feingold's Early Fundraising Breaks Longtime Campaign-Finance Pledge," *The Atlantic*, August 13, 2015, https://www.theatlantic.com/politics/archive/2015/08/feingolds-early -fundraising-breaks-longtime-campaign-finance-pledge/435132/.

185 *the currency of corruption:* Reporter Carter Yang described how casino interests split $6.5 million between the two parties in the mid- to late 1990s and walked away with a $316 million tax break. The Senate nixed some pesky regulatory legislation after Big Tobacco doled out $5.5 million, mostly to Republicans. The pharmaceutical industry funneled more than $14 million to the GOP, which proceeded to kill a bill the industry opposed that would have guaranteed Medicare recipients a prescription drug benefit. In January 2001, after credit card and finance companies had doled out $3.6 million in soft money during the previous cycle, Senate Majority Leader Trent Lott told incoming Republicans their first priority would be to vote on an industry-sponsored bill that would make it a lot harder for ordinary people to declare chapter 7 bankruptcy. The bankruptcy overhaul was "bought and paid for" by the credit card industry, Larry Noble, then executive director of the Center for Responsive Politics, told Yang. The bill that ultimately passed—in 2005—did not, however, prevent wealthy Americans from using complex trusts to shield assets from their creditors. See Carter M. Yang, "Does 'Soft Money' Really Matter?" ABC News, January 7, 2006, https://abcnews.go .com/US/story?id=93793&page=1.

186 *no more than $2,800 per two-year election cycle:* But PACs can give $5,000: "Contribution Limits," United States of America Federal Election Commission, https://www.fec.gov/help-candidates-and-committees /candidate-taking-receipts/contribution-limits/.

186 *soft money contributions quintupled:* "Soft Money Backgrounder," Open Secrets.org, https://www.opensecrets.org/parties/softsource.php.

186 *This amounted to money laundering:* Carrie Levine, "Soft Money Is Back—And Both Parties Are Cashing In," *Politico Magazine*, August 4, 2017, https://www.politico.com/magazine/story/2017/08/04/soft-money -is-backand-both-parties-are-cashing-in-215456.

186 *"legalized bribery":* Christopher Robertson, D. Alex Winkelman, Kelley Bergstrand, and Darren Modzelewski, "The Appearance and the Reality of *Quid Pro Quo* Corruption: An Empirical Investigation," *Harvard Law School Journal of Legal Analysis* 8, no. 2 (Winter 2016), https://academic .oup.com/jla/article/8/2/375/2502553.

186 *its sentiment was the same:* "Bipartisan Campaign Reform Act," Ballot-pedia, https://ballotpedia.org/Bipartisan_Campaign_Reform_Act.

186 *Thanks largely to Don McGahn:* David Arkush and Craig Holman, Letter to President Barack Obama, "RE: The FEC: An Enforcement Agency Walking Away from Enforcement," Public Citizen, February 18, 2011, https://www.citizen.org/wp-content/uploads/open-letter-to-obama-re-fec-20110218.pdf.

186 *FEC . . . abandon its mission:* Andy Kroll, "What the FEC?" *Mother Jones*, April 18, 2011, https://www.motherjones.com/politics/2011/04/fec-cazayoux-citizens-united/.

187 *Soft money was back!:* The cases in question were *Wisconsin Right to Life, Inc. v. FEC*, in 2008, *Citizens United v. FEC*, in 2010, and *McCutcheon v. FEC*, in 2014, in which SCOTUS struck down McCain-Feingold's spending limits. The "possibility that an individual who spends large sums may garner 'influence over or access to' elected officials or political parties . . . does not give rise to quid pro quo corruption," Chief Justice John Roberts wrote for the majority. For a different take, see: Robertson et al., "The Appearance and the Reality of *Quid Pro Quo* Corruption: An Empirical Investigation."

187 *"We're not going to let them do it!":* Author interview with Russ Feingold, May 1, 2020.

188 *state lawmakers agreed to a one-year moratorium:* Guy Gugliotta, "A Wonder Drug or a Threat?," *Washington Post*, June 24, 1990, https://www.washingtonpost.com/archive/politics/1990/06/24/a-wonder-drug-or-a-threat/fc5e5065-a42d-4a13-b0ad-7a19fd4fc78f/.

188 *a "victory for food terrorists":* Robert Imrie, "Wisconsin Legislature Passes Temporary Ban on Growth Hormone," Associated Press, March 22, 1990, https://apnews.com/1a931a1cd2818dd2eb26e7c5f92f7a78.

188 *Tommy Thompson vetoed a subsequent bill:* Cindy Simmons, "Thompson Vetoes BGH Ban," United Press International, November 22, 1991, https://www.upi.com/Archives/1991/11/22/Thompson-vetoes-BGH-ban/9748690786000/.

188 *fancy restaurants like Charlie Palmer steakhouse:* Restaurant names provided by *Mother Jones* political reporter Tim Murphy. Here's an earlier piece on such establishments: Paul Bedard, "Top 10 Places to Eat with D.C. Big Shots," *U.S. News and World Report*, April 1, 2009, https://www.usnews.com/news/blogs/washington-whispers/2009/04/01/top-10-places-to-eat-with-dc-big-shots.

188 *schmoozed with lobbyists and power brokers:* Former Republican House

majority leader Eric Cantor famously spent almost $226,000 at BLT Steak and Bobby Van's during his 2014 primary. OpenSecrets.org, https://www.opensecrets.org/members-of-congress/expenditures?cycle=2014&cid=N00013131&type=I.

189 *Wealthy people . . . significantly more conservative on economic issues:* Even within this relatively small sample, the wealthiest subjects tended to be the most conservative: Page, Bartels, and Seawright, "Democracy and the Policy Preferences of Wealthy Americans."

189 *These differences transcend party affiliation:* In another study, Boston University behavioral economist Raymond Fisman looked at the "distributional preferences" of a group of elite liberals (Yale law students), who identified as Democrats by a margin of more than ten to one. Fisman used his own twist on the Dictator Game (see chapter 12), in which subjects are given points redeemable for cash and are told they can give as many points as they like—or none—to an unidentified fellow participant. A person who is equally willing to share whether doing so is cheap or expensive—akin to making the same charitable contribution whether or not it is tax deductible—is "equality-minded." But if you are "efficiency-minded," you are more generous when told you only have to sacrifice ten points for the other guy to get twenty—much like a matching charitable contribution—and less generous if you have to give up twenty tokens so the other person can get ten. The balance between efficiency and equality can be used, say, to predict the likelihood that a person will vote for a candidate who favors redistributive tax policies. Despite their political leanings, 80 percent of the Yale kids were efficiency-focused, as compared to 50 percent of a public sample. The young libs were also less likely to be classified "fair-minded" and more likely to be classified "selfish." These results "offer a potential new explanation for the muted policy response to increased income inequality in the United States," Fisman wrote, because "the policymaking elite" are "far less inclined than is the general population to sacrifice efficiency to promote equality." See Raymond Fisman, Pamela Jakiela, Shachar Kariv, and Daniel Markovits, "The Distributional Preferences of an Elite," ScienceMag.org, September 18, 2015, http://www.umass.edu/preferen/You%20Must%20Read%20This/Distributional%20Preferences.pdf.

190 *whether a politician's personal wealth might affect:* Michael W. Kraus and Bennett Callaghan, "Noblesse Oblige? Social Status and Economic Inequality Maintenance Among Politicians," *PLOS ONE*, January 21, 2014,

https://journals.plos.org/plosone/article?id=10.1371/journal.pone
.0085293.

190 *more than one hundred times that of their constituents*: And yet, there's
wealth inequality in Congress, too. See David Hawkings, "Wealth of
Congress: Richer Than Ever, but Mostly at the Very Top," *Roll Call*,
February 27, 2018, https://www.rollcall.com/2018/02/27/wealth-of-con
gress-richer-than-ever-but-mostly-at-the-very-top/.

CHAPTER 14: THE SNOW BALL GROWS

192 *"That all men are born to equal rights is true"*: Joseph J. Ellis, "John
Adams' Fears About America's Future Feel Pretty Darn Prescient Today,"
Mother Jones, October 18, 2018, https://www.motherjones.com/politics
/2018/10/john-adams-thomas-jefferson-wealth-inequality-american
-dialogue/.

192 *usually make double or triple their base salary*: Steven Clifford, "How
Companies Actually Decide What to Pay CEOs," *The Atlantic*, June
14, 2017, https://www.theatlantic.com/business/archive/2017/06/how
-companies-decide-ceo-pay/530127/.

193 *wanted to see how everyday Americans would answer that question*:
Michael I. Norton and Dan Ariely, "Building a Better America—One
Wealth Quintile at a Time," *Perspectives on Psychological Science* 6, no. 1
(2011): 9–12 (includes additional articles), https://sdsuwriting.pbworks
.com/w/file/fetch/71890982/ariely_wealth_distrib_DEBATE_GREAT.pdf.

193 *At the time of the experiment*: It took place in 2001, but the paper took
years to get into print, according to Norton.

194 *an early nineteenth-century correspondence*: Adams and Jefferson ex-
changed dozens of letters during this period. Quotes from Joseph J. Ellis,
American Dialogue (New York: Penguin Random House, 2018), 71–101
(excerpted in Ellis, "John Adams' Fears About America's Future Feel
Pretty Darn Prescient Today").

194 *"no distinction among the upper ten thousand"*: Nathaniel Parker Willis,
The Complete Works of N. P. Willis (New York: J. S. Redfield, 1846), 735.

194 *coined amid the Great Recession*: The Nobel Prize–winning economist
Joseph Stieglitz published a *Vanity Fair* essay that year, titled "Of the
1%, by the 1%, for the 1%," May 2011, https://www.vanityfair.com/news
/2011/05/top-one-percent-201105. Occupy Wall Street activists then
launched a Tumblr with posts highlighting the economic struggles of

everyday Americans: https://wearethe99percent.tumblr.com/. The press picked up on the phenomenon, and before long families were debating class warfare around the dinner table.

194 *remained busy foreclosing on them:* Andy Kroll, "Fanny and Freddie's Foreclosure Barons," *Mother Jones*, August 3, 2010, https://www.moth erjones.com/politics/2010/08/david-j-stern-djsp-foreclosure-fannie -freddie/.

194 *Inequality was a major theme in the 2012 presidential race:* A record-ing of Mitt Romney saying privately that 47 percent of Americans "are dependent on government" and "believe they are victims" and "pay no income taxes" may have cost him the election. David Corn, "SECRET VIDEO: Romney Tells Millionaire Donors What He REALLY Thinks of Obama Voters," *Mother Jones*, September 17, 2012, https://www.mother jones.com/politics/2012/09/secret-video-romney-private-fundraiser/.

196 *can barely contemplate the next rung:* Author interview with Nick Hanauer, June 10, 2019.

196 *"they're seeing Kochs and Buffetts and Gates":* Author interview with Jerry Fiddler, August 18, 2015.

197 *"the Snow ball will grow as it rolls":* Joseph J. Ellis, *American Dialogue*, 82.

197 *would need 163 Monopoly sets:* In 2019, per U.S. adult, average 0.001 per-cent wealth was ~$1,812,787,600 and average middle-class wealth (50th–90th percentiles) was ~$270,360, a ratio of 6,705-to-1. So, if the poor player gets $500, the rich one gets $3,352,544. Divide by the amount of money in a Monopoly set ($20,580), round up, and we get 163 sets.

198 *almost four football fields:* Bezos's net worth hit $200 billion that day. Dividing by average middle-class wealth from above we get a ratio of 739,754-to-1. If a middle-class player gets $500, Bezos gets just short of $370 million. Divide that by the amount of money in a set and round up, and you get 17,973 Monopoly sets. Each has 210 bills and each bill is 4 inches × 2 inches, so the cash in one set covers 1,680 square inches. Multiply by 17,973 sets and we get 30,194,640 sq. in. = 209,685 sq. ft. A football field is 57,600 sq. ft., so we divide and get 3.64 football fields.

198 *He's a 5 percenter:* Author interview with Gabriel Zucman, April 25, 2019.

198 *has kept class warfare squarely on America's front burner:* Jim Tankersly and Ben Casselman, "The Liberal Economists Behind the Wealth Tax Debate," *New York Times*, February 21, 2020, https://www.nytimes.com /2020/02/21/us/politics/the-liberal-economists-behind-the-wealth-tax -debate.html.

198 *inspired Bernie Sanders and Elizabeth Warren:* Ibid.

198 *"rank and birth, and tinsel aristocracy":* Ellis, *American Dialogue*, 82.

199 *the equity distribution Tim O'Reilly encountered:* See chapter 7.

199 *about $2.8 million in 2019:* Based on data from Gabriel Zucman and Emmanuel Saez.

200 *better access to quality medical care:* Bruce Link, Jo Phelan, and Parisa Tehranifar, "Social Conditions as Fundamental Causes of Health Inequalities: Theory, Evidence, and Policy Implications," *Journal of Health and Social Behavior* 51(S) (2010): S28–S39, http://www.rootcausecoali tion.org/wp-content/uploads/2017/07/Link-and-Phelan-2010.pdf.

200 *an extraordinary financial toll:* Mark Follman, Julia Lurie, Jaeah Lee, and James West, "The True Cost of Gun Violence in America," *Mother Jones*, April 15, 2015, https://www.motherjones.com/politics/2015/04/true-cost -of-gun-violence-in-america/.

200 *Ross . . . has a tax-exempt private foundation:* "Ross School Foundation," Ross School, https://www.rossschoolfoundation.org/.

200 *Rich families can borrow more easily and at lower rates:* Author interviews with Jerry Fiddler, August 18, 2015, and Zell Kravinsky, December 21, 2019. Auto lenders are notorious for gouging low-income borrowers. See Gary Rivlin, "'They Had Created This Remarkable System for Taking Every Last Dime from Their Customers,'" *Mother Jones*, April 4, 2016, https://www.motherjones.com/politics/2016/04/car-subprime -bubble-auto-loans-credit-acceptance-don-foss/.

200 *"it's harder to borrow $15,000 than it is to borrow $150,000":* Author interview with Zell Kravinsky, December 21, 2019.

201 *payday lenders serving as the primary financial institutions:* For a fascinating deep dive into these predatory industries, read Gary Rivlin, *Broke, USA* (New York: Harper Business, 2011).

201 *six times as likely to receive a pedestrian citation:* Topher Sanders, Kate Rabinowtiz, *ProPublica*, Benjamin Conarck, and *Florida Times-Union*, "Walking While Black," *ProPublica*, November 16, 2017, https:// features.propublica.org/walking-while-black/jacksonville-pedestrian -violations-racial-profiling/.

201 *put you on probation:* Celia Perry, "Probation Profiteers," *Mother Jones*, July 21, 2008, https://www.motherjones.com/politics/2008/07/pro bation-profiteers/.

201 *or even throw you in jail:* Topher Sanders, "A Lawsuit Over Ferguson's 'Debtors Prison' Drags On," *ProPublica*, May 31, 2019, https://www.pro publica.org/article/a-lawsuit-over-ferguson-debtors-prison-drags-on.

201 *workers at highest risk of infection:* Beatrice Jin and Andrew McGill, "Who Is Most at Risk in the Coronavirus Crisis: 24 Million of the Lowest-Income Workers," *Politico*, March 21, 2020, https://www.polit ico.com/interactives/2020/coronavirus-impact-on-low-income-jobs-by -occupation-chart/.

201 *among the most likely to see their jobs go away permanently:* Heather Long, Andrew Van Dam, Alyssa Fowers, and Leslie Shapiro, "The COVID-19 recession is the most unequal in modern U.S. history," https://www.washingtonpost.com/graphics/2020/business/coronavirus -recession-equality/, *Washington Post*, September 30, 2020.

201 *their fortunes had bounced back to pre-pandemic levels:* Michael Mechanic, "America's Ultrawealthy Already Got Their V-Shaped Recovery," *Mother Jones*, October 9, 2020, https://www.motherjones.com /coronavirus-updates/2020/10/coronavirus-ultrawealthy-pandemic -recovery/. As of fall 2020, my wealthy subjects were faring well, including Michael, who had remarried and was finishing his PhD dissertation. He and his wife had hired a live-in nanny to help with their kids so they could work.

202 *requires average household earnings of $481,000:* Income and wealth thresholds vary by location. Thomas Piketty, Emmanuel Saez, and Gabriel Zucman, "Distributional National Accounts: Methods and Estimates for the United States," *Quarterly Journal of Economics* 133, no. 2 (2018): 553–609 (updated September 2020).

202 *"a reallocation of rents to shareholders in a decelerating economy":* Daniel L. Greenwald, Martin Lettau, and Sydney C. Ludvigson, "How the Wealth Was Won: Factor Shares as Market Fundamentals," NBER Working Paper, May 17, 2020, https://www.nber.org/papers/w25769.pdf.

202 *In 2019 . . . the same worker made $19,105—$93 less:* From the Piketty-Saez-Zucman dataset, converted to 2019 dollars.

202 *inflation nibbled on the carcass:* Broadly speaking, real wages declined from 46 percent of GDP in 1989 to 43 percent in 2019. See: "Compensation of Employees: Wages and Salary Accruals/Gross Domestic Product," Federal Reserve Bank of St. Louis, https://fred.stlouisfed.org/graph /?g=2Xa.

202 *stalled at $7.25 for more than a decade:* To this day, waiters, bartenders, taxi drivers, and casino and hotel workers in some states are only guaranteed a federal "tipped minimum wage" of just $2.13 an hour. This ultra-low-wage group includes millions of Americans. See "Tipped Workers in the United States," GovDocs, June 3, 2014, https://www.govdocs.com

/tipped-workers-united-states/. Bosses are obligated to make sure these workers earn at least the federal minimum after tips, but that doesn't always happen: Dana Liebelson, "The Minimum Wage Loophole That's Screwing Over Waiters and Waitresses," *Mother Jones*, May 12, 2014, https://www.motherjones.com/politics/2014/05/minimum-wage-tip-map-waiters-waitresses-servers/.

202 *less than $10 an hour before taxes:* "State Minimum Wages: 2020 Minimum Wage by State," National Conference of State Legislatures, August 20, 2020, https://www.ncsl.org/research/labor-and-employment/state-minimum-wage-chart.aspx.

202 *Howard Schultz would still be rich:* For the investor class, growth has been nearly exponential. See: "S&P 500 Index—90 Year Historical Chart," Macrotrends, https://www.macrotrends.net/2324/sp-500-historical-chart-data.

202 *helped enact a $15 minimum in SeaTac:* Molly Ball, "A Plutocrat's Case for Raising the Minimum Wage," *The Atlantic*, December 28, 2015, https://www.theatlantic.com/magazine/archive/2016/01/a-plutocrats-case-for-raising-the-minimum-wage/419130/.

203 *miserly wages:* A decades-long decline in union membership has only exacerbated the wage-and-benefits gap. Numbers here: "Union Members Summary," U.S. Bureau of Labor Statistics, January 22, 2020, https://www.bls.gov/news.release/union2.nr0.htm.

203 *Marginal income tax rates . . . were slashed:* "Historical Highest Marginal Income Tax Rates," Tax Policy Center, February 4, 2020, https://www.taxpolicycenter.org/statistics/historical-highest-marginal-income-tax-rates.

203 *He came up short:* Thomas L. Hungerford, "Taxes and the Economy: An Economic Analysis of the Top Tax Rates Since 1945," Congressional Research Service, September 14, 2012, https://www.democrats.senate.gov//files/documents/CRSTaxesandtheEconomy%20Top%20Rates.pdf.

203 *the nation's four hundred richest individuals pay an average of 23 percent:* Emmanuel Saez and Gabriel Zucman, *The Triumph of Injustice* (New York: W. W. Norton, 2019), 13–20.

203 *get most of their income not in wages but lower-taxed investment:* This is also why the fortunes of ultrawealthy Americans bounced back so fast from the pandemic—many did exceedingly well as the Federal Reserve propped up public markets. See Mark Helenowski, "Billionaires Have Made an Absolute Killing During the Pandemic. The Number Is Staggering," *Mother Jones*, August 10, 2020, https://www.motherjones.com

/politics/2020/08/billionaire-coronavirus-wealth-animation-covid-685
-billion/; also see: Peter Eavis, "These Companies Gave Their C.E.O.s
Millions, Just Before Bankruptcy," *New York Times*, June 23, 2020,
https://www.nytimes.com/2020/06/23/business/ceo-bonsues-before
-bankruptcy-coronavirus.html.

204 *max out at annual earnings of $142,800:* Social Security Administration,
"Contribution And Benefit Base," https://www.ssa.gov/oact/cola/cbb
.html.

204 *less than 7 percent of the wealth of 1 percenters:* Edward N. Wolff,
"Household Wealth Trends in the United States, 1962 to 2016: Has
Middle Class Wealth Recovered?," NBER Working Paper 24085, Table
10, p. 53, https://www.nber.org/system/files/working_papers/w24085
/w24085.pdf.

204 *Sales taxes, too, favor the rich:* Saez and Zucman, *The Triumph of Injustice*, 15–18.

205 *"record and photograph the latitude and longitude readings":* Raleigh P.
Watson, "Offshore Closings," *Marlin*, October 26, 2018, https://www
.marlinmag.com/offshore-closings-state-sales-tax/.

205 *Boat buyers in Florida pay a maximum of $18,000:* "Sales and Use Tax
on Boats: Information for Owners and Purchasers," Florida Department
of Revenue, https://floridarevenue.com/Forms_library/current/gt800
005.pdf.

205 *New Jerseyites pay $20,000 tops:* "Sales and Use Tax for Boats and Vessels," State of New Jersey, https://www.state.nj.us/treasury/taxation/s_u
_boat_vessels.shtml.

205 *in South Carolina, you'll pay no more than $500:* "Maximum Sales and
Use Tax," South Carolina Department of Revenue, https://dor.sc.gov/tax
/max-tax.

205 *most consumer goods are taxed:* Saez and Zucman note that excise taxes
on alcohol and tobacco are based on quantity, not price, which means
you pay as much tax on a bottle of Trader Joe's "two-buck Chuck" as a
wealthy oenophile pays when he plops down $1,600 for a bottle of Chateau Latour.

205 *which the Republicans are desperate to repeal:* See chapter 15.

205 *our elders should be willing to sacrifice their lives:* Bess Levin, "Texas
Lt. Governor: Old People Should Volunteer to Die to Save the Economy," *Vanity Fair*, March 24, 2020, https://www.vanityfair.com/news
/2020/03/dan-patrick-coronavirus-grandparents; Katie Shepherd, "'I
would rather die than kill the country': The conservative chorus push-

ing Trump to end social distancing," *Washington Post*, March 25, 2020, https://www.washingtonpost.com/nation/2020/03/25/coronavirus -glenn-beck-trump/.

CHAPTER 15: DYNASTY

206 *45 million American families would pass along $68 trillion:* "The Great Wealth Transfer," Cerulli Associates, https://info.cerulli.com/HNW -Transfer-of-Wealth-Cerulli.html.

207 *"For thousands of years, being rich involved being armed":* Jeffery A. Winters, "Wealth Defense and the Complicity of Liberal Democracy," *Nomos* 58 (2017): 158–225, American Society for Political and Legal Philosophy, https://www.jstor.org/stable/pdf/26785952.pdf?seq=1.

207 *join forces when necessary:* For instance, the push to lobby Congress to make sure family offices were exempt from a provision of the Dodd-Frank legislation that called for regulating "private wealth managers." See Brody Mullins, "Family Trusts Lobby to Avoid New Rules," *Wall Street Journal*, October 21, 2009, https://www.wsj.com/articles /SB125608740329797917. (One of the lobbyists family offices hired was Jake Sehar, a longtime Joe Biden aide: https://littlesis.org/person/26999 -Jake_Sehar.) The dynasties have also come together to try and kill the estate tax. See Emily Myers, "Billionaires' Bluff: How America's Richest Families Hide Behind Small Businesses and Family Farms in Effort to Repeal Estate Tax," Public Citizen, June 25, 2015, https://www.citizen.org /wp-content/uploads/billionaires-bluff-estate-tax-report.pdf.

207 *to prevent wealthy families from leaving large fortunes to grandchildren:* Julie Garber, "How the Generation Skipping Transfer Tax Exemption Works," *The Balance*, May 24, 2020, https://www.thebalance.com /exemption-from-generation-skipping-transfer-taxes-3505526.

207 *Ernst & Young predicted would be worth nearly $70 trillion by 2021:* "The EY Outlook for Asset Management in 2018," Ernst & Young Global Limited, https://eyfinancialservicesthoughtgallery.ie/asset-management -2018/.

208 *"private tax system, catering to only several thousand Americans":* Noam Scheiber and Patricia Cohen, "For the Wealthiest, a Private Tax System That Saves Them Billions," *New York Times*, December 29, 2015, https:// www.nytimes.com/2015/12/30/business/economy/for-the-wealthiest -private-tax-system-saves-them-billions.html.

208 *the special tax treatment of offshore insurers:* Hal Lux, "The Great Hedge

Fund Reinsurance Tax Game," *Institutional Investor*, March 31, 2001, https://www.institutionalinvestor.com/article/b15134hfvkpsy7/the -great-hedge-fund-reinsurance-tax-game.

208 *The law is the law:* Author interview with an IRS spokesman who asked not to be quoted by name, May 6, 2019.

208 *The Republican Party has waged open warfare on the IRS:* Paul Kiel and Jesse Eisinger, "How the IRS Was Gutted," *ProPublica*, December 11, 2018, https://www.propublica.org/article/how-the-irs-was-gutted.

208 *the IRS was auditing fewer than one in ten of the nation's richest taxpayers:* "SOI Tax Stats—Examination Coverage: Individual Income Tax Returns Examined—IRS Data Book Table 9b," Internal Revenue Service, https://www.irs.gov/statistics/soi-tax-stats-examination-coverage -individual-income-tax-returns-examined-irs-data-book-table-9b.

208 *Obamacare and the taxes it imposed on the 1 percent:* "Affordable Care Act Tax Law Changes for Higher Income Taxpayers," Tax Act Blog, https://blog.taxact.com/tax-law-changes-for-higher-income/.

209 *"What in the world were you thinking of?":* Kelly-Koskinen House hearing, see p. 104: "Hearing Before the Subcommittee on Oversight of the Committee on Ways and Means U.S. House of Representatives," U.S. Government, April 22, 2015, https://docs.house.gov/meetings/WM/WM06 /20150422/103354/HHRG-114-WM06-Transcript-20150422.pdf.

209 *cost the agency more than one-fifth of its workforce:* "IRS Budget & Workforce," https://www.irs.gov/statistics/irs-budget-and-workforce.

209 *tax debt the IRS formally wrote off . . . more than doubled:* OECD's Tax Administration 2019 report numbers provided by the IRS spokesman cited above.

209 *It can "take months to identify the person who represents the partnership":* James R. White, "Growing Population and Complexity Hinder Effective IRS Audits," GAO Testimony Before the Permanent Subcommittee on Investigations, Committee on Homeland Security and Governmental Affairs, U.S. Senate, July 22, 2014, https://www.gao.gov/assets/670/66 4917.pdf.

209 *Virtually no partnerships were audited in 2018:* Pass-through entities don't pay taxes; only the owners do. The problem is that partnerships are deliberately opaque—a partner in a fund can be another partnership, whose own partners are yet other legal entities, etc. Auditing a partnership can require auditing hundreds of individual partners—if the IRS can figure out who owns what. A 2018 rule change should make such audits easier: "BBA Centralized Partnership Audit Regime," IRS, https://

www.irs.gov/businesses/partnerships/bba-centralized-partnership
-audit-regime.

209 *just 0.03 percent of $10 million–plus taxpayers:* IRS Data Book Table 17a,
"Examination Coverage and Recommended Additional Tax After Examination, by Type and Size of Return, Tax Years 2010–2018," IRS, updated
June 29, 2020, https://www.irs.gov/statistics/soi-tax-stats-examination
-coverage-and-recommended-additional-tax-after-examination-by
-type-and-size-of-return-tax-years-2010-2018-irs-data-book-table-17a.

209 *still owed $46 billion:* "High-Income Nonfilers Owing Billions of Dol-
lars Are Not Being Worked by the Internal Revenue Service," Treasury
Inspector General for Tax Administration, May 29, 2020, https://www
.treasury.gov/tigta/auditreports/2020reports/202030015fr.pdf.

210 *The estate tax exemption is at its highest level in decades:* Prior to Election Day 2020, estate lawyers were alerting clients the situation might
not last if the Democrats took over Congress. Julie Garber, "How the
Federal Estate Tax Exemption Changed from 1997 to Today," *The
Balance*, June 7, 2020, https://www.thebalance.com/exemption-from
-federal-estate-taxes-3505630.

210 *"It's really that they have access to more opportunities to cheat":* Author
interview with Gabriel Zucman, April 25, 2019.

210 *"Families haven't always been pushing back":* The relevant video has been
removed from the Family Office Association website, but I verified the
quote: Author email with Patricia Angus, December 15, 2020.

211 *up to $11.7 million:* The exemption is adjusted periodically for inflation.
Unless Congress intervenes sooner (which is likely under Democratic
control), the exemption is set to revert to half the current amount in
2026.

211 *gifts of up to $15,000:* For 2021. Federal gift exemption limits are period-
ically adjusted for inflation.

211 *Those gifts needn't be reported:* "Frequently Asked Questions on Gift
Taxes," IRS.gov, https://www.irs.gov/businesses/small-businesses-self
-employed/frequently-asked-questions-on-gift-taxes.

211 *goes to our heirs tax-free:* Another perk is the "step-up in basis" rule. Say
your parents bought five thousand shares of Amazon the day after the
IPO, and never sold. If they die and leave you that stock and you sell it
right away, you pay no capital gains tax, because the stock's "cost basis"
is reset to the current market value upon the owner's death, so there is
no profit from that sale. Your parents paid about $15,000 for the stock.
As of September 2020, it was worth more than $14 million. And neither

you nor they will ever pay a dime on those gains: https://www.irs.gov
/faqs/interest-dividends-other-types-of-income/gifts-inheritances/gifts
-inheritances.

211 *a state with its own estate tax:* Most states lack this tax, but exemptions
in Massachusetts and Oregon are only $1 million, and Washington State
charges a 20 percent estate tax in addition to the federal tax. Nebraska
charges 19 percent.

212 *a "family limited partnership":* There will be gift tax implications, but if
the child gets a stake early on, when the value of the assets is low, those
assets will henceforth grow estate-tax-free, as with a dynasty trust.

212 *forever immune from inheritance taxes:* This applies only to the portion
that is initially tax-exempt. If a couple puts $50 million into a dynasty
trust in 2020, $23.4 million (and the future proceeds from that money)
are exempt forever. However, they *would* be charged estate tax on the remaining $26.6 million—and proceeds from investing that portion would
be included in their beneficiaries' taxable estates.

212 *These tactics . . . can backfire:* Attorney Amy Shelf offered some exam-
ples: The insurance trust I cite keeps life insurance proceeds out of your
taxable estate, but the money you put into it usually applies to your gift-
tax limit, so you can't give the beneficiaries additional money without
tax liability. Like GRATs, CLATs, etc., the personal residential trusts—
useful when interest rates are high—work only when you outlive the
trust term. A family limited partnership requires some contribution
from the children or else the "grant" will be considered a gift. But if you
do as Sam Walton did, and create the partnership before your company
becomes super-valuable, there's a lot of upside.

212 *Clifford Crummey beat the IRS on a technicality:* D. Clifford Crummey
et al., Petitioners, v. Commissioner of Internal Revenue, Respondent, 397
F.2d 82 (9th Cir.1968), Justia Law, June 25, 1968, https://law.justia.com
/cases/federal/appellate-courts/F2/397/82/360188/.

213 *the initial $5 million . . . is paid back to him:* GRATs are done a bit differ-
ently these days. Read on.

213 *what one source calls the "table rate":* That's attorney Richard Covey. It
is officially called the Section 7520 Interest Rate. See "Section 7520 Interest Rates," IRS.gov, https://www.irs.gov/businesses/small-businesses
-self-employed/section-7520-interest-rates.

213 *a wee bit more complicated:* Thanks to inflation, the $5 million Jeff gets
back within ten years is worth only ~$4 million. The IRS considers the
difference a taxable gift to his beneficiary at the outset. At the maximum

gift tax rate of 40 percent, Jeff would owe $400,000. If the table rate is identical to the actual investment return rate on that money, Preston gets about $1.4 million, but Jeff will owe $400,000 in gift tax, and the whole thing is a wash—he may as well have just handed Preston $1 million and paid the gift tax.

213 *$3.3 million is exempt from gift taxes:* I based this example on calculations by Megan M. Burke (see "increasing payments," Tables 1 and 2), "Great Time for a GRAT," *Journal of Accountancy*, October 1, 2019, https://www.journalofaccountancy.com/issues/2019/oct/wealth-transfer-grantor-retained-annuity-trusts.html.

213 *Zuckerberg and Dustin Moskovitz set up what appear to be GRATs:* Items (3), (6), and (18) of "Principal and Selling Stockholders," S-1 Registration Statement, Securities and Exchange Commission, February 1, 2012, https://www.sec.gov/Archives/edgar/data/1326801/000119312512034517/d287954ds1.htm.

213 *The Walton clan, with combined assets of $215 billion:* Tom Metcalf, "These Are the World's Richest Families," *Bloomberg*, August 1, 2020, https://www.bloomberg.com/features/richest-families-in-the-world/.

213 *is renowned for its tax-avoidance prowess:* Via *Bloomberg News*, "$100 Billion: How America's Richest Family Avoids Taxes, Maintains Its Wealth," *Los Angeles Daily News*, August 28, 2017, https://www.dailynews.com/2013/09/13/100-billion-how-americas-richest-family-avoids-taxes-maintains-its-wealth/.

213 *granted each child a 20 percent share:* "How Wal-Mart's Waltons Keep the Tax Man at Bay," *Dallas Morning News*, September 14, 2013, https://www.dallasnews.com/business/retail/2013/09/14/how-wal-marts-waltons-keep-the-tax-man-at-bay/.

214 *curb the abuse of another kind of trust:* A grantor-retained *income* trust is different from a GRAT. It distributes income (such as dividends and interest) to its creator during the lifetime of the trust, but the body of the trust assets go to the beneficiary, not back to the creator. At the outset the creator of the GRIT is assessed a gift tax based on that month's table rate (see page 213). Wealth managers realized that when the table rate is higher than actual market yields, the government underestimates the gift value of the trust at the outset, so it under-taxes the trust's creator.

214 *"they loosened up on the law":* Author interviews with Richard Covey, October 22 and October 29, 2020. To reverse the error, Covey says, would require Democratic control of the Senate, the House, and the presidency, which has only happened three times since 1990: during the

first two years of Bill Clinton's and Barack Obama's presidencies—and now under Joe Biden (hint, hint).

214 *she owed gift taxes on $7.6 million: Walton v. Commissioner*, 115 T.C. 589 (2000)," Leagle, https://www.leagle.com/decision/2000704115aotc 5891664.

214 *a no-risk proposition:* If you put stock into a two-year GRAT (considered the minimum term), you'll get back about half the shares each year. You can then roll those shares into another two-year GRAT, and so on. If the stock doesn't appreciate during a given period, no harm done. But if it spikes, your heirs will cash in. For this reason, there's more upside to setting up a series of interlocking short-term GRATs than using a long-term one.

214 *transfer at least $7.9 billion to his heirs:* Zachary Mider, "Accidental Tax Break Saves Wealthiest Americans $100 Billion," December 16, 2013, https://www.bloomberg.com/news/articles/2013-12-17/accidental-tax -break-saves-wealthiest-americans-100-billion.

214 *"the culmination of five decades of Walton's selective breeding":* "Record $3.2 Million for Walton's Rocking W Ranch Dispersal," *Quarter Horse News*, September 29, 2015, https://www.quarterhorsenews.com/2015 /09/record-3-2-million-for-walton-s-rocking-w-ranch-dispersal/.

214 *the world's richest woman:* MacKenzie Scott (Bezos) briefly held the title in September 2020.

215 *was bankrolled by a series of "Jackie O trusts":* Zachary Mider, "How Wal-Mart's Waltons Maintain Their Billionaire Fortune: Taxes," *Bloomberg News*, September 13, 2013, https://www.bloomberg.com/news/articles /2013-09-12/how-wal-mart-s-waltons-maintain-their-billionaire -fortune-taxes. (Free version via *Los Angeles Daily News*: https://bit.ly /33K6biu.)

215 *Jacqueline Kennedy Onassis famously set one up for her heirs:* Paul Sullivan, "A Trust Surges, Heirs and Taxes in Mind, but Mind the Details," *New York Times*, July 22, 2011, https://www.nytimes.com/2011/07 /23/your-money/estate-planning/charitable-lead-trusts-draw-renewed -interest.html.

216 *"one day, if I work really hard, I could live in that mansion'":* "CNN Larry King Weekend Interview with Bono," CNN.com, December 1, 2002, http://transcripts.cnn.com/TRANSCRIPTS/0212/01/lklw.00.html.

CHAPTER 16: WHO WANTS TO HAVE IT ALL?

217 *a celebrity mega-landlord and motivational speaker:* https://grantcar
done.com.

217 *"Who wants a better life?":* Quotes and descriptions are from author interviews and observations at the Real Estate Wealth Expo in San Mateo,
California, September 10, 2019.

221 *According to its website:* When I checked back in September 2020, the
Expo website was offline. Fortunately, we have the Wayback Machine:
https://web.archive.org/web/20190516031641/https://www.realestate
wealthexpo.com/.

221 *the McDonald's of the continuing-education industry:* Cotten Timber-
lake, "'How To' Courses Leading 30-Year-Old to Riches," *Los Angeles Times*, January 24, 1985, https://www.latimes.com/archives/la-xpm
-1985-01-24-fi-11443-story.html.

221 *a pillar of Tony Robbins's events:* "The History of Firewalking," Tony Robbins: Firewalker, January 6, 2017, https://tonyrobbinsfirewalk.com/the
-history-of-firewalking/.

221 *a "raise" to $1.5 million:* Andrew Kaczynski and Christopher Massie,
"That Time Trump Said He Had World's Highest Speaking Fee and Everybody Went with It," Buzzfeed News, August 11, 2016, https://www
.buzzfeednews.com/article/andrewkaczynski/the-art-of-the-spiel.

222 *Trump admitted under oath he was getting $400,000:* David A. Fahr-
enthold and Robert O'Harrow Jr., "Trump: A True Story," *Washington
Post*, August 10, 2016, https://www.washingtonpost.com/graphics/pol
itics/2016-election/trump-lies/?utm_term=.a332ca213040.

222 *"cost me over $40 million, and it cost me my reputation":* "Alex Rodriguez
on PED Suspension: 'How Stupid Can You Be?,'" ESPN.com, October 13,
2017, https://www.espn.com/mlb/story/_/id/21016687/alex-rodriguez
-says-jackass-using-performance-enhancing-drugs-career.

222 *agreed to pay $25 million to settle class-action lawsuits:* Camila Domo-
noske, "Judge Approves $25 Million Settlement of Trump University
Lawsuit," NPR, March 31, 2017, https://www.npr.org/sections/thetwo
-way/2017/03/31/522199535/judge-approves-25-million-settlement-of
-trump-university-lawsuit. (The official settlement was delayed until
2018.)

222 *entice attendees to sign up for "advanced" seminars:* Global Learning Alliance, LLC, the mysterious entity overseeing the Expo I attended, shares
the same physical address in Cottonwoods Heights, Utah, as two other

seminar businesses that were accused of misleading their customers. One, Zurixx, LLC, was the subject of a September 2019 complaint by the Federal Trade Commission and Utah's Department of Consumer Protections accusing Zurixx of deceptive practices identical to those described. (A federal court granted a preliminary injunction, and Zurixx is in receivership. But the case was still pending as of December 2020.) https://www.ftc.gov/system/files/documents/cases/zurixx_complaint.pdf.

222 *these pitchmen covered their behinds:* According to its (now offline) website, the Expo is operated by the "Global Learning Alliance," a Utah-based LLC that has virtually no web presence and, on paper, does not appear to be connected with Zanker. (Neither Zanker nor the lawyers who registered the LLC responded to my outreach and questions.) But the GLA has an intriguing trail of connections I'll likely be covering on my author website: ReadJackpot.com.

223 *in search of riches that didn't pan out: The Records of the Virginia Company of London,* "The Change in Character from 1606 to 1609," Library of Congress, 1906, http://www.virtualjamestown.org/exist/cocoon/jamestown/virgco/b000451042; also see: "Jamestown Settlement," from "Africans in America: The Terrible Transformation, Part I: 1450–1750," WGBH, October 1998, https://www.pbs.org/wgbh/aia/part1/1p261.html.

223 *willing to drop all else:* James Rawls, Richard Orsi, and Marlene Smith, *A Golden State: Mining and Economic Development in Gold Rush California* (Berkeley: University of California Press, 1999), 185–86, https://archive.org/details/goldenstateminin0000unse/page/186/mode/2up.

223 *California wasn't even American turf in January 1848:* "Treaty of Guadalupe Hidalgo," Wikipedia, https://en.wikipedia.org/wiki/Treaty_of_Guadalupe_Hidalgo.

223 *The state's population . . . swelled to one hundred and fifteen thousand:* Andrew Rolle and Arthur C. Verge, *California: A History* (Arlington Heights, IL: Harlan Davidson, 1987), 110.

223 *"Gold! Gold! Gold! From the American River!":* Douglas S. Watson, "Herald of the Gold Rush: Sam Brannan," *California Historical Society Quarterly* 10, no. 3 (1931): 298–301.

223 *$15 for gold pans he'd acquired for twenty cents:* Frank K. Martin, *A Decade of Delusions* (San Francisco: Wiley, 2011), 21, footnote.

223 *miners were paying $100 for shovels and picks:* Hubert Howe Bancroft, *History of California, Volume 6; Volume 23,* 93, footnote 16, https://

books.google.com.bz/books?id=h4Go1kZ-TuoC&q=Samuel+Brannan
#v=snippet&q=prices&f=false.

223 *who "mined the miners"*: Steve Boggan, "Gold Rush California Was Much
More Expensive Than Today's Tech-Boom California," *Smithsonian*,
September 30, 2015, https://www.smithsonianmag.com/history/gold
-rush-california-was-much-more-expensive-todays-dot-com-boom
-california-180956788/.

224 *$1,484 all told:* It was $43 then, and the consumer price index in 2020
was 34.5 times what it was in 1849, using this calculator: https://www
.measuringworth.com/datasets/uscpi/.

224 *"A pretty expensive breakfast, thought we!":* Edward Gould Buffum, *Six
Months in the Gold Mines* (London: Richard Bentley, 1850), 105; search-
able on Google Books.

224 *genocide and seizure of land from Native Americans:* Notably, the FBI
was born as the result of a federal investigation into a series of murders
of the Osage people, who became wealthy after oil was discovered on
their Oklahoma reservation, causing much local white resentment. The
Osages were, of course, driven off their land. David Grann tells the story
masterfully in his bestseller, *Killers of the Flower Moon* (New York: Penguin Random House, 2017).

224 *a hereditary institution:* Not until slavery was made a for-profit business was the child of an enslaved person enslaved for life. And slavery
was *insanely* profitable. Michael Mechanic, "We Watched Roots With a
'Roots' Expert," *Mother Jones*, May 31, 2016, https://www.motherjones
.com/media/2016/05/new-history-roots-recap-episode-1/.

224 *gave rise to . . . mass incarceration:* This is well documented in David
Blackmon's *Slavery by Another Name* (New York: Anchor Books, 2008);
also see Shane Bauer, *American Prison* (New York: Penguin Random
House, 2019).

224 *turned Florida . . . into a vacation getaway:* "The Forgotten Real Estate
Boom of the 1920s," Harvard Business School Historical Collections,
https://www.library.hbs.edu/hc/crises/forgotten.html.

224 *It transformed western North Dakota:* Caroline Cournoyer, "North Dakota's Oil Boom Is a Blessing and a Curse," Governing.com, August 2011,
https://www.governing.com/north-dakotas-oil-boom-blessing-curse
.html.

224 *our fledgling nation was a "commercial republic":* Joseph J. Ellis, "John
Adams' Fear About America's Future Feel Pretty Darn Prescient Today,"

Mother Jones, October 18, 2018, https://www.motherjones.com/politics /2018/10/john-adams-thomas-jefferson-wealth-inequality-american -dialogue/.

225 *"Everyone was a temporarily embarrassed capitalist":* John Steinbeck, "A Primer on the 30's," *Esquire*, June 1, 1960, https://classic.esquire.com /article/1960/6/1/a-primer-on-the-30s.

225 *63 percent . . . were satisfied with their opportunities:* Frank Newport, "Majority in U.S. Satisfied with Opportunity to Get Ahead," Gallup, March 7, 2018, https://news.gallup.com/poll/228914/majority-satisfied -opportunity-ahead.aspx.

225 *Americans were significantly more optimistic than their European counterparts:* Alberto Alesina, Stefanie Stantcheva, and Edorado Teso, "Intergenerational Mobility and Preferences for Redistribution," *American Economic Review*, February 2018, https://pubs.aeaweb.org/doi/pdfplus /10.1257/aer.20162015.

225 *Americans . . . are "over-optimistic":* The cruel irony is that some of the regions where mobility is the least likely, such as in the Deep South, are where people cling especially tightly to the mobility myth. See Patricia Cohen, "Southerners, Facing Big Odds, Believe in a Path Out of Poverty," *New York Times*, July 4, 2019, https://www.nytimes.com/2019/07/04 /business/economy/social-mobility-south.html.

225 *doing better than your parents—is no longer assured:* Raj Chetty, David Grusky, Maximilian Hell, Nathaniel Hendren, Robert Manduca, and Jimmy Narang, "The Fading American Dream: Trends in Absolute Income Mobility Since 1940," National Bureau of Economic Research, December 2016, http://www.equality-of-opportunity.org/papers/abs _mobility_paper.pdf; for a related read, see Ben Steverman, "Harvard's Chetty Finds Economic Carnage in Wealthiest ZIP Codes," *Bloomberg Businessweek*, September 24, 2020, https://www.bloomberg.com/news /features/2020-09-24/harvard-economist-raj-chetty-creates-god-s-eye -view-of-pandemic-damage.

226 *weaponized the term "welfare queens":* Bryce Covert, "The Myth of the Welfare Queen," *The New Republic*, July 2, 2016, https://newrepublic .com/article/154404/myth-welfare-queen.

226 *52 percent . . . cited "lack of motivation" as a key cause of poverty:* "American Attitudes About Poverty and the Poor," Population Reference Bureau, https://www.prb.org/americanattitudesaboutpovertyand thepoor/.

226 *urban Black men were "not even thinking about working":* Igor Volsky,

"Paul Ryan Blames Poverty on Lazy 'Inner City Men,'" ThinkProgress, March 12, 2014, https://thinkprogress.org/paul-ryan-blames-poverty-on-lazy-inner-city-men-6448050b3059/. More recently, Donald Trump's coddled advisor and son-in-law Jared Kushner gave an interview in which he seemed to question the aspirations of Black Americans. Annie Karni, "Kushner, Employing Racist Stereotype, Questions if Black Americans 'Want to Be Successful,'" *New York Times*, October 20, 2020, https://www.nytimes.com/2020/10/26/us/politics/kushner-black-racist-stereotype.html.

226 *64 percent of Republican respondents . . . said poverty was caused more by "a lack of individual effort"*: "Society or the Individual: Root Causes of Poverty in America," College of Mount Saint Vincent, January 5, 2016, https://mountsaintvincent.edu/society-or-the-individual-root-causes-of-poverty-in-america/.

226 *anyone could achieve the American Dream by working hard*: RealClear Opinion Research, February 22–26, 2019, https://www.realclearpolitics.com/docs/190305_RCOR_Topline_V2.pdf.

226 *children as young as four can distinguish "rich" from "poor" people using visual clues*: Kristin Shutts, Elizabeth L. Brey, Leah A. Dornbusch, Nina Slywotzsky, and Kristina R. Olson, "Children Use Wealth Cues to Evaluate Others," *PLOS ONE*, March 2, 2016, https://www.ncbi.nlm.nih.gov/pmc/articles/PMC4774995/.

226 *the children rated the rich characters more favorably*: Carol K. Sigelman, "Rich Man, Poor Man: Developmental Differences in Attributions and Perceptions," *Journal of Experimental Child Psychology*, November 2012, https://www.ncbi.nlm.nih.gov/pubmed/22858091.

227 *"Yes. I worked very hard for it"*: Tim Hains, "Bernie Sanders to Mike Bloomberg: You Have a 'Grotesque and Immoral' Amount of Wealth," *RealClearPolitics*, February 19, 2020, https://www.realclearpolitics.com/video/2020/02/19/bernie_sanders_to_mike_bloomberg_you_have_a_grotesque_and_immoral_amount_of_wealth.html.

227 *"Mobility optimists may . . . express hostility"*: Jeff Manza and Clem Brooks, "Why Aren't Americans Angrier About Rising Inequality?," Stanford University, 2016, https://inequality.stanford.edu/sites/default/files/Pathways_Presidential_Anger.pdf.

228 *both authors came from well-established families*: Timothy Noah, "The Mobility Myth," *The New Republic*, February 7, 2012, https://newrepublic.com/article/100516/inequality-mobility-economy-america-recession-divergence.

228 *The Ragged Dick tale . . . "conveys three basic messages":* Harlan Dalton, *Racial Healing* (New York: Anchor Books, 1995), 261, https://amesocia lissues.files.wordpress.com/2016/06/horatio-alger.pdf.

228 *"I came from the projects":* Marc Fisher, "Howard Schultz Says He Grew Up in a Poor Rough Place. Those Who Lived There Called It the 'Country Club of Projects,'" *Washington Post,* March 13, 2019, https://www.wash ingtonpost.com/politics/howard-schultz-says-he-grew-up-in-a-poor -rough-place-those-who-lived-there-called-it-the-country-club-of -projects/2019/03/13/4f26b800-39e9-11e9-a06c-3ec8ed509d15_story .html.

228 *white people have used his success to justify the stories:* Author interview with Darren Walker, December 16, 2019.

CHAPTER 17: THRIVING WHILE BLACK

229 *It took all of about five seconds for Erwin Raphael to realize:* All quotes and details about Raphael's experiences are from author interviews with Erwin Raphael, July 14, 2019, and May 2, 2020, plus follow-up emails.

230 *Whites lacked "the critical mass to dominate the society":* Author emails with Franklin Knight, May 12, 2020.

231 *"'You're at the wrong bar, n—!'":* Raphael used the N-word, so why am I not spelling it out? See MichaelMechanic.com/blog.

231 *steps away from a row of multimillion-dollar yachts:* Richard Gillam, a pal of one of the club's owners and a close friend of Raphael's, stops by our table. Gillum, once a nationally ranked pairs figure skater, hit his jackpot as cofounder and CEO of Direct Sports Network, a website where fans pay to stream exclusive content from pro leagues. Raphael is on DSN's board with Leigh Steinberg. I ask Gillam what one of these rowboats would knock me back. "The blue one here is a little over $20 million," he says, but the similarly sized yachts a couple of berths over would run four to five. As with airplanes, the price depends as much on age and speed and amenities as size. "They vary wildly," he says. "Unfortunately the slip prices don't." Ah, the classic coastal 1 percenter quandary. When Raphael lived in Dana Point, he informs us, he and his wife flirted with buying a boat. It would be a poor investment, they concluded, since they know people who own yachts and almost never use them. "One of the selling points of the boat, which was overpriced, was you get the slip with it, be- cause slips aren't available," he says. "So you can buy a boat for less money or buy a much nicer boat and you've got no place to park it."

232 *we all have a tendency to emphasize obstacles:* S. Davidai and T. Gilovich, "The Headwinds/Tailwinds Asymmetry: An Availability Bias in Assessments of Barriers and Blessings," *Journal of Personality and Social Psychology* 111, no. 6 (2016): 835–51, https://psycnet.apa.org/record /2016-56495-001; also see: L. Taylor Phillips and Brian Lowery, "The Hard-Knock? Whites Claim Hardships in Response to Racial Inequity," *Journal of Experimental Social Psychology* 61 (2015): 12–18, https:// www.ltaylorphillips.com/publications/PhillipsLowery_HardKnockLife _2015JESP.pdf.

232 *downplay our own luck and privilege:* Random luck—even just the place and month we are born and the first letter of our last names—can have a big impact on our financial prospects: Robert Frank, "Are You Successful? If So, You've Already Won the Lottery," *New York Times*, May 20, 2016, https://www.nytimes.com/2016/05/22/upshot/are-you -successful-if-so-youve-already-won-the-lottery.html.

232 *ten times the wealth of Black households:* Rakesh Kochhar and Anthony Cilluffo, "How Wealth Inequality Has Changed in the U.S. Since the Great Recession, by Race, Ethnicity and Income," Pew Research Center, November 1, 2017, https://www.pewresearch.org/fact-tank/2017 /11/01/how-wealth-inequality-has-changed-in-the-u-s-since-the-great -recession-by-race-ethnicity-and-income/.

232 *50x and 25x, respectively:* This study excluded durable goods from the Federal Reserve's Survey of Consumer Finance data, which makes the numbers more meaningful, according to coauthor Chuck Collins. By his team's calculations, median Black family wealth ($3,600) was only 2 percent of median white family wealth, and median Latino family wealth ($6,600) was 4 percent of the white figure: Chuck Collins, Dedrick Asante-Muhammed, Josh Hoxie, and Sabrina Terry, "Dreams Deferred," Institute for Policy Studies, January 15, 2019, https://ips-dc.org/racial -wealth-divide-2019/.

232 *Such results cannot . . . be attributed to differences in natural talent:* Andrew Van Dam, "It's Better to Be Born Rich Than Gifted," *Washington Post*, October 9, 2018, https://www.washingtonpost.com/business/2018 /10/09/its-better-be-born-rich-than-talented/.

232 *the "Black tax":* Raphael says he read Rochester's book "in one sitting." See https://blacktaxed.com/.

232 *COVID-19 kills Black Americans at nearly twice the rate:* And the virus infects these groups at more than three times the rate it infects whites. See "The Color of Coronavirus: COVID-19 Deaths by Race and Ethnic-

ity in the U.S.," APM Research Lab, September 16, 2020, https://www
.apmresearchlab.org/covid/deaths-by-race.

232 *though never a Trump supporter:* "What is it that you could possibly find
attractive?" he says.

233 *"This is not a talent issue, but an access issue":* Derek T. Dingle, "There
Are Only 4 Black CEOs at Fortune 500 Companies. Here's How the ELC
Is Changing That," *Black Enterprise,* October 16, 2019, https://www
.blackenterprise.com/elc-increase-number-black-ceos-nation-largest
-public-companies/.

233 *the United States had 788 billionaires:* "Billionaire Census 2020,"
Wealth-X, p. 11.

233 *a posh three-story Manhattan apartment:* American Luxury Staff,
"Billionaire Robert F. Smith Closes on $59M Triplex in Manhattan,"
American Luxury, May 8, 2018, https://www.amlu.com/2018/05/08
/billionaire-robert-f-smith-closes-on-59m-triplex-in-manhattan/.

233 *"I can't have a Black guy buy me dinner":* Nathan Vardi, "Richer
Than Oprah: How The Nation's Wealthiest African-American Con-
quered Tech And Wall Street," *Forbes,* March 6, 2018, https://www
.forbes.com/sites/nathanvardi/2018/03/06/richer-than-oprah-how-the
-nations-wealthiest-african-american-conquered-tech-and-wall-street
/#4a717eea3584.

233 *He pledged to personally wipe out the student debt:* Marjorie Valbrun,
"A Clean Loan Ledger for New Graduates," *Inside Higher Ed,* September
23, 2019, https://www.insidehighered.com/news/2019/09/23/billionaire
-robert-smith-follows-through-pledge-pay-morehouse-students-loan
-debt.

234 *a $1.6 trillion problem:* Now it's a $1.7 trillion problem. See "Consumer
Credit Outstanding," Federal Reserve, updated Dec. 7, 2020, www.fed
eralreserve.gov/releases/g19/HIST/cc_hist_memo_levels.html.

234 *Smith would later admit to big-time tax evasion:* In October 2020,
Smith signed a deal with federal prosecutors alleging that he knew that
Houston businessman Robert Brockman, who invested $1 billion into
Smith's first private equity fund, had concealed that money from the IRS.
(Brockman was indicted the same month for allegedly evading about
$2 billion in federal taxes—he has pleaded not guilty on all counts.)
Smith admitted he had personally used overseas accounts to evade taxes
for fifteen years, and had filed false statements with the IRS. To avoid
federal prosecution, he agreed to pay $139 million in back taxes and
penalties, and promised to cooperate with Brockman's prosecutors for

five years. See David Voreacos and Neil Weinberg, "Billionaire Robert Smith Admits Evading Taxes for Years," *Bloomberg*, October 15, 2020, https://www.bloomberg.com/news/articles/2020-10-15/billionaire -robert-smith-admits-he-cheated-on-taxes-for-15-years. Also see: Dave Michaels and Miriam Gottfried, "Houston Software Executive Robert Brockman Charged With Tax Evasion," *Wall Street Journal*, October 15, 2020, https://www.wsj.com/articles/houston-software-executive-robert -brockman-charged-with-tax-evasion-11602790834.

234 *lack the resources to weather a catastrophe:* "Report on the Economic Well-Being of U.S. Households in 2018—Dealing with Unexpected Expenses," Board of Governors of the Federal Reserve System, May 2019, https://www.federalreserve.gov/publications/2019-economic-well-being -of-us-households-in-2018-dealing-with-unexpected-expenses.htm.

234 *about twenty times more likely to have negative wealth:* Collins, Asante-Muhammed, Hoxie, and Terry, "Dreams Deferred."

234 *Florida "condo king" Jorge Pérez:* Chris Morris, "5 Self-Made Hispanic Immigrant Millionaires," CNBC, June 12, 2017, https://www.cnbc.com /2017/06/12/5-self-made-hispanic-us-immigrant-millionaires.html.

234 *388,000 enslaved Africans:* Henry Louis Gates Jr., *100 Amazing Facts About the Negro* (New York: Knopf Doubleday, 2017), 416.

234 *well over 4 million brown-skinned people:* 4.4 million by 1860, of which 3.9 million remained enslaved: Ibid.

235 *"the people, in general, cannot bear very much reality":* James Baldwin, "Mass Culture and the Creative Artist: Some Personal Notes," in *The Cross of Redemption: Uncollected Writings* (New York: Pantheon, 2010), 3.

235 *the nation's second most valuable capital asset:* Perhaps even the *most* valuable. Yale historian David Blight compares the slave trade in America to oil in Saudi Arabia. Listen to "The South's Cotton Economy," starting at 40:00: https://oyc.yale.edu/history/hist-119/lecture-2.

235 *a 4 percent annual profit for each Black child:* Henry Wiencek, "The Dark Side of Thomas Jefferson," *Smithsonian*, October 2012, https:// www.smithsonianmag.com/history/the-dark-side-of-thomas-jefferson -35976004/.

235 *The Homestead Acts weren't explicitly racist, but the outcome was:* See Trina W. Shanks (citation below). Historian Keri Leigh Merritt also wrote about race and the Homestead Acts in *Masterless Men* (Cambridge, UK: Cambridge University Press, 2017). Brief summary here: Keri Leigh Merritt, "Land and the Roots of African-American Pov-

erty," Aeon, undated post, https://aeon.co/ideas/land-and-the-roots-of
-african-american-poverty.

236 *"The acquisition of property was the key":* Shanks also cites this quote
from Everett Dick, *Lure of the Land* (Lincoln: University of Nebraska
Press, 1970), p. 2.

236 *Homesteading was no cakewalk:* Trina Williams Shanks, "The Home-
stead Acts: A Major Asset-Building Policy in American History," in
Inclusion in the American Dream, ed. Michael Sherraden (New York:
Oxford University Press, 2005), 20–41.

236 *a foundation for intergenerational wealth:* Trina Williams, "Asset-building
Policy as a Response to Wealth Inequality: Drawing Implications from
the Homestead Act of 1862," *Social Development Issues* 25 (2003),
47–58, http://ww1.insightcced.org/uploads/assets/Shanks_Trina/Shanks
_Article.pdf.

236 *more than 48 million living Americans:* Shanks (Williams) kindly updated calculations from her 2005 book chapter cited above, using 2018
census data for adults ages 25–85.

237 *to preserve conditions much as they were under slavery:* Richard Wormser, *The Rise and Fall of Jim Crow* (New York: St. Martin's Press, 1999),
7–8. Read the entire first chapter (pages 1–17) for a brief yet solid summary of the crucial postwar period, 1865–1877.

237 *a brief, sweet respite from the madness:* Eric Foner, "Why Reconstruc-
tion Matters," *New York Times,* March 28, 2015, https://www.nytimes
.com/2015/03/29/opinion/sunday/why-reconstruction-matters.html;
Timothy Murphy, "That Time Domestic Terrorists Took Back the South,"
Mother Jones, May 2, 2017, https://www.motherjones.com/politics
/2017/05/donald-trump-civil-war-reconstruction-eric-foner-history/.
For a deeper dive, read Eric Foner, *Reconstruction,* updated edition (New
York: HarperCollins, 2014).

237 *an estimated two thousand African Americans held public office:* Henry
Louis Gates Jr., *Stony the Road* (New York: Penguin Press, 2019), p. 8.

238 *"less capacity for governing than any race on Earth":* Wormser, *The Rise
and Fall of Jim Crow,* 7. Lincoln wasn't a fan of equal rights, either.
He professed as much during a Senate bid against incumbent Stephen Douglas. See "The Lincoln-Douglas Debates of 1858: Excerpts,"
Academicamerican.com, November 14, 2011, https://www.stjoe.k12.in.us
/ourpages/auto/2011/11/14/53458274/Lincoln-Douglas%20Debates
_%20Excerpts.pdf.

238 *slaughtered hundreds of Black citizens:* Tim Murphy, "That Time Domestic Terrorists . . ."

238 *seized control of New Orleans for several days:* Wormser, *Rise and Fall of Jim Crow*, 1–17.

238 *for the white media if not angry mobs:* For a full account of these fascinating Black lives, read Shomari Wills, *Black Fortunes* (New York: HarperCollins, 2018).

238 *Richard Rothstein provides a full accounting:* Richard Rothstein, *The Color of Law* (New York: W. W. Norton, 2017), 39–75.

239 *Homeownership was a stretch even for the white middle class:* Ibid., 63–67.

239 *discouraged lending in older or urban areas:* Ibid., 64–65.

240 *Black veterans got dramatically less benefit from the GI Bill:* David Callahan, "How the GI Bill Left Out African Americans," Demos.org, November 11, 2013, https://www.demos.org/blog/how-gi-bill-left-out -african-americans; see also: Erin Blakemore, "How the GI Bill's Promise Was Denied to a Million Black WWII Veterans," History.com, September 30, 2019, https://www.history.com/news/gi-bill-black-wwii -veterans-benefits.

240 *the Justice Department sued Fred Trump and his son Donald:* The Trumps ultimately signed a consent decree in which, per standard practice, they were not required to admit guilt. See "Complaint for Injunction Pursuant to Fair Housing Act of 1968," *USA v Fred C. Trump, Donald Trump, and Trump Management Inc.*, October 15, 1973, https:// www.clearinghouse.net/chDocs/public/FH-NY-0024-0005.pdf.

240 *white homeownership today is about 76 percent:* "Quarterly Residential Vacancies and Homeownership, Third Quarter 2020" (Table 7), United States Census Bureau, July 28, 2020, https://www.census.gov/housing /hvs/files/currenthvspress.pdf. In 2000, per this older census report, the median value of homes owned by non-Hispanic whites was nearly $43,000 more than that of homes owned by African Americans. https:// www2.census.gov/library/publications/decennial/2000/briefs/c2kbr -20.pdf.

240 *human lenders . . . assigned higher mortgage interest rates:* Racist lending practices were a big contributor to the 2008 mortgage meltdown, for which some lenders, including major banks, were later taken to task: Rick Rothacker and David Ingram, "Wells Fargo to Pay $175 Million in Race Discrimination Probe," Reuters, July 12, 2012, https://www.re

uters.com/article/us-wells-lending-settlement/wells-fargo-to-pay-175
-million-in-race-discrimination-probe-idUSBRE86B0V220120712.

240 *$750 million per year in excess payments:* Robert Bartlett, Adair Morse,
Richard Stanton, and Nancy Wallace, "Consumer-Lending Discrimination in the FinTech Era," UC Berkeley, February 2019, https://haas
.berkeley.edu/wp-content/uploads/Consumer-Lending-Discrimination
-in-the-FinTech-Era.pdf.

240 *a nationwide racial "assessment gap":* Andrew Van Dam, "Black Families Pay Significantly Higher Property Taxes Than White Families, New
Analysis Shows," *Washington Post*, July 2, 2020, https://www.washing
tonpost.com/business/2020/07/02/black-property-tax.

240 *pay 10 percent to 13 percent more property taxes:* They also pay more
for car insurance, regardless of their driving record: Julia Angwin, Jeff
Larson, Lauren Kirchner, and Surya Mattu, "Minority Neighborhoods
Pay Higher Car Insurance Premiums Than White Areas with the Same
Risk," *ProPublica*, April 5, 2017, https://www.propublica.org/article
/minority-neighborhoods-higher-car-insurance-premiums-white-areas
-same-risk.

240 Newsday *revealed widespread discrimination by white realtors:* Ann
Choi, Keith Herbert, and Olivia Wislow, "Long Island Divided," *Newsday*, November 17, 2019, https://projects.newsday.com/long-island/real
-estate-agents-investigation/.

242 *whose 250,000 members may have included the governor:* Gov. Edward J.
Jackson "was a Klan supporter if not a member," Columbia University
historian Kenneth Jackson (no relation) told me in an email.

245 *Joe Biden was even talking about this:* This is something I don't recall
hearing from previous mainstream candidates, including Obama. Here's
one clip: https://www.youtube.com/watch?v=1NzooejAFJs.

245 *took out a full-page ad:* It ran on Sunday, June 14, 2020. You'll find the
text (scroll down) at https://opusunited.com/.

246 *"'No way! We just finally got access to these'":* On a related note, see
Bernie Becker, "Black Business Owners Backing GOP Estate Tax Repeal Bid," *The Hill*, March 25, 2015, https://thehill.com/policy/finance
/domestic-taxes/236982-black-business-owners-backing-gop-estate
-tax-repeal-bid.

CHAPTER 18: WOMEN ON TOP

247 *female CEOs in the Fortune 500 was at an all-time high:* Emma Hinchliffe, "The Number of Female CEOs in the Fortune 500 Hits an All-Time Record," *Fortune,* May 18, 2020, https://fortune.com/2020/05/18/women-ceos-fortune-500-2020/.

247 *more than twice the poverty rate of male single-parent households:* "Income and Poverty in the United States: 2019," Table B-2, U.S. Census Bureau, Sept. 15, 2020, www.census.gov/library/publications/2020/demo/p60-270.html.

247 *the pandemic has worsened that divide:* In July 2020, based on industry mix and workforce participation, McKinsey estimated that American women should have suffered 43 percent of pandemic-related job losses—but they accounted for 54 percent. "COVID-19 and gender equality: Countering the regressive effects," McKinsey & Co., www.mckinsey.com/featured-insights/future-of-work/covid-19-and-gender-equality-countering-the-regressive-effects#.

247 *men outnumbered women by more than nine to one:* In 2019, 90.1 percent of the world's 290,720 ultrawealthy were male, and 32 percent were American. (Gender was not broken out by country.) Wealth-X, "World Ultra Wealth Report 2020," p. 28.

248 *half-time was forty hours a week:* From past and recent conversations with my parents.

248 *resembles the Black story:* Women of color get the twofer.

248 *not have the boss grab your ass:* This happened to one prominent woman I interviewed.

248 *even simply to vote:* Terence McArdle, " 'Night of Terror': The Suffragists Who Were Beaten and Tortured for Seeking the Vote," *Washington Post,* November 10, 2017, https://www.washingtonpost.com/news/retropolis/wp/2017/11/10/night-of-terror-the-suffragists-who-were-beaten-and-tortured-for-seeking-the-vote/.

248 *more than three times as likely as men to have gotten their fortunes entirely by inheritance:* Wealth-X, "World Ultra Wealth Report 2017," 33–34.

248 *women accounted for just one in five employees:* "Women in Alternatives," Prequin Impact Report, February 2020, https://go.preqin.com/women-in-alternatives.

248 *the same proportion one finds at the equity-partner level of corporate law firms:* Marc Brodherson, Laura McGee, and Mariana Pires dos Reis, "Women in Law Firms," McKinsey & Company, October 2017,

https://www.mckinsey.com/~/media/mckinsey/featured%20insights /gender%20equality/women%20in%20law%20firms/women-in-law -firms-final-103017.ashx.

248 *more funds initiated by men named David than by women:* Miles Kruppa, "The 'David' Problem," *Absolute Return* newsletter, September 2018, https://www.chiltontrustcompany.com/wp-content/uploads /2018/10/Absolute-Return_Chilton-Investment-Company.pdf.

248 *funds with at least one female manager were more likely to fail:* But surviving women-led funds outperformed their male-led counterparts. Rajesh K. Aggarwal and Nicole M. Boyson, "The Performance of Female Hedge Fund Managers," Northeastern University Review of Financial Economics, February 3, 2016, https://papers.ssrn.com/sol3/papers .cfm?abstract_id=2726584.

249 *"that's saying something is wrong with the capital allocation process":* Lindsay Fortado, "Women-Led Hedge Funds Try to Crack the Boys' Club," *Financial Times*, May 15, 2019, https://www.ft.com/content /73698e76-7293-11e9-bf5c-6eeb837566c5.

249 *"you're out in the cold, and that's just a fact":* Author interview with Kim Polese, June 18, 2020.

249 *every potentially lucrative new niche becomes a bro culture:* Capitol Hill remains so. In the 117th Congress, women comprise less than one-third of voting House representatives and only 24 percent of senators, and have yet to breach the ultimate glass ceiling. "Results: Women Candidates in the 2020 Elections," Center for American Women in Politics, Rutgers University, November 4, 2020, https://cawp.rutgers.edu /election-analysis/results-women-candidates-2020-elections.

250 *more than 85 percent of their employees . . . were men:* Charlie Custer, "Blockchain's Gender Divide: A Data Story," LongHash, https://en.long hash.com/news/blockchains-gender-divide-a-data-story.

250 *The after-party was held at a Miami strip club:* Nellie Bowles, "Women in Cryptocurrencies Push Back Against 'Blockchain Bros,'" *New York Times*, February 25, 2018, https://www.nytimes.com/2018/02/25/busi ness/cryptocurrency-women-blockchain-bros.html.

250 *"Otherwise the men are going to get all the wealth, again":* Ibid.

250 *female investors performed better in the long term:* Brad M. Barber and Terrance Odean, "Boys Will Be Boys: Gender, Overconfidence, and Common Stock Investment," *Quarterly Journal of Economics*, April 20, 2000, https://papers.ssrn.com/sol3/papers.cfm?abstract_id=219240.

250 *Public universities . . . began coeducating men and women as early as*

1856: "University of Rochester History: Chapter 13, Enter the Ladies," River Campus Libraries, https://rbscp.lib.rochester.edu/2319.

250 *a Radcliffe degree opened fewer doors:* Not to suggest Radcliffe women were unsuccessful, but this was the general state of affairs at the time.

251 *Malkiel . . . chronicles some of the pushback:* Nancy Weiss Malkiel, *Keep the Damned Women Out* (Princeton, NJ: Princeton University Press, 2016). The cited quotes are from Nancy Weiss Malkiel, "When Women Were Admitted to Ivy League Schools, the Complaints Sounded a Lot Like a Trump Tweet," *Los Angeles Times*, October 21, 2016, https://www .latimes.com/opinion/op-ed/la-oe-malziel-when-women-claim-male -roles-20161021-snap-story.html.

251 *The incrementalism of the Ivies . . . may have contributed:* Author emails with Nancy Weiss Malkiel, June 2020.

251 *banks refused to loan money . . . without a male cosigner:* Author interview with Susan Davis, June 9, 2020. See also: Suzanne McGee and Heidi Moore, "Women's Rights and Their Money: A Timeline from Cleopatra to Lilly Ledbetter," *The Guardian*, August 11, 2014, https://www .theguardian.com/money/us-money-blog/2014/aug/11/women-rights -money-timeline-history.

251 *female Ivy League graduates . . . make only seventy cents per dollar:* Caroline Kitchener, "The Ivy League's Gender Pay-Gap Problem," *The Atlantic*, February 2, 2017, https://www.theatlantic.com/education /archive/2017/02/the-ivy-leagues-gender-pay-gap-problem/515382/. Inflexible workplace policies prevent low-wage parents (mothers mainly) from fulfilling their earning potential. Women in high-paying professions face a similar problem despite flexible policies. Harvard economists Lawrence Katz and Claudia Goldin found that high-earning professionals who took advantage of such policies paid a price. They looked at the outcomes of Harvard students from the classes of '69 through '92, most of whom went on to earn advanced degrees. Women who had experienced the equivalent of an eighteen-month "job interruption" (think child rearing) within fifteen years of earning their undergraduate degrees were slapped with an "earnings penalty" of 41 percent for MBAs, 29 percent for lawyers and PhDs, and 16 percent for MDs. The data suggested that women MBAs who tried to stay on the fast track after bearing a child found it all but impossible. Three to four years after a first birth, even MBAs who hadn't had a second child were working 24 percent fewer hours and making far less money than those who hadn't taken a break. "The corporate and financial sectors impose heavy pen-

alties on deviation from the norm," Katz and Goldin concluded. (The norm is what the male bosses say it is.) Claudia Goldin and Lawrence F. Katz, "The Cost of Workplace Flexibility for High-Powered Professionals," *The ANNALS of the American Academy of Political and Social Science* 638, no. 45 (2011), https://scholar.harvard.edu/files/goldin/files/the_cost_of_workplace_flexibility_for_high-powered_professionals.pdf.

251 *Some studies suggest that these wage-gap figures are misleading:* "The State of the Gender Pay Gap in 2020," PayScale, https://www.payscale.com/data/gender-pay-gap.

252 *Fair enough, but why is that?:* Robert Hohman, "This Is the Biggest Myth About the Gender Wage Gap," *Fortune*, April 12, 2016, https://fortune.com/2016/04/12/myth-gender-wage-gap/.

252 *women take on the lion's share of domestic work:* Arlie Hochschild, *The Second Shift* (New York: Viking, 1989), 1–4.

252 *37 percent of computer science degrees . . . were going to women:* Marissa Fessenden, "What Happened to All the Women in Computer Science?," *Smithsonian*, October 22, 2014, https://www.smithsonianmag.com/smart-news/what-happened-all-women-computer-science-1-180953111/. Also see: Code.org, "Women Computer Science Graduates Finally Surpass Record Set 17 Years Ago, but Percentages Lag Behind," Medium.com, May 11, 2020, https://medium.com/@codeorg/women-computer-science-graduates-finally-surpass-record-set-17-years-ago-20a79a76275.

252 *the snarky post in question:* Now appended to the author's mea culpa: Eric Jackson, "Apology to Sheryl Sandberg and Kim Polese [Updated]," *Forbes*, May 23, 2012, https://www.forbes.com/sites/ericjackson/2012/05/23/apology-sheryl-sandberg-kim-polese/#1bda298c664e.

253 *Time magazine's 1997 list of the 25 Most Influential Americans:* "TIME's 25 Most Influential Americans," *Time*, April 21, 1997, http://content.time.com/time/magazine/article/0,9171,986206-2,00.html.

253 *Polese had received a similar treatment:* Melanie Warner, "The Beauty of Hype: A Cautionary Tale of Silicon Valley," *Fortune* (via CNN Money), March 1, 1999, https://money.cnn.com/magazines/fortune/fortune_archive/1999/03/01/255816/index.htm.

254 *in Cupid costumes:* Gary Rivlin, "Dot-Com Uses 'Guerrilla' Marketing to Get Noticed,'" *The Industry Standard* (via IDG/CNN), August 4, 2000, https://www.cnn.com/2000/TECH/computing/08/04/marketeer.cult.idg/index.html.

254 *banged out a response then and there:* Caroline Howard, "Kim Polese:

Stop Comparing Female Execs and Just Let Sheryl Sandberg Do Her Job," *Forbes*, May 25, 2012, https://www.forbes.com/sites/caroline howard/2012/05/25/stop-comparing-female-execs-and-just-let-sheryl -sandberg-do-her-job/#78b2b4d73efc.

254 *women she didn't even know had come to her defense:* Some men did, too: "Kim Polese Is a Cautionary Tale?," Workbench, https://workbench.ca denhead.org/news/3680/kim-polese-cautionary-tale.

254 *a subsequent apology post:* Jackson, "Apology to Sheryl Sandberg and Kim Polese [Updated]."

254 *had appeared on the cover of* Fortune: Rana Foroohar, *Don't Be Evil* (New York: Penguin Random House, 2019), 38. No book is error-free, of course. You might even find a few errors in this one!

254 *the claim that Marimba had "flamed out":* Ibid., 78.

254 *What really happened:* The IPO took place two years and two weeks after *Time* published its list.

254 *Marimba went public:* George Anders, "Marimba Triples on First Trading Day as Investors Shrug Off Operating Losses," *Wall Street Journal*, May 3, 1999, https://www.wsj.com/articles/SB925478358510469053.

255 *the company was taken private:* Stacy Cowley, "BMC to Buy Marimba for $239 Million," *Computerworld*, April 29, 2004, https://www.comput erworld.com/article/2803126/bmc-to-buy-marimba-for-239-million .html.

255 *"There's very much a code of conduct":* Author interview with Tracy Gary, January 5, 2020.

255 *"There's an automatic presumption that you did not earn the money":* Author interview with "Annika," June 15, 2020.

256 *"Women don't come with the confidence":* Author interview with Tracy Gary, January 5, 2020.

256 *helped launch nearly two dozen nonprofits:* "Philanthropist and Movement Builder Tracy Gary Receives Shaw-Hardy Taylor Award for Advancing Women's Philanthropy," Indiana University Lilly Family School of Philanthropy, March 15, 2017, https://philanthropy.iupui .edu/news-events/news-item/philanthropist-and-movement-builder -tracy-gary-receives-shaw-hardy-taylor-award-for-advancing-women's -philanthropy.html?id=223.

257 *"Literally, the wives were often told nothing":* Author interview with Susan Davis, June 9, 2020.

257 *Harris Bank, which the federal government had sued:* Phillip Shenon, "Chicago Bank to Pay $14 Million in Resolving Discrimination Case," *New*

York Times, January 11, 1989, https://www.nytimes.com/1989/01/11/us/chicago-bank-to-pay-14-million-in-resolving-discrimination-case.html.

CHAPTER 19: GIVING IT AWAY

259 *"'I would as soon leave to my son a curse as the almighty dollar'"*: Andrew Carnegie, "Wealth," *North American Review*, No. CCCXCI, June 1889, https://www.swarthmore.edu/SocSci/rbannis1/.

259 *"'in the process you're going to destroy some of them'"*: Author interview with Richard Watts, June 13, 2019.

261 *Between half and two-thirds of U.S. households donate:* Interestingly, the proportion that gave to charity (including religious giving) declined from almost 68 percent in 2002 to 53 percent in 2016. See "16 Years of Charitable Giving Research," Lilly Family School of Philanthropy Panel Study (p. 8), Indiana University, 2009, https://scholarworks.iupui.edu/bitstream/handle/1805/21470/gfl-research191212.pdf. Gallup, whose "self-reported" survey numbers are higher than those of the Lilly School, found a nadir in April 2020, particularly among people earning less than $100,000 a year. (See citation below.)

261 *three in five volunteer time and effort:* Jeffrey M. Jones, "Percentage of Americans Donating to Charity at New Low," Gallup, May 14, 2020, https://news.gallup.com/poll/310880/percentage-americans-donating-charity-new-low.aspx.

262 *The average rent for a one-bedroom apartment in Oakland:* "Rent Trend Data in Oakland California," Rent Jungle, https://www.rentjungle.com/average-rent-in-oakland-rent-trends/.

262 *whose union-busting efforts resulted in deadly violence:* In 1892, workers at Carnegie's steel plant in Homestead, Pennsylvania, sought a pay increase and were rewarded instead with a pay cut by the plant's general manager, Henry Frick, who, along with Carnegie, was determined to break the workers' union. During the ensuing standoff, Frick, with Carnegie's knowledge and support, shut workers out of the plant and brought in thousands of strikebreakers and hundreds of armed Pinkerton agents, resulting in violence that left ten dead and hundreds injured. Here's one brief account: "The Strike at Homestead Mill," *American Experience*, PBS, undated article, https://www.pbs.org/wgbh/americanexperience/features/carnegie-strike-homestead-mill/.

263 *built thousands of free public libraries:* Carnegie created 2,509 libraries, 1,679 in the United States: "Andrew Carnegie: Pioneer. Visionary. Inno-

vator," Carnegie Medal of Philanthropy, undated, https://www.medalof
philanthropy.org/andrew-carnegie/.

263 *$791 million in federal taxes on $26.5 billion in profits:* It paid nothing
in 2019, despite profits of $11.2 billion. Christopher Ingraham, "Amazon
paid no federal taxes on $11.2 billion in profits last year," *Washington
Post*, February 16, 2019, https://www.washingtonpost.com/us-policy
/2019/02/16/amazon-paid-no-federal-taxes-billion-profits-last-year/.

263 *Bezos himself spent $100,000:* John Cook, "Steve Ballmer, Jeff Bezos
fund effort to defeat state income tax," *Puget Sound Business Journal*,
September 20, 2010, https://www.bizjournals.com/seattle/blog/tech
flash/2010/09/ballmer_bezos_fund_effort_to_defeat_state_income
_tax.html.

263 *Amazon played hardball:* Maya Kosoff, "Amazon Crushes a Small Tax
That Would Have Helped the Homeless," *Vanity Fair*, June 12, 2018,
https://www.vanityfair.com/news/2018/06/amazon-seattle-repeal-head
-tax-homelessness.

263 *The city council's "hostile approach":* Jason Del Rey, "Amazon Is Questioning Its Future in Seattle After the City Voted for a New Tax on Big Business," *Vox*, May 14, 2018, https://www.vox.com/2018/5/14/17354420
/amazon-seattle-head-tax-employee-vote-homelessness-construction.

263 *would have discouraged companies from hiring impoverished people:*
Antony Davies and James R. Harrigan, "Stop BEZOS and a Lesson in
Economics," *InsideSources*, September 11, 2018, https://www.inside
sources.com/stop-bezos-and-a-lesson-in-economics/.

263 *Stop Bad Employers by Zeroing Out Subsidies Act:* Matthew Yglesias,
"The Controversy Over Bernie Sanders's Proposed Stop BEZOS Act,
Explained," *Vox*, September 12, 2018, https://www.vox.com/policy-and
-politics/2018/9/11/17831970/stop-bezos-bernie-sanders.

264 *the more plausible explanation was that Amazon hoped to reap positive press:* Eric Levitz, "Why Amazon Raised Its Minimum Wage to
$15," *New York*, October 2, 2018, https://nymag.com/intelligencer/2018
/10/why-amazon-raised-minimum-wage-to-15-dollars-jeff-bezos-act
-bernie-sanders.html.

264 *Jeff published a Medium post:* Jeff Bezos, "No Thank You, Mr. Pecker," Medium, February 7, 2019, https://medium.com/@jeffreypbezos/no-thank
-you-mr-pecker-146e3922310f.

264 *one of the world's richest women:* Kristin Stoller, "The Top 10 Richest
Women," *Forbes*, 2020, https://www.forbes.com/sites/kristinstoller/2020
/04/07/the-top-10-richest-women-in-the-world-2020/#503eddfa4776.

264 *worth almost $68 billion as of October 13, 2020:* She'd already given some of her fortune away by then, however. I chose a specific date because Scott's net worth moves around so much. In September 2020, Scott even snatched the "richest woman" title away from Alice Walton, who promptly snatched it back: Emma Hinchliffe, "MacKenzie Scott is now the wealthiest woman in the world," *Fortune*, September 2, 2020, https://fortune.com/2020/09/02/mackenzie-scott-bezos-net-worth-richest-woman-in-world-wealthiest-women-amazon-stock-jeff-bezos-billions/.

264 *She signed the Giving Pledge:* "Mackenzie Scott," The Giving Pledge, May 25, 2019, https://givingpledge.org/Pledger.aspx?id=393.

264 *216 billionaires and would-be billionaires . . . had signed on:* "The Giving Pledge Welcomes 13 New Signatories," press release, December 21, 2020, https://givingpledge.org/PressRelease.aspx?date=12.21.2020.

264 *Notably absent: Jeff Bezos, the Waltons, and the Trumps*: Laurene Powell Jobs is also notably absent, but she has independently pledged to give away her entire fortune or thereabouts.

264 *Only about 1 in 13 of the world's 2,825 billionaires:* Billionaire population from "Billionaire Census 2020," Wealth-X, 10–11.

265 *more assets in August 2020 than they did when the pledge was created:* Only 11 of 62 saw their net assets shrink due to giving or market losses since 2010, the IPS reports; in fact, the combined wealth of these pledgers nearly doubled, from $376 billion to $734 billion in 2020 dollars. Chuck Collins and Helen Flannery, "Gilded Giving 2020," Institute for Policy Studies, August 2020 (see p. 7), https://ips-dc.org/wp-content/uploads/2020/07/Gilded-Giving-2020-July28-2020.pdf.

265 *would hand out 99 percent of their Facebook stake:* Vindu Goel and Nick Wingfield, "Mark Zuckerberg Vows to Donate 99% of His Facebook Shares for Charity," *New York Times*, December 1, 2015, https://www.nytimes.com/2015/12/02/technology/mark-zuckerberg-facebook-charity.html.

265 *Zuckerberg owned 400,468,692 shares of Facebook:* "Form SC 13G/A Facebook Inc [Amend] Statement of Acquisition of Beneficial Ownership by Individuals," Securities and Exchange Commission, February 14, 2020, https://sec.report/Document/0001193125-20-038147/.

265 *Zuckerberg has substantial investments in Asana:* T. K. McDonald, "Mark Zuckerberg's Portfolio," Investopedia, July 18, 2020, https://www.investopedia.com/articles/personal-finance/042516/what-mark-zuckerbergs-portfolio-looks-fb-msft.asp.

265 *seven hundred acres of prime waterfront land in Kauai:* Katherine Clarke, "Unraveling Mark Zuckerberg's Secret Deal for a $59 Million Tahoe Compound," *Wall Street Journal,* May 2, 2019, https://www .wsj.com/articles/unraveling-mark-zuckerbergs-secret-deal-for-a-59 -million-tahoe-compound-11556811876.

265 *"He should be everybody's hero":* Niall O'Dowd, "Chuck Feeney, Bill Gates' and Warren Buffett's Hero, Honored by Ireland Fund," Atlantic Philanthropies, March 12, 2016, https://www.atlanticphilanthropies .org/news/chuck-feeney-bill-gates-and-warren-buffetts-hero-honored -by-ireland-fund.

266 *Feeney was reluctant to join:* Charles F. Feeney, "Letter to Bill Gates," February 3, 2011, https://givingpledge.org/Pledger.aspx?id=195.

266 *nearly $9 billion to his philanthropic pursuits:* $8,117,059,368 in grants and $808 million in overhead for thirty-eight years of operations in seven countries, per author email with Atlantic Philanthropies CEO Christopher Oechsli, October 26, 2020.

266 *homemade sandwiches at night on fraternity row:* This and most other details about Feeney's youth and early business doings are from Conor O'Clery, *The Billionaire Who Wasn't* (New York: PublicAffairs, 2007 and 2013), 3–22.

266 *"the holy grail of grouse moors":* Annika Purdey, "Best grouse estates for the Glorious Twelfth," *Tatler,* August 5, 2019, https://www.tatler.com /article/best-grouse-estates-for-the-glorious-twelfth.

266 *two of his daughters married princes:* O'Clery describes Miller's estate and lifestyle in excruciating detail.

267 *"I can only wear one pair at a time":* Author interview with Harvey Dale, March 5, 2019.

267 *Duty Free Shoppers . . . was obsessed with secrecy:* O'Clery, *The Billionaire Who Wasn't,* 115–32.

267 *a charitable entity he'd set up in Bermuda:* Feeney and Dale chose this location because, unlike the U.S., Bermuda let foundations oversee for-profit businesses and made it easier for Feeney to maintain anonymity. Ibid., 100.

267 *he was unaware who Feeney was:* Author interview with Chris Oechsli, December 11, 2018.

268 *the* New York Times *finally outed him:* Judith Miller, "He Gave Away $600 Million and No One Knew," *New York Times,* January 23, 1997, https://www.nytimes.com/1997/01/23/nyregion/he-gave-away-600 -million-and-no-one-knew.html.

268 *Ian Parker profiled him for the* New Yorker: Ian Parker, "The Gift: Zell Kravinsky Gave Away Millions. But Somehow It Wasn't Enough," *The New Yorker*, July 26, 2004, https://www.newyorker.com/magazine/2004 /08/02/the-gift-ian-parker.

268 *"I never buy clothes"*: All quotes from author interview with Zell Kravinsky, December 21, 2019.

269 Law & Order *and* House *based episodes on his story: Law & Order: Criminal Intent* ("Ex Stasis") portrayed him as a monster, Kravinsky said, whereas *House* ("Charity Case") made him more like a saint.

270 *"'She's going to slam the door in his face'"*: "She would! My wife would!" Kravinsky insisted. "She doesn't care how good-looking he is or how big a celebrity."

270 *fewer than 150 . . . had ever been performed:* This is based on data provided by the United Network for Organ Sharing, which has records dating back to 1988, when it tallied its first nondirected donation. By 2002, 111 such surgeries had been done, all told. There were seventy -five in 2003, the year Kravinsky donated his kidney, and because he did it during the summer, I estimated thirty-eight of them had been done before his. But from January 2016 through October 2020 (despite COVID), there were an average of 286 nondirected kidney donations per year.

273 *"a reputation-laundering exercise"*: Author interview with Rob Reich, June 8, 2020.

273 *contributed to the deaths of hundreds of thousands of Americans:* "Overdose Death Rates," National Institute on Drug Abuse, https://www.dru gabuse.gov/drug-topics/trends-statistics/overdose-death-rates.

273 *giving at least $60 million to universities:* Collin Binkley and Jennifer McDermott, "Prestigious Universities Around the World Accepted More Than $60M from OxyContin Family," *USA Today*, October 3, 2019, https://www.usatoday.com/story/news/nation/2019/10/03/sackler -family-donations-imperial-college-london-university-sussex-yale /3849912002/.

273 *the Louvre, the Met, and the Guggenheim:* Michael Posner, "The Sacklers: Charitable Giving Does Not Excuse Improper Business Conduct," *Forbes*, March 31, 2019, https://www.forbes.com/sites/michaelposner /2019/03/31/the-sacklers-charitable-giving-does-not-excuse-improper -business-conduct/#40f7835e77b6.

273 *These institutions pledged to take no more gifts:* Elizabeth A. Harris, "The Met Will Turn Down Sackler Money Amid Fury Over the Opioid Crisis,"

New York Times, May 14, 2019, https://www.nytimes.com/2019/05/15
/arts/design/met-museum-sackler-opioids.html.

273 *Tufts . . . stripped the family name off one of its buildings:* Kate Taylor,
"Sackler Family Members Fight Removal of Name at Tufts, Calling It
a 'Breach,'" *New York Times*, December 19, 2019, https://www.nytimes
.com/2019/12/19/us/sackler-opioids-tufts.html.

273 *Purdue announced it would plead guilty to criminal federal conspiracy
charges:* "Justice Department Announces Global Resolution of Criminal
and Civil Investigations with Opioid Manufacturer Purdue Pharma and
Civil Settlement with Members of the Sackler Family," DOJ press release,
October 21, 2020, https://www.justice.gov/opa/pr/justice-department
-announces-global-resolution-criminal-and-civil-investigations-opioid;
from the bottom of the page you can download Purdue's plea agreement
and criminal settlement, and the Sacklers' civil settlement. Regarding
the fraudulent transfers, New York's attorney general separately alleged
that some $1 billion of Purdue funds had been wired into Swiss bank
accounts controlled by the Sacklers. See "Attorney General James' Statement On Purdue Pharma Bankruptcy Filing," press release, September
16, 2019, https://ag.ny.gov/press-release/2019/attorney-general-james
-statement-purdue-pharma-bankruptcy-filing.

274 *paying miserly wages and shortchanging employees:* For a few exam-
ples, see "Discounting Rights," Human Rights Watch report, May 2007,
https://www.hrw.org/reports/2007/us0507/index.htm; also: "Wal-Mart
Workers to Receive More Than $33 Million in Back Wages," Department
of Labor press release, January 15, 2007, https://www.dol.gov/news
room/releases/esa/esa20070125; and "Wal-Mart must pay $188 million
in workers' class action," Reuters, December 16, 2014, https://www.re
uters.com/article/us-walmart-lawsuit/wal-mart-must-pay-188-million
-in-workers-class-action-idUSKBN0JU1XJ20141216.

274 *dedicated a foundation to "hunger relief and healthy eating":* Walmart
boasts that it donated 640 million pounds of food in FY2019, of which
more than 55 percent was meat and produce (that is, perishable) and
worked to improve access to SNAP and WIC, government entitlements
some underpaid Walmart workers have relied on to get by. https://fcon
line.foundationcenter.org/fdo-grantmaker-profile?key=WALM001.

274 *consolidate power and foment genocidal campaigns:* Jamelle Bouie,
"Facebook Has Been a Disaster for the World," *New York Times*, September 18, 2020, https://www.nytimes.com/2020/09/18/opinion/facebook

-democracy.html; also see Alexandra Stevenson, "Facebook Admits It Was Used to Incite Violence in Myanmar," *New York Times*, November 16, 2018, https://www.nytimes.com/2018/11/06/technology/myanmar-facebook.html.

274 *Facebook established a $15 minimum wage in 2015:* Akanksha Rana and Arjun Panchadar, "Facebook Raises Minimum Wage for U.S. Contract Workers to $20/Hour," Reuters, May 13, 2019, https://www.reuters.com/article/us-facebook-wages/facebook-raises-minimum-wage-for-us-contract-workers-to-20-hour-idUSKCN1SJ1TQ.

274 *to explicitly target . . . "Jew haters":* Julia Angwin, Madeleine Varner, and Ariana Tobin, "Facebook Enabled Advertisers to Reach 'Jew Haters,'" *ProPublica*, Sept. 14, 2017, https://www.propublica.org/article/facebook-enabled-advertisers-to-reach-jew-haters; Julia Angwin and Terry Parris Jr., "Facebook Lets Advertisers Exclude Users by Race," *ProPublica*, October 28, 2016, https://www.propublica.org/article/facebook-lets-advertisers-exclude-users-by-race; Ariana Tobin and Jeremy B. Merrill, "Facebook Is Letting Job Advertisers Target Only Men," *ProPublica*, September 18, 2018, https://www.propublica.org/article/facebook-is-letting-job-advertisers-target-only-men. For more on the problems Facebook poses for American media and democracy, see Monika Bauerlein and Clara Jeffrey, "How Facebook Screwed Us All," *Mother Jones*, March/April 2019, https://www.motherjones.com/politics/2019/02/how-facebook-screwed-us-all/.

274 *"Russian actors created 80,000 posts":* Samidh Chakrabarti, "Hard Questions: What Effect Does Social Media Have on Democracy?," Facebook, January 22, 2018, https://about.fb.com/news/2018/01/effect-social-media-democracy/.

274 *amid public pressure and an exodus of advertisers:* Suzanne Vranica and Deepa Seethearaman, "Facebook Tightens Controls on Speech as Ad Boycott Grows," *Wall Street Journal*, June 26, 2020, https://www.wsj.com/articles/unilever-to-halt-u-s-ads-on-facebook-and-twitter-for-rest-of-2020-11593187230; also see Elizabeth Culliford and Sheila Dang, "Facebook Will Label Newsworthy Posts That Break Rules as Ad Boycott Widens," Reuters, June 26, 2020, https://www.reuters.com/article/us-facebook-ads-boycott-unilever/facebook-tightens-hateful-conduct-policies-as-ad-boycott-gains-steam-idUSKBN23X2FW.

275 *"should a few of us have all this dough?":* Author interview with Nick Hanauer, June 10, 2019.

275 *one of the nation's first . . . general-purpose charitable foundations:* Most

charities then, including Carnegie's Foundation for the Advancement of Teaching, were more narrowly focused: "Foundation History: The Early Years," Carnegie Foundation, https://www.carnegiefoundation.org /about-us/foundation-history/.

275 *"Your fortune is rolling up . . . like an avalanche!":* This and the quotes from Taft, Roosevelt, and Holmes come from Rob Reich, *Just Giving* (Princeton: Princeton University Press, 2018) 1–7.

276 *averaging just 4.2 percent from 2010 to 2016:* Chuck Collins and Helen Flannery, "The Case for an Emergency Charity Stimulus" (p. 9), Institute for Policy Studies, May 11, 2020, https://inequality.org/wp-content/up loads/2020/05/Brief-CharityStimulus-Revision-May12-FINAL.pdf.

276 *expended 6 percent of their assets:* This figure is for "independent" grant-making foundations (see below), and excludes corporate, community, and "operating" foundations: "Key Facts on U.S. Nonprofits and Foundations," Candid, April 2020, https://www.issuelab.org/resources/36381 /36381.pdf.

276 *the S&P 500 clocked a 29 percent gain:* (assuming dividend reinvestment) "2019 S&P 500 Return," DQYDJ, September 6, 2020, https://dqydj.com /2019-sp-500-return/.

277 *nearly 108,000 independent grantmaking foundations:* Candid, April 2020, https://www.issuelab.org/resources/36381/36381.pdf. These are private "nonoperating" foundations endowed by wealthy families and individuals. In December 2019, they held a combined $948 billion in assets. The number of such foundations, according to Candid's records, nearly doubled from 41,751 in 1998 to 79,558 in 2018, but this excludes the ones that didn't give any grants during the year in question. Candid's 2019 count includes foundations that gave that year and ones that didn't—hence the significantly higher number.

277 *$120 billion now stashed in donor-advised funds:* Collins and Flannery, "The Case for an Emergency Charity Stimulus."

277 *remain sequestered in the charitable portfolios of our wealthiest citizens:* Will Hobston, "Zombie Philanthropy: The Rich Have Stashed Billions in Donor-Advised Charities—but It's Not Reaching Those in Need," *Washington Post,* June 24, 2020, https://www.washingtonpost.com/lifestyle /style/zombie-philanthropy-the-rich-have-stashed-billions-in-donor -advised-charities—but-its-not-reaching-those-in-need/2020/06/23 /6a1b397a-af3a-11ea-856d-5054296735e5_story.html.

277 *at best about one-third of charitable giving serves that purpose:* The proportion of U.S. households giving to basic needs charities declined from

about 31 percent in 2006 to about 25 percent in 2016. See p. 16 of the Lilly report cited below.

277 *spent about 10 percent of their charitable dollar on "basic needs" giving:* Reich relied on 2005 data from the Lilly Family School of Philanthropy at Indiana University: Rob Reich, *Just Giving*, 89. Panel data the school provided me for 2001–2017 was less conclusive. In that dataset, families earning $50,000 or less directed about 15 percent of their giving to basic needs, on average, versus about 17 percent for families earning $250,000 or more, but in Reich's analysis it was only at very high incomes that basic needs giving dropped off (and arts and education giving increased). The Lilly School declined to provide data for donors with $1 million–plus salaries, citing inadequate sample sizes.

277 *can deduct charitable gifts totaling up to 60 percent:* "Charitable Contribution Deductions," IRS.com, https://www.irs.gov/charities-non-profits /charitable-organizations/charitable-contribution-deductions.

278 *fewer than 14 percent of taxpayers itemize:* 13.7 percent in 2019, estimates the Tax Foundation, mostly 10 percenters and up. Scott Eastman, "How Many Taxpayers Itemize Under Current Law?," Tax Foundation, September 12, 2019, https://taxfoundation.org/standard-deduction -itemized-deductions-current-law-2019.

278 *where the "big bets" . . . ended up:* William Foster, Gail Perreault, Alison Powell, and Chris Addy, "Making Bets for Social Change," *Stanford Social Innovation Review*, 2016, https://www.sandlerfoundation.org/wp -content/uploads/Making_Big_Bets_for_Social_Change.pdf.

279 *religious, charitable, scientific, literary, or educational purposes:* "Charitable Contribution Deductions" (p. 2), IRS.gov, https://www.irs.gov /charities-non-profits/charitable-organizations/charitable-contribution -deductions.

279 *"fostering appreciation" for camellias:* "About American Camellia Society," American Camellia Society, https://www.americancamellias.com /about-american-camellia-society.

279 *"promoting the medium of American mime":* "American Mime, Inc.," Facebook, https://www.facebook.com/pg/cjcBarbour/about/?ref=page _internal.

279 *anti-LGBTQ, anti-Muslim, and anti-immigrant:* The NCF won't comment on the specifics of where its donors direct their money. Alex Kotch, "America's Biggest Christian Charity Funnels Tens of Millions to Hate Groups," *Sludge*, March 19, 2019, https://readsludge.com/2019/03/19

/americas-biggest-christian-charity-funnels-tens-of-millions-to-hate
-groups/; also see: Philip Rojc, "Big Money, Quiet Power: A Look at the
National Christian Foundation," *Inside Philanthropy*, August 21, 2017,
https://www.insidephilanthropy.com/home/2016/10/3/big-money
-quiet-power-a-look-at-the-national-christian-found.html.

279 *Among the NCF's leading recipients:* 0.66 percent of the NCF's 2019 total
giving went to Alliance Defending Freedom, a spokesman said—that's
more than $10 million.

279 *a network... the Southern Poverty Law Center has designated a hate group:*
Zack Ford, "Is Alliance Defending Freedom a Hate Group? Just Look at
Their Work," ThinkProgress, August 18, 2018, https://thinkprogress.org
/adf-hate-group-3302dd95ace4/; also see: Rebecca Damante and Brennan
Suen, "The Extremism of Anti-LGBTQ Powerhouse Alliance Defending
Freedom," Media Matters, July 26, 2018, https://www.mediamatters.org
/alliance-defending-freedom/extremism-anti-lgbtq-powerhouse
-alliance-defending-freedom#death.

279 *collects tens of millions in tax-exempt donations each year:* "Alliance Defending Freedom Form 990 for Period Ending June 2018," *ProPublica*,
https://projects.propublica.org/nonprofits/display_990/541660459
/05_2019_prefixes_53-56%2F541660459_201806_990_20190522163
33362.

279 *charities that promote racial animus and white nationalism:* David J.
Herzig and Samuel D. Brunson, "White Supremacist Groups Don't
Deserve Tax Exemptions," *New York Times*, August 29, 2017, https://
www.nytimes.com/2017/08/29/opinion/white-supremacists-tax
-exemptions.html.

279 *Dylann Roof... was motivated by "black on white" crime propaganda:* "I
have never been the same since that day," notes his purported manifesto.
"There were pages upon pages of these brutal black on White murders.
I was in disbelief." http://media.thestate.com/static/roofmanifesto.pdf.

279 *Council of Conservative Citizens:* a 501(c)(4) charity, per Nonprofit Ex-
plorer: https://projects.propublica.org/nonprofits/organizations/36335
4434.

279 *the like-minded New Century Foundation:* Alex Kotch, "Nation's Biggest
Charity Is Funding Influential White Nationalist Group," *Sludge*, November 22, 2019, https://readsludge.com/2019/11/22/nations-biggest-charity
-is-funding-influential-white-nationalist-group/. Reached by phone, Taylor said he disagreed with Roof's motive of starting a race war ("that's im-

moral"), but said "his grievances were understandable." He disputed the SPLC's characterization of CCC and New Century as white nationalists: "I call myself a 'race realist' and a "white advocate.'"

279 *VDARE Foundation . . . has collected more than $5 million:* "VDare Foundation—Nonprofit Explorer," *ProPublica,* May 9, 2013, https:// projects.propublica.org/nonprofits/organizations/223691487.

279 *"Six Out of Eleven Mass Shootings in 86% White Wisconsin":* James Fulford, "Milwaukee Shooting: Six Out of Eleven Mass Shootings in 86% White Wisconsin Are by Minorities or Immigrants," VDARE.com, February 27, 2020, https://vdare.com/posts/milwaukee-shooting-six-out -of-eleven-mass-shootings-in-86-white-wisconsin-are-by-minorities -or-immigrants.

280 *"NYPD Releases Pic of Suspect in Tessa Majors Killing":* James Fulford, "NYPD Releases Pic of Suspect in Tessa Majors Killing. Guess What? He's Black," VDARE.com, December 20, 2019, https://vdare.com/posts /nypd-releases-pic-of-suspect-in-tessa-majors-killing-guess-what-he-s -black.

CHAPTER 20: PERFECT STORM

281 *Darren Walker gets it:* All quotes and details in this chapter come from author interviews with Darren Walker, December 16, 2019, and February 13, 2020, and follow-up emails.

283 *he was later hired as chief operating officer:* From Darren Walker's LinkedIn, https://www.linkedin.com/in/darrencwalker/, and Ford Foundation page, https://www.fordfoundation.org/about/people/darren -walker/.

285 *Walker composed an open letter:* Darren Walker, "Toward a New Gospel of Wealth," *Equals Change Blog,* Ford Foundation, https://www.ford foundation.org/ideas/equals-change-blog/posts/toward-a-new-gospel -of-wealth/.

286 *"the American Dream . . . has been diminished":* Only 27 percent of respondents in this February 2019 poll said the American Dream is "alive and well" for them: https://www.realclearpolitics.com/docs/190305 _RCOR_Topline_V2.pdf. Periodic public surveys by the Public Religion Research Institute found that the share of U.S. adults who believe the American Dream "still holds true" declined from half in 2010 to less than one-third in 2015, a year in which 14 percent of the Black respondents said the dream has "never held true." See: "A Window of Opportunity II:

Perceptions About Income Inequality and Equal Opportunity," Key Findings, Section 3.2, Opportunity Agenda, 2016, https://www.oppor tunityagenda.org/explore/resources-publications/window-opportunity -ii/income-inequality-equal-opportunity.

286 *groups such as Patriotic Millionaires:* See "Resources," p. 297.

286 *"nearly $1.7 billion in unrestricted gifts":* MacKenzie Scott, "116 Organizations Driving Change," *Medium,* July 28, 2020, https://mackenzie-scott .medium.com/116-organizations-driving-change-67354c6d733d.

287 *pledged $200 million to racial equity groups:* Susan Sandler, "My Cancer Milestone and My Philanthropic Legacy," Medium.com, September 14, 2020, https://medium.com/@susansandlerfund/my-cancer-milestone-and -my-philanthropic-legacy-a338d03bfc94.

287 *A survey of major foundations:* Council on Foundations, "Shifting Practices, Sharing Power," September 2020, https://www.cof.org/content /shifting-practices-sharing-power-how-us-philanthropy-responding -2020-crises.

287 *Scott made headlines again in December 2020:* Michael Mechanic, "Giving Away Billions of Dollars Is Hard Work—Just Ask MacKenzie Scott," *Mother Jones,* December 4, 2020, https://www.motherjones.com/politics /2020/12/giving-away-billions-of-dollars-is-hard-work-just-ask-mack enzie-scott/.

287 *"where guests pay $100,000 for a table":* Darren Walker, "Are You Willing to Give Up Your Privilege?," *New York Times,* June 25, 2020, https:// www.nytimes.com/2020/06/25/opinion/sunday/black-lives-matter -corporations.html.

288 *"Trumpism is pitchforks":* Author interview with Nick Hanauer, June 10, 2019.

290 *$1.2 million with interest:* Gary also made a prescient early investment in Celestial Seasonings, the tea company, which left her even more money to give away.

292 *a cage with gilded bars:* Author interview with Doug Holladay, May 9, 2019.

INDEX